Compositional Subjects

Laura Hyun Yi Kang

Compositional Subjects

Enfiguring Asian/American Women

Duke University Press

Durham and London

2002

© 2002 Duke University Press

All rights reserved

Printed in the United States of America

on acid-free paper ∞

Designed by C. H. Westmoreland

Typeset in Bembo

by G&S Typesetters, Inc.

Library of Congress Cataloging-in-

Publication Data appear on the last

printed page of this book.

For our *harmoni*, Han No Bun

contents

acknowledgments

In the final throes of writing *Compositional Subjects*, I received an inspiring, handwritten note from my six-year-old niece Elyssa: "Good luck in finishing your book. I hope you make a good grade!" This well-wishing nicely captures the long journey of writing this book, which would not have been possible without the guidance and encouragement of many people. I have been blessed with a relay of amazing feminist mentors. First and foremost, I would like to thank Elaine H. Kim, who has taught me so much and given me many key opportunities. As will be amply evident in reading this book, my work here would not be possible without the prolific body of scholarship that she has produced with such courage and foresight. At the University of California–Santa Cruz, Judy Yung was an early anchor for my interests in studying Asian/American women and a peerless model of pedagogical excellence. Angela Davis inspired me to "stay in school" with her calm genius and guided my passage toward dissertation writing. As the chair of my dissertation committee, Donna Haraway offered me the perfect balance of freedom and incisive interrogation to craft the early full draft of this book; her indelible influence on *how* I think about thinking is inscribed throughout this monograph. As my senior mentor at the University of California–Irvine, Leslie W. Rabine has been an oasis of steadfast support and wise counsel on all matters of work and life. Last but not least, Lisa Lowe has guided me well at several key junctures with her admirable combination of intellectual rigor and prudence. In addition, several other faculty members in History of Consciousness helped me to conceive and write early versions of certain sections in this book: Jim Clifford, Barbara Epstein, Stephen Heath, and Hayden White.

Many friends eased and enriched the process with their fine minds, finer souls, and great camaraderie: Caren Kaplan, Inderpal Grewal, Rachel Lee, Brian Albert, Eungie Joo, Mimi Kim, Claudia Castañeda, Anjie

Rosga, Leslie Bow, Elena Creef, Nora Okja Keller, Thelma Foote, Bob Moeller, Ketu Katrak, Jane Newman, David Lloyd, Elora Shehabuddin, Heidi Tinsman, Chungmoo Choi, Yong Soon Min, and Jin-me Yoon, who made the generous gift of her artwork for the cover of this book.

The early writing of this book was made possible through financial support from the University of California President's Postdoctoral Fellowship and a University of California–Irvine School of Humanities Faculty Career Development Award. At Duke University Press, Ken Wissoker has been an ideal editor for both his early commitment to my manuscript and his enduring patience in allowing me the time that I needed to finally let go of it. Pam Morrison's sharp editorial skills helped greatly in the final stages of production.

Finally, I must thank my large and extended family for their love and tolerance of the willful feminist bookworm in their midst: my mother, Mae Ja Kang, and my father, Jin Yong Kang; my sister Linda and brothers John and James; Justin, Elyssa, Nathan, Ryan, and Darren for making me play with them and not think about my work. I want to also thank the Yi family, especially Yun Hui and Chon Kyu Yi and the late Ho Nam Chang. Paul Yi has kept me loving company throughout this long adventure through fine cooking, passionate conversations, and unflappable faith in my zany ideas.

Compositional Subjects is dedicated to our *harmoni,* Han No Bun. She raised five children alone amid the ruins of postcolonial, postwar Korea, then raised twelve grandchildren in the different rubble of immigrant America. Her enduring strength helped me keep in perspective that a book is just a book.

Thank you each and all.

Introduction

The people of the State of California represented
in Senate and Assembly do enact as follows:
Section 1. It shall not be lawful from and after the time when this act takes
effect, to bring or land, from any ship, boat or vessel, into this State, any
Mongolian, Chinese or Japanese females, born either in the Empire of
China or Japan or in any of the Islands adjacent to the Empire of China,
without first presenting to the Commissioner of Immigration evidence
satisfactory to him, that such female desires voluntarily to come into this
State, and is a person of correct habits and good character, and thereupon
obtaining from such Commissioners of Immigration, a license or permit
particularly describing such female and authorizing her importation or
immigration.—AN ACT TO PREVENT THE KIDNAPPING AND IMPORTA-
TION OF MONGOLIAN, CHINESE, AND JAPANESE FEMALES, FOR CRIMI-
NAL AND DEMORALIZING PURPOSES (Approved, 18 March 1870)

In 1834, the American Museum in New York put Afong Moy on public
display under the billing of "Chinese Lady."[1] The marked turn from a
curious look at an imported spectacle to a legislative measure to stave off
an unseemly throng of immigrating females suggests several significant
shifts in the intervening thirty-six years. First, in contrast to the temporary
rarity of Afong Moy, the 1870 act presupposes and indeed attempts to respond to an invasive plurality that would more permanently inhabit the social geography. In addition to the earlier specification of "Chinese," an enlarged litany merges into one suspect category not only "Mongolian" and
"Japanese" but also those ambiguously identified as "born in any of the Islands adjacent to the Empire of China." This clustering predates by almost

exactly a century the composition of "Asian American women" as an emergent identity at several universities in the State of California during the 1970s.

Transfigured as both proliferating collectivity and social problem, these "Mongolian, Chinese, or Japanese females" are cast as objects of concerted investigation and certification. Ambiguously positioned in relation to prevailing standards of "correct habits and good character," the difference to be discerned is turned outside in, from spectacular surface to dubious interiority.[2] Rather than precluding any and all entrance, the 1870 Act placed these women under a more penetrating gaze that would ascertain a personhood worthy of admission and possibly permanent residence. Even as it presumes a largely coercive transnational traffic in female bodies, the wording nevertheless allows for the possibility that some *could* qualify for entry. What seems crucial here is not that an applicant for entry possessed a properly volitional self, but that she was able to adequately *demonstrate* one to the Commissioners of Immigration. A legislative tactic to limit, if not wholly exclude, the physical presence of these "females" hinges their acceptability—permissible for entrance—on a convincing performance for this masculine, bureaucratic gaze and its descriptive inscription.[3] This enactment marks the troublesome place of Asian women in the United States at the crisis-ridden intersection of social difference and its controlled surveillance and documentation.

When it is considered against this genealogy of collective naming and selective authorization, how can we make critical sense of the contemporary proliferation of social, political, cultural, economic, and pedagogical endeavors in the name of two linked and often interchanged groupings— "Asian women" and "Asian American women"? In tracking the variant terms and conditions of their emergence and legibility, *Compositional Subjects* examines the intimate but often mutually vexing protocols of identity and disciplinarity. The intervening slash in Asian/American women is a diacritically awkward shorthand for the cultural, economic, and geopolitical pressures of the continental (Asian), the national (American), and the racial-ethnic (Asian American) as they come to bear on an implicitly more solid gendered ontology (women). Starting from the arguable premise that Asian/American women have been profusely represented, my critical engagement is impelled by a different directionality. Rather than a further descent into some hidden interiority or a more encompassing coverage of their gender, sexual, class, ethnic, and national identities, I stress what the contradictory claims made about, by, and for Asian/American women might suggest about the instability and inadequacy of those generic delineations of individuality and collectivity. Against the unqualified demands for greater presence and accuracy within a range of social and discursive arenas, this study explores how existing accounts that pose Asian/American women as particular objects of knowledge and subjects of consciousness and action might tell another tale about the peculiar protocols of inclusion and representation in that instance. A comparative study of such shifting productions and combinations necessarily spotlights how it is possible to say *some* thing about *any* body under certain settled procedures of recognition and demonstration.

Each of the first four chapters focuses on four rather stock figures— writing self, desiring body, national citizen, and transnational worker—as they have cohered in certain disciplines: literary criticism, film studies, history, and anthropology. In heralding a particular object of study or domain of inquiry, such disciplinary names bear a burden and an alibi. On the one hand, their very generic designation binds these knowledges, at least nominally, to account for the immense heterogeneity of human figures that might produce but also are made by these objects and domains. On the other hand, their very epistemological commitment to a particular object of study or domain of inquiry acquits them from full, total coverage of every possible kind of personhood. Considered against this paradox, how are Asian/American women inducted within and across these disciplinary demarcations? How does the impulse to incorporate them as newly visible incarnations of social, cultural, or corporeal particularity interface with the investment in the discipline as ultimately unprejudicial in its special epistemological purchase on a (transhuman) object of study and domain of inquiry? The sometimes facile but more often fraught attempts to account for Asian/American women could underscore how different disciplines privilege particular modes of subjection. My critical approach in each instance is directed less at an unveiling of some truth that has been misrepresented than a foregrounding of the particular historical circumstances, ideological suppositions, and methodological tactics that enable and constrain that compositional instance.

While questions of difference and diversity may be more readily conjured for Asian/American women, this study demonstrates that they also pose problems of disciplinarity, representation, and knowledge production. Despite the weight of tradition and scientific aura they enjoy and foster, academic disciplines are also particular, partial, and ever-shifting formations:

> The modern connotation of *disciplinarity* is a product of the nineteenth century and is linked with several forces: the evolution of the modern natural sciences, the general "scientification" of knowledge, the industrial revolution, technological advancement, and agrarian agitation. As the modern university took shape, disciplinarity was reinforced in two major ways: industries demanded and received specialists, and disciplines recruited students to their ranks. . . . Formalization of the pursuit of knowledge in various fields—history in 1884, economics in 1885, political science in 1903, and sociology in 1905—paved the way for the "professionalization" of knowledge in the twentieth century.[4]

Part and parcel of their historical contingency, disciplines have been made and sustained by the peculiar *social* exchange of discriminating practitioners. The animating struggle within a discipline is not so much *about* fidelity/infidelity to an external object of study but *around* internalized rules and norms of a "methodological field" that binds but also fractures its practicing agents, or "disciples."[5] Disciplines are made, sustained, and transformed by these disciples as much as these practices also discipline these knowing subjects. A discipline must also be situated as a particular political economy of material resources and human labor.[6] To sum up, disciplines and disciplinarity are historical, social, and political economic constructs.

In relating academic disciplinarity to the question of social and cultural diversity in the U.S. academy, Arjun Appadurai perceives that "diversity is typically the voice of the 'minor' whereas disciplines claim, generally successfully, the voice of the major (in all senses of the senior, the larger, the more important). Here is where the tension between historicity and authority comes in."[7] The calls for the inclusion of and attention to minoritized subjects can easily result in a bifurcation of the academy in which diversity, minority, and historicity are lined up on one side, helping to preserve the other chain of associations between disciplinarity, majority, and authority. The prevailing reduction of Asian/American women as belated and still minor objects of study within established disciplines works to preserve those disciplines' authority as a progressivist accumulation of knowledge of all subjects within liberalism's promise of universal representation. Against such a redoubled consolidation of disciplinarity through a further minoritization of difference, Appadurai suggests that we "invoke the minor and minority in the landscape of disciplines, not just as part of a program of distributive or affirmative reform, but as a way to destabilize the authority and establish the historicity of the 'major' in whatever textual and interpretive world we inhabit" (35).

To make the case for Asian/American women as a productive figure *for* such destabilizations, it is important to begin with a critical genealogy of its "historical specificity and cultural limits."[8] In spite of its now settled meaning and common proliferation, "Asian American women" emerged as a political and syntactical formulation not all at once, but in dispersed and sometimes linked fits and starts at the agonistic intersections of feminist, antiracist, and anti-imperialist social movements in the late 1960s and 1970s. The designation "Asian American," was composed through conjoined political mobilizations *for* civil rights in the United States and *against* American imperialism in Asia, most pointedly through the Vietnam War. A sizable U.S.-born generation of mostly Chinese and Japanese but also Filipina/o and Korean descent formulated an "Asian American panethnicity," accenting the *American* in repudiation of the alien connotations of the then-prevailing racial category of "Oriental."[9] Concurrently, a "second wave" of U.S. feminism mobilized around and fought over the identification of "women" as a historical and political category, cross-cut by racial, ethnic, class, and sexual differences.[10] The political and discursive construction of "Asian American women" thus offers a promising nexus for studying the synchronic-diachronic calibrations of the categories of "Asian," "American," and "women."

If the earliest efforts to name "Asian women" and later "Asian American women" as a distinct group were riddled with confusion and dissension, they would soon be followed and largely eclipsed by more confident claims and declarations. Often compelled to redress a negative inheritance of exclusions, suppressions, and misnomers, these efforts were also unable to foresee or fully determine the political trajectories and discursive sedimentation of the desire to name and to have a name. As the following chapters will detail, the certainty and authority of a naming of, by, and for "Asian/American women" could also discourage alternative possibilities of identification and knowledge production.

Although there have been some attempts to name a particular "Asian American women's movement," alternately and sometimes interchangeably referred to as the "Asian women's movement," it is difficult to pin down the exact time-space coordinates of its emergence. Localized clusters of mostly Chinese and Japanese but also some Filipina and Korean women formed consciousness-raising and study groups devoted to a collective examination of a shared identity as "Asian women" and later as "Asian American women." Colleges and universities, especially in California but also in the Midwest and on the East Coast, provided significant sites for these incipient endeavors, which sometimes led to the formation of service organizations. Susie Hsiuhan Ling recounts how Asian Sisters was formed in July 1970 in response to a perceived "epidemic" of drug overdoses among young Asian women in the Los Angeles area (104). These student activists also sought representation within their university curricula by agitating for—and often designing and running—courses on "Asian women" or "Asian American women" and by publishing their own research and creative writings.

In 1971 a student collective at the University of California, Berkeley, published a magazine-format collection titled simply *Asian Women*. The editorial board wrote in the introduction,

> Most of us met in Asian Studies 170, a Proseminar on Asian Women given by Asian Studies at U.C. Berkeley. We came to the course seeking knowledge and relief to the uneasiness in being Asian women. We faced a dilemma. We were not satisfied with the traditional Asian roles, the white middle-class standards, or the typical Asian women stereotypes in America. We wanted our own identity. . . . we saw that we faced a double oppression as being women but also as Asians. The white middle-class woman's liberation movement was not totally relevant to our lives. We had to create roles as Asian women.[11]

To confront these desirous but hesitant words over three decades later as the now-archived remnants of a particular point of emergence unsettles the now facile legibility—and marketability—of "Asian American women" as a distinguished social body. Already evident are rudimentary shreds of several discursive struggles to follow in the 1970s and 1980s. The enumeration of plural oppressions grapples with the fraught *intersectionality* of gender, race, and class, which would be articulated more complexly and confidently but was not yet an available terminology or analytical framework. More specifically, the inadequacy of "the white middle-class woman's liberation" to speak to and for "Asian women" presages a strikingly dissonant and recursive array of subsequent apportionments of the racial, class, and sexual contours of feminism. But if this marks a difference and agonistic tension amongst American women, the category of "Asian women" can be more internationally expansive. Likely shaped by the housing of the proseminar in "Asian Studies," the volume displays a significant geopolitical scope; a section on "Third World Woman" includes essays on such far-ranging topics as "Indochina Women's Conference," "Arab Women's Liberation," "Women in Iran," and "Chairwoman of Chongsan-Ri (A cooperative farm in North Korea)." The inclusion of Arab and Iranian women under the rubric of "Asian women" is particularly noteworthy as they often drop out in later transfigurations into "Asian American women." Finally, the editors' expressed "uneasiness in being Asian women" coupled with a compulsion "to create roles as Asian women" against prevailing cultural and social scripts renders a palpable confusion, mixing, and collision amongst the ontological, the experimental, and the performative. Their call for an active *construction* of an alternate identity is carried out in the anthology's broad and heterogeneous mix of creative writings, archival research, literary criticism, oral history, political manifestos, and sociological studies.

Then, in May 1976, another group of students at Stanford University published a volume titled *Asian American Women*. Posing the question, "Why a journal on Asian American women?" in the introduction, Leigh-Ann Miyasoto responds, "I felt my own confusion about my knowledge and beliefs about my culture, about feminism and how it relates to me as a woman of color, and about economic and political analyses of American society from an Asian American perspective." [12] This unique *perspective,* taken for granted here in a way that it is not in the 1971 volume, attests to the increased currency of "Asian American" in the intervening five years. [13] Filtered through the identification of "woman of color," the feminism invoked here is clearly something more encompassing and complicated than the earlier "white middle-class woman's liberation movement." While thus asserting a sharper political affiliation based on interlocking racial and gender formations within the United States, there is no significant attempt to examine the international differences and possible connections between

"Asian American women" and "Asian women." Finally, compared to the multidisciplinary range of *Asian Women,* "a common theme expressed is the intense, personal nature of the experiences of Asian American women" (7). While several pieces note the importance of a broader social analysis, much of the volume attends to a more privatized exploration and expression of this social identity.

Throughout the 1970s and into the 1980s, numerous women, working as individual writers and artists and as organized collectives, mobilized around the sometimes distinguished, sometimes interchangeable identifications of "Asian women," "Asian American women," and "Asian Pacific American women" through various social, political, and cultural endeavors.[14] They helped establish and sustain such groups as Asian Women United of San Francisco, Organization of Asian Women in New York, Pacific Asian American Women Writers-West (PAAWWW), and Unbound Feet, a radical-feminist writing and performance collective. Impelled significantly by these political and cultural activist efforts, "Asian American women" became a distinct social body of official recognition by local, state, and national government agencies. As early as 1974, the State Department hosted a delegation of women from Africa, Europe, and Asia on a tour of the United States. As Katheryn Fong recalled in 1978, "I was invited to sit on a panel of American women of color to brief these visitors about our histories in America."[15] Then, in 1975, President Gerald Ford "established a commission to gather data, make recommendations, and represent the country" at the United Nations–sponsored International Women's Year Conference to be held later that year in Mexico City. As a consequence of "the enthusiasm and interest generated by the Mexico City conference," Congresswomen Patsy Mink and Bella Abzug subsequently introduced "a bill proposing that a conference be held in every state and territory to identify issues and elect delegates to a U.S. national women's conference, the historic Houston Conference in November 1977."[16] The election of female representatives in national politics and the emergent conceptualization of "women" as a newly recognizable international social class converged with domestic racial politics to produce an acknowledgement of and interest in specific constituencies of American women. Various government agencies responded by organizing national gatherings and publishing their proceedings. In August 1976, the National Institute of Education sponsored what was billed as a "National Conference on the Educational and Occupational Needs of Asian and Pacific American Women" in San Francisco, which resulted in a publication under the same title. Other government agencies commissioned and published studies on more particularized issues perceived as significant to Asian/American women.[17] The state's sudden interest and activism in gathering data on Asian/American women—and women more broadly—in turn motivated and enabled the creation of several Asian/American women's organizations through local, state, and federal grants.[18]

A small number of scholarly and journalistic efforts to document the lives of specific groups of women, past and present, were also published during this period, mainly through the Asian American periodicals *Gidra, Amerasia Journal,* and *Bridge: An Asian American Perspective.*[19] Two back-to-back special issues of *Bridge* on "Asian American Women," which were published in 1978–79, merit closer examination. The brief editorial that introduced the first issue declares that "while the American woman today battles for the Equal Rights Amendment, the Asian American woman grapples with the double dilemma of being yellow and female."[20] Describing the featured writings in the special issue as addressing "those concerns that are universal to women yet unique to Asian women," the editors add, "Their poems search, their dialogue sears, their historical and personal self-analysis delineate a shape, form a composite woman we all recognize in varying degrees and textures—the yellow woman." This sense of a multifaceted composite is clearly evident in the generic and social range of the contents. Alongside interviews and oral histories that focus on an individual woman or a particular ethnic group of women, these special issues featured two very differently pitched pieces that explore the limits and possibilities of the panethnic assembly of "Asian women" and "Asian American women." The "dialogue" with Barbara Noda, Kitty Tsui, and Z. Wong titled "Coming Out: We Are Here in the Asian Community" appeared in the first issue, while the autobiographical essay by Mitsuye Yamada titled "Invisibility Is an Unnatural Disaster: Reflections of an Asian American Woman" was included in the second. Taken together, these two compositions illustrate an ongoing tension between acknowledging internal heterogeneity and dissonance, on the one hand, and imposing a more coherent identity and legibility of and for Asian/American women, on the other. Finally, the divergent reroutings of these documents beyond these initial publications are noteworthy for considering why and how certain articulations become more or less occluded while others survive to become more or less canonical, especially as they concern minoritized subjects.

"Coming Out: We Are Here in the Asian Community" is introduced as a transcription of a conversation amongst Noda, Tsui, and Wong: "We got together to talk about our lives—as Asians, as women, as lesbians—to shed light on and dispel some myths about what it means to be a gay Asian woman."[21] Despite this avowed frankness and intimacy, the very dialogical format of the piece resists any univocal coherence of the "gay Asian woman" and, by implication, the discreteness of the broader categories of Asians, women, and lesbians. While the trouble of their linkage into one identity is considered in "Coming Out," it is more pointedly extended into another published exchange. In 1980 Barbara Noda would go on to write her own review of the two special issues for *Conditions,* subtitled "a magazine of writing by women with a special emphasis on writing by lesbians."[22] Opening with a somewhat apprehensive characterization of her critical assessment as "a discussion among ourselves that we are allowing others to listen to," Noda early on expresses "fear of alienating my own peer group" in doing so. While she lauds the two issues for making a "serious attempt to include women's perceptions," Noda concludes by saying that she is "disappointed" at the "lack of support for a feminist perspective," which leads ultimately to what she sees as "an imbalanced and narrow picture of who we are." She asks, "They do not have to proclaim themselves feminists or lesbians, but where in their words do they acknowledge whole-heartedly the strength, assertiveness and success in their lives as women"? There is a clear contestation over the very identification of "women," which overlaps and veers from the other collective identifications of "feminists" and "lesbians."

Nellie Wong's response to Noda's critical review, published in the following issue of *Conditions,* directly cites the above question in accusing Noda of "baiting her Asian sisters who are heterosexual."[23] Quoting from Barbara Smith, Wong then emphatically declares, "As a feminist, I do not leave my ethnicity behind," and urges further that "feminism must coalesce with the struggles against racism, class oppression, economic ghettoization as well as against sexism and homophobia." These agonistic deliberations on the linkages—and breakage—amongst gender, racial, ethnic, and sexual identifications have been largely effaced for several reasons, most significantly, I would venture, because of their appearance in now-extinct sites of periodical publication. I re-collect them here in order to suggest several alternative temporalizations to the more commonly recited version of the assertions of racial, class, and sexual *difference* as not only coming after an initial feminist consolidation around the category of "women" but comprising distinct offshoots of political mobilization.[24] Insofar as both Noda and Wong figure feminism as a distinct perspective and affiliation, which resides beyond the "Asian American," the critical review and its own dissenting response show the category of "Asian American women" as animated by social differences and ideological conflicts in the earliest instances of self-nomination.

Considered against the effacement of these provocations and contestations, the longer and more memorable discursive career of Mitsuye Yamada's essay, which appeared in the second special issue of *Bridge,* demands some critical scrutiny. Titled "Invisibility Is an Unnatural Disaster: Reflections of an Asian American Woman," the essay would be republished in 1981 as part of *This Bridge Called My Back: Writings by Radical Women of Color* edited by Cherríe Moraga and Gloria Anzaldúa, which extended and further solidified the category of "Asian American women," especially as one of the four main racial-ethnic groupings under "women of color." In this essay, Yamada describes at length how she came to identify herself as an "Asian American woman." Relating the surprised response of colleagues when she filed an antidiscrimination grievance procedure at a community college where she taught, she adds, "One of the administrators suggested someone must have pushed me into this, undoubtedly some of 'those feminists' on our campus, he said wryly."[25] Confronted by this charge of the impossibility of her particular body to stand for, to be, the authentic agent of feminist action, Yamada concludes: "In this age when women are clearly making themselves visible on all fronts, I, an Asian American woman, am still functioning as a 'front for those feminists' and therefore invisible. . . . the most stereotyped minority of them all, the Asian American woman is just now emerging to become part of [the multicultural history of our country]. It took forever. Perhaps it is important to ask ourselves why it took so long. We should ask ourselves this question just when we think we are emerging as a viable minority in the fabric of our society . . . it took so long because we, Asian American women, have not admitted to ourselves that we *were* oppressed. We, the visible minority that is invisible" (12). While this narrative of how one subject came to realize who she was through certain social and institutional confrontations with racism and sexism underscores the forceful and contextual constructedness of any body's identification as an "Asian American woman," Yamada's essay contends that there *is* such an identity that has been merely submerged and hidden, especially from its own members. In exhorting that supposed natural collectivity—"we, Asian American women"—to recognize themselves as such, this paradoxical manifesto also begs the question of why and how such a particular grouping is "a viable minority" at that particular historical juncture. Why these peculiar dimensions of both specificity and generality for configuring a collective alliance based on a shared perception and admission of oppression? Why *not* all "Asian Americans," or all "women of color," or all "Asian women"?[26] Instead, she proposes at the end of the essay, "To finally recognize our own invisibility is to finally be on the path toward visibility. Invisibility is not a natural state for anyone." This implicit teleology of invisibility-to-visibility, which affirmatively structures visibility as the desired, penultimate goal, works to imbue "we Asian American women" with a presence and coherence that were missing and contested in the earlier compositions. Recalling the embodied visibility, the objectifying to-be-looked-at-ness of Asian female bodies before and after this writing, I would ask at this juncture, is emergence into a field of vision (optical and/or political) so natural and beneficial, and if so, for whom?

By the late 1980s "Asian American women" would become a widely recognized term and group identity throughout academic institutions, the publishing industry, and some public-policy circles. "Asian American women" was approved as a Library of Congress subheading on 11 February 1986.[27] Since its founding in 1976, Asian Women United of California has been one of the most productive and enduring forces in the discursive construction and proliferation of "Asian American women." Under several shifting configurations of authors and editorial committees, this group has produced and distributed a series of pedagogical print and visual materials throughout the 1980s, culminating in the 1989 publication of an anthology titled *Making Waves: An Anthology of Writings By and About Asian American Women*.[28] As the editors recall in the preface to its 1997 sequel, "Frustrated by what we saw as a lack of voice and visibility in all walks of American life for the rapidly growing community of Asian American women, members of Asian Women United had been talking about producing a book since the late 1970s" (xi). They were able to start actively working on it in 1984 after the group received a federal education grant to produce curriculum materials for Asian American girls and young women under the mandate of the recently passed Women in Education Equity Act. The final impetus for publication came from a commercial press:

> We had not been successful in finding ways to disseminate our earlier materials in the public schools, although the videos were shown on public television and the books were sold to individuals. By the late 1980s, many public funding sources for nonprofit organizations like ours had been phased out. Then, at the very moment when the *Making Waves* manuscript had been completed, an editor from Beacon Press visited the Asian American Studies program at U.C. Berkeley to ask if there were any published materials about Asian American women. . . . Because it was published by a commercial press, *Making Waves* found its way into many college course reading lists across the country.[29]

I quote this retrospective narration of bibliogenesis at some length because it foregrounds the convergence of several social, political, and economic forces in the making of not only the anthology but the textual production of "Asian American women" as a distinct object of knowledge through the partial interests and chance collisions of grassroots activism, ethnic studies in the university, state-sponsored knowledge production on girls and women in response to feminist efforts, and a commercial publisher's interest in a timely, profitable "topic of interest." Following the lead of Michael Omi and Howard Winant that "Asian American" is a "racial formation,"[30] I propose "Asian American women" as an overlapping but also distinct *racial-gender formation* at the nexus of higher education, cultural politics, grassroots and institutional activism, and both national and international state policies.

Making Waves is disciplinarily and generically heterogeneous in its composition, with pieces ranging from familiar poems, short stories, and autobiographical essays to a critical analysis of the representation of "Asian women" in Hollywood films, a historical study of Filipinas growing up in the United States during 1930s, and more contemporary sociological accounts of Asian immigrant women workers in the garment industry, the phenomenon of "mail-order brides," and the traumas of forced migration and resettlement suffered by Vietnamese refugee women. Even as its publication signals the growing social salience of "Asian American women" at the end of the 1980s, the editors of *Making Waves* were mindful to point to the instability of that very category. Defining it as "those women in America who can trace their roots to Asia—China, Japan, Korea, the Philippines, South Asia, and Southeast Asia," the editors further explain the ethnic subcategories: "Most of the ethnic groups we write about are familiar—Chinese, Filipino, Japanese, and Korean Americans. Others, however, may need some explanation. By South Asian women, we mean those whose roots extend to India, Pakistan, Bangladesh, and the other countries in that area. The term Southeast Asian refers to women from the Indochinese Peninsula—Vietnam, Cambodia, and Laos—as well as women from Burma and Thailand" (ix–x). In her "General Introduction: A Woman-Centered Perspective," Sucheta Mazumdar writes, "The experiences of a Southeast Asian working-class woman and what she may perceive as the major cause of her oppression will differ greatly from those of a professional, middle-class Japanese American woman."[31] In addition to accentuating such ethnic, national, and class heterogeneity, Mazumdar's example further broaches the identification of "Asian American women" between its plural "experiences" and a more individualized "perception" of a singular "major cause of oppression."

The close of the 1980s also saw a continued staging of an agonistic tension between "Asian American women" as a now more readily assumed social collectivity and feminism as a particular consciousness and politics. Esther Ngan-Ling Chow's article published in the sociology journal *Gender and Society* offers an illustrative instance. Opening with the confident assertion that "like other women of color, Asian American women as a group have neither been included in the predominantly white middle-class feminist movement, nor have they begun collectively to identify with it," Chow goes on to ask on the following page, "What are the social conditions that have hindered Asian American women from developing a feminist consciousness, a prerequisite for political activism in the feminist movement?"[32] The "Asian American women" presumed here has a categorical outline that is both missing and missed in the earlier compositions. Arguing that a "gender consciousness" must precede and pave the way for the development of a "feminist consciousness," Chow goes on to outline the "social contexts in which the gender consciousness of Asian American women has developed":

Domination by men is a commonly shared oppression for Asian American women. These women have been socialized to accept their devaluation, restricted roles for women, psychological reinforcement of gender
stereotypes, and a subordinate position within Asian communities as well
as in the society at large. Within Asian communities, the Asian family (especially the immigrant one) is characterized by a hierarchy of authority
based on sex, age, and generation, with young women at the lowest level,
subordinate to father-husband-brother-son. The Asian family is also characterized by well-defined family roles, with father as breadwinner and decision maker and mother as compliant wife and homemaker. While they
are well protected by the family because of their filial piety and obedience,
women are socially alienated from their Asian sisters. Such alienation may
limit the development of gender and feminist consciousness and render
Asian women politically powerless in achieving effective communication
and organization, and in building bonds with other women of color and
white feminists. (286)

By figuring the "Asian family" as so powerfully suppressing these women's
"gender consciousness," its homogeneity is merely announced as a social
and cultural fact, not open to analysis or alternative representations. However, a difference at least in degree is implied in the parenthetical "(especially the immigrant one)." Even in the most confident declarations of
"shared oppression," there is a distinction and blurring between the categories of "Asian American women" and "Asian women." But what about
the other women? Inasmuch as Chow situates the subjects of her study
in a "not yet" moment in relation to "feminist consciousness," I would
venture that these "Asian American women" are imbued with an ontological solidity precisely through their lack of what some other American
women already possess. A shared identification with "the predominantly
white-middle-class movement" slides rather seamlessly into the more generic "feminist consciousness." In this slippage, I would argue, feminist
consciousness is constricted to mean consciousness about white, middle-
class feminism. Consequently, "Asian American women" cannot but be
belated subjects of feminism.

What is more remarkable about this article is its bibliography. Chow
acknowledges, "My ideas are a synthesis of legal documents, archival
materials, and census statistics; participant observation in the civil rights

movement, feminist movement, Asian American groups, and Asian American organizations since the mid-1960s; interviews and conversations with Asian American feminists and leaders; and letters, oral histories, ethnic newspapers, organizational newsletters, films, and other creative writings by and about Asian American women." Even as this litany of source material attests to the many and varied forms of data that already existed and could be additionally gathered on the subject, it raises the more interesting question of what that implies in relation to the prevailing demarcations of disciplinary division and epistemological authority.

The increased output of textual productions in the 1990s has further magnified this internal heterogeneity and disciplinary multiplicity. Most anthologies and edited collections have pivoted on a more focused axis of shared identity. A group of undergraduate students at U.C. Berkeley published *Our Feet Walk the Sky: Women of the South Asian Diaspora* in 1993. In the following year, Sharon Lim-Hing edited *The Very Inside: An Anthology of Writing by Asian and Pacific Islander Lesbian and Bisexual Women*.[33] Finally, with the emergence of a sizable number of self-identifying "Asian American women" scholars as well as the gradual legitimation of "Asian American women" as objects of knowledge in specific disciplines of study, there has been an increased representation within both collections that are more broadly conceived along the lines of gender, sexuality, and nationality and in special issues of journals devoted to "Asian American women" in history, sociology, and political economy.[34] Even the anthologizing of creative writings has become specified by genre so that there are collections of short fiction or plays.[35] In turn, these efforts call into question the rationale for a more broadly conceived textual composition like the earlier *Asian Women* or *Making Waves*.

In addition to the increased specification of the *kinds* of "Asian American women," there has been a greater proliferation and refinement of the ways of rendering them visible and legible. One particularly striking epistemological development has been the unquestioned importation of the very category into certain medical and scientific discourses that treat them as an already physiologically and psychologically distinct grouping. Even a cursory bibliographic search under the title words "Asian American women" produces a sizable and growing list of studied publications that claim to measure narcissism or variations in their waist/hip ratio and hormonal secretion.[36] These forays into minds and corporealities risk the evacuation of "Asian American women" from the jagged historicity that I have sought to highlight throughout this critical genealogy. At this moment of an unprecedented number and range of knowledge-claims and representations, *Compositional Subjects* proffers a pause for some critical reflection of the terms and conditions by which Asian/American women have been rendered legible, visible, and intelligible.

The interested observation, recording, and categorization of individualized human bodies and their differential inclinations and aptitudes in the academic disciplines are intimately bound up with the constitution of disciplined subjects necessary to the functioning and growth of militarized capitalism. Foucault's formulation of the role of the "examination" in this intertwined making of the human as both a productive body and an intelligible body sounds useful warnings to the recent effusion of compositional efforts about Asian/American women.[37] He outlines three linked aspects. First, even as it becomes more elusive, power is exercised through imposing what he calls "a principle of compulsory visibility" on to the subject bodies: "It is the fact of being constantly seen, of being able always to be seen, that maintains the disciplined individual in his subjection" (187). Second, this forceful and insistent surveillance transcribes these visible bodies into a "field of documentation" and "a network of writing." If, as Foucault clarifies, this "turning of real lives into writing" is "a procedure of objectification and subjection," I would align this with the first compulsion to visibility by calling it "a technology of compulsory composition." Two epistemological possibilities follow from this transcription: "firstly, the constitution of the individual as a describable, analysable object . . . under the gaze of a permanent corpus of knowledge; and secondly, the constitution of a comparative system that made possible the measurement of overall phenomena, the calculation of the gaps between individuals, their distribution in a given 'population'" (190). The calculation of each person no longer against some inner truth but in relation to other subjected individuals doubly secures the objectification of humanity into manipulable units of knowledge. Thirdly, then, surveillance and documentation enable a refined and endless specification with "the fixing, at once ritual and 'scientific', of individual differences, as the pinning down of each individual in his own particularity . . . the gaps, the 'marks' that characterize him and make him a 'case'" (192). The knowledges constructed through these triply compulsory techniques of recognition, documentation, and encased specification in turn increase the powers of other disciplinary mechanisms—the prison, the factory, the classroom—in what Foucault alternately describes as a "circular process" or a "double process": "an epistemological 'thaw' through a refinement of power through the formation and accumulation of new forms of knowledge" (224). One final detail to note about this "disciplinary regime" of power/knowledge is that its "individualization is 'descending'" (193). The degree of specification marks the extent of subjection so that "the child is more individualized than the adult, the patient more than the healthy man." For from an indifference to social, political, and economic hierarchies, power courses through the unevenly linked encasements of differently marked subjects.

Another train of destabilizing disciplinary knowledges have been launched through various "interdisciplinary" research and teaching projects. Over the past decade, both the adjective "interdisciplinary" and the noun "interdisciplinarity" have been deployed with greater frequency as well as greater dissension. Many of these divergent estimations derive from the fact that "interdisciplinary" can be attached to a diverse range of projects, so that there have been various efforts to distinguish several degrees and kinds of interdisciplinarities.[38] Some have called for a "critical interdisciplinarity," distinguished from "mere interdisciplinarity" or a "vacant interdisciplinarity," which brings together a critique of disciplinarity and a critical interrogation of social diversity.[39] Lisa Lowe writes, "Interdisciplinary studies disrupt the narrative of traditional disciplines that have historically subordinated the concerns of non-Western, racial and ethnic minority peoples, and women, insofar as they hold the potential to transform disciplinary divisions that guarantee the self-evidence of these narratives."[40] Lowe poses the significance of Asian immigration to the United States, with its contradictory combination of labor exploitation and exclusion from both political citizenship and national culture, as both "a racial formation and an epistemological object" against the limited terms of its legibility in the academy.[41] The scant attention paid to Asian immigration does not simply mirror the sociohistorical exclusion of and disempowerment of Asian Americans outside of the academy but speaks to how it troubles the production and organization of knowledge in the academy within a capitalist liberal nation-state:

Asian American history narrates the breakdown of the explanatory power of the abstract divisions of society into the political, the economic, and the cultural. Thus, studies of the "Asian American" engage with traditional disciplines of history, literature, the arts, and fields of social sciences, and in the process, require a revision of the objects and methods in these fields. (41)

More than a compromised shuttling between two disciplines or a naïve reach for some organic wholeness of knowledge, such simultaneous and conjoined investigations of history, culture, and political economy can also critically re-member the partiality of disciplinary divisions and their knowledge-making practices.

Part of that critique necessitates an attentiveness to how the current formation of knowledges under the banner of the various identity-based interdisciplinary "studies" are bound by certain disciplinary protocols as well as possibly complicit with disciplinary power's penchant for surveillance, documentation, and categorization. The itemizing attentiveness to human diversity, summed up by Foucault as "a political anatomy of detail," has been fundamental to the expanded operations of social, political, and economic power. The 1870 act cited above stunningly bears this out, rendering its "Mongolian, Chinese, and Japanese females" as individual case studies to be seen, documented, and categorized. To be triply subjected in this way evokes comparison to the common identification of Asian/American women as being "triply oppressed" along the axes of race, class, and gender. This echo should warn us that the marginalized can "claim a voice" or "come into visibility" as a distinct subject under the most insidious compulsions. Whether by affirming familiar truths or giving rise to new certainties, the increasing discursive proliferation about and categorical specification of Asian/American women are more often bound up with, not liberated from, disciplinary regimes of codification and documentation. Especially because those subjects who produce knowledge along the specific axes of their own social difference and disempowerment are seen to derive their institutional agency and epistemological authority from merely *being* who they are, there needs to be a sustained critique of the many possible redeployments of these knowledges that emerge in the name of women, racialized communities, or immigrant workers. Wahneema Lubiano has forcefully articulated this occult time-space wherein certain socially disempowered and alienated subjects are actively producing knowledges about "themselves" or their "communities":

> We should remember that the military and the prisons, for example, places where the state is present, both create and rely on knowledge produced by the universities about marginal groups. Radical multiculturalism offers the possibility of countering the state's use of intellectual and cultural productions of and about marginal groups and thus offers institutionally transformative possibilities for middle-class people of color, who, as I've suggested, are also bound up with this state-sponsored knowledge.[42]

Inasmuch as women's studies or ethnic studies might impel a "worlding" of the academy, Lubiano points to how the knowledges produced there come to bear upon the world in ways that cannot be foretold or determined by the producers. The repeated rallying cries of "breaking silence," "coming to voice," and "making visible" presuppose some absence, repression, and marginalization as the ontological rationale and political motivation for particular articulations of self and community. As more and more Asian/American women study and make knowledge claims about (other) Asian/American women, it is important to be mindful that this making of "subjects" and "objects" is multiply idiosyncratic and not necessarily liberatory.

Keeping in mind the crucial link between disciplinary regimes and academic disciplines, I press for thinking through the growing discursive productions around specific social identities in a more expansive and skeptical manner through what I have elsewhere called a "trenchant interdisciplinarity."[43] In its implications of both keenness and marginality, the "trenchant" qualifier of interdisciplinarity signals an agonistic but nevertheless situated relation to prevailing disciplinary forms of knowledge formation and reproduction and their historical intimacies with tactics of political domination and social control over even the most peripherally delineated subjects. Here I would like to zoom in on the prefix (*inter-*), which has been predominantly figured in spatial terms by both advocates and detractors of interdisciplinarity. It has been alternately characterized as a crossing amongst various disciplines imagined as bounded arenas, as a combination of methods and objects taken from two or more fields of knowledge, and then too as the interstices outside of disciplinary demarcations. Indeed, Klein's concerted examination of the rhetoric of interdisciplinarity concludes "the dominant image . . . is that of geopolitics. The major activity is dispute over territory."[44] I would argue that this territorial figuration of interdisciplinarity imbues disciplines with a substance and fixity while it has drowned out the other possibility of the prefix to signal a temporal in-betweenness, as an *interregnum*. This other sense of being "in the midst of" better signals the primary interest of each chapter here in studying the negotiated terms and conditions of *emergence* into disciplinary legibility. A trenchant interdisciplinarity also marks out the differential historical status accorded to those knowledge formations organized around social differ-ence, such as women's studies and ethnic studies, which are often figured as belated additions to or corrections of "older," "traditional," or "estab-lished" disciplinary fields of study. Rather than an innovative or finished achievement, I would cast their widely heralded "interdisciplinarity" as an ongoing problematic and contestation about their proper and most productive location in relation to the academic disciplines. The significant proliferation of knowledge-claims about Asian/American women in the past two decades has troubled any clean distinction between traditional disciplines and interdisciplinary fields such as women's studies, Asian Amer-ican studies, and Asian studies. Increasingly, many are produced and dis-seminated *within* established disciplines such as literature, history, and so-ciology.[45] At the same time, the institutionalization of ethnic studies and women's studies has often necessitated that these fields "formalize and le-gitimate themselves in terms of established criteria" (Lowe, *Immigrant Acts,* 41); this institutionalization renders these fields as more multidisciplinary than critically interdisciplinary since faculty positions and courses are often delineated in established disciplinary terms. Still, other objects and subjects of study are further banished to the institutional and epistemological out-sides of both disciplines and interdisciplines. Keeping this ambivalent ten-sion in mind eschews interdisciplinary fantasies of achieving wholeness-through-integration against disciplinary fragmentation or of transcending disciplinary limitations.[46]

I propose Asian/American women as a productive configuration for such trenchant interdisciplinarity. Indeed, the combination of their multi-ply delineated specificity and their scattered appearances *as* Asian/Ameri-can women across a diverse range of discursive terrains allows me both a point of entry and a sustained focus for a critical inquiry into the shifting terms of their emergence and legibility. The aim is to analyze how par-ticular enfigurations enact and reconcile the vexing tug-of-war between identity and difference along the lines of gender, race, class, sexuality, and nationality. The shifting and yet problematically recurrent representations of Asian/American women can, in turn, shed critical insights into the changing and often contradictory understandings of those social and onto-logical categorizations across different epistemological frameworks. Hold-ing the dissonance and resonance of these overlapping discourses in per-sistent tension can further enable a critical revisioning of their specifically disciplined modes of knowledge construction and representation.

To begin, chapter 1 maps out the multiple discourses that have been generated by the apprehension of one "Asian American woman writer" as autobiographical presence in and through her textual productions. I open with the question of autobiographical representation and interpretation since this particular compositional act, a self-writing about that very same self, appears to hold out the promise of the most intimate truths about Asian/American women. I begin by surveying a range of critical interpre-tations of one text in particular, Maxine Hong Kingston's *The Woman War-rior*, focusing on the generic fixations of the book as autobiographical document and on the author as a representative spokesperson for her eth-nic community. Starting with autobiographical criticism as it is organized around the rubrics of nation and gender, I move on to examine a few note-worthy instances of its critical deployment in other disciplinary contexts: namely, as ethnography and historiography. Noting how the autobio-graphical categorization has proven to be both immensely productive and limiting, I seek to reframe these readings as revealing of the preoccupations of a particular site of reading/rewriting, especially as they foreground a particular axis of social difference. From there, I discuss at length the more ambivalent readings generated in relation to the emergent field of Asian American literary studies, specifically in the tension between a disciplinar-ily legible and legitimating alignment with literary studies and the socially and politically validating alignment with an interdisciplinary Asian Amer-ican studies. Keeping in mind the fantastic travels and travails of *The Woman Warrior* as object of rivalry, envy, and then, too, a certain camaraderie ex-pressed along both disciplinary and identity-based lines, I end by consid-ering the possibility of reading *The Woman Warrior* against the rigid bound-aries of genre and discipline, of self and nation.

Building on the precaution that even the most personal gesture of self-representation is contingent, situated, and liable to various appropriations, chapter 2 proceeds outward to look at the cinematic representations of Asian/American women as desirable and desiring bodies. The first part of this chapter presents a critical exegesis of three narrative films—*Thousand Pieces of Gold, Come See the Paradise,* and *The Year of the Dragon*—that feature an "Asian American" heroine as a central character. My critical retelling focuses on their concerted construction of a familiar and reassuring white American masculinity in the 1980s, an era marked by the gains and demands of feminism, growing ethnic and cultural diversity through immigration from Asia and Latin America, and declining U.S. hegemony against the intense globalization of capitalism. All three films reduce these struggles and antipathies to the manageable realm of interracial, heterosexual romance between a white male and an "Asian American woman," thereby reconfiguring racial conflict and sexual domination as complementary difference.

The second part of chapter 2 considers these portrayals in relation to the discipline of film studies. As I attempt in chapter 1 for literary studies, I point to the variously ambivalent efforts to incorporate the challenge of racial, sexual, and national *differences* that have resulted in highly uneven developments of socially particularized subfields, which foreground one particular axis. An institutional and epistemological consequence of such multiple trajectories has been what I see as an even more emphatic separation of disciplinarity and identity. I point to how a more recent skepticism toward identity-based film studies—often noted as "stereotype criticism"—lacks the theoretical sophistication and methodological rigor to contribute to what really matters about the discipline. Insofar as many of the existing critical discussions of cinematic images of Asian/American women have concerned themselves largely with how these images affect the "real" perceptions and especially the self-perceptions of Asian/American as a distinct and homogeneous social body, they reinforce these disciplinary prejudices. Even the narrative and ideological analyses of interracial romance miss a more interesting problem of enfiguration—how to render and discern an "Asian American woman" through a particularly *American* cinematic apparatus and political economy?

While the first two chapters explore the process of enfiguration across the inner self–outer embodiment divide, from a penetrating discernment of interior depths and the play of visible bodies and their desires, the next two chapters are linked on a different axis of time-space. Chapter 3 traces the jagged emergence of "Asian *American* women" over a hundred-year span of U.S. history while chapter 4 tracks the geopolitical assignations of Asian/American women as labor force for global capitalism. Chapter 3 traces the ways in which Asian women have been identified as/not U.S. citizens and "Americans" from the purported first arrival of Afong Moy in 1834 to more recent legislations on immigration and citizenship. Against the loving fantasies of their incorporation and complementarity in films, I counterpose a more forceful and contentious historical narrative of the placement of Asian/American women in and against American nationhood. The first part chronicles how different clusters of Asian women have been delineated away from a U.S. citizenship, which broaches the settled and cohesive conception of the "American people" as discontinuously bound up with and indeed dependent on the exclusions and minoritizations of Asian/American women. To weave this disjointed and conflicted narration of nation, I invoke some rather scattered—both in the moments of their production and the arenas of their later circulation—accounts of legislative acts and judicial rulings that have historically thwarted yet also shaped the emergent contours of the "Asian American women" as a distinct social body for the state's recognition and documentation in the 1970s.

The second part of chapter 3 casts a critical gaze on the writing of this history. Even as the first two chapters of the book critique the erasure and displacement of historical realities in the representational logic at work in literary interpretations and cinematic narratives, I direct my critical lens upon historiographical practices as they come to bear upon Asian/American women. I focus upon those very Asian women prostitutes who came to the United States in the nineteenth century with whom I began this introduction. Rather than offering an authoritative description of these women, I analyze how they pose moral, political, but also methodological challenges to their disciplined inscription, which in turn shed critical insights into the writing of several histories: women's history, American history, and Asian American history. Comprising the great majority of the first wave of Asian women to come to and work in the United States, these "prostitutes" must be accounted for in the political and historiographical strategy of laying claim to an oldest possible history of "Asian American women" and indeed of the general Asian American population as "Americans." In addition to the moral ambivalence provoked by such a genealogy, writing these women into history proves methodologically vexatious; these accounts must concede many "unknowables" about this socioeconomically marginalized and politically subject population, who had little access to and even less control over what would survive as the material traces of their existence in those officially sanctioned and disciplinarily legitimated archives. I analyze how such moral and methodological ambivalence is negotiated through two interrelated historiographical tactics: (1) emphasizing external coercion in explaining how these women came to be "prostitutes" in the United States and then positing marriage and reproduction as both the ideal and the only viable alternative, and (2) conferring on these women a knowable interiority, most significantly a "desire" to escape prostitution and become wives and mothers who can be readily absorbed into the narration of nation as monogamous reproduction. What becomes elided in this willful subjectivization is the profoundly undemocratic (re)production of the archives, which by their own partial construction can never speak *for* these women. Instead, I urge that any effort to recall these women must also be a *historical* remembering of the imbricated exclusion and marginalization of Asians and particularly Asian immigrant women workers from both legal citizenship and archival presence in the United States.

If chapter 3 is thus concerned with questions of national citizenship, chapter 4 looks at the deployments of Asian women as "transnational labor" in the circuits of assembly-line manufacturing, military prostitution, and sex tourism. In an effort to denaturalize these political-economic phenomena, I begin with a summary description of the historical formation of these laboring sites located in various Asian countries, emphasizing the coordinated planning and forceful implementations that have sustained them. In addition to pointing out the definitively international aspects of these mobilizations of Asian women workers in Asia, the chapter also invokes the situation of many Asian immigrant women who perform similar work *within* the nation-state borders of the United States to challenge the salience of national identity as a unifying point for political mobilization and thus to further contest any unqualified "Americanization" of Asian/American women.

From there, chapter 4 critically examines another kind of "transnational labor," specifically the symbolic and rhetorical practices deployed in select texts describing and analyzing various Asian women workers and their laboring circumstances. I am especially interested in uncovering the ways in which some key texts that map a discourse about the global assembly line, sex tourism, and military prostitution rationalize and naturalize the exploitation of the Asian women workers. On this note, the chapter presents a critical analysis of how Asian women have been embodied as the most proper, if not ideal, transnational workers through the following arrested representational practices: (1) recurrent visualization, whether through the descriptive language or through photographic reproductions, and (2) positioning them too securely at a spatial and temporal distance, away from both the scholar-writer and the reader of the text.

Following the analyses of the resonant and divergent ways in which Asian/American women are imagined, enfigured, recruited, and disciplined, the fifth chapter examines some selected instances of Korean women's scholarly, literary, artistic, and cinematic articulations that creatively engage with the *problematic* of both identification and representation that preoccupies the first four chapters. Locating themselves in specific historical and social milieus of Japanese colonization, American military imperialism, transnational emigrations, resettlement, and forceful acculturation under often inhospitable circumstances, shifting patriarchal traditions, and class relations, I highlight how these particular explorations of identity acknowledge the constitutive power of, even as they often subvert, hegemonic prescriptions of race, ethnicity, gender, sexuality, class, and nationality. Such an explication demands critical attention to not only the content but the form of these works; therefore, I foreground those representational tactics and strategies that actively contend with—rather than simply reject or bypass—those methods of *fixation on* the figure of the Asian/American woman and *containment of* Asian/American women that I analyzed in the first four chapters. I end the chapter by considering how Asian American women belong to those intellectual-institutional sites of knowledge production that are already demarcated by identity such as women's studies, Asian studies, or Asian American studies.

The book thus concludes by pointing to how a multivalent critical examination of Asian/American women can unsettle and reformulate the given boundaries of social identification, cultural representation, and knowledge construction. The impossible questions of "What is she?" and "Who are they?" are turned around into other queries: How have Asian/American women been conjured, interpreted, and missed? What constituent parts make up Asian/American women? How are they enfigured differently within and across particular sites of representation? Even further, how can a "trenchant interdisciplinarity" be deployed to reveal and to contest the thematic coherence, ideological suppositions, and rhetorical tactics of each of those locations? Beyond the telos of represented object to representing subject, the *compositional subjects* of my title clench the tension of these three qualifiers: composed, composite, and positional.

chapter 1

Generic Fixations

Reading the Writing Self

> One of my growing convictions, founded upon the last 20 or so of my
> more than 40 years of teaching at Yale University, is that the life of the
> mind and the spirit in the United States will be dominated by Asian Amer-
> icans in the opening decades of the 21st century. The intellectuals—the
> women and men of literature and the other arts, of science and schol-
> arship, and of the learned professions—are emerging from the various
> Asian-American peoples. In this displacement, the roles once played in
> American culture and society by the children of Jewish immigrants to the
> United States are now passing to the children of Asian immigrants, and
> a new phase of American literature will be one of the consequences.
> —Harold Bloom, *Asian-American Women Writers*

Composing the lifeline of national culture as an ethnically marked succession of dominance, recession, and another emergence, this confident prog-
nosis opens Bloom's editorial introduction to a 1997 compilation of various published critical writings on "Asian-American women writers," part
of a series on "Women Writers of English and Their Works." As if in an-
ticipation of the bewilderment as to why and how this particular critical
authority has come to append his proper name to such a specified bibliographic and editorial project, Bloom takes some pains to situate himself in
relation to the writing subjects of this collection. An intriguing short essay
that precedes the introduction, is titled simply "The Analysis of Women
Writers" and begins,

I approach this series with a certain wariness, since so much of classical feminist literary criticism has founded itself upon arguments with that phase of my own work that began with *The Anxiety of Influence* (first published in January 1973). Someone who has been raised to that bad eminence—The Patriarchal Critic—is well advised that he trespasses upon sacred ground when he ventures to inquire whether indeed there are indisputable differences, imaginative and cognitive, between the literary works of women and those of men. If these differences are so substantial as pragmatically to make an authentic difference, does that in turn make necessary different aesthetic standards for judging the achievements of men and women writers?[1]

But this is no naïve and open-ended investigation of the relationship between social identity and disciplinary specialty, for, as Bloom declares on the following page, "The consequences of making gender a criterion for aesthetic choice must finally destroy all serious study of imaginative literature as such." After quoting a comment by Elizabeth Bishop, which begins by acknowledging the significance of gender in artistic production and ends by emphasizing that "art is art and to separate writings, paintings, musical compositions, etc., into sexes is to emphasize values in them that are *not* art," Bloom concludes: "Gender studies are precisely that: they study gender and not aesthetic value."[2] Instead, Bloom would subsume considerations of gender's significance in literature to a more disciplinarily legible and generically specified "biographical criticism," which "like the different modes of historicist and psychological criticism, always has relied upon a kind of implicit gender studies."

This charge against identity-based delineation of literature as displacing the aesthetic and formal concerns that should be the centering object of proper literary study is, by now, a familiar mode of protectionism. What *is* intriguing is how Bloom conjoins this disciplined resistance to feminism to a critical acclaim of "Asian-American women writers." Indeed, Bloom sets up the titular subjects of this collection to mediate an intriguing triangulation amongst three other compositional subjects that he names as: (1) "American literature," (2) "feminist literary criticism," and (3) "the Asian-American peoples."[3] In betting the future of this national body of writings on an ethnically specific constituency of writers, Bloom would relegate the work of the unspecified but implicitly not "Asian-American" feminist literary study to a misguided past. To chart one genealogy of this prodigious body of writing subjects, this chapter studies the travels and travails of the most heralded of "Asian-American women writers"—Maxine Hong Kingston—through the profuse murmur of interpretations and commentaries about one particular textual production, *The Woman Warrior: Memoirs of a Girlhood Among Ghosts.*

Named the best work of nonfiction in 1976 by the National Book Critics Circle, it was reviewed favorably in the *New York Times, Washington Post, Newsweek,* and *Time.* A vibrant second wave of U.S. feminism also created a receptive context for a woman-authored book whose title so rousingly named a generic subject-position of female empowerment. A reviewer for *Ms.* magazine praised it as being "almost a psychic transcript of every woman I know—class, age, race, or ethnicity be damned" while demonstrating "the real meaning of America as melting pot." [4] In addition, the publication and reception of *The Woman Warrior* would prove singularly notable in relation to an emergent "Asian American" social collectivity and the literature produced and interpreted under that name. In a 1998 review of "Asian American Literary Studies," King-kok Cheung distinguishes it as "the first Asian American work to receive astounding national acclaim." [5]

The generic classification of the book as an autobiography *of* Maxine Hong Kingston has crucially shaped the contours of its critical acclaim and prolific representativeness. A much-circulated "origin story" traces its "nonfiction" labeling to editors at Alfred Knopf, the publishers of the first 1976 printing, who "felt it would sell better as autobiography." [6] This marketing strategy proved successful, both commercially and critically, by inviting the text to be read as a transparent window onto Maxine Hong Kingston and her family. In a particularly visceral collapsing of a textual detail and its author's lived body, "Kingston has been asked in radio interviews to explain how her mother cut her frenum." [7] Even as late as 1990, after she had published two more books, both centered on male protagonists, Maxine Hong Kingston continued to be enfigured *as* "Woman Warrior." [8]

By metonymic extension, numerous book reviews and critical essays have heralded this book as speaking for a range of overlapping social, cultural, and political constituencies: ethnic Americans, women, immigrants, the Chinese people, all Asian Americans, Chinese women, Chinese Americans, Asian American women. [9] The *New York Times* praised it as "an account of growing up female and Chinese-American in California, in a laundry of course."[10] When Kingston's second book, *China Men,* published four years later in 1980 but focusing on a range of Chinese immigrant male characters, again garnered the National Book Critics Circle Award for Nonfiction, it further cemented the reputation of Kingston as ethnic spokesperson. One journalist, in characterizing the two texts as "chronicles of Chinese-Americans," confidently declared, "In both, the author was passionately concerned with her roots and the achievements of the immigrant Chinese, many of them her relatives, who faced the challenge of finding a secure place in American history and culture".[11] In contrast, Kingston's purchase as spokesperson for "women" or even for "American women" has been more fraught and discontinuous. While *The Woman Warrior* continues to be heralded as a cross-culturally resonant articulation of women's oppression and feminist empowerment, the other two texts, focused on male characters and often narrated from their points of view, have been less amenable to such a mimetic and political reading.[12]

These generic fixations in the popular press have carried over into critical literary studies. *The Woman Warrior's* canonical stature and pedagogical prominence in literary studies are notably demonstrated by the 1990 publication of the edited collection *Approaches to Teaching Kingston's "The Woman Warrior,"* published by the Modern Language Association in a series of "approaches" to such disciplinary brand names as Chaucer, Milton and Shakespeare. Most discussions in this volume and elsewhere in academic criticism take for granted and uphold the classification of autobiography. One such instance goes so far as to brand Kingston as an "autobiographer" who "immerses herself in her ethnic girlhood by recalling discrete narratives of Chinese-American women."[13] The classification of the book as "autobiography" is even more striking in those instances in which the critics acknowledge the conventional and constructed nature of this genre. If one were to take seriously all of these confident and contending interpretations, then the person named Maxine Hong Kingston would seem to have led multiply contradictory lives.

Although it is a key genre in literary classification, autobiography can also be disciplinarily muddying, comprising an uneven mixture of novel, diary, journalistic reportage, native testimony, familial genealogy, political statement, and oral history. Even Georges Gusdorf, one of its early renowned theorists, must resort to an extradisciplinary metaphorical reach in arguing that "the appearance of autobiography implies a new spiritual revolution: the artist and model coincide; the historian tackles himself as object."[14] Indeed, the autobiographical branding of *The Woman Warrior* has enabled a multidisciplinary scope in scholarly interpretation. As Elaine H. Kim noted in 1990, "Critical essays explore the book from the point of view of anthropology, folklore, sociology, linguistics, theology, history, and psychology."[15] The book has also been frequently discussed under the rubric of two "interdisciplinary" fields, women's studies and especially Asian American studies where the book's autobiographical status has been persistently contested less as a matter of literary genre and more as an impasse of representation in a broader discursive struggle against racism.

In tracking the multiply dispersed yet also interpretively constrained critical circulation of the text, this chapter is primarily interested in measuring the shifting pressures of disciplinary location and social identification within and across two sites, in particular, literary studies and Asian American studies. Tellingly, the book's generic classification and disciplinary belonging have been more easily assumed when it is read as exhibiting a social or cultural *difference* from some privileged, primary axis of identity. For instance, in literary studies Kingston's gender is emphasized under "American autobiography," whereby its consideration also affirms the project of the inclusion of women writers even as the book is heralded for its ethnic specificity under the rubric of women's writing. In contrast, the generic categorization has been vociferously contested in Asian American studies because the text threatens to stand for *sameness,* thereby displacing other literary representations and critical studies by and about Asian Americans. However, an inverse tension around disciplinary classification follows from this. Under the most confident rubric of literary criticism, *The Woman Warrior* is read for much more than its aesthetic merits; it is often read instead as a sociological or ethnological document. In contrast, in the ongoing critical debate waged by Asian American studies scholars, there is a certain lament that the text is not being read as "literature," further raising the question of whether there is or can be a discrete field of "Asian American literature" or "Asian American culture" apart from the identity-based demands of fidelity to historical, ethnological and linguistic verities. Noting how the autobiographical categorization has proven to be both immensely productive and constrained, these readings could tell another tale, having little to do with Maxine Hong Kingston or *The Woman Warrior* and much more with the preoccupations of a particular site of reading/rewriting.

The Proper Name of Autobiography

The discursive career of the tripartite name Maxine Hong Kingston has far exceeded the sentient individual and the productive writer. In attempting to locate a criterion by which to distinguish autobiography from fictional writing, Philippe Lejeune suggests, "Autobiography (narrative recounting the life of the author) supposes that there is *identity of name* between the author (such as he figures, by his name, on the cover), the narrator of the story, and the character who is being talked about." [16] Although it never appears beyond the title page, the proper name of the author is readily attached to both the perceived narrator and female protagonist of *The Woman Warrior*. Many critics refer to a "Kingston" as a discernible textual figure, eliding any distinctions among the protagonist, narrator, author, and, what Lejeune calls, the person of "vital statistics." Here, I would point out that one of the text's most striking aspects is the near absence of any proper names. Most of the characters featured in the five differently titled sections of the book are unnamed; indeed, the title of the first section is "No Name Woman." The most prominent exceptions are "Brave Orchid" and her sister, "Moon Orchid," but the relationship between these named protagonists and their narrator is unstable and admittedly mediated. [17] By familial extension, Brave Orchid and the "No Name Woman" are often referred to as "Kingston's mother" and "Kingston's aunt." [18] Despite his stated aversion to emphasizing any aspect of an author's social identity and existence, Harold Bloom's editorial introduction to the section on the critical scholarship on the works of Maxine Hong Kingston asserts, "The Kingstons' tradition of passing down myths and family history profoundly influenced the future author, who would incorporate much of these memories into her novels" (37). He also adds, "the text is in fact populated by numerous characters drawn from the Chinese-American community of Kingston's youth." In other extreme instances of this (auto)biographical collapsing of author and textual figure, the perceived girl narrator is called by her more informal and intimate first name: "The struggle of the artist/protagonist is defined a few pages into the book, in the chapter 'No Name Woman,' where Maxine engages in an imaginative reconstruction of the life and suicide of her father's sister in China."[19] One critic goes so far as to study the arrangement of the three parts of the author's name and concludes, "As her name reveals, Maxine Hong Kingston is somewhat distanced from her Chinese-American origins by marriage to a Caucasian."[20]

Through recourse to the ontological uniqueness and solidity afforded by the proper name of "Maxine Hong Kingston," the prevailing axes of social formation, in which a self bears one each of a given array of gender, sexual, cultural, national designations, mutually shape and reinforce the presumed referential solidity of autobiography. I would add furthermore that this generic fortification also affirms two sides of the larger literary critical enterprise: (1) penetrating interpretation of *a* self who writes, and (2) appropriate classification of the *kinds* of selves who come to write but, moreover, who come to be legible as writers. But what gets displaced in this embrace of identity and disciplinarity? As Biddy Martin has pointed out about "lesbian autobiography," the composite alignment of the social nomination with the generic categorization "brings out the most conventional interpretation of each, for the *lesbian* in front of *autobiography* reinforces conventional assumption of the transparency of autobiographical writing. And the autobiography that follows lesbian suggests that sexual identity not only modifies but essentially defines a life, providing it with predictable content and an identity possessing continuity and universality."[21]

Inasmuch as it constrains the interpretive possibilities of the text, the proper name of a writing self also enables and affirms other extratextual claims. In tracking the question of authorship as "a privileged moment of individualization in the history of ideas, knowledge and literature," Michel Foucault focuses on "the singular relationship that holds between an author and a text, the manner in which a text apparently points to this figure who is outside and precedes it."[22] In contrast to earlier times when texts were "accepted, circulated, and valorized without any question about the identity of the author" (125), the author now plays a social role that exceeds the limits of any individual writer, a productive capacity that Foucault calls an "author-function":

The author explains the presence of certain events within a text, as well as their transformations, distortions, and their various modifications (and this through an author's biography or by reference to his particular point of view, in the analysis of his social preferences and his position within a class or by delineating his fundamental objectives). The author also constitutes a principle of unity in writing where any unevenness of production is ascribed to changes caused by evolution, maturation, or outside influence. In addition, the author serves to neutralize the contradictions that are found in a series of texts. Governing this function is the belief that there must be—at a particular level—a point where contradictions are resolved, where the incompatible elements can be shown to relate to one another or to cohere around a fundamental and originating contradiction. (128)

Proposing that we keep in mind the noncorrespondence of narrator, writer, and author, Foucault then adds, "It would be as false to seek the author in relation to the actual writer as to the fictional narrator: the 'author-function' arises out of their scission—in the division and distance between the two" (129). In seeking to uncover some truth about an individual either in the form of biographical details or her original genius as an artist, the "author-function" attempts to surmount what he deems as the "pervasive anonymity" of discourse. On that score, the proper name comes to play a crucial role: "Obviously not a pure and simple reference, the proper name (and the author's name as well) has other than indicative functions. It is more than a gesture, a finger pointed at someone; it is, to a certain extent, the equivalent of a description" (121).[23]

If "Maxine Hong Kingston" points a finger at something other than a someone, what happens to the author-function as it is preceded and specified in a nomination such as "Asian-American Women Writers"? One critical impulse is to protest the exclusion of "Asian American women" from the metaphysical-ideological tradition that posits the author as a knowing Western, white bourgeois male subject. Indeed, as many have convincingly documented, the seeming stability and power of this normative authorial identity have accumulated through its definition against various other bodies that are imprinted with a contrasting lack of self-possession and authority and thus the impossibility of authorship. In addressing this dilemma, Trinh T. Minh-ha writes,

Being merely "a writer" without doubt ensures one a far greater weight than being "a woman of color who writes" ever does. Imputing race or sex to the creative act has long been a means by which the literary establishment cheapens and discredits the achievement of non-mainstream women writers. She who "happens to be" a (non-white) Third World member, a woman, and a writer is bound to go through the ordeal of exposing her work to the abuse of praises and criticisms that either ignore, dispense with, or over-emphasize her racial and sexual attributes.[24]

Distinguishing two kinds of writing, between "a scriptive act—the emergence of writing itself" and "a consolidation of writing from the self," Trinh points to their differential commodification: "The two often overlap, but the type that inundates the market is without doubt the second one: write-about autobiographies or novels through whose stories the woman author constitutes an identity" (29). The pressures to account for racial and gender difference are met by the highlighting of one or both of these attributes of the author in espying an unmediated expression of a real presence embodied as such before and behind the text. But that said, what does one wish for "a woman of color who writes"? To be disencumbered of the "happens to be" as a way to accede to being "merely 'a writer'"? Why is "a writer" not a burdensome marker of encased specificity?

I lay out these questions in order to clarify that my critical tracking of the various readings of Maxine Hong Kingston as a textual presence and a confessional subject is *not* composed in the hopes of eventually qualifying her as "merely a writer." Can a writing subject ever become unmarked when the case for its considerate inclusion is preceded by and often premised on the claims of its particular absence or exclusion? I would argue that the very desire to pass as a socially unmarked writing self and not as a marked body presumes and affirms the universality of certain disciplinarily delineated subjects such as writer, body, citizen, and worker. Indeed, a discipline's ability to absorb such "emergent subjects" as "Asian American women writers" fortifies the neutrality and soundness of its original object of study. Far beyond the effect of the author's creative intention or the publisher's profit motivation, the generic fixation of *The Woman Warrior* has been compelled by and sedimented through a much larger circuit of reading practices and "writing technologies."[25]

While some mention of *The Woman Warrior* appears in many, if not most, very broadly conceived explorations of autobiography, its inclusion and induction are most steadfast in more narrowly delineated subcategorizations of autobiographical criticism in terms of nation, ethnicity, and gender. I would even venture to say that an approving acknowledgment, if not an extended exegesis, of the text appears obligatory and pro forma in broad considerations of American autobiography, women's autobiography, and ethnic autobiography. In many of these instances, *The Woman Warrior* is touted as an archetype of the subgenre and/or positioned as the final text in the critical analysis. In the sections below, I have chosen to highlight select readings in each terrain, which attempt to expand and complicate the definitional parameters of both the generic and the social axes under consideration.

American Autobiography

Elaine H. Kim has noted, "*The Woman Warrior* has achieved status as an American classic; a top profit maker for its publishers, the book is used as a standard text in American literature courses across the country."[26] Its induction and inclusion under the nation- and genre-specific rubric of "American Autobiography" is manifest in titles of critical studies such as *First Person Singular: Studies in American Autobiography, American Autobiography: Retrospect and Prospect,* and *Multicultural Autobiography: American Lives.* G. Thomas Couser, the editor of *Altered Egos: Authority in American Autobiography,* posits, "The values of the genre and those of American culture have long seemed to be in close congruity; and the notion of a special compatibility between American culture and autobiographical criticism has become a commonplace of criticism" (14). Couser is nevertheless careful to point out that autobiographical inscription has not been equally available to all of the nation's subjects, and he faults other critics for "ignoring its remoteness from, or inaccessibility to, minority groups within the larger population" (20). Given such a breach between these generic "minority groups" and autobiography as a nationally compatible genre of writing, Couser would hold Maxine Hong Kingston up alongside Richard Rodriguez for traversing that divide:

Indeed, both suggest that the writing of their autobiographies required defiance of ethnic prescriptions since autobiography had little or no warrant in Chicano and Chinese-American culture. The emergence of "minority autobiography" may signal the contact of particular individuals with the dominant culture or even a subtle form of cultural imperialism, rather than the development of generic preconditions in minority cultures. (20)

While Couser's invocation of "cultural imperialism" might appear to bespeak a certain attention to power relations in literary production, publication, and critical interpretation, this exceptionalist and individualistic figuration of two ethnically specified writers works to maintain a clear distinction between "American culture" or "the dominant culture" and the variously specified "minority cultures." Situated squarely within the first terrain, autobiography also functions as a portal through which certain individual ethnic writing subjects can cross into the nation's cultural center from their marginal origins.

Even as Couser ends his study with a reading of *The Woman Warrior* as an example of a "contemporary" American autobiography that "ultimately achieves a novel accommodation between minority and mainstream culture," its author must be figured as existentially encumbered with a particularized body and identity. Furthermore, this biculturalism is not equally weighted as Couser declares, "Kingston's book is powerfully shaped by the fact that she is a member of a gender minority as well as an ethnic one; it both documents and indicts the strong constraints of Chinese-American culture on women. Perhaps the primary obstacle to the autobiography of a Chinese-American woman is Confucian exaltation of family and community over the individual, and the privileging of men's lives over women's" (227). "Kingston" becomes split temporally between a younger ethnically burdened girlhood and a now mature, strategic agent of writing: "What she experienced, as a girl, as irreconcilable, even unutterable differences, she exploits, as an autobiographer, as elements of a vibrant and multivocal discourse" (230). "Instead of conceiving her identity and her story in terms of conventions of the dominant culture," Couser continues, "Kingston . . . challenges and deauthorizes the discourse of the cultures— Caucasian, Chinese, and patriarchal—that threatened to condemn her to silence, to marginality" (231). This litany of past threats identifies the "dominant" as a more racially specified "Caucasian" but also approximates the "patriarchal" to the Chinese. Consequently, Couser is able to preserve the emancipatory promise of the "American" from all three hazards as he goes on to argue, "Only by taking American liberties with the story [of "No Name Woman"] can she establish a significant relationship with her proscribed relation" (232). To affirm this point about the constraints of ethnicity, especially on the female writing subject, Couser later writes, "Insofar as autobiography involves the forthright naming of names and the location of the self in a matrix of verifiable assertions, such discourse opposes its author to ethnic and familial custom. To put it differently, conformity to minority mores would seem to militate against authoritative autobiography" (244–45). The enabling force of "American liberties" also enables Kingston to transcend the restrictions of gender. Couser's earlier observation—that "genre is clearly gender-bound: women may be the subjects of stories but not their authors" (232)—can be reframed in the end as, "Insofar as it inscribes her story in relation to those of mute foremothers, her narrative also manages to elude the gender trap and to authorize a woman's Life" (245). Even as the author's presumed ethnic and gender differences might be the very premise for the book's benevolent inclusion in this survey of American autobiography, to be legible as a generic American is to demonstrate the desire and the ability to transcend the constrictions of both one's racial and gender specificity.

Women's Autobiography

The Woman Warrior has been discussed at length or at the least obligatorily acknowledged in most monographs and edited collections of criticism in the subgenre of "Women's Autobiography" and, even more specifically, in "American Women's Autobiography" in the past two decades.[27] That the book has been included in the earliest critical surveys and theoretical explorations of women's autobiographical writings, which form around the same time as the book's publication in 1976, distinguishes this common induction from the more belated attention to the book as an "American autobiography." The collection *Women's Autobiography: Essays in Criticism,* edited by Estelle C. Jelinek and published in 1980, contains not one but two essays that feature *The Woman Warrior* in their titles.[28] Even when one critic chooses to consider the book as a "memoir" in accordance with what she discerns as Kingston's expressed preference in the subtitle, she adds that it "shares many aspects of the form of female autobiography."[29] If the publication of Kingston's second book focused on male protagonists could possibly trouble this neat alignment of gender and genre, Suzanne Juhasz claims, "Taken together, *The Woman Warrior* and *China Men* compose a woman's autobiography, describing a self formed at the source by gender experience" ("Toward a Theory of Form," 173). Juhasz continues, "For it is as a Chinese American woman that Kingston seeks to define herself" (174). Here, the more ontologically solid noun, *woman,* modified by the ethnic-national adjectives, enables the apperception and critical construction of a single self as manifest in and through two different texts.

The matter of the relation between gender and genre has been more ambivalently worked out by various other feminist literary critics. While some have defended and even celebrated autobiographical writings by women as liberating and galvanizing, others have been more circumspect toward a legacy of exclusion from traditional conceptualizations of "autobiography" as a literary genre. In addition, the *autos* of women are seen as distinguished from the canonical autobiographical texts of male authors. Bella Brodzki and Celeste Schenck argue, for example, "The (masculine) tradition of autobiography beginning with Augustine had taken as its first premise the mirroring capacity of the autobiographer: *his* universality, *his* representativeness, *his* role as spokesman for a community."[30] They continue: "No mirror of *her* era, the female autobiographer takes as a given that selfhood is mediated; her invisibility results from her lack of a tradition, her marginality in male-dominated culture." In contrast to how these canonized male-authored works "do not admit internal cracks and disjunctures, rifts and ruptures," Shari Benstock observes, "The self that would reside at the center of the text is decentered—and often is absent altogether—in women's autobiographical texts."[31] In the same volume, Susan Stanford Friedman leans on the theoretical insights from Sheila Rowbotham and Nancy Chodorow to argue that women's selves are more contextual and relational than men's selves. Such gendered differences are manifest in autobiographical theory and criticism so that Friedman opens her essay by asserting that "the individualistic concept of the autobiographical self that pervades Gusdorf's work raises serious theoretical problems for critics who recognize that the self, self-creation, and self-consciousness are profoundly different for women, minorities, and many non-Western peoples" (34). She explicates that "the emphasis on individualism does not take into account the importance of a culturally imposed group identity for women and minorities." But, what is this singularly imposing group identity and where does "a woman of color who writes" fit in the space of "women and minorities"?

In her exploration of "a poetics of women's autobiography," Sidonie Smith surveys over six centuries of Anglo-American autobiographical writings from Margery Kempe (ca. 1370) to Harriet Martineau (1877) and ends with a reading of *The Woman Warrior.* Given the century-wide gap between Martineau and Kingston's textual production and their more glaring differences of nationality, Smith goes to some lengths to explain her choice to conclude with this book.[32] Declaring emphatically that "for me, at least, no single work captures so powerfully the relationship of gender to genre in twentieth century autobiography," she goes on, "And so it is fitting to conclude this discussion of women's autobiography with *The Woman Warrior: Memoirs of a Girlhood Among Ghosts,* which is, quite complexly, an autobiography about women's autobiographical storytelling. A post-modern work, it exemplifies the potential for works from the marginalized to challenge the ideology of individualism, and with it the ideology of gender."[33] Whatever the critical potential of marginality, it is ultimately constrained by so securing the book to one definitive tradition of writing. In order to minimize the different historical conditions under which *The Woman Warrior* was produced and circulated, Smith conjoins it to the earlier autobiographical texts by positing a transhistorically shared experience of gender, namely the mother-daughter relationship: "For Kingston, then, as for women autobiographers generally, the hermeneutics of self-representation can never be divorced from cultural representations of woman that delimit the nature of her access to the word and her articulation of her own desire. Nor can interpretation be divorced from her orientation toward her mother, who, as her point of origin, commands the tenuous negotiations of difference and identity in a drama of filiality that reaches through the daughter's subjectivity to her textual self-authoring" (150). If the category of "women autobiographers" is significantly predicated on a generic daughterhood, Smith's repeated tendency to emphasize an ethnically specific patriarchal culture contradicts such deracinating gender identification. As in many other readings of *The Woman Warrior,* there is much critical explication of the misogyny and gender inequality *within* "Kingston's family," the "Chinese culture," or the "Chinese American community."

> Kingston recalls the repetition of commonplace maxims that deny female significance ("Feeding girls is feeding cowbirds"; "When you raise girls, you're raising children for strangers"; "Girls are maggots in the rice"); the pressures of a language that conflates the ideographs representing the female "I" and "slave"; the images "of poor people snagging their neighbors' flotage with long flood hooks and pushing the girl babies on down the river" (62). All these signs and stories of her culture equate her identity as "girl" with failed filiality and engender in her a profound sense of vulnerability and lack. (160)

In reciting these textual details and not others that illustrate instances of racism, Smith foregrounds not only gender marginalization but a specific terrain of gender oppression in "her culture." This selective accenting also elides how the autobiographical subject here is also a subject of "American culture," an identification that might have been more fruitful to bridge the geographical and historical distance between Kingston and the earlier Anglo-American women autobiographers.

Recent work in feminist autobiographical criticism has trained greater attention to the geographical and social specificities of women's autobiography. In their introduction to *De/Colonizing the Subject: The Politics of Women's Autobiography,* Julia Watson and Sidonie Smith point out: "Western autobiography functions as an exclusionary genre against which the utterances of other subjects are measured and misread. While inviting all subjects to participate in its practices, it provides the constraining template or the generic 'law' against which those subjects and their diverse forms of self-narrative are judged and found wanting."[34] *The Woman Warrior* somewhat disproves such a broadly framed account of exclusion, especially because so many critical readings herald the book as exemplary of the genre itself. This accent on the genre's exclusionary and coercive mechanics against all "other subjects" exists in tension with Smith and Watson's editorial decision to include discussions of *some* women's autobiographies but not others.[35] They explicitly acknowledge that their "selections" are "clustered in some areas at the expense of others" (xxii). For instance, they note how "the Indian subcontinent, with its history of British colonization, is the only area of Asia explored in depth here" while they seek to represent "the range and specificity of women's identities in the United States and North America." To that end, they explicate at length their inclusion of works about "the African American community" and "Native American ethnicities," but preface it by pointing out how "the most notable gap is in Chicana autobiography" (xxxiii, xxxiv). Although there is a notable lack of commentary on the inclusion or absence of "Asian Americans" and "Asian American women writers," Maxine Hong Kingston and *The Woman Warrior* are significantly featured in several places in the volume. A focused, extended reading by Lee Quinby will be discussed more closely in a later section of this chapter, but I want to draw attention here to how Smith and Watson slot it with a group of essays that they characterize as "mappings of the territorialization and transgression of autobiographical theory" (xxvi). This might suggest that *The Woman Warrior* has been able to rise from any racial-ethnic particularity to a more gender-representative and even *theoretical* currency in the study of women's autobiography. However, the only other place in which *The Woman Warrior* is significantly invoked proves otherwise.

Julia Watson's essay begins: "In women's autobiographies, naming the unspeakable is a coming to voice that can create new subjects, precisely because women's marginality may be unnameable within the terms or parameters of the dominant culture."[36] The constraining "culture" takes a seamless but significant turn in the very next sentence: "Maxine Hong Kingston introduces the category of the unspeakable in *The Woman Warrior* to describe the lack of identity that surrounds the first-generation Chinese-American children who want to name and therefore erode the boundaries of ghostly silence that guard the old culture's hegemony." After citing a passage from *The Woman Warrior* that describes an intergenerational struggle for and against silence, which if read in the full context of the book has been imposed by *political* and *economic* forces *within* the "new country," Watson declares even more confidently:

> Refusing to name the unspeakable not only protects what is sacred in Chinese tradition by enshrouding it in silence, guarding it from the uninitiated; it also marks cultural boundaries within which what is operative does

not need to be spoken. For the immigrant or multicultural daughter, naming the unspeakable is at once a transgressive act that knowingly seeks to expose and speak the boundaries on which the organization of cultural knowledge depends and a discursive strategy that, while unverifiable, allows a vital "making sense" of her own multiple differences. (139–40).

In footnotes, Watson provides yet another textual instance when "Kingston again refers to the unspeakable as the unnamed of traditional Chinese discourse," and then adds, "Writing the book names the 'secrets' on whose repression the perpetuation of traditional culture depends" (165). This unabashedly culturalist reading of speech suppression portrayed *in The Woman Warrior* but also transgressed *by* Maxine Hong Kingston, the writer, inaugurates Watson's very differently focused attempt "to locate women's autobiographies with respect to sexual demarcations along an axis of sexualities, and to read their speaking of sexual identity as complex statements that may challenge or rethink contemporary ideologies of gender" (140). This simultaneously particularized and generic positioning of *The Woman Warrior* in relation to women's autobiography studies is most provocatively staged in the footnotes of the essay where Watson narrates this history of the field: "In the last ten years, a series of canons have emerged in women's autobiography, initially privileging texts by *literary women autobiographers* (Mary McCarthy, Lillian Hellman, Virginia Woolf, and Gertrude Stein, as well as earlier spiritual autobiographers), that has now shifted toward *autobiographers of marginality* (the work of Maxine Hong Kingston, Zora Neale Hurston, Maya Angelou, women's slave narratives)" (165n6; my italics). Returning to the editorial introduction, it is noteworthy that despite their stated misgivings about the exclusionary legacy of the genre, Smith and Watson affirm that "for the marginalized woman, autobiographical language may serve as a coinage that purchases entry" (xix), which recalls Couser's heralding of autobiography as an enabling portal through which the ethnically suppressed subject can pass into an American agency of writing. From this consumerist figuration, Smith and Watson continue, "To enter into language is to press back against the disarticulated status of the spectral other that [Rey] Chow calls the 'dominated object.'" While the sense of discursive struggle as a "pressing back against" rather than expressing from within is suggestive, it remains to be asked, toward what? To emerge and become articulated as "the marginalized woman" among women?

If literary studies, disciplinarily charged with the literariness of text, is thus dominated by interpretive reaches into sociological and anthropological verities, it should not surprise that *The Woman Warrior* is circulated as a mimetic document in other disciplines that claim a more objective relationship to historical, cultural, and social realities. In an essay included in *Writing Culture: The Poetics and Politics of Ethnography,* Michael M. J. Fischer reads the book, along with Charles Mingus's *Beneath the Underdog* and Marita Golden's *Migrations of the Heart,* among other texts, in proposing that "ethnic autobiography and autobiographical fiction can perhaps serve as key forms of exploration of pluralist, post-industrial, late twentieth century society." [37] Designating his discussion of *The Woman Warrior* with the subtitle "Dream-Work," Fischer characterizes it as "an archetypal text for displaying ethnicity processes analogous to the translation of dreams" (108). This emphatic declaration commences an assured reading of Maxine Hong Kingston *as the* Woman Warrior. This autobiographical fixation is reinforced throughout in the very grammar of Fischer's analysis, which repeatedly discusses the book through a passive construction of both text and author:

> Kingston's text is developed as a series of fragments of traditional stories, myths and customs imposed by parents, but not adequately explained, at critical points of her childhood, which thus are embedded in consciousness to be worked out through, and integrated with, on-going experience. This process of interrogation is analogous to that experienced by the analysand in psychoanalytic therapy, who must translate from the imagery of dreams into verbal discourse so that both he and the analyst can reason through it. (208)

In transfiguring Kingston-as-textual presence from confessional subject to object of scrutiny. Fischer's reading effects an ellipsis from "her childhood" to *his* dreams. As a studied and insightful analyst, this reader can interpret and diagnose a literal attempt to forge a self as if it were unfolding before him. He writes, referring to the first section, titled "No Name Woman": "The obscure story gains force as Kingston *considers* the alternative possible interpretations it might contain" (209, my italics), and further relates, "The story, *says* Kingston, was told to warn young girls . . . but also to test the

American-born children's ability to establish realities." By establishing such stable and unbroken lines of narration and reception—there was a story, it was told to Kingston to teach her, she in turn tells this experience of listening to the reader *of The Woman Warrior*—Fischer renders Kingston less as a scriptive agent and more as an aural-to-oral conduit, that transmits to a more discerning critic, who interprets her self and her life in the end. This diminished figuration of Kingston as synchronic and oral presence, subject to another's critical examination and inscription, resonates with what Michel de Certeau has identified as a founding operation of ethnology in which the Western investigating subject distinguishes itself through a display of literacy in ethnographic accounts that construe and construct a purely oralized other as object of study and inscription.[38]

From such premise, Fischer's essay interprets the book as above all an earnest expression and exploration of ethnocultural *identity:* "The process of articulating what it means to be Chinese-American, for Kingston, is the process of creating a text that can be integrated and made coherent" (208). The legibility of this individual identification, in turn, enables this ethnographic reader to comment on a broader ethnic collectivity that Kingston belongs to but must also leave behind. He underscores "the unreal devaluation of girls in her Chinese communal setting, from which she finds an escape into American society, where she can become a strong person in her own right" (209). But this is not a permanent exit and entry into "American society," but a more temporary time-space of personal growth and empowerment, as he adds: "Like Fa Mu Lan, she feels she must stay away until strong enough to return and reform the stifling Chinese immigrant community" (209). The autobiographical and sociocultural transparency of *The Woman Warrior,* which Fischer assumes in such statements, is striking since the essay readily acknowledges the poststructuralist critiques of language as mediation. In superinscribing his own ethnographic observations over this oralized account by a "Chinese-American," Fischer mobilizes *The Woman Warrior* and the other texts for an ethnic "bifocality," which, he adds, "has always been part of the anthropological rationale: seeing others against the backdrop of ourselves, and ourselves against a background of others" (199). Ultimately, what is demonstrated here is not any truth about *The Woman Warrior,* Maxine Hong Kingston, or "the stifling Chinese immigrant community" and its culture—or even the American society that offers freedom of individual realization—but the power of this reader-ethnographer to decipher, apprehend, and inscribe them all within the expandable yet coherent boundaries of his own encultured study.

While each critical reading is proffered as a more complicated and expansive framing of American autobiography, women's autobiography, and ethnic autobiography, these progressive gestures rely on the "author function" of Maxine Hong Kingston as a particular Other. This generic classification further supports the presumed stability of the demarcations of national, gender, and ethnic difference. However, in foregrounding the defining significance of one identity over another, some part of the nexus of "Asian American woman writer" must be crucially left out or subsumed to produce the confident readings of *The Woman Warrior* as a proper example of national narration, women's self-writing, or native ethnography.

Eschewing Autobiography, Reinscribing the Autobiographical

In critiquing the generic fixation of *The Woman Warrior* and its prodigious power not only to belong to but to stand for and even to redeem the disciplined and identity-based study of autobiography, I am not headed toward another, more fitting generic classification. Indeed, even in those instances, which explicitly reject the autobiographical categorization, there is a lingering tendency to fall back on the ontological guarantee offered by the proper name of Maxine Hong Kingston. Noting how the book is "often discussed as unproblematically autobiographical in both mainstream and feminist discussions of autobiographical writing," Liz Stanley chooses to "treat it as fiction, albeit fiction that is autobiographical."[39] Even as she seeks to differentiate "the girl narrator" from "the young Maxine Hong Kingston" in contradistinction to other readers who assume their "synonymity," the discussion ends by recourse to the textually discernible figure of an adult Kingston who writes. Describing the narrator's language as marked by silences and even a "muteness," Stanley claims, "Yet, as soon as readers know this, share the silence, so we also have foreknowledge that the future holds a triumphant kind of speaking in a different and authoritative voice: that is, the author, whose realities we participate in on her own terms" (71). In empowering the now older Maxine Hong Kingston and the author of *The Woman Warrior* as really in charge of the terms of the book's reading, Stanley mutes her own critical projection of their synonymity.

Noting a "crisis in the critical approaches to the discourses of women's self-representation," Leigh Gilmore explains how the privileged linking of gender and genre has induced an impoverished reading of women's autobiography.[40] In addition to how "a focus on gender may theoretically diminish the significance of sexuality, race, and class," Gilmore adds that it also fixes the interpretive possibilities of gender within "autobiography's discursive nexus of identity, representation, and politics":

> Gender is interpretable through a formalist logic by which the sex one can see becomes the gender one must be. According to the formalist logic of gender, the binary of sex (of which there are only two: male and female) is the "natural" ground onto which gender as a cultural construction is layered. Autobiography, then, according to this logic of development, would translate the fact of sexual difference through the experience of gender to its subsequent representation. In this dynamic of production, autobiography is the last domino to fall: sex becomes gender becomes experience becomes book. (11)

Against this expressive and mimetic reading of women's autobiography, Gilmore offers the term "autobiographics" to note instances which are evidently "over-written" in a way that emphasize textuality or "writing itself as constitutive of autobiographical identity" such that "the autobiographicality of the *I* in a variety of discourses is emphasized as a point in self-representation" (42 and 45, original italics). As to the matter of gender, Gilmore points to lesbian autobiography in particular as offering "a historical and cultural account of how gender and sexuality are not simultaneously known, experienced, lived, and represented," and adds that "their self-representational projects perform cultural work through autobiography focused in how sex does *not* become gender become heterosexual desire become female subjectivity" (12, original italics). I find all of the above points highly suggestive for a different reading of *The Woman Warrior,* and Gilmore indeed devotes an entire chapter to this book.

The chapter is replete with anchoring the "Chinese-ness" of Maxine Hong Kingston as alternately a "fictive self, a writing self, and an historical self," all discernible through the text. Asserting early on that "Maxine

Hong Kingston creates a myth of identity," the terms by which Gilmore describes this creation process are striking: "The swordswoman Fa Mu Lan of ancient Chinese lore and the young Kingston, who wants to score well on exams so she can go to college, are pulled from different rhetorical situations and bound together through talk-story, her mother's name for storytelling. Kingston's mother's talk-story is one of the technologies of autobiography in relation to which Kingston must represent herself" (172). When she gets around to the matter of gender, Gilmore espies only a culturally specific struggle: "Kingston describes the ambivalence in the Chinese discourse of gender identity as profoundly unsettling. The practices of female infanticide and female slavery, however, more accurately represent the daily life of women in the China from which the talk-stories are drawn. Kingston offers a litany of epithets suggesting the value of women in no uncertain terms" (172). The ethnicity the feminist critic can see is the ethnicity the female autobiographer must be.

Placing the text within and against an American tradition of what she calls "personal-political narratives," Malini Johar Schueller explains her decision to devote the final chapter of *The Politics of Voice: Liberalism and Social Criticism from Franklin to Kingston* to *The Woman Warrior*: "it is not only a personal-political narrative by a marginal writer, written through the perspective of marginality, but also a radical narrative which questions the unified and autonomous subject of liberal capitalism and demonstrates the effectiveness of a politics of difference."[41] Displaying a fair amount of awareness about the history of Chinese exclusion and disenfranchisement in the United States, from which she derives her repeated focus on Kingston's marginality, Schueller also departs from some of the other critics of American autobiography by emphasizing the "radical instability (of the narrative voice) which questions the very notions of identity and universality." (144). Given this more informed and sophisticated critical interrogation, Schueller nevertheless reads *and* inscribes Kingston as a distinctly autobiographical figure. Defining the book as "a collection of 'memoirs' of Kingston's experiences of growing up in an immigrant family in Stockton, California," Schueller goes on to observe how "Kingston *reveals* the squalor and poverty of Chinatowns, the endemic racism, the traumas of acculturation in a hostile environment, and her own attempt to subvert gender hierarchies by imaginative identification with the woman warrior" (144–45, my italics). Presuming an empirical reality of "experiences" that undergirds the book, the choice of the verb "reveals" is itself revealing of the assumption of access to some hidden sociological community and individual psychology. Already present in the above passage, such active psychologizing of the figure of Maxine Hong Kingston is more forcefully brought out in the subsequent discussion of the thematic of silence and voicing. Reading the "vivid accounts of being tortured by silence" in the book as "metaphors for the particular limitations the marginal writer must overcome in order to be heard," Schueller adds, "Kingston's voicelessness is a symbolic expression of the culture's refusal to give her voice legitimacy" (148). However, Schueller knows enough to immediately qualify: "But the alternative to disempowerment, Kingston knows, is not to create a 'true' Chinese woman's voice or to define a singular Chinese identity to celebrate, but to question the very political structures that make positions of power and powerlessness possible":

> . . . the voice Kingston speaks through is not isolated and autonomous. It refracts, echoes, and is creatively conjoined with the numerous voices with which it interacts. The undefined basis of narration dramatizes *Kingston's determination* not to create singular definitions of ethnic identity in order to combat the impoverishing stereotypes to which Chinese-Americans are subject. She *does not wish* to postulate the foundations of a new hierarchy. (145, my italics)

The italicized phrases assume that the discerning critic possesses certain access to a knowing and interrogating consciousness of the author.

Schueller's often complex critical reading of *The Woman Warrior* is further compromised by her ascribing to Maxine Hong Kingston a fixed and discrete location of marginality. While she credits Kingston the author for challenging and undoing racial and sexual oppositions, she does so by ascribing a racially and sexually generic subject-position: "Kingston's questioning of oppositions and her resistance to definition are intensely political struggles. For *the Asian woman* who is often pathologized by a singular definition (most commonly as the 'passive,' unemancipated woman), such a dialogic stance is a strategy of survival" (152, my italics). In privileging *The Woman Warrior* as an expression of both oppressed marginality and its strategic resistance, in contrast to the other authors of "personal-political narratives" whom Schueller sees as operating *within* the liberal, bourgeois tradition, she heralds but does not adequately account for the historical conditions that could have enabled this shift. Furthermore, Schueller assumes the task of prescribing the literary responsibilities of "the marginalized writer" when she writes, "if marginalized groups are to be effective, they have to subvert the concepts of unity, coherence, and universality and force a recognition of the values of multiplicity and diversity upon the dominant culture" (144). Her positing and overvaluation of a space of marginality that nevertheless remains in thrall to the dominant center could use some further elaboration. Ultimately, *The Woman Warrior* is positioned not against but *within* the development of this "American" tradition. The space of marginality thus idealized makes *The Woman Warrior* not so much a critique of the liberal national tradition but a renarration of the nation as more truly inclusive and productive of its (radical) margins. This reading then *naturalizes* the book and its author.

In an essay titled "The Subject of Memoirs," Lee Quinby has written the most telling instance of an explicit resistance to the autobiographical classification, which nevertheless relies on the assurance of the proper name.[42] Citing Foucault's admonition that "maybe the target nowadays is not to discover who we are but to refuse who we are," Quinby credits Kingston for her "refusal" of the totalizing individuality of the modern era and "the fields of representation that have promoted that subjectivity" (297). Placing emphasis on the expressed identification of "memoirs" in the book's subtitle, he further quotes a 1982 interview in which Kingston claimed that she "is not writing history or sociology but a 'memoir' like Proust" (264). Dating the production of "modern memoirs" back two centuries before the appearance in 1809 of the first known autobiography, Quinby "heralds the older genre," for "it promotes an 'I' that is explicitly constituted in the reports and proceedings of others." Against the individualized and self-interested recounting of autobiographical inscription, Quinby favors *memoir,* which names "a type of writing that is a composite of several generic discourses" (300). This might be extremely suggestive for my line of inquiry in this chapter and in this book as whole except for the emphatic declaration that shortly follows: "*The Woman Warrior* is precisely such a composite." The move away from one generic fixation leads to yet another.

Tracing the strange etymology of "memoir," Quinby reads how the word itself may be understood as "a metonym of Kingston's particular discursive position" (300).[43] He continues to explain, "A Chinese-American, her linguistic heritage is informed by two different language systems. As a woman, she is a 'somewhat anomalous' memoirist, using a grammatically feminine term that has been colonized by a masculine form." From this considerate delineation of ethnic and gender differences in language systems and grammatical rules, the slide from discursive position to Kingston as an ontological person, expressing her self and life through the book, is fairly seamless. "Kingston represents her girlhood as triply displaced" is followed by, "The idea of ghosts suggests the profound confusion she felt as a child" (301). Consequently, "She is haunted by the stories of China that her mother told her, stories of women's oppression and female infanticide." In perhaps the most extreme instance of autobiographical fixation, Quinby observes, "The memoirs recount extensively Kingston's own difficulties with language, focusing on them as a feature of the conflict of cultural impulses within Chinese-American culture generally and her Chinese-American family specifically" (303).

This second cluster of critical readings *against* autobiography privileges and reifies certain categorical delineations of nation, gender, ethnicity, and culture in ways that ultimately, and especially when taken together, necessitate the autobiographical fixation of *The Woman Warrior.* When these accounts are considered alongside the other interpretations that take for granted the autobiographical status of *The Woman Warrior,* the proper name of Maxine Hong Kingston would seem not only to have led multiple lives as multiple selves, but also to have waged multiple struggles with and against multiple problems of language. It is certainly not reducible to the vital statistics of one person. In certain respects, the critical interpretations render a presumed autobiographer into a biographee—the person about whom a biography is written. To push the point even further, this particular "Asian-American woman writer" is an anomalous *autobiographee*—the person about whom an autobiography is read. However, I would argue that the generic impossibility of *The Woman Warrior* is announced by the very possibility of the production and proliferation of such discretely positioned readings. Furthermore, inasmuch as the assumptions of its autobiographical truthfulness have served to shore up the disciplinary borders of literary study as flexible and accommodating of social difference, those very profuse and scattered attempts to herald the text as a distinctive genre of literary production leak beyond "the serious study of imaginative literature as such" in the apprehension of *The Woman Warrior* as transmitting extratextual realities about *a* self, *a* community, or *a* culture.

The "Autobiographical Controversy" of
Asian American Literature

If it has spurred on *and* consolidated a host of differently confident interpretations in literary studies, the generic classification of *The Woman Warrior* has been figured in the interdisciplinary terrain of Asian American studies as a defining and persistent controversy. Here, the name "Maxine Hong Kingston" has come to stand for and point to one side of a conflict around the proper politics and poetics of an "Asian American literature" while the other side has been identified by the name "Frank Chin." A playwright who had achieved some critical acclaim for *The Chickencoop Chinaman* (1972), Frank Chin sought to establish a distinct "Asian-American literature" by coediting the anthology *Aiiieeeee!: An Anthology of Asian-American Writers* (1974) with Jefferey Paul Chan, Lawson Fusao Inada, and Shawn Wong. According to one widely cited origin story titled "Word Warriors" and published in the *Los Angeles Times,* "In 1976, Kingston and her editor asked Chin to endorse her soon-to-be-published book," which initiated a "barrage of correspondence" that centrally revolved around the racist implications of literary genres: "Chin wrote Kingston that her prose was moving and lyrical. But he couldn't back this book that purported to be a non-fiction account of a Chinese American. He argued that autobiographies by Asian Americans were cloying bids for white acceptance. 'I want your book to be an example of yellow art by a yellow artist,' he wrote 'not the publisher's manipulation of another Pocahontas.'"[44] The "literary duel" between the two authors extended and expanded into a "pen war that raged between the defenders of Kingston on the one side and Chin and his supporters on the other."[45]

While Frank Chin, Jefferey Paul Chan, and Benjamin Tong have couched their criticisms of the book as motivated by an antiracist resistance to assimilationist pressures, a range of feminist literary scholars have foregrounded the thoroughly gendered, heterosexual, and often sexist assumptions that undergird their charges. Elaine H. Kim casts the controversy as a struggle between "men and women in Asian American literature," which itself is borne of the uneven disenfranchisement of collectively racialized but differentially gendered social subjects in the United States: "Relative and limited increases in options for Asian women in American society have been made possible largely because Asian patriarchy was pushed aside or subsumed by an American patriarchy that did not, because of racism, extend its promise to Asian American men. Deprived of the rewards of patriarchal legitimacy, some Asian American men have responded by attempting to reassert male authority over the cultural domain and over women by subordinating feminism to nationalist concerns."[46] Political and economic inequalities are the primary historical forces that shape the attitudes, aspirations, and prohibitions that come to be expressed in the realm of culture. Literary production is then an important site of social and ideological struggle.

In her framing of what she calls a tension between "feminist and ethnic literary theories," Shirley Geok-lin Lim similarly argues that "Asian American literature (restricted here to Japanese, Chinese, and Korean American literature) has been an active site of masculinist views and feminist resistance."[47] Characterizing the writings of Asian/American women as "symptomatic of the struggle to figure the subject between the often oppositional demands of ethnic and gender identity," Lim would reconfigure the terms of the debate as not so much about the demographics of "who should be read—female or male *writers*," but rather a more literary struggle "over how representation of the subject is negotiated between ethnic and feminist *thematics*" (573, my italics). Unlike Kim's emphasis on the defining significance of broader social inequalities in the United States, Lim attempts to anchor this struggle of gender representation to "Asian" tradition: "The polarities between feminist and masculinist assertions of identity were already in place in the traditional east Asian patriarchal constructions of society" (573).

Lisa Lowe sees not so much an all-encompassing conflict between nationalist men, on the one side, and feminist women, on the other, but a more localized "debate in which Chin and others stand at one end insisting upon a fixed masculinist identity, while Kingston, Tan, or feminist literary critics like Shirley Lim and Amy Ling, with their representations of female differences and their critiques of sexism in Chinese culture, repeatedly cast this notion of identity in question."[48] Pointing out how the strident ethnonationalism articulated by Chin "obscures" important gender and class distinctions among "Asian Americans," Lowe further clarifies that the controversy is "more properly characterized as a struggle between the desire to essentialize ethnic identity and the fundamental condition of heterogeneous differences against which such a desire is spoken." Going beyond a binary of men and women, feminists and nationalists, then, Lowe's figuration of critical desires cannot be firmly moored in opposing dyads of gendered bodies or ideological positions. Situated instead within the constraints of a larger discursive struggle, the proper name of "Maxine Hong Kingston" and the proper vocation of "Asian-American woman writer" just may be unbound from their generic fixations.

This productive possibility has been significantly curtailed by the ways in which the "autobiographical controversy" over *The Woman Warrior* has itself taken on a sociological solidity through its repeated invocation as *the* defining debate within Asian American literary studies. In "Re-Viewing Asian American Literary Studies," King-kok Cheung characterizes this "pen war" as "the most notorious and protracted" debate in the field. While many of these accounts have often focused upon the proper and preferred role of the "Asian American woman writer," two other kinds of *reading* subjects have emerged as significant figures: the Asian/American "feminist critic" and the "white reader." In the essay "The Woman Warrior versus The Chinaman Pacific," King-kok Cheung explicitly frames the cultural debate as a case of divided critical loyalties, asking in the subtitle, "Must a Chinese American Critic Choose Between Feminism and Heroism?" Citing Frank Chin's hyperbolic condemnation of autobiography as a feminized and irredeemably capitulatory genre, Cheung characterizes Chin and his fellow male writers as attempting to assert their "Asian American manhood" by recovering the heroic tradition of Chinese myth and literature. To this cohort, Cheung opposes those who "believe that women have always appropriated autobiography as a vehicle for asserting, however tentatively, their subjectivity."[49] This cross-ethnic collectivity of "feminist critics" applaud the book for its female-specific mode of self-writing in contrast to those ethnically specified "Chinese American critics—mostly male but also some female—who tax Kingston for misrepresenting Chinese and Chinese American culture, and for passing fiction for autobiography" (238). Far from questioning the book's generic classification, Cheung invokes "feminist scholars of autobiography" to situate Kingston within a tradition of "women's autobiography" in which "women writers often shy away from 'objective' autobiography and prefer to use the form to reflect a private world, a subjective vision, and the life of the imagination" (239). In the end, this reading exonerates Kingston as autobiographical subject through a reframing of "Kingston's autobiographical act," which, according to Cheung, "far from betokening submission, as Chin believes, turns the self into a 'heroine' and is in a sense an act of 're-venge' . . . against both the Chinese and white cultures that undermine her self-esteem" (239). The critic's dilemma posed in the essay's title is thus resolved in the heroism *and* feminism displayed in the text and by the author. Rather than deconstruct the terms of their opposition, Cheung reifies them by figuring their reconciliation as the particular psychic and political burden of a Chinese American feminist critic, thereby emphasizing the "racial and sexual attributes" of a critical position.

Is Kang's project de-constructive???

In a very resonant exploration of this debate in terms of a tension between filiation and affiliation whereby feminism is positioned as a betrayal of ethnic loyalties, Leslie Bow notes, "The Kingston/Chin debate suggests a binarism into which bodies can easily be read: to do any kind of feminist work is to be an assimilationist."[50] This begs the question of the failure of feminism to marshal the pull of belonging and any consequent betrayals in the way that ethnic affiliation is presumed to do. However, Bow, like Cheung, transposes the binary as the particular onus of a critical subject: "In examining the ways in which the opposition between cultural nationalism and feminism is constructed, I realize that as an Asian American feminist literary critic I am likewise implicated in this betrayal." She then asks, "Am I an Asian Americanist or a feminist?" She further suggests that for an "Asian American feminist literary critic" to speak of the debates in a critical register is itself "a violation of 'family' codes" and represents "a kind of betrayal, paralleling the dynamics that arise in the literature when Asian American women are forced to choose between familial and sexual alliances or between gender collectivity and Asian cultural identity" (36–37).

In a more recent configuration of competing critical loyalties, Jinqui Ling is able to figure feminism as a betrayal of ethnic communality by narrating a linear development of Asian American literature as established first and foremost as a unified antiracist project with the publication of *Aiii-eeeee!* in the early 1970s.[51] In attempting to situate how its four editors "angrily affirmed their Americanness through a discourse of citizenship,"

Ling argues that "we see that it constituted, for the first time since the mid-nineteenth century, a public claim on rights that Asian Americans were entitled to but denied historically" (25).[52] Crediting the anthology's editors with this primary protest, Ling claims that "Kingston virtually started a revolution within a revolution" with the writing and publication of *The Woman Warrior*. Ling recounts: "Shortly after the formation of a narrowly defined and counterhegemonic Asian American literary discourse represented by Chin and the other editors of *Aiiieeeee!*, Kingston's Chinese American feminist discourse defiantly branched out from the larger community-based Asian American literary revival and drew support from the mainstream feminist movement" (115). As evidence of how Kingston, as a historical person writing in the 1970s, was nurtured by feminism, Ling cites the instance in *The Woman Warrior* when the narrator points to the interchangeability of the Chinese word for the female "I" and for "slave." Rather than anthropologically mirroring Chinese culture, as Sidonie Smith would cast this detail, Ling transfigures this "appropriation of the Chinese language by Kingston" as having "derived from its rhetorical form from two [other] interrelated cultural contexts." Ling describes one such cultural context as "an important argument made by 'mainstream' American feminists in the late 1960s and early 1970s for consciousness-raising—that is, women's oppression is a form of enslavement—an argument that emphasized the moral urgency of women's liberation through invoking scenarios of American slavery" (116).[53] If feminism is a recitation of a prior racial discourse of enslavement and freedom, Kingston's "Chinese American feminist discourse" is doubly removed from the "Asian American community" in the itinerary Ling maps here from ethnically marginalized origin to "mainstream" feminist destination. Thus he can confidently declare, "This formative moment created a context ripe for betrayal."

Ling is able to reconcile this gendered straying and contamination by a redoubled ethnic solidarity-in-commonality. In addition to privileging an originary, "community-based Asian American literary revival" against a belated, imported feminism, Ling's own critical allegiance to the editors of *Aiiieeeee!* is expressed through his approbation of the more "overtly oppositional" writings of Chin and his cohorts, whom Ling further credits with having "strategically raised Asian American's angry voice publicly" (115). This antiracist defiance is buttressed further by aligning it as "congruent with and partly shaped by the black protest and counterculture movements" (115). In consideration of such origins, Ling warns that their criticisms of *The Woman Warrior* should not be dismissed as "merely sexist": "Rather, these varying responses should be viewed as illustrations of how the articulation of Chinese American women's oppression is caught up with that of Chinese American men's" (114). It is telling that, at this point, this cross-gender affiliation is called for in ethnically specified terms whereas Ling deploys "Chinese American" and "Asian American" interchangeably throughout the book.

But how to resolve the lingering legacy in which the proper name of Maxine Hong Kingston has been so singularly overinvested with the taint of ethnic betrayal? How to explain why one particular text, *The Woman Warrior,* has been so singularly heralded as the mark and the measure of both "Chinese American" and "Asian American" literary achievement? Ling writes, "the reception of *The Woman Warrior* reflects both the epistemological and ontological difficulties posed for a woman writer of color, whose ability to speak—and whose chance to be heard—was severely limited by given racial, gender, and class power structures" (114). This apparently more sympathetic portrait of one "woman writer of color" reduces the very profuse and tangled web of readings and writings, which I have attempted to map above, to a lone struggle of orality and aurality. Displaced from the political economy of literary production and criticism but amplified through the corporeal intimacies of *speaking* and *hearing,* Ling privatizes broader political and discursive contradictions as the onus of being and of knowing for one racialized and gendered individual: "The challenge that faced Kingston, one may speculate, was how to carry out the task of articulating Asian American women's concerns and still locate common grounds with Asian American men's interests, and how to strengthen rather than weaken an evolving Asian American cultural voice through women's interventionary moves that could also be culturally rigorous and politically constructive" (117). In this yet another generic fixation, Maxine Hong Kingston is absolved of the charges of betrayal and transfigured into a properly representative, if suffering, Asian American writing self.

Some body or some thing else must then take a place at the outer limits. The "f" word not accidentally drops out in this reconciliation. In the reach for an "Asian American" commonality and solidarity, which can only and properly be expressed through a singular, coherent "cultural voice," any feminist articulation that does not share or support a "common ground" with "men's interests" can be neither rigorous nor constructive. If Maxine Hong Kingston is to be embraced back into the folds of an ethnically communal politics, the bearer of feminist critique shifts to a broader social body that Ling earlier identifies as "some Asian American feminist critics," who "continue their impassioned exchange with Chin, mostly in reaction to the obviously simplistic aspects of his position, with the aid of analytical tools available from posthumanist discourses" (113). These critics are outcast in their feminist *and* posthumanist borrowings.

Another repeated tactic of recusing the author from the critical (mis)-readings of her text is through shifting the focus to the generative yet mistaken interpretive impulses of particular constituencies of readers. If King-kok Cheung has affirmed *The Woman Warrior* as autobiography in line with other feminist critics, other commentators on this debate have sought to disavow its autobiographical status as produced and propagated largely by "white" readers.[54] This social body is frequently distinguished from but more often interchanged with "non-Asian" or "non–Asian American" readers.[55] To be sure, such racialized identifications first pop up in and through efforts to *describe* the resistance to "white readers" in the diatribes by Frank Chin and others. This delineation of a distinctly "white" reading position also recurs in the critical scholarship. Elaine H. Kim declares, "There is no doubt that many non-Asian readers, completely ignorant about Chinese Americans, take Kingston's metaphors as Chinese 'facts,' viewing them only according to a flat-footed facticity."[56] On the next page, Kim becomes more specific in pointing out how "white readers of *The Woman Warrior* have indeed found in it ways to reinforce their stereotypes about Asian Americans" (80). Similarly, Robert G. Lee attributes resistance to the book partially to the fact that "it exoticizes the Chinese aspect of the Chinese American experience, thereby catering to the Orientalist prejudices of its white audience."[57] While conceding that "few public places and events in the outer world are recognizable from what we know about Kingston's life," Sau-ling Wong adds that "all else is recollection, speculation, reflection, mediation, imagination."[58] She continues: "Presumably, then, the readers who do not pay sufficient attention to the narrative intricacies of *The Woman Warrior,* especially white readers with biased expectations, will mistake fiction for fact" (252). While whiteness may be somewhat divested of the prestige of rightness here, this specific attribution of misreading reinstalls a racial binary of otherness and sameness. Even as "white" confidently points to some unified and homogeneous social body and its interpretive proclivities, the elision between "white readers" and "non-Asian readers" inscribes the insignificance and even the erasure of nonwhite, non-Asian reading publics. It further presumes that all "Asian American" readers of the book get it right. If the critical discourse on and around *The Woman Warrior* is to move beyond the constraints of its generic fixation by those who would extract truths about the author as well as her culture, the prodigious effects of the text should not be foreclosed by epistemologically privileging—or blaming—*any* body.

The confident figuration of an ontologically and epistemologically "white" audience, against which more culturally sensitive and knowing "Asian American" readings are to be measured, uncannily hearkens back to the representational dilemmas of early autobiographies. In her foundational study, *Asian American Literature,* Elaine H. Kim provides a rich and detailed analysis of the writing and circulation of the autobiographical writings by Asians in the United States as shaped by specific historical conditions. For instance, the systematic exclusion and socioeconomic marginalization of Asian immigrants in the nineteenth century precluded the development of a substantial population of writers as well as a market demand for their literary productions. Many of the earliest writings published in the first half of the twentieth century were authored by elite "Ambassadors of Good Will," who aimed to ally themselves with readers, often by differentiating and distancing themselves from the poorer, less educated Asian immigrants.

> Until recently, published Asian American writers presented the Asian American experience lightly and euphemistically, even humorously, without significant expression of concern about the manifestations of social injustice. Bitterness against Asian cultures and values, and Asian American values and life styles, were far better tolerated by publishers and a predominantly white readership, which has been traditionally more receptive to expressions of self-contempt and self-negation on the part of members of racial minorities than to criticisms of problems in American society. Limited as they were by such a climate, and often by their own ignorances as well, it should not be surprising that those early Asian American autobiographers who did publish accepted the "cultural bridge" (be-

tween Asia and America) role while at the same time expressing the ar-
dent desire for acceptance in American society by any means necessary,
and under almost any conditions.[59]

While their descriptions of their native lands fed a growing popular fascination with Orientalist exotica during this period of the United States' first
imperialist forays into Asia, these autobiographical efforts to harmoniously
reconcile the "East" and "West" militated against the cultural threat of permanent Asian presence by affirming *American* values of individualism,
hope, and success. Following the assimilationist logic that one becomes
more "American" as one sheds and/or disavows any marker of racial difference and ethnic affiliation, such "bids for acceptance" (89) continued
well into the autobiographical writings of U.S.-born Japanese Americans
in the 1970s. Kim further underscores the market-driven motivation behind such ethnic *de*-composition: "The more complete the process of self-
negation, the more likely that the autobiography will be hailed as a 'success story'" (81).

This inverse ratio of ethnic distinction and self-assertion to national
legibility and literary success foregrounds the compromising and paradoxical status of autobiographical classification for Asian American literary
production and criticism. First, the writing and circulation of Asian American autobiographies are enabled and constrained by the changing dictates
of a larger political economy of publishing and criticism, which are in turn
shaped by shifting definitions and valuations of Asian, American, and Asian
American identities. Writing more recently in 1998 about how "we need
to question whether there is some unspoken formula for Asian American
literary success that prevents those who deviate from it from being heard,"
King-kok Cheung asks, "Why, for instance, is there such a preponderance
of autobiographical works by Asian Americans?" ("Re-viewing," 17). The
self-negation that is necessitated by appealing to such situational pressures
(dis)qualifies the generic categorization of these texts and their consequent
critical reception as unmediated expressions of the *autos* and the *bios* of one
ethnic individual. If the genealogy of "Asian American autobiography"
foregrounds those writings not of the self but of differential stagings of self-
negation and self-conversion, I want to ask what it would mean for autobiographical studies and American literary studies at large to take this history and political economy of literary production seriously. First, the *autos*

could not be easily matched to either a writing subject or to one "person of vital statistics." Second, it would trouble the alliterative alignment of "America" and "Autobiography." If we recall Thomas Couser's figuration of autobiography as a portal of Americanization, the distinct *autos* of American autobiography may itself have to be socially and historically degraded.

But where could such an investigation fit within prevailing demarcations of different scholarly domains? The repeated casting of this debate as *the* defining controversy of an "Asian American literary studies" works to particularize what I would frame as a broader clash of disciplinarity and social difference. Put differently, while the focus on the particular figures of "Asian American woman writer," "Chinese American feminist critic," and "white reader" appears to reference socially and politically distinctive persons, I would reframe the contentions around the generic status of *The Woman Warrior* as a problem of disciplinary un / belonging in relation to literary studies and interdisciplinary Asian American studies.[60] Here, I would direct attention to two prevalent modes of classification in literary studies: according to literary genres and, more recently, according to social identities, as in "Asian American literature." A frequent tactic of disciplinary representation implicitly rests on the sociological correspondence of certain select texts with real "Asian American" bodies and lives, mostly in terms of the racial, ethnic, and gender identification of the author. Lisa Lowe claims: "*The Woman Warrior* is the target of such criticism because it was virtually the first 'canonized' piece of Asian American literature" (*Immigrant Acts,* 76). Rather than a racist or culturally ignorant mistake, the autobiographical fixation of the book has been crucial to this canonization by affirming the socially inclusionary capacities of literary studies. I would extend this to suggest that the book's canonization has paved the grounds for the later establishment of "Asian American literature" as a legible and legitimate field of literary study.

If the book's generic fixation affirms the inclusionary desires at play in the more disciplinarily entrenched subfields of "American autobiography" or "women's autobiography" precisely by authorizing the text to shine under the rays of racial, ethnic, cultural *difference,* it is telling that the generic label has been so strenuously disavowed and worried over when *The Woman Warrior* is placed under the banner of racial-ethnic *sameness,* without any other specific protocols of legibility. Here, it may be useful to distinguish in rather stark terms the two anxieties that are expressed at this

Recast debate in terms of disciplines

Autobio fixation crucial to canonization of book & est. of AA literature impasse of identity and disciplinarity. I have related at length the antipathy toward how the autobiographical classification qualifies the book to be read as *other than* literature by literary critics and scholars who would see a mimetic, representative account of "Chinese American" or "Asian American" history, culture, and experience. However, there is an attendant desire for the inclusion within literature and literary study of texts that can *speak for* a particularly marginalized group, which Sau-ling Wong describes as "the premise that a definitive version of the life of an ethnic group exists, one which is the ethnic writer's moral responsibility to represent."[61] As Wong goes on to explicate, this "definitive version" bears more than a demand for mimetic faithfulness so that it "would represent the given ethnic group in a favorable light, purged of annoyingly 'unique' features, and free of useless fantasy which diverts attention from the sordid facts of oppression in American society." More recently, with the growth of "Asian American literature" as an increasingly legible and in-demand subfield of literary studies, there has been an increasing apprehension that inasmuch as the book has enabled a cross-disciplinary reach into history, anthropology, and sociology, the autobiographical categorization *disqualifies* the book from being counted *as* literature. This is a dilemma that haunts the disciplinary legitimacy of "Asian American literature" and its critical scholarship, for, as King-kok Cheung notes, "The die hard tendency to value Asian American works primarily as autobiography and ethnography has perhaps prevented these works from being taken seriously as literature" ("Re-viewing," 19).

Shirley Lim's work has been perhaps most insistent and consistent in attempting to accent the "literature" in "Asian American literature." Characterizing it as composed from the beginning with an interdisciplinary component, namely, "a strong concern with its immigrant history," she continues, "Unsurprisingly, therefore, it draws heavily upon the resources of autobiography, biography, and history, provinces in which writing reflects more faithfully personal experiences, social observations, and memory."[62] Distinguishing Kingston's first two books as "histories" in a litany of other Asian American writings that she categorizes as autobiographies, short stories, and novels, Lim notes that they all "share a concern with sociological texture in their attempts to rewrite a past; as such they exhibit in different degrees a burden of referentiality in which the texts demand to be read for their relevance to an outside historical meaning." In contrast to the disciplinary murkiness effected by such obligation toward the socio-logical and historical, Lim privileges the "self-enacting, self-reflexive ver-bal structures" of a *literary* modernism. She continues, "In Asian-American writing, insofar as these works appear composed to meet external referen-tiality, be it of explanation of ethnic identity to an unknowledgeable au-dience or of fidelity to sociological and historical-based memory, they are less powerfully literary constructions" (58). In response to this disciplinary impasse, Lim would argue for "Asian-American writing"—and here her repeated emphasis on the more active "writing" over the more thinglike "literature" becomes crucial—as first and foremost *literary* constructions: "These writers [such as Kingston] have become self-conscious; they have begun to deal with problems of textuality instead of given racial stereo-types. When imaginings of self occur together with awareness of functions of text, Asian American writers liberate themselves from commonplace notions of the exotic. Moving away from sociological documentation, much contemporary Asian-American writing now aspires to the power of the literary artifact" (58).

Such literary aspirations exist in tension with the ways in which *The Woman Warrior* has often been invoked within interdisciplinary Asian American studies as illustrative of both Maxine Hong Kingston and the various ethnic or gendered constituencies she is seen to belong to. Fur-thermore, the debate over its generic categorization has itself been figured as a broader cultural, social, and historical feature of the "Asian American community." Chin's denouncements of Kingston and *The Woman Warrior* have often been cast in terms of a patriarchal Chinese or Asian *culture*, when one could also frame his misogynistic and homophobic rhetoric as very much congruous with established protocols of masculinist authorization displayed by many canonical *American* male writers.[63] In citing King-kok Cheung's essay "The Woman Warrior versus The Chinaman Pacific" to discuss how Asian American men have been "forced into 'feminine' sub-ject positions," Yen Le Espiritu generalizes the Kingston vs. Chin debate as one manifestation of a broader Asian American social and psychic phe-nomenon: "The Asian American men who can see only race oppression, and not gender domination, are unable—or unwilling—to view them-selves as both oppressed and oppressor. This dichotomous stance has led to the marginalization of Asian American women and their needs. Concerned with recuperating their identities as men and as Americans, some Asian

[handwritten margin note: lit deliv to est. legit exist in tension w/ AA studies]

American political and cultural workers have subordinated feminism to nationalist concerns."[64]

Stephen Sumida surveys the "autobiographical controversy" by holding both the text and Maxine Hong Kingston up against Asian American history. Sumida maps an ethnically delineated suspicion toward autobiography in an unbroken lineage of writings by Chinese immigrant women in the nineteenth century to Kingston as one "Chinese American" woman writing in the 1970s:

> As elsewhere in missionaries' campaigns to convert "heathen" people, in California, the act of teaching English literacy to rescued women was aimed at enabling the converts not only to read the Bible but also to confess their sinful, pagan pasts and to make way for a new Christian life. Whatever the Chinese American convert's past, it was thus intertwined with a culture that "rescuers" considered to be not simply inferior, but sinful. Writing such an "autobiography" for the missionaries had to be quite different from "confessing" to people of the same culture; for the Chinese American autobiographer—to save her very life, if she had been a caged prostitute in San Francisco—had to deal with, by the writing, being considered a representative of her culture for an audience that believed their own culture and notions of individual virtue to be superior to hers. In such an autobiography, a confession implied an apology to a higher authority.[65]

He continues, "Chinese American autobiography today inherits this history." However, besides a shared nomination as "Chinese American autobiographer," the nameless Christian convert was and is a very different kind of writing subject, *especially* if she had been a caged prostitute writing to save her life. But *how* can such writing be categorized as "autobiography" in relation to other textual instances of the genre? Given the heavily mediated and even coercive dimensions of such inscription, circulation, and reception, one could argue that such a textual articulation does not securely qualify as autobiography. Such transhistorical bridging also neglects to consider that these nineteenth-century compositions would certainly *not* be inducted into literary studies in the way that *The Woman Warrior* has been in the late twentieth century. However, the burden of this history must be borne by Maxine Hong Kingston and other "Asian-American women writers" who must write against it. Following this rationale, Sumida is able to explain Chin's criticisms against *The Woman Warrior* as "raising questions about how Asian American first-person narratives affirmed, suggested ignorance of, or were indifferent to cultures and literary histories not only of racist depictions of Asians but also of coaching books and converts' autobiographies and the like." While providing a historical ground for Chin's position, the passage above does not allow for the possibility that an act of confession *within* one's own culture might also be constrained and submissive, albeit to a different set of expectations and forms. And what gives this "culture" the prerogative to define a person's belonging and intelligibility above all?

A less confining tactic has been to emphasize the unrepresentative and un-generic possibilities of *The Woman Warrior.* In the same essay cited above, writing against the tendency to read the book as "a clear revelation by means of explicit, descriptive statement of what it means to grow up Chinese American and female," Sumida proffers a reading of the book as "a critique of its narrator, a fictional first-person 'I' meant to be questioned so that her confusions about Chinese American identity and the causes and consequences of her American ignorance of China might be understood" (403). Robert G. Lee would defend Kingston against the charges of inauthenticity by calling for a vigilant distinction of "Asian American literature" from "Asian American history":

> The damage wrought by racist stereotyping and the urgent need to rediscover lost texts and buried histories notwithstanding, we should not let ourselves be pushed into a blind empiricism in which the distance between Asian American literature and Asian American history is foreshortened by a demand for literal correspondence.
>
> This position is ultimately a reductionist one that leads to an ethnographic reading of literature in which we follow the paths set by colonial administrators and anthropologists and end up by simply extracting data on subject peoples. The reduction of literature to its data not only strips the text of its subjectivity but also prevents us from seeing its complexity as a locus of social contradictions. As a result, we may fail to recognize that history is itself a terrain on which struggles for meaning are continuous. (55)

I would venture that the "debate" over *The Woman Warrior* is symptomatic of the problem of delineating what counts as "Asian American literature," how "Asian American literature" always fails to stand for "Asian Americans." While the text has been an oft-cited touchstone, the demands and questions posed to its inability to be representative could be posed for all Asian American literature. This also troubles the ready induction of the text as American autobiography or women's autobiography as a measure of the subfields' own ethnic inclusiveness and diversity.

In contrast to Lim's advocacy for a particular telos of increasing disciplinary eligibility for "Asian American literature," Lisa Lowe emphasizes its critical resistance to secure disciplinary belonging or its "canonization." Citing David Lloyd's argument that the "Anglo-European function of canonization is to unify aesthetic culture as the domain in which material stratification and differences are reconciled," Lowe sets up in direct tension how "the study of Asian American literature has been historically an endeavor committed to a consideration of the work in terms of its material contexts of production and reception."[66] Citing Elaine H. Kim's *Asian American Literature,* Lowe continues, "If we evaluate Asian American literary expression in canonical terms, it reveals itself as an aesthetic product that cannot repress the material inequalities of its conditions of production" (54). The study of "Asian American literature" demands critical deliberation on the shifting yet unequal alignment of all three constituent parts.

If the "cultural nationalism" of Asian American literature is figured as protesting against, even as it seeks to lay claim to, a broader national literature and culture, it might be useful to recall the many-sided historicity of "American literature" itself. David R. Shumway writes in *Creating American Civilization,* "Perhaps the most taken-for-granted 'truth' of the discipline of American literature was literature itself, a timeless category considered the natural outgrowth of language under the conditions of advanced human civilizations."[67] Following from this assumption, Shumway reminds us that American literature itself was borne by the agonistic passion "to certify to the achievement of a national civilization," which could be distinguished from European and specifically English literatures. Interestingly, Shumway refers to this disciplinary formation of "American literary studies" as impelled by "a new cultural nationalism" (21). In addition to contending positions on what it means to be "American," there has been a shifting ideological valence and social significance of what constitutes "literature." When the technological innovations of the printing press combined with the opening up of education to greater numbers of people, "the mere ability to read lost its status as did readable objects" (27). This intensified a need to make distinctions amongst both "readable objects" and their respective readers. Shumway concludes, "'Literature' in the modern sense is the ultimate product of this need for distinction." He then adds, "But if 'literature' comes to mean only superior works in certain genres of writing, its specification is also partially a cultural demotion, for 'literature' . . . is no longer the equivalent of knowledge" (27). After losing this equivalent status, "along with the other fine arts, [literature] was now understood as a bearer of moral truth and therefore as being a means of social amelioration." The special warrant of literature would suffer yet another epistemological demotion by the challenge posed by the ascendance of the social sciences which "substituted science for the wisdom of the ages": "The possibility of modern academic criticism emerged when literature lost to the social sciences its function of social guide and became defined primarily as an aesthetic enterprise" (28). This enclosure did not afford disciplinary coherence for, as Shumway also recalls, there were multiply inflected contestations over the meaning of the term "literary" at the turn of the century. While some elitists deployed it positively as a marker of class distinction from emergent popular cultural forms such as the magazine, mass market publishers wielded it more pejoratively "to designate what they considered the effete products and practices of their opponents." Such imputation of class, gender, and sexual properties suggests that disciplinary objects and domains—and not just social bodies—can also be made to bear particularized social identifications. Considering such discursive struggles, Shumway accents that the disciplinary formation of literary studies and its more nation-specific manifestation as "American literature" are thoroughly imbricated with the socioeconomic phenomenon of "academic professionalization," specifically "the formation of a national association [MLA] with its attendant central journal" (57). Finally, Shumway's point that bibliographical research and literary history dominated the discipline—and this was necessary to establish a distinctly American national literary tradition and corpus—and that "criticism of American literature remained outside of American literature as a discipline" (57) insists on the shifting historicity of literary studies.

This chapter has studied the ways in which the generic fixation of *The Woman Warrior* has unleashed a host of interpretive claims that are enabled but also significantly constrained by prevailing disciplinary protocols and identity markers. Alongside the preceding account of "literature" as a nationally located, historical, social, and political economic construct, I would like to end by reciting an account of *The Woman Warrior* in a transnational frame. Early on in this chapter, I pointed to the publication by the MLA of the edited volume *Approaches to Teaching Kingston's "The Woman Warrior"* as part of a series on "Approaches to Teaching World Literature." Preceding the very diverse seventeen critical essays is an intriguing "Personal Statement" by Maxine Hong Kingston. Noting how "readers often ask how she [Kingston's mother] feels about my writing," she offers this response:

> Well, since she doesn't read English, she can't get the fullest impact and power of my work. She reads the translations that have been pirated in Taiwan, Hong Kong and China. Since pirates work fast, they use ready-made literary forms. They do not take the care to experiment with language or to try new shapes—to find the new shapes that I'm working in. The easiest given form is soap opera, which fakes passion and revelation. I suppose my mother thinks I am strong on plot and very entertaining, like her favorite American book, *Gone With the Wind*. She takes the world's praise of my work at face value and assumes that she and our family come off well.[68]

In further expanding the circulation routes of *The Woman Warrior* as object of interpretation, admiration, and contempt within and across both disciplinary and identity-based fields of study, which I have tracked in this chapter, the passage above suggests other possible positionings of the "Asian American woman writer" beyond any one origin or destination.

chapter 2

Cinematic Projections

Marking the Desirous Body

Literally, colonization operates by taking over land and bodies. On a symbolic level, it works on bodies because physical anatomies become the canvas onto which cultural meanings are projected. Although it is apparent that Asians, like people of color in general, are marginalized and rendered invisible in the mass media, Asian women are, through representation, "embodied" in a distinctive and at times literalized way. . . . the bodies of Asian women are palpably present in the mass media in the most physicalized and sexualized terms. . . . For Asian women especially, ideologies of gender, race, ethnicity, and sexuality place their bodies under the burden of erasure while also marking them as receptacles of projected cultural meanings.—Marina Heung, "Representing Ourselves"[1]

The bodies of Asian women, as outlined in the above passage, bear a promiscuous range of afflictions. While *they* (a collocation of like anatomies) render an inanimate, blank screen onto which meanings can be readily projected by some other cultural agent, *they* (a class of multiple ideological subjection) are effaced from some other point of view even as *they* (a three-dimensional depository of cultural meanings) house an interiority that is vulnerable to certain intrusions from elsewhere. This odd mixture of a severely constrained cinematic representation that wields both a powerfully far-reaching social effect and a penetrating force in psychic formation has been repeatedly figured as the emblematic injury of Asian/American women. Indeed, critical analyses of visual representations have been included from the very initial efforts to articulate the very categories of

"Asian women" and "Asian American women." In an earlier and still widely cited examination of "images of Asian women," Renee Tajima formulated "two basic types: the Lotus Blossom baby (a.k.a. China Doll, Geisha Girl, shy Polynesian beauty), and the Dragon Lady (Fu Manchu's various female relations, prostitutes, devious madams)."[2] While the Dragon Lady represents a special Asian mix of sexual perversity, moral depravity, and drive for domination, the submissive Lotus Blossom projects a more welcoming image of exotic difference and erotic possibilities. Their appealing bodies are often complemented by what Tajima calls their "non-language" or "uninterpretable chattering, pidgin English, giggling or silence" (310).

In his broader and more exhaustive study of Hollywood film depictions of Asians, Eugene Franklin Wong concludes that the single most stereotypical representation of Asian women has focused not so much on certain distinguishing details of speech or personality but on their being positioned in an interracial relationship with the white male protagonist. This, he explains, often had much to do with ideological projections of white masculinity as distinct from and superior to Asian masculinity:

> In romantic potential Asian males are essentially character eunuchs. In sexual potential they are depicted as primarily character rapists. . . . Asian females, in turn, are provided no alternative on the matter of sex. If the industry calls for interracial sexuality, then that sexuality will occur between a white male and an Asian female. Unlike the racist image of the threatening Asian rapist, white males are generally provided the necessary romantic conditions and masculine attributes with which to attract the Asian female's passion. Asian females are allowed to culminate their love for the white males in explicit sexual activity on the screen.[3]

Even though, as Elaine H. Kim argues, these characterizations are "a reflection of a white male perspective that defines the white man's virility," they have managed to determine a broader field of social perception in which "it is possible for the Asian man to be viewed as asexual and the Asian woman as *only* sexual."[4] Kim continues that "the Asian woman is popularly thought to be warmly sensual, imbued with an innate understanding of how to please her man and how to serve him." Therefore, as Tajima points out, the cinematic representation of Asian female characters cannot be studied in isolation from that of other racialized, gendered characters and their placement within a particular narrative structure.

In addition to revealing how various others come to view and think about Asian/American women, film and other mass media representations have a material and psychic bearing on how Asian/American women come to think of themselves through their own consumption of and identification with these images. In a more recent essay, Tajima notes how "several generations of Asian women have been raised with racist and celluloid images."[5] Implicit in this scenario of subject-formation is a deeper layer of racist and sexist injury inflicted on Asian/American women. Marina Heung has posited perhaps the most penetrating picture of this process:

> Not only does the general population accept stereotypes of Asian women as truth and then project them onto us without our consent, but we ourselves have incorporated the same images into our self-imaginings. *Internal colonization* is the process by which stereotypes infiltrate and transform our consciousness of Asian women, with dire results for how the same women view and experience themselves. ("Representing Ourselves" 85)

The hour-long documentary *Slaying the Dragon* (1987) weaves clips from numerous cinematic appearances of Asian women and men with interview sequences with various "real" Asian/American women, who testify to how the cinematically disseminated figurations of Asian femininity have affected them in different arenas ranging from their dating choices to their experiences of employment discrimination.[6] On a more ironic note, Jessica Hagedorn's essay titled "Asian Women in Film: No Joy, No Luck" declares that "as females and Asians, as audiences or performers, we have learned to settle for less—to accept the fact that we are either decorative, invisible, or unidimensional."[7] Thus, cinematic representations have shaped Asian/American women's subjective expectations of and engagements with films that feature Asian/American women.

The assumption of the productive power of these representations has, in turn, informed an array of accounts of Asian/American women as bearing certain social and psychic injuries caused by these cinematic projections; these accounts have been published in several disciplinary sites, including psychology, legal studies, sociology, and film studies, but also in lesbian studies. In a 1987 article published in the journal *Women and Ther-*

apy, Connie S. Chan argues that "Asian women have suffered from a cultural stereotype of being exotic, subservient, passive, sexually attractive and available."[8] Chan attributes a significant origin of this image to "actual" sightings during the various U.S. military forays in Asia, from as early as the wars waged in the Philippines in the nineteenth century to World War II, the Korean War, and the Vietnam War: "Asian women were perceived by American soldiers as prostitutes and sexual objects who provided rest and recreation from the war zones." Adding that this sexualized image of "Asian women" has been "portrayed and perpetuated through film and other media images," Chan explores the "psychological responses" of a group she names as "Asian-American women" to both these cultural stereotypes and the "sexual exploitation" that they foster. More recently, in a gesture that brings together work in both feminist legal studies and critical race theory, Sumi K. Cho has coined the phrase "racialized sexual harassment," to refer to "a particular set of injuries resulting from a unique complex of power relations facing Asian Pacific American women and other women of color in the workplace." She explains,

> Asian Pacific American women are at particular risk of being racially and sexually harassed because of the synergism that results when sexualized racial stereotypes combine with racialized gender stereotypes. Model minority traits of passivity and submissiveness are intensified and gendered through the stock portrayal of obedient and servile Asian Pacific women in popular culture. The repeated projection of a compliant and catering Asian feminine nature feeds harasser's beliefs that Asian Pacific American women will be receptive objects of their advances, make good victims, and will not fight back.[9]

If media projections spotlight them as particularly susceptible and even amenable to sexual harassment, they can also have the converse effect of occluding actual instances of violence against Asian/American women. Helen Zia has pointed to how a specific subset of such stereotypical images of servility that depict violence against the women has a naturalizing effect that enforces the "invisibility of Asian women and the violence they experience," even in discourses around both domestic violence and racially motivated hate crimes.[10]

These stereotypical depictions are also seen as formative of how Asian/American women demarcate the objects of their sexual desire.

While most discussions remain fixed within a racially binary but strictly heterosexual opposition between Asian/American men and white men, recent work in lesbian studies and queer studies has pointed to how such depictions reinforce a denial of bisexual and lesbian desire. Characterizing Suzie Wong as "the paradigmatic image of the submissive, exotic Asian woman," JeeYeun Lee posits how "a particular strain of Orientalist discourse [what she later terms "American Orientalism"] that constructs Asian women as hyperfeminine, exotic, passive objects of white heterosexual male desire" intersects with "the prevailing image in lesbian communities of what a lesbian looks like, an image that is constructed as white and butch" to effect an illegibility of Asian/American women and especially femme Asian American women as anything but heterosexual.[11] In a very different register that attributes perhaps too much conscious choice and agency to Asian/American women as desiring subjects, Yen Le Espiritu suggests that "Asian American women enforce Eurocentric gender ideology when they accept the feminization of Asian men and its parallel construction of white men as the most desirable sexual and marital partners."[12]

Against such analytical penetrations into the desiring psyche of individual Asian American women, which risk privatizing the problem of the cinematic stereotype, this chapter veers off in several different directions. I propose to reconsider the ways in which mediated image, perceived identity, and felt subjectivity have been too readily linked and indeed collapsed together through the presumed unity and coherence of the categories of "Asian women" and "Asian American women." In arguing for the necessity of examining the ways in which image, identity, and subjectivity do not and cannot line up with each other, I would accentuate Asian/American women as a troubling subject for both cinematic figuration and interpretation. To begin, I present a close reading of three narrative films featuring an interracial romance plot involving an Asian/American female protagonist: *Thousand Pieces of Gold, Come See the Paradise,* and *The Year of the Dragon.* Despite the visual prominence of their bodies and the apparent narrative significance of their choice between ethnic community and white male lover, each film deploys the Asian/American female protagonist as the common terrain of struggle among competing male agencies graded by ethnicity, class, and sexuality. Consequently, all three films work to project a racially and sexually reassuring American identity in a historical context of growing racial diversity through immigration and shifting gender relations and sexual positions. Through the interracial, heterosexual romance plot, these challenges and tensions can be narratively cast into a manageable economy of white American heterosexual male desire, ultimately displacing the scenes of racist and misogynist terror, violence, exclusion, exploitation, incarceration, and harassment that are strewn in these films. The emplotment of interracial romance expresses and ultimately resolves a deeper anxiety around what it means to be an "American."

This chapter then proceeds to a consideration of how Asian/American women can be rendered as objects of study for the discipline of film studies. As I attempted in chapter 1 for literary studies, I will point to how the variously ambivalent efforts to incorporate the challenge of racial, sexual, and national *differences* have resulted in highly uneven developments of socially particularized subfields, which foreground one particular axis. An institutional and epistemological consequence of such multiple trajectories has been what I see as an even more emphatic separation of disciplinarity and identity. On this point, I note a more recent skepticism toward identity-based film studies—often identified as "stereotype criticism"—as lacking the theoretical sophistication and methodological rigor to contribute to what really matters about the discipline. Insofar as many of the existing critical discussions of cinematic images of Asian/American women have concerned themselves largely with how these images affect the "real" perceptions and especially the self-perceptions of Asian/American women as a distinct and solid social body, they reinforce these disciplinary prejudices. Even the narrative and ideological analyses of interracial romance miss a more interesting problem of enfiguration—how to render and discern an "Asian American woman" as such through a particularly *American* cinematic apparatus and political economy, which have been predicated importantly on the non-equivalence of "Asian" and "American" bodies onscreen.

While many of the discussions of stereotypes that I refer to above tend to presuppose "Asian women" or "Asian female bodies" as a physiological certainty prior to and outside of representation and distortion, I suggest that a specifically cinematic signifying and industrial practices of racial, ethnic, national, and gender identification have constrained the filmic enfigurations of Asian/American women. Given that there is a now sizable body of able but also contentious work produced about the encoding of femininity, gender/and sexuality in feminist film studies, I will focus on how this audiovisual medium has sought to project nationally, racially, and ethnically discernible bodies from almost the very beginning of its own technological invention. The present cinematic contours of Asian/American women have been shaped by an older web of international politics and commercial trade, the mediations of lighting and cosmetology, and a specific industrial structure of racially and sexually skewed casting practices.

Interracial Romance and Narrative Desire

The enabling premise of Gina Marchetti's book-length study *Romance and the "Yellow Peril"* is that while there have been a number of Hollywood films that explore miscegenation between whites and other racialized groups, "the industry throughout its history seems to have taken a special interest in narratives dealing with Asians, Pacific Islanders, and Asian Americans."[13] Such geographically and socially expansive grouping is possible insofar as Marchetti's study is *not* intent on judging the accuracy, complexity, or sensitivity of these representations in relation to "real" Asians, Pacific Islanders, and Asian Americans. Arguing instead that this cinematic prevalence did not reflect some concerted effort to appeal to audiences in Asia and especially to Asian American audiences because of their small numbers in the United States, Marchetti asserts, "Rather, Hollywood used Asians and Asian Americans and Pacific Islanders as signifiers of racial otherness to avoid the far more immediate racial tensions between blacks and whites or the ambivalent mixture of guilt and enduring hatred toward Native Americans and Hispanics" (6). Marchetti focuses instead on exploring two other cinematically composed subjects: the variety of "narratives featuring Asian-Caucasian liaisons," and how they "work ideologically to uphold and sometimes subvert culturally accepted notions of nation, class, race, ethnicity, and sexual orientation."[14] The book's chapters are divided and ordered according to the following taxonomy: rape narratives, captivity stories, seduction tales, salvation stories, sacrifice narratives, tragic love stories, transcendent romances, assimilation narratives, and postmodern spectacle.[15] While the films that illustrate each of these narrative situations bear significant differences, Marchetti concludes that they *all* attempt to resolve "the same fundamental crisis of Anglo-American culture desperately trying to reconcile its credo of 'liberty and justice for all' with its insistence on white, male, bourgeois domination of the public sphere" (218). She adds, "By following this master narrative that links personal salvation and romantic love with social emancipation and progress, all these films seem to tell one story about American identity as both superficially liberal and deeply conservative with respect to racial and ethnic differences" (219).

In discerning a singular "master narrative" of national identification that informs a variety of miscegenation plots, however, Marchetti is bound to gloss over interesting tensions between racial, national, and ethnic identifications that traverse the litany "Asians, Asian Americans, and Pacific Islanders." Classifying *The World of Suzie Wong* and *Love Is a Many-Splendored Thing* as instances of "salvation stories," Marchetti alternately refers to the lead characters as "Asian women," "nonwhite women," and "ethnic female protagonist." She argues, "In fact, part of what both Suzie Wong and Han Suyin are saved from in each film is the threat that they may become like their Western sisters. Thus, the films can uphold both the gender and the racial status quo by depicting Asian women as more truly 'feminine,' content at being passive, subservient, dependent, domestic, and slaves to love" (115–16). Even when she moves on to discuss the assimilation narratives that became popular in the aftermath of World War II, she notes that "most remain based in Asia, avoiding any discussion of the depth of American racism at home." She adds, "Although interracial romance has traditionally been a staple of Hollywood fiction, the interracial domestic melodrama has not enjoyed the same popularity" (159). While she ends the book with a chapter on *The Year of the Dragon,* which is entirely set in New York City and its Chinatown, she distinguishes it from the earlier cinematic narratives of miscegenation not so much for its national location but for its formal and structural distinctions as a "postmodern spectacle":

> Interracial sexuality becomes an element of this stylistic mélange, a contrast in color, rather than either a liberal call for reform or a conservative demand for exclusionism. . . . Portions of Hollywood plot formulas involving Asian and Caucasian characters resurface and recombine into different patterns that evoke earlier rape, seduction, captivity, salvation, sacrifice, or assimilation patterns. (203)

Instead of a rupture from older narratives featuring an interracial romance, *The Year of the Dragon* marks a beginning of sorts of a resonant cluster with two contemporary films that pivot around a white male–Asian female relationship: *Come See the Paradise* (1990) and *Thousand Pieces of Gold* (1991). These films are distinguished from most of the films examined in the Marchetti book in two key respects. First, both the lovers and the love story are located not in Asia but within the nation-state borders of the United States.[16] *Thousand Pieces of Gold* depicts the arrival of the Chinese miners and prostitutes in the nineteenth century, including the harassment, exploitation, and violence to which they were subjected. *Come See the Paradise* portrays the thriving Japanese American community in 1940s Los Angeles prior to their mass internment during World War II, and their subsequent attempts to rebuild families and neighborhoods. While *The Year of the Dragon* was produced earliest of all, it is set in the most recent historical period of the 1980s in New York's Chinatown, which is pictured as an odd mix of material wealth, professional visibility, organized crime, and immigrant squalor. Second and more significantly, the spirited proud and resourceful female protagonists of these films *appear* to depart from the older "Lotus Blossom" stereotypes of Asian women as passive, incomprehensible, and doomed. Lalu, who is renamed Polly, in *Thousand Pieces of Gold* is a gutsy pioneer woman who aggressively fights off lascivious miners and engages in a nonmarital sexual relationship. Lily Kawamura in *Come See the Paradise* is an acculturated Nisei who defies her father's arranged marriage and rails against the federal government's unjust incarceration of Japanese Americans. Tracy Tzu in *The Year of the Dragon* is a well-spoken and glamorous TV news reporter.

If their bodies and faces may initially mark them as alien and exotic, their unfolding personal stories involve familiar tropes of socioeconomic mobility and forbidden love. In each of these films, the female protagonist comes into comprehensibility and narrative significance through her romantic/sexual liaison with the white male protagonist. To varying degrees, all three films appear to pose the central narrative conflict as *her* dilemma of having to choose between her filiation with her natal family and ethnic community, on the one hand, and her desire for (hetero)sexual liberation and romantic fulfillment promised by the white male protagonist. From the opening, lingering and isolated close-ups of her face and (denuded) body persistently mark her as different from the other Chinese American and Japanese American bodies that fill the diegetic landscape. Her proud,

+ describe common occurrences w the film

independent demeanor, which already marks her alienation from cultural dictates of feminine passivity and sexual submission to patriarchal rule, presages her final decision.

Recuperating the Western Frontier: *Thousand Pieces of Gold*

Thousand Pieces of Gold is adapted from a "historical novel," written by Ruthanne Lum McCunn, which is based on the life of Lalu Nathoy, later anglicized to Polly Bemis, a Chinese immigrant woman in the nineteenth century. Produced by Kenji Yamamoto and directed by Nancy Kelly, a self-identified feminist filmmaker, the film was partially financed through the American Playhouse and has aired on PBS as part of "Asian Pacific Heritage Month." The video box cover of the film heralds it as an "incredible—and true—story of a young Chinese woman torn from her homeland and forced to survive in the frontier land of America." It then outlines the film's basic character and plot structure: "An innocent woman in an Idaho mining town's thriving bordello, Lalu rebels and pays a terrible price for her fight against racism and sexism. Wagered as a piece of property, Lalu is finally handed over to her new owner Charlie, who opens the door to a whole new life for Lalu—and himself." Despite such claims to biographical authenticity, it should be emphasized that even McCunn's novelization is a partially imagined and narratively composed version taken from the available documentary traces of Lalu Nathoy. Although it bears the same title, the film differs significantly from this already constructed text. While the book spans the entire life of Lalu Nathoy, from her girlhood in China to her death in 1933, the cinematic adaptation focuses on the struggles over her body and heart among variously positioned male characters. Although the novel is ambiguous about the terms of her removal from her natal family, the film opens with a scene in which her father sells her—and his patriarchal authority—to a Chinese procurer, which sets up a long chain of her mistreatment and exchange at the hands of other men. Given this truncated depiction of her sexual positioning, I will refer to the female protagonist of the film as Polly from here on.

The film narrative pivots around an ethnically and economically scored triangle of possible romantic and sexual partners for Polly. Charlie owns the saloon, which he has leased to Hong King, who has purchased

Polly as a means to lure more customers. Then there is Jim, another Chinese immigrant male hired by Hong King to deliver her from the auction block in San Francisco to Warrens, Idaho. When Jim rides into town with Polly in tow, the camera pans a crowd of white male miners gazing at her, but then rests on the face of Charlie, who surveys this entire scene from a table that he shares with Hong King. After congratulating Hong King as a "lucky man," Charlie proceeds to give Jim an affirmative pat on the shoulder for his successful delivery. While her body is thus established at the outset as the object of exchange linking these three men across racial and class demarcations, Polly's true desire will come to matter as what ultimately distinguishes Charlie's superior *American* heterosexual masculinity.

To reach that conclusion, *Thousand Pieces of Gold* devotes a significant portion of its screen time to portraying Polly's changing relationships with Hong King and especially with Jim. The film is much more explicit than the book in portraying her rape and mistreatment by the lascivious Hong King.[17] More significantly, whereas the novel only hints at romantic stirrings between Polly and Jim, the film depicts them in full-scale sexual relationship. They develop a bond during the long trip from San Francisco to Warrens. However, even though he is fully aware of Hong King's plans for her upon delivery, Jim carries out the task, accepts his payment, and leaves her to suffer the sexual-economic designs of Hong King. Upon Jim's return after a lengthy absence, she must reassure him that she has "not gone with ghosts, only Hong King." He finds this assurance of her sexual but not interracial relations acceptable enough and proceeds to offer to buy her from Hong King with his life savings. Hong King quotes a price and then "allows" Jim to spend the night with Polly. He spies on their sexual encounter and is careful not to disrupt them, but then decides to punish her later on. Even though he has promised to sell her to Jim, his jealous resentment aroused by his perverse voyeurism drives him to hold a lottery among the white male miners, announcing that the winner can have Polly "show him the pleasures of the East." When Jim returns once again with the money and discovers her now living with Charlie, he leaves without a word. That a cinematic interpretation of "this incredible—and true—story of a young Chinese woman" departs so remarkably from a linear birth-to-death novelistic account and focuses almost exclusively on Polly's sexual liaisons with men provokes a critical consideration of the limits and possibilities of the medium and the genre.[18]

In contrast to the utter greed and remorselessness of Hong King in offering her up to the miners and the utter helplessness of Jim in defending her, Charlie is able and willing to express his disapproval about Polly's enslavement and mistreatment and assists her on occasion. However, for much of the film Charlie is clearly ambivalent and often does not intervene on her behalf. On occasion, he willingly participates along with the other miners in the sexual harassment of Polly. When she moves out of his house to be a manager at a local boarding house, Charlie and Hong King commiserate over a bottle of whiskey. Lastly, when the Chinese are being driven out of town at the end of the film, Charlie helps Hong King to escape without harm. One notable scene—from which the advertisement still for the film's theatrical run is taken—involves the indistinguishable miners, each taking turns forcing Polly to dance with them. Disgruntled after a loss to Hong King in a card game, Charlie too takes his turn with Polly. It is significant that a snapshot of this coercive situation is taken out of context and deployed as a romantic embrace to attract viewers to see this film. However, it is indicative of Charlie's moral and sexual ambivalence toward Polly, which is the driving force of the film's narrative.

Even though she has been thus constructed as the field of struggle and the sexual prize for these three men, the film ends with Polly having to make a difficult decision between staying in an obviously racist town with Charlie or joining the Chinese men who are being forcibly driven out. Initially, she refuses Charlie's offers and chooses to leave and eventually make her way back to China. Polly seems thus to be rejecting the identity and existence that her adopted nation has ascribed to her. When Li Dick, the old and wise herbalist who represents the continuing ties to ethnicity and homeland, advises her to drink from the "River of Forgetfulness" and begin a new life in the United States, she abruptly turns her horse around and heads back toward Charlie. In the next shot, Polly emerges on horseback from the crowd of faceless Chinese men who are leaving on foot. This scene splendidly visualizes her individualization from racial-ethnic anonymity and abjection. Her exceptional incorporation amidst anti-Chinese exclusion and violence is underscored as a climactic moment of personal agency. The final shot of the film shows a pastoral landscape with text that informs us that Charlie and Polly settled down to a life along the "River of No Return." But a reading of this ending as a "happy" one or as an *end* is possible only by disregarding those bodies being driven out with their backs to the camera. The nostalgic return to the wild, pristine frontier represented in the closing shot of a female figure—presumably Polly Bemis—standing on the shores of a glistening Salmon River allows a revisioning of U.S. history that not only incorporates but *relies on* this racialized female body to redeem the American myth of manifest destiny.

Redeeming the Internment: *Come See the Paradise*

Touting the film as a "deeply touching love story set against the backdrop of a dramatic and controversial period in American history," the video release synopsis of *Come See the Paradise* reads:

> It follows the romance and eventual marriage of Jack McGurn (Dennis Quaid), a hot-blooded Irish-American, and a beautiful Japanese-American, Lily Kawamura (Tamlyn Tomita), at the outset of World War II. The clash of cultures, at once painful for the two lovers, becomes insurmountable after the Japanese bomb Pearl Harbor. Lily and the Kawamuras are relocated to a bleak, outdoor internment camp in California. Jack is drafted into the Army, powerless to help the woman he loves . . . abandoning all hope of ever winning her family's approval. This gorgeously photographed film is brought faithfully to the screen by Alan Parker, the director of *Mississippi Burning* and *Midnight Express*.[19]

Contradicting this claim of fidelity to an extracinematic subject, Alan Parker, who is also credited with writing the screenplay, has frankly admitted that he did not choose the historical setting to educate or inform the audience about the mass Internment of Japanese Americans during World War II. A newspaper interview quotes him as saying, "I set out to do an interracial love story. And that just happens to be the most significant thing that happened to that particular ethnic group, the fact that they were interned and had their civil rights taken away from them. So I just couldn't ignore it."[20] The article continues, "'So I'm suddenly responsible for telling the entire story of the internment of Japanese-Americans—as if it's my fault that no one ever touched it before or had the guts to do it,' he says indignantly." Although Parker bristles at his accountability to the historical event and ethnic group, his authorship is displaced onto the body of the beautiful Japanese American protagonist. Constructed as *her* retrospective first-person narrative, the film opens with Lily telling a story—an "origin story" of sorts—to her daughter. While Alan Parker is the proper name credited with authorship, the autobiographical filter of Lily's voice and body imbue this gorgeously photographed film with a certain personal intimacy, cultural authenticity, and historical accuracy.

The story that Lily tells begins not with her own beginning but in "Brooklyn, New York 1936" with Jack McGurn, a well-read labor activist for the Film Projectionists Union. Indeed, much of what unfolds is told from Jack's perspective. When he is implicated in the firebombing of a theater, Jack is forced to leave town and heads toward California. The film then shifts to "Little Tokyo, Los Angeles," showing a Japanese American social function replete with a full orchestra, a crooner, and a well-dressed crowd of dancers. We meet the Kawamuras, a family of eight. The Nisei children are represented from the beginning as thoroughly acculturated. The first son, Charlie, is a baseball fanatic and the second son, Harry, is a movie actor who is a small celebrity in the community even though, as someone says in the film, he can only play "Chinese houseboys." Lily, the oldest daughter, is distinguished by the detail that "she only speaks Japanese at meal times." As one reviewer has noted, "Parker is careful to make the Kawamuras as American as possible (Lily's two older brothers are 'hepcats'). It's as if he's afraid anything Old World would alienate us."[21]

But not all of the Kawamuras are bathed in the glow of this assimilationist liberalism. Mr. Kawamura, the patriarch, is portrayed as an insensitive tyrant who cares more about gambling than his family. Having amassed a large debt, he casually arranges, in the midst of a card game, for Lily to marry a much older widower. In addition to this callous patriarchal tyranny, Mr. Kawamura is further contrasted with his acculturated American children by the fact that he owns a movie house that shows films imported from Japan. When the theater's alcoholic projectionist, Mr. Ogata, commits suicide, the recently arrived Jack McGurn is hired to replace him, a suggestive reversal of the economic relations and representational authority between a native-born, white male and a Japanese immigrant male. Employed by Mr. Kawamura, Jack can only project films that have been made elsewhere and imported into the United States. There is also an interesting reversal of the common direction of acculturation; rather than a racialized alien immigrating into a familiar all-American space, a native white male enters and adapts to a racial-ethnic community. Soon Jack even learns to sing in Japanese, from showing Japanese films.

In contrast to his economic subordination to the father, Jack develops a friendly relationship with Charlie, the oldest Kawamura son. As Charlie is acquainting Jack with the theater, he comments, "The projectors are very old. So you have to treat them like a woman." When Jack asks, "With love?" Charlie retorts, "No, with patience." However, their heterosexual masculinities are in no way commensurate. In the next scene, when the two men playfully perform a masquerade dance in the theater lobby, Charlie takes on the role of a shy Japanese maiden to Jack's samurai. Even while Charlie may occupy a fraternal relation to Jack through a shared sexual objectification of women, ultimately, if one of them must be feminized to enact sexual difference, it will have to be the Japanese American male. Conversely, the white male protagonist never stops being man. I would argue further that this dramatic feminization of Charlie is made necessary precisely to offset the economic subordination of Jack to Mr. Kawamura. From heterosexual comrade to feminized substitute, Charlie goes on to pose as an ethnicized obstacle to Jack's expressed desire for Lily. Trying to dissuade Jack from pursuing his sister, Charlie reminds him, "She's *Japanese,* Jack. We'll find you a nice *American* girl." That this baseball-loving Nisei would espouse such a clear opposition between "American" and "Japanese" oddly anticipates but then displaces the racist logic of the Internment onto a Japanese American aversion to interracial desire.

Unswayed by Charlie's offer, Jack begins to woo Lily, and the rest of the film traces the development of their romantic relationship. When Mr. Kawamura learns of their affair, he fires Jack and forbids Lily to see him. Mr. Kawamura's un-American tyranny, already established in the narrative through his casual offer of Lily for marriage to repay a gambling partner, is further underscored by his possessive opposition to the truly loving and beloved Jack. In confronting the intransigent Mr. Kawamura, Jack blurts out in his frustration, "What I can never be . . . not ever . . . is Japanese." Despite his entry and acculturation into a Japanese American community, this statement asserts a racial-ethnic essence that cannot ultimately be traversed. For if Jack can say he can never be Japanese, the flip side of that essentialist declaration would be that what Mr. Kawamura can never be . . . not ever . . . is American. Once more, racism and ethnocentric prejudice are attributed to a Japanese American male body.

Against the specter of such impossibility, Lily and Jack decide to elope. As Lily tells her daughter, because of the anti-miscegenation laws in the state of California at the time, she and Jack go to Seattle and begin a new life there. The following sequence shows the two protagonists fully embroiled in the happiness of their nuclear family, with Jack working at the docks while Lily makes herself into the picture of domesticity. With the birth of their daughter, they compose the ideal American nuclear family. Jack's involvement as a labor activist begins to interfere with their marital bliss. When Lily voices her opinions to Jack—"You can't spit against Heaven"—he replies, "Don't give me that Japanese shit."

Thus rudely reminded of her ethnic difference, Lily returns to Little Tokyo with her biracial daughter only to find that Mr. Kawamura, along with many Issei men, has been arrested for possible espionage following the attack on Pearl Harbor. Lily resumes her job at the costume shop, but this time she has to take charge, as Mr. Matsui too has been taken away. Shortly thereafter, Jack appears at the shop where he and Lily consummate their passionate reunion. Jack's welcome return to Little Tokyo after the forbidding patriarchs have been forcibly removed is underscored by the following scene of a Kawamura family gathering at Christmas in which Jack takes the place of the absented patriarch. In a picture of interracial harmony and cross-cultural fluidity, the young Kawamura children dance and sing American songs while Jack chooses a sad Japanese ballad.

Come See the Paradise does attempt to cast the Japanese-bashing after the bombing of Pearl Harbor as unjust and hysterical. The film does point somewhat to the human costs of the Internment. As the Kawamuras prepare to leave, they must burn their letters and books in Japanese and sell their belongings at low prices. There is also the gradual but total displacement of the adult Japanese American males. Mr. Kawamura slowly loses his sanity and dies a lonely death in the camps. Charlie, who becomes a "no-no boy," is relocated to Tule Lake and later repatriated to Japan. Henry, the second son, decides to serve in the U.S. military to prove his loyalty, only to die in combat. While such displacements did occur historically, they take on a symbolic force here by being so concentrated in a single family and within one filmic narrative. The film ends with the happy reunification of Jack, Lily, and their daughter. One reconstituted family

no-no boy → Jap. Am ? who refuse to serve in US army
-"no-no" stand for 2 categories Jap Am shortage in loyalty oath

with its white male head-of-household is celebrated, displacing the ruptures wreaked upon numerous other Japanese American families by the Internment.

Reforming Chinatown: *The Year of the Dragon*

Before the opening scene of a Chinese New Year's Parade unfolds onscreen, a text disclaimer insists that *The Year of the Dragon* does not represent any real "Asian American" persons or situations.[22] This ethnic celebration is suddenly disrupted by a gang confrontation in which a Chinese community patriarch is assassinated. Tracy Tzu first appears onscreen and in the film narrative as she is covering the funeral procession of this slain leader, Jackie Wong. Born and raised in the San Francisco Bay Area, Tracy is also accented as culturally more *American* than Chinese, declaring, "I like Italian food better." The camera shifts from a shot of Tracy interviewing a police officer and comes to rest on the face of Stanley White, a New York City police detective who has just been promoted to be the new head of the Chinatown precinct. His first act on the new job is to invade a meeting of Chinatown community leaders. When they remind him of the long-prevailing collusion between the police department and the Chinatown leadership, Stanley declares in the language of another invasion, "new marshal in town, new marshal means new rules." The next scene shows Stanley at a police department meeting where he articulates his theory of how the Chinese are poised to take over New York City, with their first target being the Italian organized crime syndicate: "The Mafia concept is not even Italian. It's Chinese." This positioning of Chinese invasion against white ethnicity is especially telling in that we learn that, despite his surname, Stanley White himself is not an Anglo-Saxon Protestant but Polish.

A later scene finds Stanley in a meeting with Tracy at a Chinese restaurant. The sarcastic banter signals that theirs will be a classic love-hate relationship. She shows a good grasp of her own family history and how it has been affected by racist exclusion laws and economic exploitation. Both her grandfather and great-grandfather worked on the construction of the transcontinental railroad but returned to China because they were discouraged from staying on permanently. Stanley shows himself to be already well informed about Chinese American history. He proceeds to give Tracy a revisionist history lesson on Chinese exclusion and marginalization in the United States. He ends with a resolute critique of the erasure of this history: "No one remembers, that's the problem." Tracy responds to this by telling Stanley that he sounds just like her father. Having established this connection, Stanley presents himself as a social reformer and proposes that Tracy conduct a series of exposés of Chinatown corruption. Assuming the position of "good father," he enlists her assistance in overthrowing the "bad fathers" of Chinatown, those Chinese men of the implied mafia. Earlier in the conversation, he has complimented her on her greater sexual appeal compared to that of "other journalists." His choice of Tracy to do the exposé is certainly related to her feminine appeal; but, as he points out later, the primary motivating factor is her ethnicity and the authenticity it guarantees: "If it's some white broad, they would say it's racism. With you, it looks like it's on the up and up." Stanley is knowledgeable about the codes of authenticity in the multiracial, multicultural era. It is he, not Tracy, who knows the corrupt secrets of Chinatown and wants her only to be his credible mouthpiece.

At the end of this conversation, a gang attacks the restaurant. While the masses of patrons run amok in terror, White is shown as the only one who bravely fights back and pursues the attackers. For her part, Tracy hides herself in a phone booth. When White finally locates her, she is blabbering and nearly hysterical, and it is in this state of terror and disarray that Stanley first kisses her. He is the lone brave hero who rescues and comforts this Chinese woman from the irrational acts of violence and destruction perpetrated by a faceless gang of young Chinese men.

Their next meeting finds the pair in Tracy's penthouse apartment, elegantly furnished in white. They continue their love–hate verbal exchange. Stanley tells Tracy:

> The first time I saw you I hated your guts. I think that I hated you even before I met you. *I hated you on TV. I hated you in Vietnam.* You know what's destroying this country. It's not booze. It's not drugs. It's TV. It's the media. It's people like you, vampires. I hate the way you make a living by sticking microphones in everyone's faces. I hate the way you lie every night at six o'clock. I hate the way you hide real feelings. I hate everything you stand for. Most of all, I hate rich kids and I hate this place. So why do I want to fuck you so bad?

Note how his soliloquy moves quickly from racism to an attack on the media and then a rant on class differences. Like Lily to Jack, Tracy is everything that Stanley can never be; her differences are what repel and attract him to her. It is evident in this scene that he has already been watching her and has judged her authenticity. His hateful voyeurism is at once revealed and justified since she, as a television news reporter, has already offered herself up to his gaze. That she is a trained performer leads him to suspect her of conscious dissemblance. Tracy provokes multiply exacerbated anxieties in Stanley because of the many axes of socioeconomic difference that she embodies for him. In his eyes, she is a hostile, foreign country, a lost war, a manipulative social mechanism, and elitist. He must bring her within the terms of his comprehensibility and sexual agency.

When he tries to initiate sex, she stops him, claiming that she is tired from having "just spent all afternoon with her boyfriend." He responds to her rejection first with surprise and then indignation. He then subjects her to this line of questioning:

> STANLEY: So, what's his name? Is he rich?
> TRACY: You want to know if he's Chinese, right? That's what you want to know. So ask it.
> STANLEY: Yeah . . . so that's the question.
> TRACY: He's white all right. He went to Princeton. His name is Roger and he's a lawyer.
> STANLEY: Well, I hate lawyers and I wouldn't want to make love to a woman who just got done screwing a lawyer anyway. So does he have a lot of money, this Roger Pumpernickel III?
> TRACY: Well, yes and he's not a crackpot racist.
> STANLEY: Oh yeah. What does he do? Play tennis, golf, go out sailing on a yacht. What's with all these machines here? What are you with AT&T? What? Do you got everyone in town jumping in and out of bed? . . . I'm gonna go home to a woman who at least acts like a woman. If this Roger's so great, how come he didn't want to marry you. What he didn't want a slant eyed Roger IV at Princeton?

This barrage reveals that White is concerned not so much with Tracy as how her body mediates his own identification in relation to the Chinese male, the WASP elite-class male, and ultimately the white female.

The subsequent purging of Chinatown that Stanley commands compensates his anxiety around social identity and sexuality. A montage sequence reveals the seamy and illicit depths of Chinatown beneath the surface of Orientalist exotica. In one scene, Stanley literally goes underground to cavernous structures that process some strange meat product amidst damp darkness. He proceeds to close down garment sweatshops and restaurants for health violations and thus presents himself as the face of law and order against this decrepit ethnic ghetto. Stanley's efforts at purification are revealed not as selfless social reform but as an act of retribution against another battle waged against another Asian ethnic group. Even when other police officials criticize his ruthless zeal for reform, he remains resolute, arguing, "This is a fucking war. And I'm not going to lose it. Not this one. This is Vietnam all over again. It's all about politics. Nobody wants to win this one. Not all the way." Not only is he unable to distinguish between Vietnam and Chinatown, New York City a decade later, the perceived loss in the Vietnam war is the lens through which he sees Tracy as well. He tells her, "It's Nam all over again. We lost because *you* were smarter than us." She has become a metonymic figure for the early loss of face of both American masculinity and national identity. Despite this close association and its attendant hostilities directed at Tracy, he can express his need for her in the same breath, and she lovingly responds. However, he will not be easily rehabilitated by his romantic counterpart. When Tracy tells him that she "loves" him after having sex, his response is to assert her alienness again: "There's no Chinese word for love." Stanley's sadistic desire for Tracy is a harsher version of Charlie's and Jack's ambivalence toward Polly and Lily.

To retaliate against Stanley's aggressive reforms, Joey Thai, the new Chinatown leader, orders some young Chinese gang members to rape Tracy. It is the trauma of this experience that finally propels her to tell Stanley the truth about herself—that there is no Roger and that she made the whole thing up. Stanley's purging of Chinatown has indirectly effected the purging of Tracy Tzu as well. Having solved her mystery and thus resolved any anxiety about a bourgeois competitor, he uses the rape of Tracy as the impetus to pursue his reform efforts even more zealously. In the end, he coordinates the death of Joey Thai, signifying both his superior virility, retribution for the rape, and his victory in the war against the corrupt Chinatown leadership. As she has been denuded of her own secret, Tracy finally decides to conduct the exposé of Chinatown. The last scene of the film returns to yet another mass gathering in Chinatown. An angry uncontrollable mob of Chinese attacks Stanley but Tracy intervenes on his behalf. She has chosen to save him this time, from the irrational mob violence of her ethnic community. The embracing lovers begin to walk away as the credits roll. This closing image of interracial affiliation blocks the earlier scenes of sexual violence, racial hatred, and the havoc raised in an ethnic community under siege.

While each of these films appears to offer an "Asian/American woman" as the central subject of conflict and choice, the narrative that frames her choice in all three films is after all *his story*—the transformation of Charlie, Jack, and Stanley through their interactions with Polly, Lily, and Tracy. Building on Vladimir Propp's analysis of plot structures in Western discourse, Teresa de Lauretis's groundbreaking essay "Desire in Narrative" points to the recurrence of the story of a male hero who undergoes some passage and transformation.[23]

> Characters can be divided into those who are mobile, who enjoy freedom with regard to plot space, who can change their place in the structure of the artistic world, and cross the frontier, the basic topological feature of this space, and those who are immobile, who represent, in fact, a function of this space. Looked at topologically, the initial situation is that a certain plot-space is divided by a single boundary into an internal and external sphere, and a single character has the opportunity to cross the boundary. Inasmuch as closed space can be interpreted as "a cave," "the grave," "a house," "a woman" (and correspondingly, be allotted the feature of darkness, warmth and dampness), entry into it is interpreted on various levels as "death," "conception," "return home" and so on; moreover all these acts are thought of as mutually identical. (118)

Extending this outline, de Lauretis concludes, "In this mythical-textual mechanics, the hero must be male, regardless of the gender of the text-image, because the obstacle, whatever its personification, is morphologically female and indeed, simply, the womb" (119). She then declares more emphatically that "if the work of mythical structuration is to establish distinctions, the primary distinction on which all others depend is not, say life and death, but rather sexual difference."

Consistent with this paradigm of "the single figure of the hero who crosses the boundary and penetrates the other space" (121), the white male protagonist of each of the three films undergoes some type of incursion into a territory demarcated as other. In contrast to earlier Asian–white miscegenation narratives, however, these "other spaces" are located *within* the nation–state borders of the United States. Although *Thousand Pieces of Gold* is set in a historical era of severe racial segregation and anti-Chinese violence, Charlie Bemis easily moves in and out of the small Chinese settlement at the outskirts of Warrens, where he receives acupuncture from wise Li Dick and learns to say a few words in Chinese. During their courtship, he accompanies Polly to what he calls a "Chinese shindig"—a New Year's celebration, complete with fireworks and a dragon dance. Blacklisted for his union activities, Jack McGurn is forced to leave his Irish, working-class community in New York and settles in Little Tokyo, Los Angeles. Hired as the projectionist of the Japanese movie house owned and run by the Kawamura family, Jack quickly befriends Lily's brother and learns to sing in Japanese. (The racial privilege of his physical and social mobility is even more strikingly depicted later in the film when Lily and their daughter are imprisoned in an Internment camp and Jack visits them dressed in his U.S. military uniform.) In the most extreme illustration, in *The Year of the Dragon,* Stanley White is a New York police detective who obsessively prowls and probes Chinatown on a mission to uncover and destroy corruption and organized crime.

While each male character enters the ethnically demarcated enclaves, the Asian/American woman does more than define the space for another traveling subject. Complicating the strict binary of what de Lauretis identifies as "the two positions of sexual difference thus conceived: male-hero-human, on the side of the subject; and female-obstacle-boundary, on the other," each female protagonist also undergoes significant passage and transformation. Indeed, Polly is forcibly brought to Warrens, and she must work to adapt to her new environment. She soon learns to speak English and even to make apple pie (from a German immigrant prostitute who befriends her). Upon learning from a black man that slavery has been abolished in the United States, she realizes her legal right to freedom, which is economically secured for her by Charlie in a gambling session with Hong King. After achieving her economic self-sufficiency by doing laundry for the white and Chinese male miners, Polly goes on to manage a boarding house whose male tenants had harassed her when she was indentured at the saloon not long ago. She forcibly earns their respect by threatening them with a huge buck knife, eventually meriting the honorary identification of "not Chinese" even as the same men strategize about a racist attack on the town's Chinese residents. When Lily elopes with Jack to Seattle, her passage from ethnic girlhood in Little Tokyo to interracially married womanhood is conspicuously illustrated in a scene of the newlyweds crashing another wedding party, where Lily dances exuberantly with a series of its white male guests. After Jack utters a racist slur during an argument, Tracy returns home to Los Angeles, only to be herded off to an Internment camp in the desert with her family. Finally, as an Ivy League–educated television reporter, Tracy Tzu lives in her own modern penthouse, which is tastefully decorated in white and, more significantly, located well outside the dreary confines of New York's Chinatown. For Tracy, her challenge is not to leave the ethnic enclave but to pass into it from a detached standpoint of both acculturation and professionalization.

Consequently, I have had to rethink my own earlier reading of these three films as primarily *not about* the prominently figured Asian/American woman but rather as symptomatic of an anxiety around white American masculinity in the 1980s and 1990s.[24] In my own critical desire to disavow these films as in any way representative of real Asian/American women and their divergent sexual orientations, I, along with other critics of images of Asian/American women, neglected to consider the terms and conditions of the cinematic representability of Asian/American women as such. In the following section, I propose to recast these films as projecting the *problem* of the cinematic legibility of an "Asian American woman" against two linked histories of its institutionalized impossibility. First, a series of legislative acts and judicial decisions on immigration, naturalization, and citizenship, which I will examine in great detail in the following chapter, have sought to preclude the formation of that very identity. Second, a dense archive of Hollywood films has induced a certain visual-racial code that marks Asian bodies onscreen as distinctly alien and inassimilable. As I will describe later, this selective sighting has been buttressed by certain Hollywood industry practices of race- and gender-biased casting, which have prevented Asian/American actors from portraying Asian/American characters.[25] Given this dual legacy, I would argue that the narrative arc of passage and transformation is crucial to the cinematic rendering of "Asian American woman." Rather than attempting some mimetic correspondence to actual living, desiring Asian/American women, each effort must struggle against previous cinematic markings of their racial and sexual alterity.

By repetitively casting these figures into interracial, heterosexual relationships, these films suggest that the only way to project them as *Americans* is to render each such visible body as genuinely desiring and finally choosing this particular union. Werner Sollors has pointed to how the concept of "forbidden romantic love" was a recurrent theme in many early literary texts, and was often cast as the dilemma of a female protagonist in relation to the custom of arranged marriages.[26] The conflict of a daughter torn between her personal choice of a lover and her father's prescription of a prospective husband symbolized the desire of "American" independence from the controlling powers of the "Old World": "American allegiance, the very concept of citizenship developed in the revolutionary period, was—like love—based on consent, not on descent, which further blended the rhetoric of America with the language of love and the concept of romantic love with American identity" (112). Related to this typology of forbidden love is the metaphor of the nation as melting pot, a peaceful fusion of different ethnic groups into a single "American people." These two themes converge in what Sollors names as "melting-pot love" to refer to "a marital union or a love relationship across boundaries that are considered significant, and often in defiance of parental desires and old descent antagonisms" (72). Rather than attempting historical or sociological accuracy, the destruction of her natal family and her ethnic community, which facilitates and also affirms the "Asian American" woman's individuating disavowal, is narratively necessary to attest to her choice and passage. Although the complementary composition of Asian-white and woman-man through the interracial dyad *attempts* to bring closure, I would press for a more open-ended and even dystopic speculation, in which the Americanization of these women is not fully secured but projected with struggle and force.

To that end, consider how the white male protagonist does not come already formed as a national subject into this encounter with the Asian/American woman. I would argue that inasmuch as the abstraction of U.S. citizenship resists anchoring in a particularized body with a discernible appearance, "American" is less a congenital ontology or an achieved state than a struggle of *becoming,* one that the moving image can especially demonstrate or repeatedly dramatize as unfixed. Consequently, narrative can be said to be necessary to encode the "white male body" as "American" by way of its emplotted self-realization through interracial, heterosexual desire. In presuming that a white American masculinity preexists and responds to the challenges posed by the racial, ethnic, and gender difference, earlier narrative analyses (mine included) miss this more suggestive possibility. Another look at Charlie, Jack, and Stanley shows all three men as initially positioned at various sites that are marginal to a Protestant, Anglo-American, middle-class norm. Charlie is an amoral, unkempt, and aimless gambler and drunk who transforms into a polite, clean-cut pioneer. Jack is a "hot-blooded Irish-American" and labor-agitator-on-the-run who becomes a loving father and man-in-uniform at the film's end. Stanley starts out as a crude, resentful, and possibly impotent Polish-American who becomes the "new marshall in town," proving himself worthy of the loving protection of Tracy. In so doing, he raises himself to the ranks of his imaginary rival, Roger Pumpernickel III. All three achieve their "'American'" manhood in the course of their interracial romances, and their personal growth takes place crucially against the backdrop of the disintegration of the respective ethnic locales. To be sure, Stanley is the most active in this process, but Charlie and Jack are complicit in varying degrees with the breakdown of the Asian-ethnic communities. While the feminist theorizations of a masculine subject-position of narrative desire have been critiqued for an inattention to racial, class, and sexual differences amongst women, they can also be reapproached as ceding perhaps too much to the security and stability of the white masculine subject. Put another way, the bimodal sexual differentiation of feminine spectacle and masculine vision and narrative agency is secured precisely through a monoracial, monoethnic dyad. If all three films end with a visual and narrative staging of the lovers' reunion, this is not enough to justify and to erase the preceding scenes of racial persecution, sexual violence, labor exploitation, mass incarceration, and police harassment. Although these scenes needed to be staged to mark a point of departure, a more ignominious past that the present and future orientation of the interracial romance works to transcend, they also attest to the social formations and forces that preclude the emergence of a self-possessed and willful "Asian American woman." While narrative analyses—as suggested by Marchetti and de Lauretis—might be more amenable to linear emplotments of conflict-resolution or binary oppositions of male passage–female boundary, they are unable to account for either the intersection of different axes of social existence or the composition of specific forms of disciplinary legibility for Asian/American women.

If the historical tension between social bodies and cinematic bodies has been one scored by awkwardness and not accuracy, how might this impinge on how one can think about a present tension between identity and disciplinarity in relation to the field of knowledge called "film studies"? Richard Dyer opens his "Introduction to Film Studies" with an almost weary observation of the excessive proliferation of knowledge formations that mark our historical moment: "Anything that exists can be studied, and in these last years of the twentieth century it may well seem that virtually everything is."[27] "Yet," he continues, "only some things become organized into disciplines and institutionalized into departments and conferences; if everything has its web site, only some things have their boards of examiners, refereed journals, and employed enthusiasts, or possess the (often insecure) cultural capital of being understood to be 'studies'." This accent on the significance of institutional contexts of publication and peer evaluation resonates with Timothy Lenoir's picture of a "political economy" of disciplinarity. Further undermining the hold of the putative "object of study" as what makes a discipline, Dyer acknowledges how "the history of film studies, as of any other discipline, makes clear that there are different ways of deciding what it is you attend to, and how you attend to it, when you 'study' something." What conjoins such multiple variables of *what* and *how* "it" is, according to Dyer, is "the conviction, one that must be made or made to be widespread, that it matters. It is the terms of such mattering that then characterizes the changing forms of study." In Dyer's introduction to film studies, what matters about film has "tended to be affirmed in one of two ways: the formal-aesthetic and the social-ideological. The first argues for, or assumes, the importance of film in terms of its intrinsic worth, whereas the latter focuses on film's position as symptom or influence in social processes." Note here the echo of Bloom's dismissal of "feminist literary criticism" as emphasizing things that are *not* literature.

As suggested in the table of contents of *The Oxford Guide to Film Studies,* the study of identity in film has proceeded along overlapping but distinguished axes of gender, race, and sexuality. A section titled "Film Text and Context: Gender, Ideology, and Identities" contains separate essays on "Marxism and Film," "Feminism and Film," "Gay and Lesbian Criticism," "Queer Theory," "Pornography." "Race, Ethnicity, and Film," and "Film and Cultural Identity." Patricia White's unit on "Feminism and Film" refers to feminist film studies as itself a "discipline" and cites how "most histories . . . find a starting-point in the appearance of several book-length popular studies on women IN films in the United States in the early 1970s."[28] This initial focus on image critique was almost immediately followed by the work of "cinefeminists" who were more invested in "theorizing the structure of representation" (118). White then relates the influential place of Laura Mulvey's 1975 essay "Visual Pleasure and Narrative Cinema," which foregrounded the ways in which narrative cinema privileged male spectatorship of women's bodies and called for its deliberate rejection in favor of formal ruptures and innovations. Mulvey's essay set off much feminist scholarship that "went on to elaborate cinema's seemingly necessary and massive exclusion of the female subject position," and over two decades later White adjudges that "in articulating the problem of dominant cinema so very exactly, the feminist psychoanalytic paradigm risked being trapped within the monolith." This totalizing paradigm of gender difference failed to account for significant sexual, racial, and ethnic differences among women, whether as bodies, characters, or viewers. Characterizing the work on "lesbian spectatorship" as "a particularly revealing challenge to psychoanalytic theory's seeming equation of 'sexual difference' with heterosexual complementarity," White describes the "unexamined ethnocentrism" of feminist film studies thus: "Insofar as sexual difference is the organizing axis of subjectivity in psychoanalysis, Lacanian feminist film theory was ill-equipped to theorize the intersection of gender with racial, ethnic, class, national, or other differences—whether in visual and narrative codes or in spectatorial response."[29] She then adds, "The institutionalization of the field reinforced this structuring omission." White does not follow this up, but it provokes an explication of *how* the institutionalization of feminist film studies as a discipline might further brace the impossibility of intersectional analysis and theorization. Which terms and conditions of becoming a "studies" might not necessitate such monolithic conceptualizations of identity along one and only one axis of difference? Furthermore, one might also wonder about why a concerted study of film along the axes of race and ethnicity did not develop concurrently.

In the editorial preface to the groundbreaking 1991 collection *Unspeakable Images: Ethnicity and the American Cinema,* Lester Friedman begins by mapping the formation and growth of feminist film criticism, which "began with studies of images, moved to discovering a lost history of women artists, evolved to the introduction of new critical theories and methodologies, and finally emerged as an accepted academic field that produces its own scholars." [30] In contrast, he notes, "Looking at this evolution of feminist criticism as a paradigm of how ethnic criticism might develop, we immediately note that most current thinking exists in the earliest phase. In this stage ethnic groups demand equal access to the symbolic order." In her essay in this volume, Ella Shohat speculates more pointedly about the marginalization of "issues of racial and ethnic representation" in film studies as attributable in large part to "the assumption that such narrowly 'sociological' matters are somehow unworthy of the discipline's newly achieved formal sophistication." [31] She further clarifies that "the disciplinary assumption that some films are 'ethnic' whereas others are not is ultimately based on the view that certain groups are ethnic whereas others are not." Shohat attributes both assumptions in part to prior studies of ethnic representations in films, which tended to focus on "character stereotypes and social mimesis" within a strict binary of a minority group against "a fixed, white-American power structure." Instead, Shohat advocates an "intercultural" approach that would espy and analyze "the *inferential ethnic presences,* that is the various ways in which ethnic cultures penetrate the screen without always being literally represented by ethnic and racial themes or even characters" (223).

Such movement away from a beginning marked by a focus on stereotype analysis is more thoroughly recommended in Ella Shohat's 1994 book, *Unthinking Eurocentrism,* coauthored by Robert Stam. A chapter titled "Stereotype, Realism, and the Struggle over Representation" starts out:

> Much of the work done on ethnic/racial and colonial representation in the media has been "corrective," devoted to demonstrating that certain films, in some respect or other, "got something wrong" on historical, biographical, or other grounds of accuracy. While these "stereotypes and distortions" analyses pose legitimate questions about social plausibility and mimetic accuracy, about negative and positive images, they are often premised on an esthetic of verisimilitude. [32]

In footnotes, Shohat and Stam cite the 1978 essay by Steve Neale that pointed out how "stereotypes are judged simultaneously in relation to an empirical 'real' (accuracy) and an ideological 'ideal' (positive image)." While they acknowledge three "indispensable" contributions of what they call "the stereotype-centered approach," Shohat and Stam devote much of the chapter to detailing several "theoretical-political pitfalls," which they dub as a linked series of *essentialism, ahistoricism, moralism* and *individualism*.[33] After detailing each problematic tendency, Shohat and Stam add, "A privileging of social portrayal, plot, and character often leads to a slighting of the specifically cinematic dimensions of the films; often the analyses might as easily have been of novels or plays. A thoroughgoing analysis has to pay attention to 'mediations': narrative, structure, genre conventions, cinematic style. . . . lighting, framing, mise-en-scene, music" (208).

This sense that a focus on bodies and identities detracts from the specificities of the disciplinary object is again expressed toward the end of the decade by Robyn Wiegman in a chapter on "Race, Ethnicity, and Film," also included in *The Oxford Guide to Film Studies*. The essay opens by declaring, "It is rare to find a film studies scholar who would assert that the study of race and ethnicity has little or no bearing on the discipline."[34] Wiegman immediately qualifies this assessment of increased disciplinary legibility: "And yet, it is difficult to speak of race and ethnicity as constituting a fully formed field within film studies," in contrast to the ways in which Patricia White "convincingly offers a history and theoretical agenda that constitutes feminist film criticism as a coherent field within the broader disciplinary area of Anglo-American film studies" (158). What then could speed up the developmental pace of the study of race and ethnicity in cinema so that it might qualify as a coherent field? Echoing Shohat's earlier observation of the differential perception of only certain groups as "ethnic" and invoking the work of scholars who interrogate "the implicit segregation of race and ethnicity to non-white and non-WASP others," Wiegman provocatively asks, "What would it mean to think of race and ethnicity in ways that both critique and exceed the 'minority' rubric? What aspects of formal cinematic analysis might be affected by considering race and ethnicity as critical categories irreducible to bodies?" (159) Even as these questions are meant to trouble the minoritization of race and ethnicity, I would ask whether and how irreducibility to bodies is necessary qualification for critical efficacy and theoretical sophistication, especially given that what *matters* about how cinema represents race is the illusion of human *bodies*.

In writing about the unprecedented sense of resemblance enabled by the photographic apparatus, Rey Chow notes, "Whether what is captured is a human face, a body, an object, or a place, the illusion of presence generated is such that a new kind of realism, one that vies with life itself, ag-gressively asserts itself." [35] This intense effect is "punctuated with an equally compelling sense of melodrama—of technologically magnified move-ments that highlight the presences unfolding on the screen as artificial and constructed experiments. Melodrama here is not so much the result of sen-timental narration as it is the effect of a caricatured defamiliarization of a familiar form (the human form)" (169). Insofar as the moving, speaking, gesturing figures projected by film are not only severed from, but also fun-damentally *not lived* by, discretely centered subjects, the human body as such is defamilarized. The material preproduction, the gestural perform-ance, the mechanized film-making, and the intervened projection of cer-tain cinematic figures as less human, less willful, and less penetrable acts to disguise this fact for all cinematic bodies:

> Film, precisely because it signifies the thorough permeation of reality by the mechanical apparatus and thus the production of a seamless semblance to reality itself, displaces once and for all the sovereignty of the so-called original, which is now often an imperfect and less permanent copy of it-self. . . . This image signifies the end of the aura of the sacredness that used to be attached to the original human figure, to the human figure as orig-inal. . . . As the effects of mechanicity, filmic images carry with them an inhuman quality even as they are filled with human contents. (173)

If film is such a displacement of the originality of the generic human body, this brings into question the agency and authenticity of all cinematically reproduced and projected bodies. Conceiving the move away from partic-ularized social bodies as a move toward greater disciplinary centrality and pertinence forgets this problem of origin for the study of film. In chapter 1, I questioned the implicit desire for disciplinary legibility as an unmarked "author" as premised on a disencumbering of markers of corporeal and so-cial specificity. Such critical impulses seem even more ironic for film stud-ies, where the primary object of study, as Chow emphasizes, *is* the visual illusion and the narrative lubrication of human bodies.

This division of social difference and disciplinary significance inhibits a conjoined analysis of cinema as an apparatus of visual representation, an ideologically powerful discourse, and a political economy of production, distribution, and consumption. According to the intradisciplinary division of film studies between the formal-aesthetic and the social-ideological,

Return to this page + re-read

which Dyer sets up even if to argue that they need to be bridged, the study of "identity" must be slotted under the latter. Consequently, the attention to specifically named human bodies and social identities can never be fully disciplinary in ways that can address and contribute to "what matters" about the socially unencumbered object of film studies. The charge that an excessive focus on the kinds of bodies competes for attention with the "specifically cinematic dimensions of films" could be recast as expressing another disciplinary anxiety for film studies in relation to literary studies: the critical explication of film involving as it does a transcoding of moving image to immobile text is closer to literary explication than the object of study. Since lighting, framing, sound, and editing cannot be relayed or cited in the form of their original appearance to the viewer-scholar, it has to be described in words, not very unlike stage directions or novelistic descriptions. All film criticism then involves "a slighting of specifically cinematic dimensions of film." Asian/American women figure as objects worthy of investigation for their compounded social difference in not one but two developmentally staggered subfields of film studies: "feminist film criticism" and "stereotype criticism." While their belated incorporation may seem to expand both areas, it also forestalls the recusal of the other centered object of disciplinarity—film as such or, in the words of Richard Dyer, what *matters* about film.

To open up the field of analytical vision beyond such enclosures, I would ask, How is an Asian/American woman discernible as such? While much of the discussion presumes a ready and readily discernible female ontology outside of and prior to its being mechanically captured and reproduced, I would argue that cinematic representations themselves have crucially dictated how we can recognize such a body. To consider this productive dynamic, let us restart by exploring how a body's Asianness has been cinematically encoded and is consequently decodable. The cinematic representation and indeed representability of racial difference is implicated in a broader problematic of race as a visible sign, which has been premised largely on the chromatic axis of black/white. Robyn Wiegman has shown how "the history, function, and structure of visibility that underwrites [this] binary formation" in modernity is scored by "the epistemology of perception that simultaneously equates the racial body with a perceptible blackness, while defining, in its absence, whiteness, as whatever African blackness is not."[36] If, as she then contends, "this black/white axis works to secure the tenuousness of race to a framework of social boundaries," which relies on and reproduces a "cultural trust in the objectivity of observation," I propose that the interposition of "yellow" could distend and buckle this chromatic-racial binary. Let me clarify.

While linked to much older figurations of invading Mongols and seventeenth- and eighteenth-century Orientalisms, this particular chromatic measure of Asianness is most prominently traced back to the virulent discourse of the "Yellow Peril" or the threat of the "yellow hordes" in the latter half of the nineteenth century. While the assignation of "yellow" might have enabled a ready slotting into a more expansive and global spectrum of racial categorization based on skin color, initial perceptions of the *difference* of Asian bodies did not always focus on their pigmentation. In an 1890 essay recounting how "the coming of the Asiatic" was "regarded as a novelty, and most amusing to the curious Californians," Hubert H. Bancroft described "the fresh-imported and cleanly-scraped Chinaman, with his half-shaven head, his long braided queue, his oblique almond eyes, his cat-gut voice, his plain blue frock, or, if a man of consequence, arrayed in a flashy silk tunic."[37] The focus on the eyes as a prominent marker of difference was also highlighted in an 1878 novel by Atwell Whitney, titled *Almond-Eyed,* which ends with the image of Chinese as "pouring in, filling the places which should be occupied by the Caucasian race."[38] That "yellow" skin coloring was rather unremarkable as a racial distinction is also evident in the cartoons and drawings for newspapers in the nineteenth century wherein Chinese figures are illustrated as such by their eyes, the queue, and details of costume. Even with the later introduction of color printing, there is not a sustained differentiation between the skin color of white and Chinese bodies.[39]

Considering these instances, I would venture that the "Yellow Peril" imperiled not only the racial hegemony of whiteness but also the very black/white binary, which helped to define whiteness against a singularly black racial other. Toni Morrison observes that "race has become metaphorical—a way of referring to and disguising forces, events, classes, and expressions of social decay and economic division far more threatening to the body politic than biological 'race' ever was."[40] In support of this metaphoricity, Wiegman points out, "Of course, bodies are neither black nor white, and the range of possibilities accruing to either designation contradicts the assurance of these categories to represent, mimetically, the observable body" (*American Anatomies,* 9). Bringing these two insights together, I suggest that "yellowness" is doubly metaphorical—a way of referring to the *assumed* visible difference of black and white that subtends racial classification, which simultaneously covers over and displaces the "of course-ness" that *sees* that bodies are not black, not white, and not yellow.[41]

This metaphoricity of "yellowness" poses a problem for the cinematic transcoding of the Asian body from linguistic description to a moving photographic image. James Snead's concept of "marking" to refer to the stubborn highlighting of skin color in cinematic representations of black figures offers an insightful point of comparison and contrast. He writes, "As if the blackness of black skin were not enough, we seem to find the color black repeatedly overdetermined, marked redundantly, almost as if to force the viewer to register the image's difference from white images."[42] To this observation, Sharon Willis adds:

> Representations that obsessively mark the "obviousness" of the visible racial difference establish its iconicity over and over, reconstructing the body as aesthetic and ideological sign. Attention to the "obvious" as overmarked, or oversignified, leads us to interrogate the potency of the very cultural and representational banalities that obsessively insist on the legibility of social differences we take to be visible and obvious, that we understand as subject to immediate appropriations at a glance: gender difference and racial difference.[43]

While differently marked, the obvious iconicity of whiteness has also been laboriously and repetitively constructed. Distinguishing the different registers of "white" as a hue, a skin color, and a constellation of symbolic connotations, Richard Dyer notes, "A person is deemed visibly white because of a quite complicated interaction of elements, of which flesh tones within the pink to beige range are only one: the shape of nose, eyes, and lips, the colour and set of hair, even body shape may all be mobilised to determine someone's 'colour.'"[44] As a concrete example, Dyer refers to how "it has been customary in the West to call the complexion of Chinese and Japanese people yellow, yet it is by no means clear that their complexions are so distinct from that of white Westerners." Instead of a difference in skin color, then, "it is generally the shape of the eyes that is critical in deciding whether someone is 'white' or 'yellow'" (42). Although Dyer neglects to explore *how* the chromatic designation of social bodies as "yellow" has come to be generally predicated on something other than skin color, I would argue that insofar as the pigmentation of "Japanese and Chinese people" is difficult to distinguish from that of "white Westerners," the cinematic figuration of Asianness *had* to zoom in on some other visible marker.[45]

Approaching this dilemma from a different angle, we could examine it as the trouble of cinematically marking the obviousness of the white body, which Dyer *does* lay out in fascinating detail. Tracing the historical development of certain technologies and conventions in film lighting and film stock, which have tended to "assume, privilege and construct whiteness," Dyer argues that "the relationship between the variously colored human subject and the apparatus of photography is not simply one of accuracy" (90). Instead, he elaborates, "Film stock repeatedly failed to get the whiteness of the white face. The earliest stock, orthochromatic, was insensitive to red and yellow, rendering both colors dark. Chris Handley, looking back in 1954, noted that with orthochromatic stock, 'even a reasonably light-red object would photograph black.' White skin is reasonably light-red. Yellow also posed problems" (91). Rather than a teleological history of cinematic technological innovations as aimed toward greater mimesis, this account underscores how the material limitations of the apparatus frustrated a desire for cinematically produced whiteness to surpass the physiological pigmentation of white persons. Dramatic make-up also posed problems. Dyer cites a lengthy passage from a 1920 edition of a cinematographic manual that decries actors' use of "chinese yellow" grease paint because "it is non-actinic and if the actor happens to step out of the rays of the arcs for a moment or if he is shaded from the distinct force of light by another actor, his face photographs BLACK instantly."[46] There were other options available, as Dyer points out. Instead of arc lights, film crews could have used not only a cooler and more portable, but also cheaper alternative: "But incandescent tungsten light has a lot of red and yellow in it and thus tends to bring out those colours in all subjects, including white faces" (92). Even blond hair posed similar problems of darkening so that "one of the benefits of the introduction of backlighting . . . was that it ensured that blonde hair looked blonde" and not black. Cinematic whiteness, therefore, had to be painstakingly staged, which, I would argue, crucially necessitated the redundant markings of both black and Asian alterity.

Characterizing the epicanthic fold as the *primary* corporeal signifier of Asianness in film make-up, Eugene Franklin Wong argued in 1978 in *On Visual Media Racism* that "of all racial minorities in motion pictures, none has so great cosmetic concern as have the Asian characters. . . . Emphasis upon slanted eyes is racially primary in the industry's cosmetic treatment of Asians, with skin color, hair texture, and so on, being largely secondary" (40). This privileging of a difference in the eyes was not so much a criterion used toward the casting of Asian actors but instead centered on the making-up of non-Asian actors to portray Asian characters. *The Technique of Film and Television Make-up for Color and Black and White,* published in 1969, advises, "The eyefold, or epicanthic fold, of the Mongolian race is one of the basic facial differences which must be created with make-up when a Caucasian type is to look Mongolian" (cited in Wong, 41). Different methods and materials used to create the appearance of the slanted eye ranged from "simple application of paint and shadow highlights" to increasingly laborious uses of spirit gum, tape, wax, and a "slick back wig." To this focus on transforming the eyes, "other affectations which do not directly come under the heading of cosmetology, may be added such as stylized body movements, pidgin English, high-pitched voice (in the case of an Asian male), and traditional Asian dress" (42).

It should be underscored that all of these surface modifications and affectations were marshaled to enable the credible illusion of Asianness as performed by a non-Asian body.[47] This practice of cosmetic transformation and cinematic illusion has been dubbed "yellowfacing," which I would argue is a misnomer. While the term draws chromatic parallels with the racial masquerade of "blackfacing," as noted earlier, there is less emphasis here on mimicking a yellow skin color than on molding the shape of the eyes. I would venture furthermore that rather than a mimetic reproduction of any physical feature shared by all Asians and not by any other kind of racial body, the exaggerated and obsessive marking of the epicanthic fold has served a double purpose: (1) to encode a body cinematically as "Oriental" or "Asian" and therefore distinguishable *at a glance* from both white and black cinematic bodies;[48] and (2) to "mark" that a white actor was *performing* an Asian character. The practices of "blackfacing" and "yellowfacing" are certainly linked but also differentially premised on a racist fortification of the unique plasticity and malleability of the white body.

Turning that around, I would say that such practices also were necessary reassurances that *only* a white body can be remade, can remake itself to "look like" its racial others. Characterizing the initial use of "cosmetized whites" in the 1920s as "a means of getting Asian characters to conform more readily to white racist perceptions and characterizations of Asians," Wong adds, "Furthermore, the incipient star system was being constructed around white performers, not Asians, who could with the assistance of the industry assume any character identity" (75–76). In spite of the time and labor-intensive trouble of "yellowfacing" as a means of producing a cinematically legible Asian body, as noted in an article in 1944, there was a definite criterion by which movie audiences could discern whether an "Oriental" character was being performed by a white actor or an Asian actor: "'We saw an Oriental on the screen and if he were a menial and his part a non-starring one, he was a real Chinese or a real Japanese. We saw an Oriental on the screen and if he were a fine, colorful character and his part a leading one, he most likely was Charles Boyer, or Paul Muni, or Walter Huston. The same with the girls. The old habit of casting occidentals as orientals will doubtless continue as far as starring performers were concerned'" (William H. Mooring, "The Sound Track," cited in Wong, 44).[49]

The practice of "yellowfacing" intersects with the predominance of Asian-Caucasian romance plots. Wong's most useful analytical contribution to this pattern of cinematic interracial relations is to emphasize that it was neither in an effort at a mimetic representation of sociological realities or the lack of available Asian actors and actresses to perform a range of other configurations of desire and sexuality. Rather it was the product of certain racist casting practices, which he calls "role segregation" and "role stratification." *Role segregation* refers to the differential mobilities enjoyed by specifically raced actors to portray a range of racial roles, which Wong dubs as "role freedom" or lack thereof. While Asian actors are prohibited from playing "those roles that are by the industry's definition designated as *white*," Wong notes, "at the same time, whites can move horizontally and cross into roles otherwise designated by the industry as *Asian,* while being secure in the knowledge that there is an industry guarantee that white roles will not be violated by Asians" (12, original italics). In this regard,

Wong specifies "role freedom" as "the cinematic right of whites to portray Asians."

Along with "role freedom," white film actors also enjoy the privilege of "role importance" through the systematic enforcement of *role stratification,* wherein the more prominent, starring roles are reserved almost exclusively for white performers while Asian actors are mostly relegated to minor roles or nonspeaking parts as extras. These intersecting axes of horizontal and vertical mobility produce a certain casting system in which the more important the Asian character role, the more likely that it gets performed by a non-Asian actor. This casting system constrained the numbers of different racial-gender configurations of Asian-Caucasian pairings, resulting in what Wong calls "the system tradition of double standardized miscegenation [which] permits of three gender relationships on the portrayals of interracial sex between Asiatics and whites":

> The first standard may allow interracial sex if the partners, both as actors and screen characters, are a white male and an Asian female. The second standard (a) prohibits the depiction of interracial sex between an *actual* Asian male actor and a white female actress, and (b) permits the *simulation effect* of interracial sex to be shown on screen so long as the Asian male character is *in fact* a white man in cosmetics. (28, my italics)

The real—actual, in fact—in this case is neither corporeal nor sociological but what I would call an *industrial* constraint on the cinematic representability of Asian female bodies and their (hetero)sexual desires. In this structural mismatch between what can be represented fictionally on film and what can actually be done in the performance of that fiction, the "simulated effect" of interracial sex is produced through the industrial prohibition of simulated sexual contact between certain acting bodies, specifically "to ensure that an 'actual' Asian actor not engage in explicit sex with an 'actual' white female actress on the screen" (Wong, 53).

Another problem of cinematic representability is that of encoding and discerning certain ethnic distinctions within the broader racial categorization of Asian, Asian American, or "Oriental." Here I would argue that the notion of an "Asian" stereotype has been produced as much, and by now more, through the language of critical discussion, which has often tended to collapse ethnic and racial distinctions. For example, in a chapter titled "The Early Years: Asians in the American Films Prior to World War II,"

Eugene Wong opens the section on the silent films by positing rather seamlessly that "Asians and Asian themes, *mostly Chinese,* found their way into the American films as early as the latter part of the 19th century" (56–57, my italics). The ethnonational specification of "Chinese" is evident in the earliest film titles that Wong relates—*The Chinese Rubbernecks* (1903), *Heathen Chinese and the Sunday School Teacher* (1904), and *Chinese Laundry: At Work* (1904). Even the 1908 film *The Yellow Peril* featured "a Chinese servant [who] disrupts a household, is thrown from a window, beaten by a policeman, and set on fire."[50] Describing how "the original Yellow Peril as perceived by white Americans and Europeans alike had been the Chinese," Wong goes on to cite from a 1969 issue of *Film Society Review,* which observed that the initial cinematic figuration of the "oriental villain" was "characteristically Chinese."[51]

If one of the more pernicious effects of cinematic stereotyping is to efface and contract the distance between ethnic specificities and a generically racialized type—"All Orientals Look Alike"—I would ask what is analytically lost by *not* maintaining a critical distinction between ethnic and racial markings, especially in order to track their problematic slippage? Inasmuch as the agglomeration of an array of varied cinematic portrayals under the rubric of one racial stereotype or one racial-gender stereotype (as in the case of the "Asian woman") might work to imbue a social coherence and even an ontological outline to the category, such gestures could also eclipse broader historical, social, political, economic, and cultural dynamics that shape significant differences. I began this chapter with a guarded departure from those who would stress the penetrating and widely dispersed force of cinematic representations to *produce* the generic contours of Asian/American women. To offer some alternative critical framings of the subject, I will suggest possible directions for study that might not only contest the limited legibility of these desiring bodies but also interrogate the investments in maintaining a separation of identities and disciplinarity.

One possible train of investigation could consider how the construction of certain reductive images and characterizations of Asians was closely linked to the earliest developments of film as a medium of popular entertainment. According to Dorothy B. Jones, "Among the early motion pictures, which have been identified from the records of the United States Copyright Office, are a number dealing with China. In 1896, the American Mutoscope Company issued two brief subjects on the visit of a Chinese celebrity to New York City—these being titled, LI HUNG CHANG AT GRANT'S TOMB and LI HUNG CHANG DRIVING THROUGH 4TH AND BROADWAY."[52] She further notes, "In this early period, too, films were being shown about the Chinese in America" naming the 1903 film *Scene in Chinatown*. As Eugene Wong recounts, "One of the most profitable and long-lasting project systems created by the industry was that of the serial or multi-part film" (75). Although the serials addressed a range of subject matter, Wong contends that their popularity and profitability lay in the fact that "not only did the earliest serials have an 'oriental villain' as a recurrent scapegoat against whom millions of Americans could vent their frustrations and even realize their racist fears, the nature of the serial structure was emotively accommodative to anti-Asianism" (75). One article on Hollywood and the First World War argues, "Because the serial structure demanded current and often sensational material and in short climactic segments, the issues in these stories were clear-cut with easily identifiable villains and heroes. The 'yellow peril' theme especially fit the purpose of the serials."[53]

I want to close by resituating the genealogy of Asian bodies in Hollywood cinema in terms of national identity and international politics and economic globalization. Here I refer at length to Dorothy Jones's 1955 study *The Portrayal of China and India on the American Screen, 1896–1955*. Commissioned by the Center for International Studies at the Massachusetts Institute of Technology as part of "a larger study of these images which [was made] as part of a program of international communications research," the report is based on content analyses of "approximately 325 motion picture features and short subjects which were shown in American theaters" and on the cases of ten films in particular, five on China and the Chinese and five on India and Indian characters. Given that "Thomas Edison . . . as early as 1898 sent a cameraman to the Far East who came back with pictures of China and India which at the turn of the century were seen on the American screen" (1), these representations were coterminous with the beginnings of film as a specific cultural medium.

While Jones is cited by later critics of cinematic representations of Asians, including Eugene Wong and Gina Marchetti, the most interesting aspect of this study is its extended account of the construction and dissemination of certain *national* figurations in film and their increasingly acknowledged significance to shifting international geopolitics and trade relations. By Jones's account, the 1920s were especially marked by such struggles over the content of Hollywood films and also their possible impact overseas on several registers. For example, Britain perceived American film as a threat to its own imperial dominance as a possible tool for the emergence of the United States as a culturally and economically hegemonic power on the global scene. Warning in a speech in 1923 against how "the film is to America what the flag was once to Britain," the Prince of Wales further predicted, "By its means, Uncle Sam may hope some day, if he be not checked in time, to Americanize the world." Two years later in a speech before the House of Lords, Lord Newton claimed even more ominously, "The Americans realized almost instantaneously that the cinema was a heaven-sent method of advertising themselves, their country, their methods, their wares, their ideas and even their language, and they had seized on it as a method of persuading the whole world that America was really the only country that counted."[54] This method of national advertising was seen as especially threatening for its appeal to British colonial subjects in Asia, especially India: "*The London Daily Chronicle* asked bluntly whether the British Empire could be conceived as 'holding together indefinitely' with American movies catering to the native crowds in Asia."[55] Linked to this geopolitical influence, there was a growing realization that "film directly influenced the currents of trade—that from Spain, the Near East, Argentina, Chile, and Brazil were coming demands for American office furniture, shoes, hardware and clothing 'like we saw at the movies',", and the American motion picture thus became a threat to foreign traders" (5).

There was also a sense that film was a powerful medium for disseminating impressions of other nations and nationalities. After the government of Mexico placed an embargo on film imports from the United States in order "to protest the large number of Mexican villains portrayed in Hollywood movies" (3), the industry promptly sent a representative to Mexico City to begin a bilateral agreement to lift the sanction.[56] The Hollywood film industry responded through other measures to prevent offending the many national sensibilities. In 1922 Will Hays, the head of the newly established Motion Picture Producers and Distributors of America, created a foreign department "whose function was to help the American motion picture companies to anticipate international problems in the making and overseas distribution of their films" (2). While he is well-known in film history for the Motion Picture Production Code (also called the Hays Code) that forbade among other things scenes of explicit sex and miscegenation, Hays could also be rather glowing in his humanistic assessments of the *international* possibilities of film:

> I do not believe I am too enthusiastic or too visionary when I say that the motion picture may be, probably will be, the greatest instrument humanity has yet known for the bringing about of better understanding between man and man, between group and group, and between nation and nation. When we know one another, we do not hate one another. When we do not hate we do not make war. . . .
>
> The motion picture knows no barrier of distance. We are apt to look upon the distant group or nations as something different from ourselves and therefore inimical. The motion picture knows no barrier of language. We are apt to regard those who do not speak our own tongue as different and inimical. But a few thousand feet of celluloid film in a metal container can be sent to the ends of the earth to speak the language which everyone understands, civilized or savage—the language of pictures.[57]

Whether in response to the threat of bans and embargoes by offended nations or in this more hopeful spirit of international understanding and peace, the self-regulating code of "Don'ts and Be Carefuls" adopted in 1927 by the Association of Motion Picture Producers (AMPP, a precursor to the present Motion Pictures Association of America), included a special provision on "International Relations." The final version, ratified in 1930, codified as Article X that "the history, institutions, prominent people and citizenry of other nations shall be represented fairly."[58] The justification for this article in the stated principle that "the just rights, history, and feelings of any nation are entitled to the most careful consideration and respectful treatment" exists in interesting tension with the absence of such considerations for the cinematic representation of certain racialized *Americans* at the same time.

This nationalized worry over offensive representations held out different consequences for the representation of different Asian nationalities. In response to the William Hearst–sponsored serial film *Patria* (1916), which depicted a villainous Japanese baron, President Woodrow Wilson expressed in a letter to Hearst, "It is extremely unfair to the Japanese and I fear that it is calculated to stir up a great deal of hostility which will be . . . extremely hurtful."[59] In contrast to a relative silence about early depictions of China and Chinese, Jones notes that the Chinese government sought to protest certain films and to intervene in the production of others in the 1930s "when China began to take her place in the community of nations and to build up a functioning foreign service" (Jones, 37). A 1932 article in the Chinese press protested, "If any Chinese character is included he has to wear a queue and Chinese boots, long discarded. Where does one find such things nowadays, except when dramas of a generation ago are presented on a stage?" (quoted in Jones, 37). Writing in 1930 about how "whenever a Chinese is portrayed on the screen he is depicted as a dope fiend, gambler, murderer or something equally bad," Paul K. Whang added a specific nationalistic critique of the casting of Japanese actors in American films about China, Chinese characters, and Chinatowns since these Japanese actors "misrepresented the Chinese for the benefit of their own country."[60] Contrary to Hays's earlier claim that film had the potential to close geographical distances and to bridge cultural-linguistic differences, Whang further argued, "Being far away from China, the public has nothing better to do than to take these misrepresentations at their face value." This also applied to (mis)representations of Chinatown, which, in turn, "will arouse the ire of the Chinese people, but will reflect no good upon the reputation of the American government." According to Ruth Vasey, "In 1930 the Chinese government banned Harold Lloyd's first talkie, *Welcome Danger,* after its portrayal of the residents of San Francisco's Chinatown as kidnappers, gamblers, and opium smugglers led to a riot at the Grand Theater of Shanghai."[61] The Chinese government took various measures of protest, from demanding that certain films be re-edited before distribution and exhibition in China, to banning entire films, to making recommendations to individual studios, to the rare instance of closing down the branch offices of the companies responsible. Following the earlier precedent set by France, Chinese representatives also tried to prevent distribution and exhibition in other nations. While others used this "diplomatic networking," Vasey says that "the Chinese probably developed this approach in its most sophisticated form" (631).

Jones describes how "Hollywood has, in the main, looked for guidance on Indian subject matter to the British Embassy and consulates in this country, to the British Board of Film Censors (BBFC) in London, and to the British India office" (66). Although the BBFC, like the AMPP, was largely focused on the cinematic representation of sex and violence, Jones notes that "one subject which was of considerable concern to the BBFC over a period of years was the portrayal of India on the screen and the role of the British in India." Given that there was not much reason for apprehension on the second point since so many films were based on written accounts that "for the most part . . . made the British role in India appear as a glorious mission in which the interests of the Indian people were at all times genuinely served," Jones notes that the stated concern of the BBFC for any possible offense to Indians was "entirely contradictory, for nothing could offend the Indians more than the glorification of British imperialism which the BBFC and the British India Office has tacitly approved" (68). As a further insult, when Hollywood studios consulted the British embassy for "advice in obtaining technical officers who would be familiar with the Indian scene," they were directed toward "officers who had served with the British army in India or officials who had been part of the British government in India" (68). In the immediate years following Indian independence, although studios were invited to shoot in India, once the Indian government representatives viewed the finished products, they "concluded that such motion pictures did not serve the interests of India for the portrayal which they gave of India to the world was not one which this young nation with its new and understandably acute sense of national pride could tolerate or accept" (69). The Indian government began to discourage the importation of such films through heavy taxes and fees.

This expansive yet dense context of international commerce, decolonization movements, and postcolonial desires has crucially determined the terms and conditions by which Asian/American women have been cinematically projected. If the skepticism toward identity-based film studies— "stereotype criticism"—would contest how they might contribute to what really matters about the discipline, I would argue that the study of Asian/American women in and through film demands but also enables such interdisciplinary attentiveness to history, international politics, economic globalization, technological innovations in film lighting, stock, and cosmetic make-up, and a specific industrial political economy of racially skewed casting practices. Rather than the claims of an especial misrepresentation and its consequent injury to the bodies and psyches of real Asian/American women, this unruly genealogy of how the elaborate staging, production, and exhibition of racial and ethnic differences have always mattered to the historical development of film opens up the possibilities for how the cinematic compositions of Asian/American women might *come to matter* for the discipline of film studies.

chapter 3

Historical Reconfigurations

Delineating Asian Women as/not American Citizens

Characterizing the then predominantly male Chinese population as a "bachelor society of 'serfs'," Reverend J. C. Holbrook wrote in an 1859 article in *Hutching's California Magazine,* "The small number of children is thus accounted for, in part, by the fact that nearly all the females are dissolute and loose in their character and habits. A large proportion of the houses of ill-fame in this city are inhabited by Chinese women. A respectable family is scarcely to be found." [1] Insofar as nuclear monandry is assumed here as the measure of a properly practicing femininity, children are significantly—and, I would add, merely—made out to be the necessary articles of proof against the charge of the women's nonreproductive and therefore excessive sexuality. Similarly penetrating claims about their "character and habits" mark a crucial pivot and relay between the fascinating display of Afong Moy and the preventative legislation against the importation of "Mongolian, Chinese, and Japanese females" I pointed to in my introduction. To the generic fixations and cinematic projections that would transfigure Asian/American women into legible subjectivities and desirous bodies, this third chapter counterposes a more contentious and disjointed account of how Asian women have been designated as alternately worthy of and ineligible for immigration, naturalization, and citizenship.

Lisa Lowe has convincingly demonstrated that throughout U.S. history "the American *citizen* has been defined over against the Asian *immigrant,* legally, economically and culturally." [2] To explore this inequality in some detail, the first part of this chapter traces a jumble of legislative acts, judicial decisions, bureaucratic procedures, and popular cultural representations that have figured specific ethnic, national, class, and sexual configurations of Asian women as distinctly *un*-American. Inasmuch as they have been subject to an array of sensational charges, anxious disavowals, and capricious qualifications, Asian/American women could also implicate the genealogy of the "American people" and its more legalistic articulation as "U.S. citizen" as a forceful, defensive, and often contradictory marking out of a national identity through shifting obsessions with and suppressions of the difference between these immigrant and native-born bodies. Rather than a teleological résumé of progressive achievements, which can be warmly inducted into the nation and its narration, this accounting of the unstable slash demarcating *Asian* from *American* reads as a chronic case study of the contingency and interdependence of both identifications.

But what then connects these un-American women of the past to "Asian American women" as a presently recognizable social category and object of study? Considering Asian/American women as significantly constitutive of American identity requires that they be dislodged from the dichotomies of exclusion vs. inclusion, otherness vs. sameness, absence vs. presence, and objectification vs. subjectivization within which they have often been cast by both dominant national histories as well as some Asian American and feminist historiographical representations. If the first part of the chapter argues for the impossibilities of a coherent and teleological narration of their Americanization, the second part further problematizes the *writing* of Asian/American women's history as partial and limited. Although I have thus far attempted to interrogate the figurations and interpretations of Asian/American women through literature and cinema, often criticizing their displacement and erasure of significant historical realities, in this chapter I now focus my critical lens on "history" as yet another vexed compositional terrain.

From Imaginary Spectacle to Public Nuisance

Well before the first known physical arrival of Chinese women in the mid-nineteenth century, particular images of them circulated in the United States through travel accounts written by traders and missionaries returning from Asia and in the dramatic staging of Orientalist caricatures that were performed by non-Asians. Referring to a staging of Voltaire's *The Orphan of China* in Philadelphia in 1755, and other such productions, James Moy points out that "the notion of Chineseness under the sign of the exotic became familiar to the American spectator long before sightings of the actual Chinese."[3] Given this context of imagined and performative hyperbolization against a corporeal absence, the first *known* Chinese women to come to the United States in the early decades of the nineteenth century were presented to a paying American public as exotic objects of curiosity who were temporarily visiting the nation. In addition to the aforementioned Afong Moy, who traveled throughout the country as part of a sideshow in 1841, the Barnum's Chinese Museum featured a Pwan Yekoo, under the billing of "a genuine Chinese lady." An article in the 21 April 1850 issue of the *New York Times* described Pwan Yekoo as "prepared to exhibit her charming self, her curious retinue, and her fairy feet (only two and a half inches long), to an admiring and novelty-loving public."[4] Even as these women were touted for the authentic and intimate impression of Chinese femininity they offered the paying public, it is important to stress that they composed a highly contrived and stylized *tableau vivant*. This spectacular display suggests an early precursor to the vexed and forceful history of the cinematic stagings of Asian/American femininity discussed in the previous chapter. The trouble of making Asianness visible through the mediations of film lighting and film stock must be recast as more than the inevitable displacements of mechanical reproduction. Pwan Yekoo's "preparation" for self-exhibition insinuates a performative element that undercuts her presentation and reception as "a genuine Chinese lady." How might one rehearse (for) a "novelty-loving" audience? This early example shows that a racial correspondence of performing and performed bodies need not produce greater authenticity.

This public fascination with the earliest Asian female bodies in the United States must have predated any suggestion of their possibly permanent residence. While the surviving testaments of these women, whether in the form of drawings or written impressions, are invariably fixated on their clear contrariety to familiar visions of American femininity, the descriptions are not yet shaped by a discourse of racial difference. Indeed, advertisement for Afong Moy attributed the variations in the women's physical appearance to the effects of their distant geographical location rather than any ethnological distinctions. The vaguely "Chinese" costumes, furniture, and other props that decorated the "viewing rooms" could have served to guarantee the properly foreign and exotic setting to which these alien corporealities securely belonged. Their physical and social confinement to the select quarters and circuits of their exhibition might have further assured (only) momentary presence in the United States, rarely provoking questions about what kinds of "Americans" or "American women" that they could become. Citing the earlier claim by Loren W. Fessler that both Afong Moy and Pwan Yekoo went on to Europe after their publicized stints in New York, and since "no historical evidence has indicated their intention to settle in the United States," Hua Liang argues, "They were, therefore, not 'immigrants' by definition."[5] According to historian Judy Yung, although Afong Moy is considered to be the first Chinese and the first Asian woman to *come* to the United States, Maria Seise was the first Chinese woman to *immigrate* to the United States in 1854 as a domestic servant for Charles V. Gillespie, an American trader.

With the discovery of gold in 1849, large numbers of Chinese men and a very few Chinese women began to arrive in California. Already by 1852 the depletion of gold heightened resentment and racial hostility from white miners, and anti-Chinese sentiment was widely and frequently expressed. An article in the 17 August 1852 issue of the *Daily Alta California* takes particular notice of the increasing public visibility of Chinese women, describing them as "queer and diminutive specimens of the human family, bunched up in bandanna 'kerchiefs,' werring blue shirts and big unmentionables, walking through the streets with as much delicacy as a turkey treading on hot ashes."[6] These plural Chinese women are figured as excessively and improperly conspicuous, both in their dress and bodily movements. Considering that the Chinese population in San Francisco in 1850 comprised 4,018 men and only 7 women, the angry tone and animalizing metaphor of this protest against these women's unrestricted mobility in public space further suggests that the earlier appeal of Afong Moy and Pwan Yekoo was premised precisely on their physical sequestering.

The popular press renderings became increasingly negative throughout the 1850s. In an 1858 article in *Harper's Weekly,* which "described in detail the 'celestial ladies' with their supposedly grotesque hair styles, bound feet, and manner of dress," the author confidently declared, "I defy any but the most catholic women worshippers to admire the women of Southern China," adding, "The taste for the baboon-like faces of Hong

Kong women is, I fancy, like that for mangoes, an acquired one. I have learned to like mangoes; but my tailor's wife still excites in me only unmitigated disgust."[7] The emphatic aversion to this Chinese woman is refracted through a strange criterion of "taste" by which this author is compelled to make some definitive diagnosis of her (hetero)sexual appeal. The metaphor of food and edibility complements the metonymic privilege of this American male subject to declare the impossibility of incorporating this immigrant alien into the national body no matter what productive role she might play in its domestic service economy.

Such eroticized gazing toward and disgusted turning away would soon reach virulent heights as all Chinese women in the United States were seen as (probable) prostitutes needing to be expelled and kept out. In addition to charging them as all "dissolute," the Reverend Holbrook also noted, "It is a singular peculiarity of the Chinese females, seen here, that they are extremely diminutive in their stature—scarcely one equaling in size the medium average of American women" ("Chinadom").The body type of the generic "American women" here is open to speculation as California was then occupied by a heterogeneous range of female bodies. Another account, also in the *Hutching's California Magazine,* characterized Chinese women as morally and sexually suspect given their position in the racial taxonomy: "Unlike the Oriental nations, the Chinese have sent hither swarms of their females, a large part of whom are a depraved class; and though with complexions in some instances approaching fair, their whole physiognomy indicates but a slight removal from the African race."[8] If the lighter skin color of these Chinese female bodies might have troubled the binary opposition of white and black, the superiority and purity of racial whiteness was reinstated by "writers and cartoonists [who] ascribed definite negroid characteristics to the Chinese stereotype."[9]

Chinese Prostitution and Immigration Exclusion

Most historical studies of early Chinese immigration concur that the great majority of Chinese women who came to the United States in the mid-1800s worked as prostitutes.[10] Lucie Cheng Hirata writes, "In 1870, among the 3,536 adult Chinese women in California, there were approximately 2,157 whose occupation were listed as prostitutes, and a majority of them

(67 percent) were concentrated in San Francisco."[11] That "prostitute" was recorded as an occupational category by census takers attests to an atmosphere of "tacit acceptance" resulting from the significant gender imbalance for all the newly arrived ethnic and national groups in San Francisco.[12] While many of "the first female arrivals [in California] were prostitutes of varying racial and national origins,"[13] journalists, politicians, and Christian missionaries were especially critical of Chinese prostitution. In April 1869, the *Overland Monthly* published an article on "Chinese Women in California," which narrated the establishment of Chinese prostitution in this way:

> Those familiar with the early settlement of San Francisco know what a crowd of people congregated from all parts of the world, and what practices were tolerated. Vice of every form reigned unchecked; and there were not wanting those who were ready to traffic in anything which might bring gain to their pockets; and amongst such were a few shrewd, but unprincipled Chinamen, who having surveyed the ground, and taken notes of the situation, returned to China; but they soon came back, bringing with them the first of those women whose numbers have since increased from year to year, and whose presence is an offence to all respectable people, and a blot on the character of their own nation. Both men and women engaged in this business; sometimes, the women as "sole traders"; and sometimes, men and women in partnership.[14]

Citing the Chinese prohibition against the emigration of women, the author asserts that "nearly all Chinese women in San Francisco are a disgrace to their nation." The article goes even further by invoking the Chinese custom of sequestering women at home, where they are segregated from men, to suspect all Chinese women who appear in public to be prostitutes: "The women who are to be seen in the gambling houses gaudily dressed, singing, and playing the guitar for the entertainment of the crowd, are of that class which, in Western parlance, would be termed 'of no account'; so, likewise, are most of those of bold and forward deportment who are seen upon the streets and frequenting the shops and the theatres."[15] This protest against an excessive public presence and visibility as itself the sign of these women's dubious character might complicate those more recent equations of visibility as liberating and empowering for Asian/American women, which were discussed earlier in the introduction.

Such outcry against this increased publicness of suspect Chinese female bodies drove lawmakers to take decisive action. As early as 1866, the California state legislature passed "An Act for the Suppression of Chinese Houses of Ill Fame," which "declared Chinese prostitution to be a public nuisance, made leases of property to brothel operators invalid, provided for the retaking of premises, and charged landlords who allowed their properties to be so used with a misdemeanor that carried a maximum penalty of $500 or six months in jail."[16] The vigorous enforcement of this law forced "the parties representing the women" to strike a compromise to stay only within "certain buildings and localities under restrictions imposed by the Board of Health and Police Commissioners."[17] Although the 1866 law would be amended in 1874 to encompass all prostitutes, this early penalization and segregation of Chinese prostitution combined with the perception of widespread gambling houses and opium dens therein to render Chinatowns as a "vice district."[18] This spatial containment of Chinese prostitutes already present in California would be buttressed four years later in 1870 by the attempt at territorial exclusion in "An Act to Prevent the Kidnapping and Importation of Mongolian, Chinese, and Japanese Females, for Criminal and Demoralizing Purposes."

The shift from Chinese to this broadened ethnonational litany is striking. Only 279 Japanese women had entered before 1890 as compared to 2,637 Japanese men.[19] Given their miniscule numbers, the specified inclusion of "Japanese females" two decades prior suggests a precautionary measure against future Japanese women's immigration.[20] This 1870 act operates out of another tension between genericity and individuality. As it is worded, the law contradicts the common presumption of innocence before proof of guilt. Although any and all Mongolian, Chinese, or Japanese women are cast as an enigma to be ascertained as to their worthiness for Americanization and duly authorized, it is not the state's obligation but the responsibility of individual women to prove that they are exceptional. Already by 1874, Chinese women en masse were cast under a general cloud of suspicion, epitomized by President Grant's claim: "Hardly a perceptible percentage of them perform any honorable labor, but they are brought for shameful purposes, to the great demoralization of the youth of these localities."[21] The properly acceptable "Chinese immigrant woman" was therefore an institutionally ascribed subject, who had to be culled carefully from a larger group of inappropriate aspirants and dangerous impostors.

A tension is set up, however, between the immigrant woman's obligation to show her "desire" for entry and the commissioner's overriding "ability" to read and to "describe" her beyond possibly false claims. While a host of third parties ranging from Christian missionaries to Chinese merchants were called to testify as to "whether it was possible to tell Chinese prostitutes from 'moral' women by their looks and clothing," the evaluative authority of the commissioner was deemed paramount.[22] The discerning power of the commissioner would be contested four years later in the U.S. Supreme Court in what is referred to as "The Case of the Twenty-Two Chinese Women." In August 1874 a steamer arrived in San Francisco from Hong Kong with eighty-nine Chinese female passengers. The commissioner of immigration deemed twenty-two of these women to be prostitutes and detained them "based on his observations of the women's demeanor and manner of dress and on the evasive and unsatisfactory responses they had given to questions put to them about their marital status."[23] His suspicion was affirmed by a Reverend Otis Gibson, who had been to China as a missionary. Observing that "the style of dress worn by several of the women detainees—handkerchiefs around the head and gaudy-colored garments embroidered with silk—corresponded with the type of dress worn by courtesans in China," Gibson further "opined that at least half of those who had been detained were prostitutes." Despite the testimony of several women on their own behalf, the court was "satisfied that the evidence showed that the women were prostitutes."[24] In addition to marking an early judicial attempt to exclude Chinese women, the "Case of the Twenty-Two Women" also involved two broader struggles. First, on appeal, the federal circuit court overturned the earlier ruling on the constitutional grounds that, in its use of the term "person" rather than the narrower "citizen," the Fourteenth Amendment assured due process and equal protection to Chinese and other foreign nationals. The ruling justice, Stephen Field, also affirmed that only the federal government, and not the state or other local governments, had jurisdiction over immigration.

In the very next year, Congress passed the Page Law, named after Horace Page, a California congressman who had argued against the influx of Chinese prostitutes. Although the Page Law also forbade the entrance of convicts and "coolie" laborers and named prostitutes generally as an inadmissible category, further declaring the importation of such women a felony, it specifically stipulated that "those convicted of importing Chinese prostitutes were subject to a maximum prison term of five years and a fine of up to five thousand dollars."[25] Since the much greater numbers of male migrants rendered the "prohibition of contract labor [as] merely symbolic," the Page Law was implemented largely against Chinese women. Furthermore, the more feasible focus on prohibiting the entry of Chinese prostitutes necessitated and thereby produced "an elaborate network of intelligence gathering and interrogation, which included American and British consular officials at Hong Kong, that city's Tung Wah Hospital Committee (an agency controlled by Chinese merchants), and port authorities in San Francisco."[26] The Page Law thus put into place a dense transnational network of surveillance, judgment, and documentation, which would later be applied to monitor and control other Chinese migrants destined for the United States.

Even as the premise of excluding prostitutes subjected *all* Chinese women who sought to enter the United States to suspicion, certain class-based distinctions were also assumed and applied. Whether a woman had bound feet or not was an oft-used criterion for adjudging her class and moral status, which were often conjoined and collapsed. Judy Yung cites one immigration official, who wrote in his report, "There has never come to this port, I believe, a bound footed woman who was found to be an immoral character, this condition of affairs being due, it is stated, to the fact that such women, and especially those in the interior, are necessarily confined to their home and seldom frequent the city districts." As an example, he describes how "the present applicant No. 14418 is a very modest appearing woman whose evident sincerity, frankness of expression and generally favorable demeanor is very convincing."[27] Despite such discerned exceptions, the prevailing suspicion that all Chinese women were prostitutes fortified the transnational apparatus of interrogating and laborious certification and effectively limited the immigration of Chinese women as a group.[28] Although the more general Chinese Exclusion Act would be passed seven years later, and 1882 is often seen as a landmark year in the history of U.S. immigration legislation, the 1875 Page Law attests to a racially biased—but on the basis of gender, class, and sexuality as well—system of restriction established several years prior.[29] Subsequent legislative efforts in 1903, 1907, and 1917 sanctioned the deportation of any Chinese woman who was suspected of being a prostitute.[30]

Even after the passage of the Page Law, medical experts, elected offi-

cials, labor unions, and xenophobic groups continued to point to the cor-
rupting and contaminating powers of Chinese prostitutes who "were believed to be infected with a particularly virulent form of syphilis that was
almost impossible to cure."[31] Such prejudicial speculation was supported
by professional medical opinion. In 1875 the American Medical Association drew up a report that characterized Chinese women engaged in prostitution as a "risk to national health":[32]

> Testifying before the congressional committee investigating conditions in
> Chinatown in 1877, Dr. H. H. Toland, founder of the Toland Medical
> College, subsequently the University of California Medical School, re-
> ported that nine-tenths of the venereal disease in San Francisco could
> be traced back directly to Chinese prostitutes. Since it was believed that
> most of the Chinese houses of prostitution were patronized primarily by
> whites, Chinese prostitution was seen as "the source of the most horrible
> pollution of the blood of the younger and rising generations."[33]

Again in 1877–78, before a Special Commission on Chinese Immigration
appointed by the California state senate, Dr. Toland, who was then a member of the San Francisco Board of Health, claimed he had seen boys as
young as eight and ten years old with syphilis.[34] Then, on 10 March 1880,
a specially appointed committee composed of the mayor of San Francisco,
I. S. Kalloch, a Dr. Henry S. Gibbons Jr., and a health officer named
J. L. Meares issued a report titled "Chinatown: Declared a Nuisance!" In
their resolution of "condemnation," approved by the city's board of health,
a subsection titled "Chinese Courtesans" begins, "In other alleys Chinese
prostitutes abound, and shamelessly ply their miserable vocation. . . . These
lewd women induce boys of all ages to enter, where he who enters is
lost."[35] From cloistered spectacle to public obscenity to a more penetrating contagion, Chinese female bodies pose a counterreproductive threat to
the national citizenry through its most prized and hopeful embodiment
and as youthful white masculinity.[36]

Such denouncements of Chinese prostitution and Chinese prostitutes
were easier to utter than to substantiate. A discursive circularity marked
this chain of medical diagnoses. Under the subheading "Dreadful Disease," the 1880 report recites the earlier testimony of Toland, specifically
his response to the committee's question regarding the source of these
infections:

In answer to the question to what extent these diseases come from Chinese prostitutes, he says: "I suppose nine-tenths. When these persons come to me, I ask them where they got the disease, and they generally tell me from China women. I am satisfied that nearly all the boys in town, who have venereal diseases, contracted them in Chinatown. They have no difficulty there, for the prices are so low that they can go whenever they please. The women do not care how old the boys are, whether five years old or more, so long as they have money." [37]

The unequal figurations of the beguiling prostitutes as "women" and their unsuspecting and vulnerable customers as "boys" contradict the testimony offered by one contemporary San Francisco police officer that "most of the Chinese houses of prostitution are patronized by whites, by young men and old ones." [38] Such changes of sexual treachery existed alongside a moral outcry against the speculation that many of the prostitutes were young "girls" who needed to be rescued, protected, and reeducated by their American sisters.

Given that Chinese prostitution served as a touchstone in the arguments for Chinese exclusion, efforts to defend Chinese immigration also specifically addressed this moral-sexual threat. In a statement addressed "To the committee on Foreign Relations of the United States," Benjamin S. Brooks argued in 1877, "There are not 500 prostitutes—no more in proportion to the Chinese population than there are white prostitutes to the *white* population." [39] Brooks's rhetorical strategy was to denounce these "white prostitutes" in the very same terms of the charges made against Chinese prostitutes: "*These* prostitutes prey upon the white population exclusively. They undermine the moral and physical constitutions of the young; plant in them the seeds of a horrible ineradicable and hereditary disease; destroy the peace of families." The main distinction between the two groups, Brooks pointed out, was their differential legal and institutional treatment: "No inspector stops *their* landing; no populace stone *them* through the streets; no laws oppress *them*." While this observation might highlight how the selective creation and enforcement of laws *produce* racially based differences amongst women and prostitutes, Brooks's defense relied on and ultimately affirmed the racial distinction and segregation of Chinese from white as well as the sexual and moral degradation of the "prostitute" within both racial-ethnic categories. In addition to arguing that because Chinese prostitutes service only Chinese men, they do not pose a significant threat to whites, Brooks conceded, "Those few miserable Chinese prostitutes are certainly *prostitutes,* and undoubtedly have intercourse and traffic with their countrymen, but certainly we cannot complain of injury to ourselves. As for the whites—few if any—whom they are able to entice to their embraces—they are not of a character to be injured, either morally or physically, even by the embraces of a Chinese prostitute" (5, original italics). After separating out the Chinese prostitutes as an undefendable group within the larger Chinese population, he ends by pointing to the presence of wives and children in Chinatown where "there are a hundred times more children [than] among the three thousand white prostitutes, their neighbors" (18).

Chinese prostitution also posed a different legal-moral dilemma in the immediate post–Civil War era. The much-rumored existence of Chinese female slavery, especially of young girls, provided a timely site onto which the anxieties of national identity, following a civil war whose victors sought to unite the nation under a banner of freedom, could be both displaced and comparatively reassured. In the aftermath of the Civil War and the formal emancipation of African slaves through a constitutional amendment, articles bearing such titles as "A Stain on the Flag" and "Chinese Slavery in America" decried Chinese prostitution as a distinctly un-American socioeconomic aberration. They often emphasized the coercive confinement of these female bodies in decrepit conditions and the speculative charge that many of these prostitutes were young girls.

Brooks's handling of the outcry against the unlawful enslavement of Chinese prostitutes here merits consideration. As if in response to those who sought to marshal these details of Chinese prostitution as demonstrating the unassimilability of the Chinese as a whole, Brooks counters, "I have never seen evidence that young girls were purchased from their parents or indentured to a life of infamy nor that prostitution was with the Chinese a legitimate or honorable pursuit" (9). While conceding that "I have heard of contracts signed by prostitutes and of transfers of such contracts, and that women were held to miscellaneous intercourse," he is quick to add, "But I have also heard of similar transactions among the white prostitutes." Following this move to acquit the Chinese by emphasizing such cross-racial similarities between Chinese and white prostitutes, he instantiates a crucial difference. Brooks draws out the inherent contradiction in which the law must serve as the privileged means through which the Chinese would become enfranchised as U.S. citizens even as it is also the coercive mechanism of their social and economic disenfranchisement in a racist political order: "Let us not charge them with being an alien population in our midst while we forbid them to naturalize. Let us not charge them with want of respect to our laws until we expunge all laws from our books that are intended to operate only against them, and thus make our laws worthy of respect" (17–18).

The vociferous sexual and moral panic around Chinese prostitution fortified xenophobic calls to ban all Chinese immigration and led to the passage of the Chinese Exclusion Act of 1882, which prohibited the immigration of Chinese laborers but exempted certain classes, specifically merchants, teachers, and students. The Exclusion Act also codified that all Chinese aliens were "ineligible for citizenship." While there were no specific provisions for Chinese women, the act produced varying ramifications for different women. Because it was implied and thus interpreted that a woman's status derived from a father or husband, "Wives of laborers, although not specifically mentioned in the act, were barred by implication."[40] Being married to a Chinese merchant, however, did not assure a woman's entry into the United States. In August 1889 the Treasury Department decreed that a Chinese woman wishing to enter the United States as a member of the exempted classes provide the same certification required of a male migrant, which was contested in an Oregon circuit court. Citing article II of the Exclusion Act, which stipulated that "Chinese subjects, whether proceeding to the United States as teachers, students, merchants, or from curiosity, together with their body and household servants . . . shall be allowed to go and come of their own free will and accord," the presiding Judge Dready ruled against the Treasury Department:

> It is impossible to believe the parties to this treaty which permits the servants of a merchant to enter the country with him, ever contemplated the exclusion of his wife and children. And the reason why they are not expressly mentioned, as entitled to such admission, is found in the fact that the domicile of the wife and children is that of the husband and father, and the concession to the merchant of the right to enter the U.S. and dwell therein at pleasure, fairly construed, does include his wife and minor children . . . the company of the one, and the care and custody of the other, are his by natural right, he ought not to be deprived of either.[41]

Even as Judge Dready noted the expressed and therefore privileged mention of "household servants" in the article, he ultimately affirms the original inattention to women by declaring that the only kind of Chinese female entrant allowed under the Exclusion Act was allowed not by the right of the woman to immigrate but by the right of a specific kind of Chinese man to "the company" of his wife. Finally, the Exclusion Act was also retroactively applied for deportation proceedings against those Chinese resident in the United States but suspected of having entered under illegal auspices. According to Sucheng Chan, "immigration officials and judges who wished to deport prostitutes . . . got rid of women by classifying them as "manual laborers'."[42] Such figurative application exposes the lack of regard for women in the conceptualization of the Exclusion Act as well as the contingent and innovative if not ludicrous methods by which that oversight was addressed in actual enforcements against certain Chinese immigrant women.

Public outcry against the special immorality and illegality of Chinese prostitution continued over a decade after the passage of the Chinese Exclusion Act. An article titled "A Stain on the Flag," published in February 1892, begins, "It was generally supposed that slavery was abolished in the United States during the administration of Abraham Lincoln; yet . . . there exists in this country, wherever the Chinese have obtained a foothold, a slavery so vile and debasing that all the horrors of negro American slavery could not begin to compare with it."[43] The author, M. G. C. Edholm, reaffirms this comparison more forcefully through invoking two generic figures: "The negro of ante-bellum days was a prince of fortune to the luckless Chinese slave." Further describing how Chinese "women and children" are "not merely sold, but imported for this purpose" by a transnational network of agents, Edholm's sensationalistic account ends: "The Chinese girls revolt at their terrible lives. But what choice have slaves? Let America blot out yellow slavery as it has blotted out black slavery. Let the Chinese woman as well as the African man point to the stars and stripes and say, No man dares do me injustice under this flag" (170). If the now-emancipated "African man" is posited as the model to which the still enslaved "Chinese girls" should aspire, even if they might lack the political and historical agency to do so, the article singles out the contributions of certain "American women" for conveying the Chinese slaves to the desired state. Referring to the work of the different Protestant mission homes, whose major fundraisers and staff workers were women, Edholm praises these "Women's Missionary societies" for "well disproving the old adage that 'woman is woman's worst enemy' for these tender-hearted women labor night and day for the amelioration of their sisters."

That same year, an editorial published in the *San Francisco Chronicle* echoes Edholm in condemning the "shameful commerce in Chinese women" as a "blot upon the escutcheon of our civilization" but is less sanguine about the possibilities of rectifying the national dilemma through legal actions. The opening of the article merits a lengthy citation:

> It is a sad commentary on the greatness of a nation where her laws are used as engines of assault on her constitution. Sadder still is the existence of such an anomaly when it not only imperils the well being of the State, but strikes a blow at the very foundations of her social system. With the abolition of slavery through the terrible medium of the war of the rebellion there came into the minds of progressive American citizens a feeling of complacency somewhat akin to that of one who has laid aside disreputable garments and donned a new set of clothes. It is not pleasant, therefore, for Americans to be told that all who seek protection under the Stars and Stripes do not breathe the air of freedom, that slavery is not altogether a thing of the past, but that human beings are today bought and sold into a worse kind of slavery than ever Uncle Tom knew of, and that the laws of our country are powerless to crush it.[44]

Worse than being merely powerless, the writer continues, "It is still more unpleasant to our ears when we are told that our processes and laws are constantly being invoked, and sometimes successfully, in aid of this nefarious traffic in human flesh." The crux of the scandal is not so much the illegality of Chinese prostitution but the very ingenuity of those who would utilize the existing laws and processes to defend and perpetuate this odious form of female slavery.

In 1897 a writer decried how Chinese prostitutes were able to bypass the restrictions by claiming to have been born in the United States because immigration officials were relatively powerless in being able to prove otherwise.[45] This foregrounds a fundamental schism of the nation-state. While the right to nationality through territorial birth affirms the national fantasy of America as territorially grounded and bounded, the state's very attempts to legislate and enforce that identity run up against its own lack of the proper technology by which to certify the truly indigenous from the foreign-born.

With the Chinese Exclusion Act in place to delimit the immigration of poor and unmarried Chinese women, anxious attention was increasingly directed against immigration from other Asian countries, especially Japan. As with the earlier wave of Chinese immigration, there was a great gender imbalance in the early Japanese immigrant population. The 1900 U.S. census recorded only 985 Japanese women in a total Japanese population of 24,326. Yuji Ichioka notes: "The small female population in 1900, numbering in the neighborhood of a thousand, included many prostitutes who, in all likelihood, comprised the majority."[46] The 1892 Supreme Court case *Nishimura Eiku v. U.S.* echoes the earlier "Case of the Twenty-Two Chinese Women" in its affirmation of the power of the commissioner to perceive and judge the acceptability of immigrant subjects over and against their own self-presentations.[47] Citing a provision in an 1882 congressional act, which ordered that "any convict, lunatic, idiot, any person unable to take care of himself or herself without becoming a public charge" be reported and detained, a California state immigration commissioner denied Nishimura Eiku and three other Japanese women permission to land in San Francisco. In spite of the fact that Eiku possessed $22, she was detained and then repatriated because, according to legal historian Hyung Chan Kim, "her story that she was accompanied by a husband turned out to be untrue, and her claim that her husband was in the United States was discredited because she did not know his address."[48] Claiming that all four women were indeed prostitutes imported by a Hasegawa Genji, "the most notorious procurer in San Francisco," Ichioka adds that Hasegawa also paid for their legal defense (5). For my purposes, I am more interested in how the category "prostitute" stands in contradistinction to the acceptable identification of "wife," which can only be proven by producing a "husband."

As with the case of efforts to exclude Chinese, the growing opposition to the unrestricted immigration of Japanese also centrally invoked the problem of Japanese prostitution in the United States. Anti-Japanese rhetoric also held up both the problem of Chinese prostitution and its solution in the exclusion law as instructive precedent, which led to a concerted strategy: "Knowing the Chinese had been excluded in 1882, both Japanese government officials and immigrant leaders looked askance at the prostitutes. Afraid the prostitutes would become the measuring rod by which white Americans would judge all Japanese in America, they self-righteously decried their presence and took measures to limit their numbers in the vain hope of avoiding the same fate as the Chinese."[49] This complex interplay of racist xenophobia, sexual moralism, class discrimination, and ethnic accommodation culminated with the United States and Japanese governments signing the 1907–08 Gentlemen's Agreement. In exchange for lifting the segregationist ban of Japanese students from the public schools of San Francisco, the Japanese government would regulate the emigration of Japanese subjects.[50] More specifically, Japan would assist in the restriction of Japanese immigration, especially of laborers, to the United States. For its part, the United States would guarantee equal and just treatment of those Japanese already residing within its borders. The Gentlemen's Agreement also led to reductions in the immigration of Korean laborers, given that Korea was under Japanese colonization at the time and the U.S. government categorized Koreans as Japanese nationals.[51]

The Immigration Act of 1917 commenced a series of even more restrictive laws regarding immigration. In addition to instituting a literacy test, intended to limit immigration from southern and eastern Europe but which also adversely affected Asian immigrants, this act prohibited immigration of laborers from what it designated as an "Asiatic Barred Zone" that covered India, Indochina, Afghanistan, Arabia, and the East Indies. According to William S. Bernard, "The act was the first step in establishing a federal policy of restriction wholly based on a rank order of eligible immigrants that favored national groups thought to be most assimilable."[52] This act most effectively halted the immigration of Indians who had been able to immigrate and become naturalized because of their standing racial categorization as "Aryans."[53]

The Immigration Act of 1924 was the most comprehensive in restricting Asian presence in the United States, barring the immigration of all "aliens ineligible for citizenship." This was a significant shift from denial of naturalization to a total ban on future Asian immigration. However, the racially neutral identification of ineligibility for naturalization helped to disguise its special consequences for Asians, especially for Asian women. The law provided for European immigrants and Euro-American citizens the right to return to their homelands, marry a foreign national, reenter the

United States, and then petition for the immigration of their spouses, who would be classified as "non quota immigrants." However, Asian women, who were now "aliens ineligible for citizenship," could not enter the country, even as wives and daughters of U.S. citizens.[54] In addition to limiting their entrance for the sake of maintaining a specious racial homogeneity belied by the very history of conquest, enslavement and territorial dispossession, the 1924 act forced Asians already living and working in the U.S. to the precarious margins of U.S. citizenry.

In an inverse manner, the history of U.S. colonial rule of the Philippines and of the national classification of Filipinas/os also contests the logic of immigration exclusion that assumes a homology between the bounded space of the nation-state and those citizens who are born and live inside its clearly demarcated borders. The history of U.S. imperialism in the Philippines shows how American nationality has not always been contained within the geographical boundaries of a contiguous land mass. Following the U.S. victory in the Spanish-American wars, the Philippines was placed under U.S. control and Filipinas/os became designated as "U.S. nationals." This, along with their earlier racial categorization as "Malays," distinguished them from East Asians categorized as Mongolians and initially exempted them from those immigration restriction laws. Consequently, after the passage of the 1924 act, Filipinas/os, mostly men, constituted the bulk of immigration from Asia to the United States, and their growing presence soon prompted vociferous and often violent anti-Filipina/o mobilizations. An odd coalition of Filipino nationalists and American isolationists and antiimmigrant racists pushed for the passage of the Tydings-McDuffie Act of 1934, which finally granted independence to the Philippines. This decolonization enabled the United States to prohibit immigration from the Philippines as it had done with the other Asian nation-states.

The ban on Asian immigration continued until World War II when, pressured by the need to project a more positive international image, the United States allowed a limited number of Asians—mainly Chinese, Filipinos, and Asian Indians—to enter. The War Brides Act of 1945 was especially significant for Asian women's immigration.[55] Initially, Asian women did not qualify, because the 1924 law that was still in effect categorized them as racially ineligible for both immigration and naturalization.[56] A special amendment to the act in 1947 allowed Asian women who married U.S. armed services personnel to immigrate. For the first time in U.S. history,

Asian women outnumbered Asian men in annual immigration figures. Many of the first war brides were Chinese wives of Chinese American servicemen. The postwar U.S. military's occupation of Japan and its later role in the Korean War (1950–53) resulted in a sizable number of international marriages and consequently the immigration of Japanese and Korean women who married U.S. soldiers. Another significant constituency of Asian immigrants in this period was Korean orphans, a majority of them girls, who were adopted by families in the United States. In one of many important historical ironies, the U.S. involvement in various imperialist wars in Asia impelled the slow removal of legislative bans on immigration from Asia. Then, in 1952, the Walter-McCarran Act lifted previous bans and allowed the miniscule number of one hundred immigrants per year— from nations in the "Asian-Pacific Triangle." Two provisions that exempted wives and children of U.S. citizens from this quota resulted in a significantly skewed gender distribution of immigrants from Asia. In the case of Koreans, those who entered the United States were predominantly female, either through marriage to U.S. soldiers or adoption. As Bill Ong Hing enumerates, "From 1959 to 1965, 70 percent were women, 40 percent of whom were 20–39." He adds, "about 40 percent were girls under the age of four, who were adopted by families moved by the large numbers of orphans left after the Korean War."[57]

Racialized and Gendered Citizenships

In addition to these measures to prevent the immigration of Asians and Asian women in particular, the genealogy of "Asian American women" has been significantly shaped by legal and political measures around citizenship and naturalization. Even after the American colonies achieved independence from English rule, the U.S. government retained many of the defining principles of British citizenship and naturalization laws, which were thoroughly inflected by racial, ethnic and gender-based discriminations. The British Parliament passed a law in 1740 that granted Jews and Protestants the right of naturalization after seven years of residence. Even though the explicit naming of Jews and Protestants was meant to exclude Catholics, Jeffrey H. Lesser argues, "the British approach was inclusionary—not exclusionary—because it demanded that in order to be acceptable for citizenship, a certain group had to be specifically included in the wording of the law. Simply put, British law assumed the undesirability of certain 'others' for citizenship."[58] In this vein, the first naturalization law passed in 1790 by the U.S. government categorically delineated a "free white person" as the only kind of immigrant eligible for naturalization. The genderless "person" here belies the gender inequalities of the rights and privileges of U.S. citizenship, since, as Eileen Boris so cogently points out, "men more often applied for naturalization when voting was the major benefit to citizenship."[59] The next naturalization law, passed nearly a century later in 1870, following the Civil War, added "persons of African nativity or descent" to this category of those to be expressly included by naturalization.[60] Contrary to arguments about the abstraction of citizenship, this inclusionary logic rests not on a discorporation of the citizen–subject but rather requires the explicit corporeal markings of only certain kinds of eligible bodies.

Although it would be another eighty years before Asian immigrants would be legislatively authorized for naturalization, various claimants sought to contest this exclusion in a series of defining court cases. As early as 1878, lawyers for four Chinese men seeking naturalization challenged the interpretive openness of the chromatic identification of "white persons" in a case referred to as *In re Ah Yup*. The San Francisco court ruled that the Chinese litigants were indeed ineligible: "The words 'white persons,' said the court, had a well-settled meaning in both common speech and scientific literature and were seldom if ever used in a sense so comprehensive as to include individuals of the Mongolian race."[61] The federal government also sought to deny the citizenship status of Chinese born in the United States in two separate cases, *In re Took Sing* (1884) and *United States v. Wong Kim Ark* (1898), in which two Chinese American males, born in the United States and having thereby obtained citizenship status, were prohibited reentry on returning from a trip to China in the aftermath of the 1882 Exclusion Act. Against the longstanding common-law principle of U.S. citizenship by territorial birth, the federal government lawyers argued that the Chinese, regardless of their place of birth, owed their primary allegiance to the Chinese Emperor.

Two notable court cases, *Ozawa v. United States* (1922) and *United States v. Bhagat Singh Thind* (1923), further affirmed that Japanese and Asian Indians respectively were not qualified for naturalization on racial grounds.

While these judicial decisions unproblematically addressed a male subject-position with little regard to the different inflections that immigration and naturalization laws may hold for women, both cases are instructive in charting the shifting tensions between racial, ethnic, and national identifications, which significantly bear on the current conceptualizations of "Asian American women." After twenty years of residence, Ozawa Takao, a Japanese immigrant, applied in 1914 for naturalization, but was rejected as a member of the Japanese race. He appealed to the Supreme Court, arguing that the authors of the 1790 and 1870 acts had meant to exclude blacks and then Chinese. Although Japanese were not nominally *included* in these naturalization acts, Ozawa's lawyer argued, "there is nothing in the laws of the United States to show that Japanese were intended to be excluded." Because "whiteness" was not a fixed linguistic designation or social category, Ozawa Takao *could* qualify as chromatically "white" and therefore entitled to naturalization as a "free white person."

The court was not convinced. The judgment against Ozawa asserted that just because "Japanese" were not specifically targeted for exclusion at the time did *not* mean that the legislators of 1790 and 1870 would have regarded them as "free white persons." The opinion declared,

> The provision was not that Negroes and Indians shall be excluded, but it is, in effect, that only free white persons will be included. The intention was to confer the privilege of citizenship upon that class of persons the fathers knew as white, and to deny it to all who could not be so classified. It is not enough to say that the framers did not have in mind the brown or yellow race of Asia. . . . It is necessary to . . . say that, had these particular races been suggested, the language of the act would have been so varied as to include them in its privileges.[62]

Although the nonexistence of Japanese immigrants in 1790 would not have warranted any consideration of them whatsoever, by a strange move of retrospective projection into the minds of "the fathers," the court could confidently assert that, even if the Japanese had been considered as possible candidates for naturalization, they would *not* have been included by the earlier legislators. That "Japanese" were not explicitly named was proof of the court's certainty of the nonequivalence of "Japanese" and "free white persons." If naturalization is not a widely assumable right but a narrowly conferred privilege, the historically shifting and politically strategic constructions of U.S. citizenship rights in 1790 and 1870 are refracted and legitimated through an organic figuration of the nation as multigenerational family headed by the original "framer-fathers."

Granting that the meanings of the original wording of "free white persons" could not be fixed, the Supreme Court had to make some attempt to address Ozawa's claim that because he was *not* "not white" as that category was envisioned in 1790 and 1870 against blacks and Chinese respectively, he could very well qualify as "white." In the ruling against Ozawa, Supreme Court Justice Sutherland declared:

> Manifestly, the test afforded by the mere color of the skin of each individual is impracticable as that differs greatly among persons of the same race, even among Anglo-Saxons, ranging from the fair blond to the swarthy brunette, the latter being darker than many of the lighter hued persons of the brown or yellow races. Hence to adopt the color test alone would result in a confused overlapping of races and a gradual merging of one into the other, without any practical line of separation.[63]

To avoid such fusions and confusions, there was then a narrowing of the more ambiguous, interpretively flexible definition of "whiteness" into the pseudoscientific category of the "Caucasian" race given that "gradations of race did not exist, only gradations of color."[64] Although his petition for naturalization was denied, the *Ozawa* case impelled a judiciary clarification of a distinction between "color" and "race," upholding the latter's scientific fixity over the perceptual heterogeneity and instability of a person's skin color. What was assumed but remained to be discussed, however, was an explicit "race test" that would be more incontrovertible than the "color test." However, as *United States v. Thind* would show in the following year, the definition of "Caucasian" itself was not so fixed and reliable.

Bhagat Thind was an immigrant from India and a World War I veteran of the U.S. Army who had been granted the right of naturalization in 1920 by an Oregon federal court, on the basis of his claims that he was "a pure Aryan" and thereby was racially qualified to become a U.S. citizen. According to Charles J. McClain, Thind and his lawyers were prepared to address the matter of his perceptible nonwhiteness: "The term, 'white,' he contended, clearly could not refer to skin color since many dark-skinned Europeans had been ruled eligible for naturalization—a point acknowledged by the Court in *Ozawa*" ("Tortuous Path," 49). Modern ethnography counted India as part of the "Aryan" race. In arguments before the Supreme Court, the U.S. attorney, who sought to cancel Thind's naturalization certificate, "conceded that Thind might technically be Aryan but contended that the privilege of naturalization should only be open to those who belonged to 'white civilization,' as that term was generally understood."[65] McClain describes the U.S. attorney's racial reconfiguration, "Indians were universally seen as belonging to a different cultural and political fellowship. The government harped on the popular, as opposed to the scientific, conception of racial identity. Whatever the Hindu might be to the ethnographer, the government argued, in popular conception the Indian was seen as alien to the white race and part of the 'white man's burden'" (49). Ozawa was rejected on the ground that though he might qualify as "white" in a chromatic sense—or at least not "not white"—he was "not Caucasian," in the pseudoscientific, ethnographic sense. However, a reverse yet complementary logic operated in the "denaturalization" of Thind, since he was deemed scientifically "Caucasian" but not "white" in the popular sense of that word in 1790.

While Lesser points out that the Thind case is significant for being the first to stress the significance of the "popular" definition of "whiteness," he does not analyze the assumptions of the American *people* underlying the notion of the "popular" here. On this point, the conceptualization of the "popular" seems intimately related to the metaphorizing of the nation as an organic *family* both in terms of a "horizontal comradeship" across space and a multigenerational link through time.[66] This is manifestly evident in the written decision:

> The words of familiar speech, which were used by the original framers of the law, were intended to include only one type of man whom they knew as white. The immigration of the day was almost exclusively from the British Isles and northwestern Europe whence they and their forebearers had come. When they extended the privilege of American citizenship to "any alien being a free white person," it was these immigrants and their kind whom they must have had affirmatively in mind. The succeeding years brought immigration from eastern, southern, and middle Europe, among them the Slavs and dark-eyed, swarthy people of Alpine and Mediterranean stock, and these were received as unquestionably akin to those already here and *readily amalgamated* with them.[67]

The criterion of "popular" acceptance revolved around the question of assimilability, which as the above reasoning shows relied on androcentric assumptions of blood and familial relations. As a prime example of the closed circularity of racist logic, the unassimilability of Indians as established by the *Thind* ruling was reinforced by reference to the 1917 Barred Zone Act, which was taken as "evidence that Congress was opposed to naturalizing persons of Asian descent." Within three years of the *Thind* ruling, over sixty Indian American citizens were denaturalized, thereby rendering them "stateless persons."[68] Such exercise of the state's prerogative and power to deprive persons of national affiliation has been necessarily occluded to maintain its more dominant image as the locus of belonging *and* its guarantor.

While these cases have been cited as instances of discrimination against Asians or Asian Americans, they also underscore how certain subjects sought to become "American" by pronouncing their measurable difference and distance from other Asians and people of color. Insofar as Ozawa's lawyers sought to qualify Ozawa under the 1790 law, I would argue, they missed the opportunity of disrupting the foundational equation of "American citizen" as "free white person," which was offered by the 1870 amendment to explicitly include those of "African ancestry." Put differently, the *Ozawa* case also implicates the Asian/American "quest for citizenship" as a "quest for whiteness" or, conversely, a repudiation of "blackness." This strategy was made most explicit in appealing the case to the U.S. Supreme Court, wherein Ozawa's attorneys "claimed that the word *free* was meant to be used in opposition to slavery, while the word *white* signified a class of individuals who did not have 'negro blood.'"[69] Adding that a *person* was any member of the human race, the lawyers argued that Takao Ozawa qualified for all three categories. In addition, Ozawa's lawyers responded to the privileging of "Caucasian" by providing "some ethnological evidence—rather dubious, it must be said—purporting to show that the Japanese were in fact part of the Caucasian race and did not deserve to be classified as belonging to the Mongolian branch of humanity."[70] Like their disjointed yet resonant conceptualization and implementation, these various bars to citizenship for Chinese, Japanese, Koreans, Indians, and Filipinos would be lifted not all at once but in staggered fits and starts, beginning with the Magnuson Act of 1943, which repealed the 1882 Chinese Exclusion Act and designated Chinese as eligible for naturalization. Three years later, in acknowledgment of their contributions as U.S. allies in the war effort, Filipinos and Indians were granted the right to citizenship in 1946, and the "Asiatic Barred Zone," was abolished by the Walter-McCarran Act of 1952. Here it should also be noted that the repeal of immigration exclusions was necessary for the projection of the United States as a leading "democracy" in the postwar world order. Citing the argument of legal scholar Neil Gotanda that this concession to the eligibility of each national group did not fundamentally challenge the core equation of "Americanness"-as-"whiteness," Lisa Lowe has cogently summarized that "through the legal enfranchisement of specific Asian ethnic groups as *exceptions* to the whites-only classification, the status of Asians as nonwhite is legally restated and reestablished. Thus, the historical racialization of Asian-origin immigrants as nonwhite 'aliens ineligible for citizenship' is actually rearticulated in the processes of legal enfranchisement and the ostensive lifting of legal discriminations in the 1950s."[71] The incommensurability of "U.S. citizen" and "nonwhite person" is also thereby sustained as the foundational core of "American" identity.

The United States also inherited key gendered discriminations from British citizenship laws. In addition to the assurance of citizenship to all those born within the territorial borders of the nation-state, it adopted the 1708 ruling by the British Parliament, stipulating that children born abroad to a U.S. citizen would also possess U.S. citizenship. However, as Virginia Sapiro is quick to clarify, "the only parent who could transmit nationality in this manner was the father. Women's blood, apparently, was not strong enough to transmit nationality unless the child was illegitimate."[72] According to the British legal tradition, the U.S. also granted primacy to a husband's nationality over the wife's, what Eileen Boris characterizes as "women's legal disabilities as *femme covert,* the fiction that married women merged their identities into that of their husbands."[73] Under the "common law of naturalization," which made the citizenship status of married women dependent on the nationality of the husband, an 1855 congressional act decreed that an alien woman who married a U.S. citizen could become naturalized. But, as Ian F. Haney-López points out, "A wife's acquisition of citizenship, however, remained subject to her individual qualification for naturalization—that is, on whether she was a 'white person.' Thus, the Supreme Court held in 1868 that only 'white women' could gain citizenship by marrying a citizen."[74] In this legal calculus, then, the ideal citizen-woman would be the "white wife of a white man." As Lauren Berlant points out in consideration of such variously stratified claims to U.S. nationality already in place in 1850, "Being an American citizen wasn't 'natural' for white men, but it involved the possession of a gendered and racialized body; it wasn't simply 'familial' or 'local,' but still involved a historical inheritance in the form of *jus sanguinis* and *jus soli*."[75]

If the fiction of femme covert enveloped the legally married and white alien "wife" within the folds of U.S. citizenship as a privilege extended through her citizen-husband, a 1907 congressional act clarified that an American citizen-woman who married a foreigner would consequently be "stripped of her [U.S.] citizenship." In the case of such denaturalizations, the once-American-but-now-alien woman could become naturalized only after her foreign-born husband acquired U.S. citizenship. Combined with their racially based disqualification from naturalization, this legal dependency of married women on the citizenship status of the husband posed special consequences for U.S.-born Chinese and Japanese women in the early twentieth century. Those Asian/American women who married noncitizens were not only stripped of their U.S. citizenship status but also lost any chance of regaining it through naturalization because they would now be categorized as "aliens ineligible to citizenship." Given such impossible choices between citizenship and/or marriage, these Asian/American women cannot be inducted smoothly under the naturalizing trope of the nation as family.

Then in 1922, in what Virginia Sapiro deems "one of the most important changes in the position of women as citizens," the Cable Act ended this legal dependency, by making a woman's citizenship status independent of her husband's status.[76] It also granted that an American mother may transmit her nationality to her children. For both reasons, this piece of legislation, immediately following the obtainment of voting power for women through the Nineteenth Amendment, has been hailed as a significant political victory in the historical struggle for women's political rights in the United States. However, the Cable Act also delineated a clear symbolic division and political power struggle between the recently enfranchised "American women" and immigrant alien women by affirming and empowering the former's citizenship rights at the expense of the latter's exclusion. As Reed Ueda describes:

Henceforth no female citizen could lose her U.S. citizenship by marriage to an alien, and no alien woman could acquire citizenship either by marriage to an American or by the naturalization of her husband. The Cable Act had been supported by those seeking to enfranchise women who had lost their citizenship through marriage, after the Nineteenth Amendment had given women the right to vote. The principle of independent citizenship would also provide protection against the political power of foreign women who had obtained citizenship, and thereby voting rights, simply by marrying U.S. citizens.[77]

A clearly racialized division *among* American women was encoded in two key clauses. One clause in Section 3 decreed, "That any woman citizen who marries an alien ineligible to citizenship shall cease to be a citizen of the United States." If marriage to an "alien male who was not racially qualified"—the racially neutral legal coding of Asian—would thus *denaturalize* such a woman, the Cable Act also assured that she could not attempt to regain her citizen status without renouncing her marital status. Another clause in Section 5 determined, "That no woman whose husband is not eligible to citizenship shall be naturalized during the continuance of the marital status."[78] Although no particular racial or national identifications were specified in the wording of the act, the series of immigration exclusion and restriction acts combined with the Supreme Court decisions against their naturalization to clarify that Asians were the most prominent immigrant aliens who were "ineligible to citizenship." Eight years later in July 1930, Congress amended the Cable Act by granting the right of naturalization to those women who had lost their U.S. citizenship through marriage to an alien before 1922, but only if the woman herself were "eligible to citizenship."

The 1922 Cable Act and its 1930 amendment presented a double bind for U.S.-born Chinese women. Existing laws prohibited miscegenation, but they risked denaturalization as a consequence of marrying a noncitizen Chinese male, with no hope of future renaturalization. Some U.S.-born Chinese women, who married Chinese citizens but did not formally apply for Chinese citizenship, became in effect "stateless persons." In a brief article categorically titled "Asian Women Lose Citizenship," Kathryn M. Fong mentions two cases, those of Lily Sung and Florence Kwan, in which Chinese *American* women were stripped of their U.S. citizenship. This state-induced denationalization of U.S. citizens marks a contradictory precursor to the U.S. Supreme Court ruling in *Trop v. Dulles* (1958), in which a soldier was dispossessed of his citizenship for desertion from the army. In the majority decision, Justice Earl Warren wrote: "We believe . . . that use of denationalization as a punishment is barred by the Eighth Amendment. There may be involved no physical mistreatment, no primitive torture. There is instead the total destruction of the individual's status in organized society."[79] Lauren Berlant observes that *Trop v. Dulles* is a landmark case because it situates citizenship in a body, "the abstract body that can, nonetheless, feel pain as well as the humiliation of being vulnerable, feminized" (13). Considering that these racialized Chinese American women were denationalized several decades earlier as punishment for their marriage choices, this latter "landmark" ruling also pronounces how U.S. citizenship adheres unevenly to differentially abstracted and concretized bodies. Stripped of their own citizen status, these women were also prohibited from conferring it to any children born outside the territorial boundaries of the nation. Such a state-enforced procedure of Asian women's "denaturalization" further rebukes the naturalizing metaphors of national affiliation in terms of both territorial birth and familial bloodlines.

The clauses that negatively affected Chinese American women would later be removed by an amendment to the Cable Act in March 1931, but it would take another forty years of legislative revisions to address the contradictions of race, gender, and citizenship unleashed by this concerted effort to delineate Asian women as distinct from both American citizens and American women.[80] Even the gradual shift to qualify Asian/Americans for naturalization in the 1940s and 1950s was scored by gender discriminations. Referring to the 1943 Magnuson Act, which repealed the Chinese Exclusion Act and instituted a quota of one hundred immigrants per year from China, Lisa Lowe explicates, "in the 1946 modification of the Magnuson Act, the Chinese wives of U.S. citizens were exempted from the permitted annual quota; as the law changed to reclassify 'Chinese immigrants' as eligible for naturalization and citizenship, female immigrants were not included in this reclassification but were in effect specified only in relation to the changed status of 'the Chinese immigrant' who was legally presumed to be male."[81] She concludes, "Thus, the administration of citizenship was simultaneously a 'technology' of racialization and gendering."

These modes of exclusion, detention, segregation, deportation, and denaturalization of the Asian female from the U.S. citizenry bring "Asian

American women" into critical relief *not* as a descendant grouping of single origin but rather as a tenuous identification situationally congealed and then too internally differentiated—according to nationality, class, sexuality—through a disconnected, even haphazard jumble of cultural constructions, local and federal legislations, and enforcement mechanisms. I want to outline several implications. First, while others have cited this composition of exclusionary measures as what unifies and gives coherence to the category of "Asian American," I have suggested how some instances could just as well be read as attempting to differentiate from and, even in some instances, to repudiate just such a panethnic, cross-gender conglomeration of bodies and identities. Second, as many others have pointed out, the exclusion and denaturalization of Asian women sought to prevent the formation and reproduction of families in the United States. In seeking to deprive Asians of the right to stake a claim to a national territory through native birth as well as to a national history through multigenerational familial lineage, these acts have rendered the "Asian American family" the product of what Katie King describes as "divergent historical constructions of heterosexuality as a political achievement for Chinese and Japanese immigrants to the United States."[82] Arrangements such as "split households," "paper sons," and "picture brides" reveal the geographically scattered and situationally invented modes of marriage and family formation for early Asian immigrant communities. These transnational practices of family construction, often under oppressive circumstances and deceptive means, further denaturalize the familialization of the United States as a geographically contained community joined by native birth. If, as Anne McClintock contends, the family figures so crucially in positioning the nation within some organic trajectory of reproduction and succession, what would it mean to insist that the "Asian American family" can *not* be vacated of its historical contingency through some invocation of an unbroken organic lineage?[83] The convoluted delineations of different Asian women as/not American citizens could unsettle, rather than corroborate, the naturalizing and unifying trope of the nation as family. Third, inasmuch as each such instance of adjudicating their differences has also helped produce and redefine the "American," Asian/American women could be recast, neither as victims of barrings and expulsions nor as willing aspirants to citizenship, but rather as seditious figures who have necessitated a more stringent definition of "we, the people" at various twists and turns of the nation's history.

Such an approach, then, might reveal more about "the nation" than at first assumed. Even though such synecdochic concepts as "the people" presume a sovereign and continuous national *presence* and although narrativizing this imputes a "fullness" to the nation that it can only have in such representations, both the subject of the narrative and the narrative itself are cobbled out of what Homi Bhabha calls the "shreds and patches of cultural signification" that are both *available* through strained negotiations among various groups and *invented* under particular historical conditions of enunciation.[84] As the reader 'may have discerned, the preceding narration has been highly speculative, full of conditional constructions of "could have been" and "might have been." I have had to rely on the citational availability of prior published studies in a range of both disciplinary and identity-based discursive contexts. This brings up the problem of the writing of those overlapping histories—"American history," "women's history," and "Asian American history"—with which any history of "Asian American women" must confer and contend. As a social category comprising a succession of ethnic, national, and gendered markers, "Asian American women" both belongs to and is differentially marginalized within each of these historiographical rubrics. Insofar as ethnic history and women's history are configured as smaller, overlapping fields within a broader national rubric, they have often been cast as filling an absence with presence or correcting a misrepresentation with a truth. However, this axis of exclusion-to-inclusion inhibits a critical awareness of the compositional mediations of historical scholarship and writing. On this point, we might keep in mind the mediated construction and political function of "American history" by recalling the frank observation of the early U.S. historian Mary Douglas that "nations need to control national memory, because nations keep their shape by shaping their citizens' understanding of the past."[85] Rather than focus on how Asian/American women have been marginalized by and within "Asian American history" and "U.S. women's history" because of their gender and ethnic differences respectively, I point to some awkward and forceful attempts to *include* them within these already specified subfields of history. Against their easy induction, I press for how Asian American women pose a broader historiographical *dilemma,* which critically interrogates the intimacy of national identification and the writing of history.

The Making of Asian/American Women's History

A prominent strand in the research and writing of "Asian American history" has foregrounded moments and mechanisms of the exclusion and disenfranchisement of successive waves of Asian nationalities, beginning with the Chinese and then the Japanese in the nineteenth century to Koreans, Indians, and Filipinas/os, Vietnamese, and other southeast Asians in the twentieth century. In highlighting the exclusion of Asians from free entry as well as full participation in U.S. society, such studies demonstrate a fundamental estrangement of the "Asian" from the "American." Because of their ascribed *racial difference,* Asians in the United States have been largely denied full and steady access to a deserving *national identity.* As Ronald Takaki points out in *Strangers from a Different Shore: A History of Asian Americans,* "coming from Asia, many of America's immigrants found that they were not allowed to feel at home in the United States, and even their grandchildren and great-grandchildren still find that they are not viewed and accepted as Americans."[86] Takaki does not specify *who* constitutes the nameless yet powerful agents of perception, permission, and acceptance. In her *Asian Americans: An Interpretive History,* Sucheng Chan defines them as "members of the host society" in explaining why the paradigm of assimilation used in studies of European immigration is not applicable: "This is not so because Asians refused to assimilate—that is, to discard their own heritage in order to adopt Anglo-American beliefs and behavior, as their detractors have claimed repeatedly—but because assimilation does not depend solely on the predilections of the newcomers. It can only occur when members of the host society give immigrants a chance to become equal partners of the world they share and mutually shape. As this books reveals, Asian immigrants were never given that chance until quite recently."[87] If their shared exclusion is what constitutes their common identity in the United States, the initial rhetorical distinction between Asians—"immigrants from Asia" or "Asian immigrants"—and Americans fades as it is ultimately directed toward a broader, pluralist integration of Asians *as* Americans or "Asian Americans." To that end, the myriad instantiations of exclusion and disenfranchisement are consistently set against the affirmation of a genuine and unmitigated desire to be recognized as Americans: "Asians resisted their exclusion and marginalization and thereby enlarged the range and deepened the meaning of American democracy."[88] The unruly delineations of Asians as "unwelcome immigrants" and unassimilable others are domesticated as temporary aberrations in a more expansively figured America as a diverse and ultimately tolerant community.

The emphasis on political and legal exclusions is extended to the matter of historiographical representation, specifically the omission or lack of Asian Americans in most accounts of U.S. history. As Takaki describes, "Many existing history books give Asian Americans only passing notice or overlook them altogether. Sometimes Asian pioneers are even excluded from history."[89] Two different valences of "history" are elided here. The first sentence obviously refers to *written* accounts while the second deployment of "history" appears to point to some extradiscursive object or phenomenon. In response to this double omission, Takaki condemns the ignorances, oversights, and suppressions of other historical accounts preceding his own narration of the history of Asian Americans: "Eurocentric history serves no one. It only shrouds the pluralism that is America and that makes our nation so unique, and thus the possibility of appreciating our rich racial and cultural diversity remains a dream deferred." The historiographical absence of Asian Americans is a false or distorted image imposed by ethnocentric bias on an actual, underlying core of plurality, which Asian Americans have been part of all along. To ameliorate this historiographical distortion, Takaki urges, "We need to 're-vision' history to include Asians in the history of America, and to do so in a broad and comparative way." To that end, Takaki's book along with many other historical accounts have documented their long habitation of the territorial United States and their significant social, economic, and cultural contributions to the nation.

Insofar as this imperative to "re-vision" history suggests a belated act of adding to and correcting the partiality of an existing set of accounts, any concerted effort to construct a fuller and more faithful narration opens up a discursive struggle over certain thematic priorities, rules of evidence, and expository modes. By foregrounding how American history has omitted a significant portion of "Americans" and going so far as to rename those accounts as "Eurocentric history," such Asian American–centered "re-visionings" also broach the disciplinary identity of history. In characterizing the interventions of social historians in the 1930s as undermining the claim of history as a disciplinary enterprise of objectivity, Joyce Appleby, Lynn Hunt, and Margaret C. Jacob write, "Social historians hoped to fill out the record by offering a more complex account of the past, but one of the main effects of their work has been to reveal how limited the previous histories were. In effect, they underlined the fact that history writing had always been intensely ideological."[90] Because such work "fostered the argument that history could never be objective," they go on to note ominously, "It is as if the social historians with their passion for breaking apart the historical record had dug a potentially fatal hole into which history as a discipline might disappear altogether."

While this scenario of disciplinary dissolution has not materialized, it suggestively maps one possible itinerary for Asian American history not merely as a reconfiguration of *who* can belong to "America" but as an exploration of how to write a genealogy of unbelonging. This would entail a critical consideration of the narrative desires, disciplinary protocols, and linguistic mediations of Asian American history itself. Instead, most accounts presume that they (more) accurately represent an extradiscursive Asian American historical reality. As much as a particular essay or book-length study seeks to document the *presence* and *significance* of Asian Americans against this double erasure, the vexatious implication that it too is a partial, situated discursive production has rarely been taken up in a sustained manner. Here I would venture that the substantive focus on legal and political exclusions conjoins the contention of prior historiographical suppressions to imbue the present accounts with an especial referential solidity. In the preface to *Strangers from a Different Shore,* for instance, Ronald Takaki reconciles this break between his own historical accounting of Asian Americans and an inaccurate, insufficient body of U.S. histories that he seeks to correct through invoking the possibility of a more faithful and complete narrative: "Their stories belong to our country's history and need to be recorded in our history books, for they reflect the making of America as a nation of immigrants, as a place where men and women came to find a new beginning" (10). The pronominal alignment of the historian with the generic American "we" against the Asian immigrant "they" here is striking. The belated yet still possible inclusion of "stories" by and about *them* can enable "our history books," which comprise an accumulative roster of differentially gendered yet equally hopeful bodies, to better reflect the realities of plural immigration. In that vein, Takaki later declares on a more positive note, "America represented liminality, and the Asian immigrants' actions enabled them to make history even in conditions they did not choose" (18). This transfiguration of Asians Americans as historical agents befitting and benefiting from such "liminality" has two implications. First, those documented instances of exclusion are aberrant and unrepresentative moments in a longer, deeper history of Asian American accomplishments. Second, their productive historical presence as documented by the book masks another "making of history"—Takaki's own historiographical mediation.

In addition to the thematic focus on exclusion/inclusion, the historiographical mediations of Asian American history have been occluded by a recurrent figuration of methodological excavation. As in other histories, archaeological metaphors infuse much of the writings of Asian American history. For instance, with reference to the exclusion of Asian Americans from "dominant" or "mainstream" histories, there are numerous calls to "recover our 'buried past'."[91] This accent on unburying posits the past as some solid, unchanged thing that is waiting for those in the present to discern its subterranean location and clear off the layers of dust suppressing it.[92] The accompanying presumption that what is found can fill out the lack of prior accounts affirms the disciplinary purchase of history to produce a faithful yet objective account of the past. Yet this ignores what remains suppressed and irretrievable or what, in the words of Michel de Certeau, must be rendered as "unthinkable" by each new historiographical revision: "In the past from which it is distinguished, it [historiography] promotes a selection between what can be understood and what must be forgotten in order to obtain the representation of a present intelligibility."[93] The very possibility of such unburying further denies that the accessibility of the past is dictated by the existing archive and the prevailing disciplinary protocols, which privilege certain forms of evidence and narration.

Any sustained critical attention to this archival problematic has been blunted by the urgent sense of political and epistemological intervention motivating efforts to include Asian/American women in both U.S. women's history and Asian American history as a retrieval and restoration. In acknowledging the "exclusion of women from the 'pages of paper'" in Asian American history, Gary Okihiro has called for a "recentering of women." However, this reinstallation conflicts with the disciplinary protocols of history: "Women were barely present in the bachelor society that typified much of the early period of Asian American history. . . . Given those statistics, how could one write a woman-centered history—the 'majority's past,' in Gerda Lerner's words—and remain faithful to the historical realities?"[94] He then proposes that those women who remained in Asia during this early bachelor period be included as significant subjects of "Asian American history":

> Asian men in America were not solitary figures moving in splendid isolation but were intimately connected to women in Asia, like the "no name" aunt of Kingston's narrator, who built and maintained the solid world of family and community. Recentering women extends the range of Asian American history, from the bachelor societies in Hawaii and the U.S. mainland to the villages and households in Asia, in an intricate and dynamic pattern of relations. Transcending American exceptionalism is but one of the consequences of a woman-centered history.[95]

In addition to the accenting of "family" and "community," Okihiro ends the chapter by a regendering of women as the transmitters of culture: "Of especial interest to me in the rise of women is the nature of women's role in the preservation and transmission of Asian culture."[96] But there is no single "Asian culture" to preserve and transmit. The following chapter, titled "Family Album History," also renaturalizes Asian American history under the banner of the family but further fixated through the visual metaphor of the snapshot.

The trope of unburying a suppressed past has also prominently marked the field of women's history. Since women have been "hidden from history," they must be "rediscovered" or "found."[97] Along with other women of color, Asian/American women have been figured as excluded or marginalized in and by women's history, imbuing them with an especially significant presence-in-absence. In seeking to transform what they characterize as "the white, middle-class canon of women's history" wherein "many groups of women, rarely explored or incorporated into women's history, await further study," Ellen Carol DuBois and Vicki L. Ruiz list three instances of "white domination," which must be addressed as part of such a "multicultural" U.S. women's history: "the dispossession of Mexican land after 1848; the genocide and relocation of Native Americans; the legal exclusion of Asian Americans."[98] In thus pinpointing certain forms of domination as specific to particular racial-ethnic groups, they go on to suggest that "a multicultural approach, one in which many pasts can be explored simultaneously, may be the only way to organize a genuinely national, a truly inclusive, history of women." But this already assumes the ability of history, and more specifically women's history, to attain some ideal of authenticity and inclusiveness. Later, they characterize "Evelyn Nakano Glenn's pioneering research on Asian Americans" [as] "a harbinger of the attention that domestic labor, paid and unpaid, will receive as women of color emerge from the shadows of women's history" (xiv). Emergence "from the shadows" is another recurrent methodological trope that is linked to the trope of excavation and supported by a metaphysics of presence and representative mimesis.[99] This has produced some very forceful or capricious constructions of what counts as "evidence." For instance, in the 1994 monograph *From the Other Side,* Donna Gabaccia narrates the experiences of a nineteenth-century Chinese immigrant woman through rephrasing the life story of Lalu Nathoy as written in Ruthanne Lum McCunn's *Thousand Pieces of Gold.* Gabaccia asserts the book's historical referentiality by generically categorizing it as "a slightly fictionalized account."[100]

Considering the problematic ways in which Asian/American women have been incorporated into both Asian American history and women's history, I think that the writing of Asian/American women's history can greatly enliven and complicate its undertaking through a concerted engagement with historiography as disciplinarily "situated" writing practice and knowledge production that must negotiate the *problem* of the archives. In defining what he calls a "historical *a priori*" as "tak(ing) account of the fact that discourse has not only a meaning or a truth, but a history, and a specific history that does not refer it back to the laws of an alien development," Michel Foucault describes the archive as "the domain of statements thus articulated in accordance with historical *a prioris.*"[101] Thus, against the desire to read these documents as transmitting "thoughts that were formed in some other time and place," they are "systems that establish statements as events (with their own conditions and domain of appearance) and things (with their own possibility and field of use)." This system involves certain prescriptions so that "the archive is first the law of what can be said, the system that governs the appearance of statements as unique events" (129). Such a conceptualization of the archive also redefines "archaeology" for

Foucault: "This term does not imply the search for a beginning; it does not relate analysis to geological excavation. It designates the general theme of a description that questions the already-said at the level of its existence: of the enunciative function that operates within it, of the discursive formation, and the general archive system to which it belongs" (131).

With this different sense of archaeology in mind, how can *a* writing of Asian American women's history *stress*—in the sense of both emphasis and pressure—the archives not as preserving the residues of the past but as displaying an ongoing crisis of what counts as reliable historical data in different presents, and how they then induce, enable, and preclude certain narrations of the past? Here I now stand to compromise the trustworthiness of the "evidence" that I have referenced in my counternarrative. For while I have tried to (re)narrate Asian American women as an integral definitional other to a normative, legal "American" citizenship, I must do so with the awareness of the figurative and intertextual nature of this construction. Indeed, the "proof" and the "records" I have been relying on are limited by their own dependence on discursive apparatuses that have, until very recently, excluded the supposed object of description from being a subject of narration and critical inquiry. Much of the information comes from court proceedings or newspaper accounts, which greatly problematizes the possibility of securing any experiential, sociohistorical solidity through these documents. A critical focus on nineteenth-century Asian immigrant women prostitutes as such troubling compositional subjects highlights the political and methodological dilemmas in the writing of an "Asian American women's history."

According to the historiographical strategy of laying claim to a long "American" lineage for Asian Americans, their earliest bodily entrance into and occupation of the national inscape must be accounted for. However, a remarkable detail of the originary moment of Asian/American women in U.S. history is scored not by their presence but their striking absence. Many historiographical accountings of women in Asian American history begin by noting the gender imbalance in most "first wave" immigration. According to what is often referred to as the "sojourner" theory, the immigrant men, physically separated from their natal families, considered themselves almost as temporary residents who would eventually return to China with the capital to buy land or to start a business. Another prominent historiographical strain attributes the low numbers of Chinese women to the cultural restrictions against female travel. For example, Lucie Cheng Hirata argues that "the Chinese patriarchal family system discouraged or even forbade 'decent' women from traveling abroad."[102] Though they may have some grounding, both the "sojourner" and "restrictive (patriarchal) culture" theories are problematic in focusing all explanatory power on the cultural milieu and individual choice of the Chinese historical actors, thereby ignoring or reducing the significance of social, political, and economic conditions in the United States.[103] Other scholars have thus pointed out that low wages and racial discrimination discouraged permanent settlement and the immigration of women and young children. Sucheng Chan argues that "efforts by various levels of the American government to restrict the immigration of Chinese women became the more significant factor."[104] After paraphrasing the published arguments about the patriarchal cultural restriction and the sojourner theses, Yen Le Espiritu argues that "labor recruiting and immigration exclusion policies were the most significant factors in restricting the immigration of Asian women."[105] Many of these historians further emphasize how the systematic restriction of female immigration was intended to preclude family formation and consequently permanent Chinese settlement in the United States. Although it may well be that all of these factors played some determining role, I want to note the implications of the existence of such multiply diverse interpretive priorities and explanations for the (impossible) search for any single, definitive account or theoretical model.

The relatively recent composite category of "Asian women" is cast backward in historical time to point to and group together ethnically diverse bodies of women, who likely did not recognize themselves and each other as part of this collectivity. So, an early article bearing the title "The Asian Women in America" begins its section on "Historical Perspectives" by proclaiming that "Asian women have been in the United States for over one hundred and twenty years."[106] The author, Gloria L. Kumagai, then traces this line of descent: "Their roots were started in the 1850s when a large influx of Chinese women came into this country." A reach back toward such predecessors in the United States yields the consensus that many if not most of these nineteenth-century Asian immigrant women were "prostitutes." Indeed, much of the published historical scholarship on Asian American women either focuses exclusively on or significantly highlights the large number of prostitutes in the initial presence of Asian women in

Against single definitive history [handwritten marginal note]

the territorial United States and in American history, especially of the nineteenth century.[107] As Lucie Cheng Hirata writes: "Among the first Chinese female residents in America allegedly was a twenty-year old prostitute from Hong Kong who landed in San Francisco late in 1848."[108] Yuji Ichioka states more forcefully, "[Japanese prostitutes] were the first significant number of Japanese women here," adding that they therefore "constitute the point of departure for any study of women in Japanese immigrant society."[109] More recently, Yen Le Espiritu notes, "Chinese and Japanese prostitutes were among the pioneers of their respective communities."[110] These historical "facts" distress much of the scholarly research and cultural production around Asian/American women in the past two decades, which has sought to counter their tenacious stereotyping as "prostitutes," sexually overcharged bodies that threaten the moral and physiological health of American manhood and, by extension, the nation itself. The very effort to locate the earliest possible embodiment of "Asian American women" must be conducted in the shadow of this enduring figuration, precluding a confident separation of the historical actuality and the present misrepresentation.[111] When undertaken in the shadow of an unfolding narration of the nation as propelled forward from some originary moment of arrival through the fecundity of nuclear family reproduction, the challenge of writing these women into history becomes a vexatious matter of domesticating these un-American bodies and sexualities into the properly gendered criteria of U.S. citizenship.

There is a second way in which the nineteenth-century Chinese—and I would add, Japanese—immigrant "prostitutes" are troubling subjects of historiographical composition, accentuating the paradox of writing *about* the past but *in* the present, bound by the archives that are both physically accessible and disciplinarily legitimate. Most striking in the various studies are the recurrent acknowledgements of the many "unknowables" about this socioeconomically marginalized population, who had little access to and even less control over what would survive as the documentary traces of their existence. Indeed, many accounts are sprinkled throughout with disclaimers on this epistemological limit. The reach toward the earliest moment of their arrival and settlement in the territorial United States is especially discouraged by the lack and unreliability of surviving data from that time, as amply demonstrated in this qualified description of the 1875 Page Law and Chinese female immigration in the nineteenth century: "A scarcity of surviving records obscures the actual occupations of Chinese women who sought to enter the United States from 1875–1882." [112] As Yuji Ichioka concedes for the case of early Japanese immigrant women:

> The small female population in 1900, numbering in the neighborhood of a thousand, included many prostitutes who, in all likelihood, comprised the majority. No documented evidence on the first appearance of the prostitutes nor precise figures of their numbers and geographical distribution exist. Oral tradition has it that they appeared in Denver, Colorado as early as the 1860s. . . . Thus, assuming the veracity of the oral tradition, it means that these women had to have departed surreptitiously from Japan before the beginning of the Meiji era in 1868. San Francisco more than likely had Japanese prostitutes prior to the 1880s, but again there is no extant evidence. [113]

My extraction of this string of knowledge claims clearly foregrounds the layers of hesitancy, hearsay, and speculation that mediate between the presently knowable and the already "surreptitious" conditions that marked the physical passage of these women to the United States. Ichioka follows up with this more confident claim: "As an historical fact, they appeared in the late 1880s. Japanese consular reports bear out their arrival." Attesting to the special force of these "consular reports" to dictate the present terms of what counts as "an historical fact," this passage also underscores all that such official state records cannot account for about these women.

Many other accounts on the topic similarly proceed in a declarative and narrative style of conventional historiography, but they are forced to this stop-and-start movement of qualified deductions, marked by "probably," "apparently," "possibly," "reportedly," "presumably." The archival "evidence" that is cited in support of these narrativizations and analyses comprises a heterogeneous range of governmental records and scholarly, literary, religious, and popular discourses written by various parties *about* these women. [114] In a rare critical analysis of preexisting historiographical representations, George Anthony Peffer points to Mary Coolidge's 1909 book on Chinese immigration to the United States in the nineteenth century as having been based on unreliable sources and evidence:

> Compilations of the testimony given in legislative hearings, most notably those conducted by Congress and the California Senate in 1876, provided

the central evidence for this area of her research. The government's involvement in such hearings always began with the identification of Chinese Americans as a problem group, whose communities demonstrated deviant behavior that seemed unaffected by traditional forces of social control, like law enforcement and progressive education. Eventually, the response of Congress to this image produced the political solution embodied in the Exclusion Act.[115]

Peffer further contests the creditability of census data, given that "they were conducted by census workers in the habit of 'correcting' responses from Chinese subjects whom they regarded as dishonest, and by immigration agents who favored the exclusion of all Chinese, except for members of the merchant class and their wives" (42–43).

Even the documentary records of the "ethnic community" are ideologically charged. As early as in the 1869 article on "Chinese Women in California," the author points to the unreliability of the documentary records of the Chinese American community, a result of its androcentric organization: "As the Six Companies were not organized with reference to the immigration of females to this country, there is nothing in their constitutions and by laws making provision in any way for them; nor do they keep any register of their names, or of the arrivals and departures; consequently there is no means of ascertaining, with any satisfactory degree of accuracy, the number of Chinese women on this coast."[116] Even those very rare accounts narrated by the women themselves must be seen as mediated by the specific conditions of their transcription, translation, and publication.[117] As documentations of such partial impressions, often in support of the exclusion of and sanctions against these immigrant women, the archives attest to the impossibilities of writing a "self"-centering history for nineteenth-century Asian prostitutes as the desire to locate their "agency" and "subjectivity" runs up against the paucity of surviving documents.[118] This, then, reveals the collusion between the exclusion of Asians and particularly Asian immigrant women workers from both legal citizenship and archival significance in the United States.

These moral and methodological ambivalences have been negotiated through two interrelated historiographical tactics to domesticate these nineteenth-century Asian immigrant prostitutes into the properly gendered criteria of U.S. citizenship, which accents marriage and motherhood.[119] One prevalent historiographical strategy has then been to reform this sexually ambivalent population of nineteenth-century prostitutes—and the majority male "bachelor societies"—within a teleological narrative that celebrates the gradual formation and survival of the Asian American "family" *in spite of* the very efforts to prevent this by the state's enactment of various laws barring Asian immigration and citizenship. This retrospective figuration has been accomplished by emphasizing external coercion to explain how these women became "prostitutes" and positing marriage and generational reproduction as the only viable alternative. This "wifeization" is complemented by a second historiographical operation that confers on these women a knowable interiority, most significantly the "desire" to escape prostitution and become wives and mothers. In one of the earliest historiographical endeavors, Joyce Wong writes, "Chinese girls and women were sold, kidnapped or deceived into prostitution or slavery. Very few came willingly into the life" ("Prostitution," 24). The following paragraphs will briefly track such historiographical operations in some of the more prominent accounts of Chinese and Asian women prostitutes in the nineteenth and early twentieth centuries.

The supporting archive behind Lucie Cheng Hirata's important 1982 essay "Free, Indentured, Enslaved" includes (1) city, state, and federal government records such as census manuscripts and transcriptions of court cases in the United States; (2) Chinese language sources ranging from a Qing dynasty official report to popular novels; (3) popular U.S. media, especially the periodicals of the day such as *Alta California;* (4) publications by missionary groups; (5) travel narratives; (6) popular histories such as Dillon's *The Hatchet Men;* and (7) academic histories and ethnographies. The essay veers between readily acknowledging the gaps and distortions of many of these sources and affirming the relative reliability of certain others: "The exact number of Chinese prostitutes in California and San Francisco during the nineteenth century is not known. Although several contemporary estimates are available, their tremendous variation indicates low reliability."[120] However, she immediately covers over this lack by invoking the greater credibility of the 1860, 1870, and 1880 government censuses that "contain social and demographic information on individuals which makes it possible to estimate the numbers and to construct a statistical profile of Chinese prostitutes for these decades." But Hirata turns right around with an extended qualification regarding the reliability of these government records:

Since "prostitution" was used as an occupational category in the 1870 and 1880 census manuscripts, we have simply followed the designation of the census taker to identify Chinese women engaged in prostitution during those two decades. Obvious distortions *may* arise from this procedure. Although the census enumerator was instructed to record what the interviewee reported to him or her, a language problem *could* lead to guessing by the census worker. It is also *reasonable to assume* that the census taker was *probably* biased toward designating a woman a prostitute because of popular racist beliefs or an inability to distinguish between concubinage and prostitution. On the other hand, the interviewee was *probably* inclined not to state that she worked as a prostitute even if she really did. Since these biases run in opposite directions, they tend to neutralize each other. (24, my italics)

Despite these multiple conjectures, Hirata is nevertheless able to conclude from these recorded figures that "the heydey of Chinese prostitution in San Francisco was around 1870, and its precipitous decline occurred just before 1880" (25). While the article stresses the broader social, economic, and political processes that shaped Chinese prostitution as a "form of labor," it frequently slips into what I would call a "subjectivizing" mode, as when Hirata writes,

> Only a few women crossed the Pacific on their own in search of better compensation for their labor in prostitution. Usually the family, not the girl, arranged the sale. Girls often accepted their sale, however reluctantly, out of filial loyalty, and most of them were not in a position to oppose their families' decision. In addition, the sheltered and secluded lives that women were forced to live made them particularly vulnerable to manipulation, and many were tricked or lured into prostitution. (6)

Significantly, no sources are cited in support of these broad and penetrating claims. This presumption about these women's feelings and motivations is strikingly combined with an implicit judgment of prostitution as social and sexual pathology when the essay ends with the confident but problematic declaration, "There can be no doubt, however, that as a result of the efforts of Cameron and others like her, many prostitutes became wives and led normal family lives" (28). Despite these dubious judgments, one of the most suggestive claims of Hirata's essay is her periodization of Chinese prostitution in the nineteenth century into an "initial period of free competition [ca. 1849–1854], during which the prostitute was also the owner of her body service" and later "a period of organized trade, during which the prostitute was a semi-slave and other individuals shared the benefits of her exploitation" (7–8).

At the opening of his monograph, *Unsubmissive Women: Chinese Prostitutes in Nineteenth-Century San Francisco*, Benson Tong distinguishes his own historiographical project from Lucie Cheng Hirata's article, which "concentrates on the impact of Chinese prostitution on the economy and how different groups profited from hawking the sole commodity members of the demimonde possess."[121] He continues: "This work, however, concentrates on the women themselves. . . . Furthermore, the focus here is on the years between 1849 and 1882, the first phase of the trafficking and vice trade." Later in the preface, however, Tong simultaneously acknowledges the historiographical problem of his project and describes his method:

> Like Hirata and most students of marginal groups, I faced the dilemma of writing a book on a group of women who had left few writings of their own. To compensate for the paucity of primary material, I relied on government publications, census schedules, newspapers, and records of missionary organizations to uncover the details of their existence. It should be noted that I have also used a few oral and written accounts of and by prostitutes who worked in the post-1882 years. That has allowed me to make some tentative comparisons of those prostitutes with their sisters who lived through the first phase of their trade. (xii)

Despite this opening admission of a limited and selective archives, Tong's book proceeds by repeatedly subjectivizing the Chinese women even though he relies on a very similar set of evidentiary documents as Hirata.[122] The book's title itself announces a knowable and common interiority of these Chinese prostitutes and this imposition of an accessible subjectivity is reenacted in chapter titles like "Unwilling Travelers to Gum Saan" and "Adjusting to Life in Chinatown." The historiographical impulse to thus "humanize" these women manifests itself throughout the text by references to them as "actors," "agents," and "survivors" who "desired," "strategized," and "chose" to leave the sex trade.[123] Indeed, a key part of this normalizing effort to elicit the reader's sympathetic investment and ethical identification with these women is to characterize them repeatedly as "unwilling" or "coerced" into prostitution, whether through kidnapping, sale by desperate parents, or false offers of employment and/or marriage.[124] Interestingly, Tong takes the lack of definitive historical data on nineteenth-century Chinese women's prostitution to contest Hirata's characterization of an initial period of free entrepreneurship: "However, it is difficult to ascertain the number of independent Chinese prostitutes living and working in California during the 1850s due to the lack of information and the scattered nature of available evidence. It is safe to infer that they made up a minority of the total number of Chinese prostitutes" (31). In addition to this inferential disavowal of "willing" and "independent" women, Tong's linear emplotment from forced prostitution to a desired escape through marriage further curtails the range of interpretive possibilities that are opened up by the dearth and unreliability of the archives. Thus Tong performs a historiographical redemption by reconfiguring these women from "prostitutes" to nascent and desirous candidates for marriage and motherhood.

In such efforts to write the nineteenth-century Asian immigrant prostitutes into the U.S. national narrative by thus conferring on them a heterosexual subjectivity and reproductive orientation, what becomes elided is the profoundly undemocratic (re)production of the archives, which, by their own very partial and limited construction and maintenance, can never simply speak *for* these women.[125] In other words, Tong's book may be an adequate history of the multiple forces determining the structure and development of Chinese prostitution as a defining moment—not an isolated, ethnicized aberration—in American history, but it is not and cannot be an unmediated account of the women's selves. This is perhaps most starkly demonstrated by the book's own appendix, which features an example of "Bills of Sale of Chinese Prostitutes." This archival document attests to the systematized estrangement of its subject from the coherent, self-possessed personhood of "American citizen." Tong's book is only the most blatant instance of the historiographical fixation of Asian/American women as wives and mothers in a narrative of family formation.

Finally, I want to end by speculating on a writing of Asian/American women's history that can critically imagine other forms of sexual existence not captured by the records of state agencies, community leaders, and official archives, which can, in turn, contest the terms of sexual citizenship for "becoming American" beyond marriage and motherhood. Against the impulse to distinguish the morally acceptable "wife" from the problematic "prostitute," we might consider how the peculiar exigencies of immigrant life might have interestingly blurred their boundaries. Joan Hori recounts the socioeconomic practice of "wife-selling" and the pimping of women by their husbands among early Japanese immigrants in Hawaii even as she acknowledges their archival marginalization: "Little information remains about their lives, although they were an important part of the pioneering Japanese society in Hawaii."[126] Lucie Cheng Hirata points out:

> Both the Chinese consulate and the Six Companies saw prostitution as one of the major causes for the anti-Chinese movement in California. Further, both were concerned about the economic loss and the image of the Chinese, so they actively collaborated with the American authorities in identifying and deporting Chinese prostitutes. In reality, however, since Chinese prostitution was not the reason for the anti-Chinese movement, their action did not thwart the hostility; but their efforts did bring about a temporary decline in the organized traffic.[127]

Both examples above signal important internal fissures of class, gender, and sexuality in Asian American history that become displaced or minimized in the call to include Asian/American women under the banner of a "family album history."

Joyce Appleby, Lynn Hunt, and Margaret Jacob have argued that "a democratic practice of history . . . encourages skepticism about dominant views, but at the same time trusts in the reality of the past and its knowability."[128] I would like to underscore how the realities of the present undertaking of Asian/American women's historical representation force an acknowledgment of certain unknowabilities, and that doing so is not undemocratic. Beyond decrying how the archives can never simply speak for these women, the task of a *critical historiography* is to foreground the *limits* of such documents as also historically significant. Here it is useful to turn to Lisa Lowe's examination of what she calls "the realist aesthetic as a regime for the production of history" and its resonant deployment in the writing of history and the novel, specifically in the ways in which "both presuppose closure (telos) and character (subject of development)."[129] In conjoining the insights of Hayden White and Dominick LaCapra with Dipesh Chakrabarty's observation of the imperialist imposition of this mode of historical representation on to the colonies, Lowe points out, "Rather than provoking cynicism about the possibility of writing history, the challenge to representation signals the need for alternative projects of many kinds and suggests that the writing of *different* histories—of non-elites, of insurgencies, of women, from the 'bottom up'—inevitably runs up against representation and linear narrative as problematic categories" (112, original italics). Lowe very usefully delineates two different modes of an Asian American cultural project, which I would extend to the disciplinary productions of knowledge about Asian/American women in the academy, specifically history. She identifies the first as "the representational project," which is "motivated by a desire to represent, to make visible the erased and evacuated histories in realist and naturalist modes" and thus operates through symbolic figurations that are propelled by "a persistent belief in a knowable social totality of which the representative figure is a reflection and in terms of which that figure can be recognized" (34–35). Benson Tong's *writing* of the nineteenth-century Chinese immigrant prostitutes commits them precisely to this representational and representable status. In contradistinction, Lowe argues for a more allegorical project of cultural representation, given that "the concept of allegory presumes that social and historical processes are not transparent, taking place through what Benjamin calls 'correspondences' rather than through figures that represent or reflect a given totality." Indeed, earlier in the chapter Lowe names such projects as "critical historiographies," in which "the 'past' that is grasped as memory is . . . not a naturalized, factual past, for the relation to that past is always broken by war, occupation and displacement" (28). As I have tried to argue, the relation to the past is dismembered by the partial and situated composition of the archives, which do not offer the reassurances of some mimetic record of unbroken continuity but the refractory clues to a breach of citizenship and history. If the hegemonic narration of nation would herald their intimately sutured articulation, the writing of Asian/American women's history could foreground that they never were or could be coherent and harmonious for certain subjects.

I want to end with a more recent delineation of Asian women as/not American citizens to once again emphasize the discontinuous and recursive aspects of this process. While the 1965 Immigration and Nationality Act has often been used to mark a liberalizing shift toward an inclusive approach to the immigration and naturalization of Asians in the United States, the relationship between "Asian woman" and "American citizen" continues to be strained and questionably circumscribed. In an insightful article, Mary Kim DeMonaco analyzes the shifting legislative measures and procedural actions over the past two decades regarding the immigration and citizenship rights of children born in Vietnam of Vietnamese mothers and American fathers. While the 1982 amendment to the 1965 Immigration and Nationality Act, known as the Amerasian Immigration Act, was a "legal breakthrough" because it marked the "first public recognition [by the United States] of its moral responsibility to these children who had been fathered by Americans abroad,"[130] DeMonaco criticizes it as meaningless and ineffectual when applied to the Amerasians in Vietnam. First, the United States and Vietnam did not yet have the formal diplomatic relations necessary to jointly process the claims of Amerasians for U.S. citizenship through patrilineage. Another shortcoming was that it granted the right of immigration only to Amerasians and not to their other family members, including their Vietnamese mothers and half-siblings: "The new law also made it mandatory that mothers of the Amerasians seeking U.S. entry sign irrevocable releases on their children before the children could be eligible for processing" (662). As DeMonaco so cogently points out, "This failure to include those people who are crucial to the Amerasian's assimilation and adjustment in the United States clearly contradicted the family reunification purpose underlying the Orderly Departure Program." I would add further that the homologies of mother and nation are completely dissolved in this effort to "naturalize" the Amerasian as an "American" *through* her/his estrangement from the Vietnamese mother and natal family.

In response to these impracticable contradictions, as part of the 1987 Resettlement Accord between the United States and Vietnam, Congress passed the Amerasian Homecoming Act, which "established a five million dollar program under the Immigration and Naturalization Service (INS)" and declared that all those Amerasians "born in Vietnam between January 1, 1962 and January 1, 1976" were eligible to apply for immigration to the United States along with any immediate family members.[131] Dubbed "Operation Homecoming," the 1987 act spurred the establishment of a transnational apparatus of documentation, evaluation, and expert testimony necessary to process the resulting claims. The U.S. federal government established offices in Ho Chi Minh City, where State Department employees could interview Amerasian claimants for immigration. The legitimacy of their claims has pivoted around a striking convergence of visible features of racialized physiognomies, new technologies of genetic testing, and corroborating acknowledgments of paternity by a U.S. citizen. DeMonaco notes that "for those applicants, possessing obvious American features, however, previous stringent requirements are relaxed in principle during the US interviewing state" (683). Another way of facilitating the applications is a direct claim by the American father on behalf of individual Amerasians: "since March of 1988, Vietnam has been permitting former U.S. servicemen to return to Vietnam to help expedite processing of their children; because of their father's actions, those Amerasians, known as documented citizens, have a claim to U.S. citizenship" (645). The privileging of the word of the father further marginalizes the political and legal status of the Vietnamese mothers. Finally, the legal categorization of these Amerasian claimants as "documented citizen" nevertheless distinguishes them from native-born and naturalized "Americans." Hearkening back to the arbitrary powers of immigration officials to judge the worth of Asian immigrant women in the nineteenth century, DeMonaco has rightly pointed out: "The new face-to-face interviewing scheme also has the effect of placing too much discretionary power in one individual. . . . In one unfortunately typical case, the State Department prevented a fifteen-year old Amerasian boy from emigrating to the U.S. to reunite with his father because he 'did not look Caucasian enough' to be the American's son" (697). While DeMonaco does not take up a closer analysis, this case strikingly illustrates the irresolvable contradiction between the inclusive trope of the nation as a multiracial "family" and the biologistic features of a more discriminating Americanness-as-whiteness—and more specifically as "Caucasian" paternity—that continues to underscore the myth of diversity-as-sameness. The ethos of "family reunification" of the liberalization of immigration laws in 1965 can be read as supporting a very particular embodiment and configuration of the family.[132]

The ambivalence of national identification, which has often split the category of "Asian American women" into "good American citizen" and "illegal Asian alien" exists, then, in contemporaneous tension with the celebrated affirmations of "Asian-American women writers" and the feisty female protagonists discussed in the first two chapters. More significantly, a critical examination of the historical and political delineations of Asian/ American women reveals the arbitrary and questionable construction of "American" identity itself. Lauren Berlant proposes that "the subject who wants to avoid the melancholy of insanity of the self-abstraction that is citizenship, and to resist the lure of self-overcoming the material political context in which she lives, must develop tactics for refusing the interarticulation, now four hundred years old, between the United States and America, the nation and the utopia" (*Anatomy of National Fantasy*, 217). As she clarifies, this vigilance against the blurring and collapsing of "America" and the historical United States need not mean a refusal of all utopian imagination, rather that "utopian social relations might be sought or effected without reference to the national frame." Both in their irreducible differences as well as in their recent interpolation into "the people," Asian American women turn the line of interrogation around to unsettle the finite boundaries of both national membership and its narration.

In addition to these concerted yet forceful and awkward efforts to include Asian/American women into U.S. history through the subfields of Asian American history, immigration history, and women's history, there have been efforts to outline an even further specified compositional grouping, as in Shirley Hune's overview volume, *Teaching Asian American Women's History*, published in 1997 by the American Historical Association. Here we may heed the observation made by Joan Scott on the odd disciplinary career of "women's history," wherein "the discrepancy between the high quality of recent work in women's history and its continuing marginal status in the field as a whole points up the limits of descriptive approaches that do not address dominant disciplinary concepts in terms than can shake their power and perhaps transform them." [133] She is careful to add later, "I do not think that we should quit the archives or abandon the study of the past, but we need to scrutinize our methods of analysis, clarify our operative assumptions, and explain how we think change occurs. Instead of a search for single origins we have to conceive of processes so interconnected that they cannot be disentangled" (42). If there must be a field of study called "Asian American women's history," it must work *through* scrutinizing—and not compensating for—the particular limits of the archives and their possible (re)narrations as tangled up with the hierarchical particularlization of national bodies and subjects.

chapter 4

Disciplined Embodiments

Si(gh)ting Asian/American Women as Transnational Labor

Her hands grasping two pairs of tweezers occupy the center of the black-and-white photograph; they cover up any distinguishable facial features. Her entire body appears molded to the task. This representation of a faceless woman worker peering into a tiny Ricoh watch part has arguably become one of the emblematic images of the global assembly line.[1] Despite such iconic prominence, this flattened composition of working woman, industrial equipment, and job task conveys little *about* the female subject. Rather, in its documentary certainty and photographic fixedness, this close-up framing eclipses a larger scene of transnational coordination—the complicated histories and the many other bodies that have shaped the meeting of the woman with the machinery in a liminal yet carefully planned space of an export-processing zone in the Philippines. What is it about the sight and site of this working body that has rendered it so visible and yet so anonymous?

To those who would uphold the human body's sensuous and sensate solidity as "an ontological thereness that exceeds or counters the boundaries of discourse," Judith Butler proposes "a process of materialization that stabilizes over time to produce the effect of boundary, fixity, and surface we call matter."[2] This materialization proceeds unevenly to produce differently bounded, fixed, and surfaced bodies so that the title of Butler's book, *Bodies that Matter,* has a double resonance. The discursively produced thereness of any body upholds and is constrained by a hierarchical taxonomy of meanings attached to different bodies through "the repeated and violent circumscription of cultural intelligibility." As Butler asks in the preface, "Which bodies come to matter—and why?" (xi). This chapter explores not only why but how "Asian women" or more accurately "Asian female bodies" have come to matter for two linked registers of transnational labor: (1) the political economies of assembly-line manufacturing, military prostitution, and sex tourism, and (2) the discursive economies of representational practices and knowledge claims about Asian women workers in those three interrelated sites.

Through the attribution of such inherent characteristics as childlike innocence and docility, digital nimbleness, physical stamina, keen eyesight, sexual largess, and muscular flexibility, Asian women have been figured as especially suited to conduct certain labor needs of transnational capitalism. To be sure, certain profit-driven agents of international commerce, manufacturing, and tourism have been especially motivated to propagate such enfigurations as a means of attracting capital investments as well as traveling bodies to these Asian locales. I am more interested in tracking how such rhetorical claims and practices insinuate themselves into those accounts that are avowedly critical of multinational capital and sympathetic to the exploited women workers. Without denying the importance of being ever mindful of local and global inequalities, I wish to trouble the positivist assumption that their complexities can be readily accessed and communicated truthfully and objectively, and, consequently, that "uncovering" and "reporting" about them are necessarily empowering and liberatory gestures. Paying close attention to the metaphors, analogies, plots, and images by which these working sites and working bodies have been rendered visible and intelligible could remind us of how the most well-intended representations are also forcefully partial and disciplinarily situated.

One particularly troubling emplotment positions exploitative working conditions in certain national political economies as a necessary phase in some inevitable trajectory of capitalist growth, which all workers must pass through. This story crosses oddly with a second narrative of global capitalist development as having entered a distinctly transnational phase of heightened mobility, flexibility, and porosity. With their supposed constitutional fitness, Asian female bodies are figured as ideal for inhabiting and working at that intersection. This propriety is often premised on their spatial remoteness and temporal detachment from the here-now of the representing subjects and their audiences. Figured not only as geographically distant but as mired in some unchanging "tradition," often an ahistorical brand of patriarchy, certain or sometimes all Asian women are inscribed by certain *American* representing subjects, including some "Asian American women," as bound to an earlier moment of a teleology of individual subject forma- tion. *Their* miserable subalternity nevertheless assures us of *our* own relative self-possession and socioeconomic mobility.

In considering what may be signified and also occluded by this dis- cursive production and circulation, I propose to emphasize contempora- neous *and* transnational circuits employing Asian/American women work- ers, which contest any such assumptions of their developmental lag and geographical circumscription to an elsewhere. To that end, this chapter focuses on three laboring sites—export-oriented manufacturing, military prostitution, and sex tourism—whose interrelated historical formation and interstitial territoriality emblematize the transnational political econ- omy of late capitalism.[3] The first part of the chapter traces their staggered yet linked composition in the 1960s and 1970s as intimately bound up with the postwar ascendance of the United States as a political, economic, and military international superpower. While a great many scholars have com- mented on these transnational interconnections during the past three decades, I recall only certain significant dimensions pertinent to Asian women in Asia and in the United States in order to attest to the far- reaching and uneven geographical dispersions of the "American." These contemporary laboring sites and their working bodies provocatively criss- cross the historical reconfigurations of Asian women as/not "American" studied in chapter 3. Although the walled-in, heavily guarded "Free Trade Zones" in Malaysia are forcibly demarcated from the rest of the country, their labor force, their working conditions, industrial machinery, and the assembled products are similar to those in a garment sweatshop in Los An- geles or an electronics assembly line in the Silicon Valley. Then too, the English neon signs, blaring pop music, and male bodies that fill the "hot spots" of military prostitution and sex tourism render these places as much "American" as "Thai" or "Korean."

The second part of this chapter examines several different visual and textual representations of Asian women workers. Looking at area studies journal articles, ethnographic studies, activist pamphlets, and avowedly feminist photographic pictorials, I examine how these compositions at- tempt to grapple with the problem of attesting to material and psychic conditions across geographical distances as well as nation-state demarcations. The section ends by exploring the representational challenge of accounting for larger political-economic structures and processes of transnational capitalism versus their more local manifestations and individual negotiations. Here I conjoin the important work of Arturo Escobar in tracing the dominance of the "economic" in development studies and the work of Aihwa Ong in emphasizing the significance of the "cultural" in studying Asian women workers and transnational capitalism through the disciplinary framework of anthropology. Although both Escobar and Ong seek to reaccent the "cultural" in the study of these phenomena, especially in the ways this emphasis can speak to the local struggles and subjective experiences of the working subjects of development and industrialization agendas, I preface this discussion with a caveat through some recent examples of how the methodological rhetoric of the social sciences has been invoked as grounds for more probing and attuned figurations of Asian women in sex tourism.

Interlocking Formations

Upon formal political independence, many former colonies throughout Asia set out to build a self-sufficient domestic industrial base that could produce the previously imported manufactured goods. However, because domestic demand was limited and therefore quickly met, these emergent industries were forced to turn to other markets.[4] The concerted push for economic autonomy through *import-substituting industrialization* (ISI), with its often overtly nationalist rhetoric and protectionist trade policies, discouraged foreign investments and the U.S. dollar exchange that were necessary to purchase machinery and to build infrastructure. A disparity in technological knowledge also precluded competitiveness with goods manufactured in the United States and necessitated an alternative economic strategy geared toward the production of goods for export and the acquisition of foreign currency. This newly postcolonial terrain was marked by the emergence of transnational corporations (TNCs), "large companies undertaking direct investment and locating production in two or more countries": "The TNCs are distinct from foreign investment in that their main power lies in the technology and skills, which they also move along with capital. Consequently, they are a new development on firms which simply engaged in uncomplicated international trade."[5] While TNCs are often figured as arriving at these Asian locales *after* the demise of ISI and its subsequent replacement with *export-oriented industrialization* (EOI), as one critical study points out, "many TNCs were able to establish themselves in the markets of these less developed countries by setting up behind the protective walls erected by LDC [less developed countries] governments as part of the ISI strategy."[6] Indeed, as the author goes on to elaborate, these early incursions were motivated by a desire to open the local markets for TNC manufactured goods and, as such, paradoxically doomed ISI to failure: "Using their considerable established technological, financial, and marketing advantages, they were often able to dominate local manufacturing in the LDCs, preempt the local 'infant industries', and remit much of their profits back to their home bases in developed countries" (23). On the last point, the home governments of the TNCs played a key role by "modifying their tariff provisions to provide for duty-free re-entry of goods assembled abroad from parts and components exported from the developed country."[7]

This shift from import-substituting to export-oriented industrialization was further facilitated and enforced by the postwar formation of an international development apparatus. Under the strong guidance of agencies such as the World Bank, the United Nations Industrial Development Organization, and the International Monetary Fund, Hong Kong, South Korea, Singapore, and Taiwan adopted EOI in the 1960s. As outlined in the pamphlet *Women in the Global Factory,* both the World Bank and the IMF made loans to these countries contingent on their adhering to a specific political and economic blueprint that combined "elimination of import tariffs that protect domestic industry but hamper multinationals, tax breaks for foreign investors and the creation of free-trade zones . . . control of wages, abolition of price controls and any subsidies for food and other necessities."[8] National economies such as Malaysia complied by offering "generous exemptions (up to ten years), minimum custom fees, and unhampered transfers of profits and capital."[9] The establishment of specifically bounded and conveniently situated "export-processing zones" (EPZS) or "free-trade zones" (FTZS), modeled after the first EPZ established in 1959 at the Shannon Airport in Ireland, was a crucial element of this recruitment package. Finally, a conjunction of several local and international factors shaped the concentration of low-paid, rigorously disciplined women workers in these export-oriented TNC factories. Motivated by the "idea that women's subordinate position stems from a lack of job opportunities," the policy banner of "integrating women into the development process" was significantly jump-started at the "United Nations Conference on International Women's Year which took place in 1975 under the tutelage of various international development agencies."[10] By 1987 the World Bank instituted a Division for Women in Development.[11]

This reorientation of specific national economies toward production of goods for export soon comprised what Rachel Grossman referred to as a "highly integrated Asian circuit of semiconductor factories" wherein "the NS [National Semiconductor] plants in Thailand, Indonesia and Penang . . . do the same work, so that political upheaval in one country will not precipitate a breakdown in the overall production cycle."[12] Given that "plants can be closed down on short notice if the political climate appears too risky or if they become economically superfluous" (3), I would argue that the concerted strategy of the TNC conjoins these national economies as much as their geographical proximity or regional identity. That such terms and conditions clearly favored the foreign multinational corporations over and against the local labor force was acknowledged in the Ascher Memorandum, "a secret World Bank report leaked to the press in late 1980," which warned, "The Bank's imprimatur on the industrial program [in the Philippines] runs the risk of drawing criticism of the Bank as the servant of multinational corporations and particularly of U.S. economic Imperialism."[13] Yet this program of export-oriented economic growth has been replicated and zealously pursued in other Asian national economies such as Thailand and more recently Indonesia and Sri Lanka.[14] As costs and wages have increased in South Korea, Hong Kong, and Singapore, the TNCs have relocated production processes to sites that promise even lower wages and less labor regulations, such as mainland China and Vietnam. This geographical proliferation of production sites has offered TNCs an even broader and more diversified field of investment and labor exploitation, which has produced both more international competition and new forms of transnational cooperation.

The success of EOI has been significantly guaranteed by the concomitant militarization of these nation-states. As Cynthia Enloe noted in 1983, "In the Philippines—as in South Korea, Taiwan, Hong Kong, Singapore, Indonesia, Malaysia and Thailand—government insecurity stems from the keen awareness that state maintenance rests on 19-year-old women factory workers and the gender ideologies of dexterity, docility and family obedience that enable foreign and local entrepreneurs to mobilize them. Patriarchy alone—without police and military reinforcement—is seen by elites as inadequate to sustain the kind of discipline they need in order to reassure foreign investors that their societies are 'good bets' for profitable investment."[15] Here too, there has been extensive U.S. involvement, from direct military engagement in World War II, the Korean War from 1950 to 1953, and the Vietnam War through 1973, to varying forms of encampment and assistance in the present. From massive engagement of troops in these conflicts to maintaining bases, selling and supplying arms, and training leaders for several national armed forces, the U.S. military has been a significant social and physical presence in many countries. Resonant with the strategic adjoining of the multinationally located EPZs through TNC production strategies, one could argue that the U.S. military involvement in these various wars has enduringly connected these far-flung sites and national histories in the twentieth century. As Saundra Sturdevant and Brenda Stoltzfus point out, "Although during the Korean War the U.S. Air Force-based squadrons on Okinawa flew bombing missions over the territory of the northern part of Korea, it was during the Vietnam War that the Okinawan R&R industry experienced its greatest growth."[16] There was also a proliferation of prostitution in Vietnam itself.

The history of U.S. military-geared prostitution in Korea offers a telling case study. Long after the end of the Korean War in 1953, the U.S. Forces, Korea (USFK) has continued to maintain a prominent place in the South Korean landscape. Katharine H. S. Moon notes, "U.S. troop presence in the 1960s, for example, stood at about 60,000 (compared to approximately 40,000 by September 1971), and the U.S. effectively had command over the Korean military through its role as head of the United Nations forces in Korea."[17] Such extensive occupation and control reflected the strategic importance of South Korea for Cold War struggles in Asia, especially given the proximity of the Soviet and Communist China-backed North Korea. Moon additionally points out that such "clear U.S. geostrategic interests and alliance commitments" coupled with "a policy of non-interference in the internal affairs of the host nation" (149) on the part of the United Nations command made it difficult to demand South Korean government oversight of the social and commercial activities of Korean nationals in relation to the occupying troops, including prostitution. This created an initial period of relative freedom and mobility for some Korean women sex workers, and despite some urging by the U.S. military command that these women be controlled and monitored, especially for venereal diseases, little or no action was taken by local authorities, given that "the Korean government considered camptown prostitution primarily a U.S. problem and a matter between GI and prostitute" (150). By contributing 50,000 soldiers to fight alongside the Americans in Vietnam, South Korea enjoyed even greater bargaining power in negotiations with the United States.

Towards the end of the Vietnam War and the withdrawal of both Korean and American troops from Vietnam, however, the balance of power would radically shift in favor of the USFK. Under the Nixon Doctrine of an overall U.S. pullout from military conflicts in Asia, the number of U.S. troops in Korea was cut by 20,000, a third of the 60,000 who were then stationed in the 1960s. The military-backed regime of Park Chung Hee, made suddenly nervous about the possibility of a total withdrawal of troops and support, established a Base-Community Clean-Up Committee (BCCUC):

> The USFK authorities also targeted Korean prostitutes as the main source, or "the reservoir" of venereal disease transmission among U.S. servicemen and, together with the Korean government, developed numerous programs to control the registration, VD examination, and quarantine (detention) of infected women. The Korean government's job was to enforce the registration, mandatory physical examination, and detention of *kijich'on* prostitutes in order to help reduce the spread of venereal disease to U.S. servicemen. The Korean Ministries of Health and Social Affairs (MOHSA), Foreign Affairs (MOFA), Home Affairs, Justice, and the National Police all expended considerable sums of money and energy to "clean up" these women. The Korean government allocated a total of 380 million *won* in 1971–2 to improve health and sanitation in camptowns. . . . [This money] financed government enforcement actions as forced "round-ups" of women for examinations as well as "mass injections" of antibiotics to "inoculate" women against VD infection.[18]

These details point not only to the systematic organization of military prostitution at the level of both domestic policy and interstate relations but also to how its terms and conditions shift according to changing historical and geopolitical circumstances within and across national borders.

Two other countries noteworthy for U.S. military prostitution are the Philippines and Thailand. Until the formal end of the U.S.-Republic of Philippines Military Agreement in 1991, the United States maintained two significant military installations there: Subic Naval Base and Clark Air Base. According to Aida F. Santos, both bases "provided operational support during the U.S. invasion of Vietnam," and sexual services constituted "the most significant economic activity around the baselands."[19] Thailand was officially designated as a "rest and recreation" (R and R) site for American troops during the Vietnam War through a 1967 treaty with the Thai government. Between 1969 and 1971, "entire hotels . . . were leased out to U.S. military personnel."[20] The sudden and intense wartime demand for R and R created an economic boom so that by 1970 the American soldiers spent $20 million, which Truong estimates was "as much as one-fourth of rice exports for that year" (161). When the United States eliminated Sydney and Hong Kong as R and R sites in the latter part of the Vietnam War, there was an even greater emphasis placed on Thailand to fulfill this role. However, the construction of more hotels, bars, and other infrastructure, much of it financed by short-term, high-interest loans, resulted in an oversupply following the gradual withdrawal of U.S. troops in the early 1970s. Having gained an international reputation as a sexual playground, the military-catered sex services industry reoriented itself toward an increasingly civilian clientele. Although there were similar shifts of sex services toward a foreign, civilian, and predominantly male clientele in South Korea and the Philippines, Thailand would assume a singularly notorious place in the formation and growth of what has alternately been called "tourism prostitution" or "sex tourism."

As noted by Elaine H. Kim in 1987, "The transformation of wartime prostitution into the expanded peacetime sex industry of the 1980s should be viewed within the context of the international tourist industry, which has become an increasingly important part of the development strategy of non-socialist countries during the last two decades."[21] Although other nationals such as the Australian mafia[22] and Japanese firms significantly shaped this transnational field of labor and consumption, the United States would play a central role in this reorientation. Given the unstable geopolitical situation in Indochina and the subsequent uncertainty of the R and R market, a more coherent policy was needed. In 1971, Robert McNamara, who had been Secretary of Defense when the R and R treaty was signed in 1967 and was then president of the World Bank, visited Thailand and brokered an agreement with the Thai government to send the bank's specialists to plan the development of Thailand's tourist industry. In 1975 the bank published a report that "recommended more public sector investment in infrastructure, i.e. airport expansion and maintenance, development of provincial sites and resorts."[23] More than offering advice, the World Bank provided "loan and equity investment for hotel construction and other tourism-related privately-owned enterprises through its International Development Association and the International Finance Corporation."[24]

The geopolitical utility of tourism had been recognized as far back as 1958 when the U.S. Department of Commerce researched Asia as a possible tourist destination partly in response to pressures from the American banking and aeronautical manufacturing sectors seeking to expand their own postwar boom beyond the domestic and European markets. In order to revive the demand for large airplanes in the postwar years and to provide new sites for capital investment abroad, the United States seized on a means of combining the creation of new travel destinations with the emerging international agenda of economic development. As cogently outlined by Truong, "To ensure adequate accommodation facilities in developing countries, large capital commitments had also to be ensured as, in many developing countries, local capital to be diverted into hotel construction was limited. As international private capital was hesitant to invest in an unpredictable new economic venture, tourism had to be tied to development purposes" (117). Through the International Travel Act of 1961, which established the United States Travel Office, the Kennedy administration proposed tourism as "a non-military instrument to contain political tension and insecurity" (117). In a speech presented to mark the opening of the Travel Office, Kennedy exhorted, "As people move throughout the world and learn to know each other, to understand each other's customs and to appreciate the qualities of individuals of each nation, we are building a level of international understanding which can sharply improve the atmosphere for world peace" (quoted in Truong, 117). This glowing pronouncement resonates with the unique power of cinema in promoting international understanding and harmony, which was hailed by Will Hays three decades earlier.

American geopolitical interests in Asia dovetailed with a broader restructuring of the international political economy in the postwar era, which included a reframing of leisure and tourism as both domestic and international commodities for individual consumption. In 1967 the United Nations declaration of "International Tourist Year" was unanimously approved by the General Assembly because "tourism is a basic and most desirable human activity deserving the praise and encouragement of all peoples and governments."[25] However, this incitement to travel as a fundamental need, the rightful fulfillment of which would unite geographically scattered humanity, presumes a measure of reciprocal exchange between places, peoples, and governments. Given the glaring contradiction between such claims and political-economic inequalities, by the following decade international tourism would be recontextualized within "the doctrine of the New International Economic Order, as a means of redistributing wealth by encouraging the rich to spend in poor countries" (117). But this still elides the intranational inequities of citizen/resident/alien status and socioeconomic resources that would prohibit many from the capital-rich countries from participating in this peculiar pursuit of world peace and harmony. If tourism-geared development was less than truly global in its reach and directionality, it was more certainly *international* in securing not only economic dependence on American capital but also ideological alliance with the U.S. policy of containing communism in Asia. "Deployed in Thailand," Truong notes, "this strategy sought to open the economy as much as possible to trade, foreign investment, grants, loans, and aid through the instrumentality of multilateral and bilateral institutions" (159). The long war in nearby Vietnam and the ultimate loss to communist forces only reinforced the importance of Thailand.

In addition to specific national governments and the World Bank, local military and business elites, international travel conglomerates, and American veterans of the Vietnam War have significantly shaped the growth and maintenance of tourism in Asia. To return to the case of Thailand, a power bloc comprised of the local business elite with military and government leaders came together in the 1950s to implement a major social and economic restructuring with the long-term goal of building an integrated manufacturing base through transnational corporate investments and a more immediate, short-term strategy of accumulating foreign exchange through leisure and service sectors geared toward international tourism. The phenomenal amount of revenue generated by the R and R boom further encouraged reinvestment in the leisure and service sectors, including the sizable commercial sex industry:

> Initial local investment in hotels and entertainment places was boosted by the incentives given to private businesses under the First Investment Act and by the loans provided by the Industrial Finance Corporation of Thailand (IFCT). IFCT is an affiliate of a consortium of international private and public financial capital, including the Bank of America Corporation, the Chase Manhattan Corporation, the International Finance Corporation, and the Deutsche Bank AG. Between 1960 and 1972 some 80 million *baht* (US$4 million) were lent out by the IFCT to seven companies providing "personal services."[26]

Other significant actors in and beneficiaries of tourism are the "travel conglomerates which sought new pastures for the expansion of their businesses in the diversification of their products" (Truong, *Sex, Money, and Morality,* 122). While international financing was directed toward "large-scale projects" such as hotel and resort construction, many smaller, individually owned sex services establishments were funded by non-Thai investors. Thai law requiring at least 50 percent Thai ownership could be bypassed through various methods; thus one of the significant investors in the infamous Patpong Road was an "American who (in 1969) transformed an existing tea-house into a luxurious nightclub" (*Sex, Money, and Morality,* 162) Attesting to significant continuity with the wartime R and R role of Thailand, one of the first bars in Bangkok, The Cowboy, was established by L. T. "Cowboy" Edwards, a retired U.S. Air Force officer. An entire district of bars is now called Soi Cowboy after Edwards. More significant than capital investment or ownership, such foreigners "have introduced new methods of operation, management skills, such as girlie bars, go-go bars and sex floor shows in the Western tradition" (162). Considering that international tourism is categorized as an export-commodity in the calculation of trade balances, its women sex workers can be said to perform a kind of export-oriented labor.

These sustained modes of American influence and presence suggest a transnational porosity between the United States and these Asian locations, which in turn qualifies the formation of these three sites of labor in Asia and the female working bodies therein as a crucial part of U.S. history.

Asian +
body
concealed
by ①

②

However, as I will detail below, these continuities and connections are displaced and veiled by two representational tendencies. Often these women workers are not only relegated to a distinct locale in a faraway place, but this geographical distance is mutually reinforced by figuring them as living in a belated moment of both global capitalist progress and feminist liberation. In addition, the forceful and strategic deployments of these women workers in these sites of transnational labor have been muted and even naturalized by their spectacular embodiment through both linguistic and photographic methods. An emblematic visibility of their bodies at work—recall the photograph of the Ricoh watch factory worker—further secures their placement within late capitalism. Furthermore, I would argue, these discursive inclinations—(1) the imprinting of remoteness and historical belatedness, and (2) visual fixation—powerfully support each other; while the first privileges the mobile, disembodied agency of capitalist accumulation, the second provides a reassuringly material embodiment of the logic of profit pursuit through labor exploitation.[27]

Spatial-Temporal Fixations

The collapsing of geographical *distance* as social, economic, political, and cultural *difference* has scored a range of discourses around globalization and transnational labor. The marking off of entire regions, economies, and peoples into First World/Third World, North/South, and core/periphery is not merely descriptive or analytic, but expresses and reinforces what Johannes Fabian calls a "political cosmology."[28] Scattered, heterogeneous yet also simultaneously interrelated political-economic situations are fixed at different points on a linear yet staggered axis of capitalist growth and maturation. Pointing out how "the notions of underdevelopment and Third World were the discursive products of the post–World War II climate," Arturo Escobar has convincingly shown how certain "poor countries" were defined as such according to a specifically "economic conception of poverty [which] found an ideal yardstick in the annual per capita income."[29] Although this measurement was "nothing more than the result of a comparative statistical operation, the first of which was carried out only in 1940,"[30] it produced a numerical marking of *lack* especially as expressed through the U.S. dollar: "And if the problem was one of insufficient income, the solution was clearly economic growth."[31] The temporal lag of these countries, economies, and peoples had to be produced to provide the compelling terrain for the work of development. From this "common starting point [where] poverty is viewed in deprivationist terms,"[32] positively oriented terms like "modernization" or "industrialization" can disguise the damaging, exploitative, uprooting consequences of such political-economic shifts or make them appear justifiable in light of other end goals. In preference to the colonialist connotation and evaluative implication of these designations, there has been a renewed emphasis on the nation-state as an organizing unit and definite locus through the alternative namings of "less economically accomplished countries" and "more economically advantaged nations."[33] Yet this paradigm of *national* economic pathways still echoes an assumption of a particular "evolutionary slope" as in the more recent designation of Singapore, Taiwan, and Korea as "newly industrializing countries" (NIC) even though they have been *industrialized* for some time. This distinction, in turn, casts a temporal shadow over the national economies of China, Vietnam, Indonesia, and Sri Lanka, which are figured as "following" or "emulating" the NICs.

Such mapping of distinct national or regional boundaries can be contested by the internal geographical and social fragmentation wrought by the transnational laboring sites in each country. The free-trade zones, U.S. military outposts, and sex tourist districts are spatially, economically, and socially demarcated from the rest of the country. Indeed, both "free trade zone" and "export-processing zone" suggest a spatialization that transcends national borders and natural territories:

> Free trade zones are like a country within a country. Cut off by barbed wire or concrete walls from the rest of the country and guarded in some cases by "zone police," the zone is an enclave in terms of customs-territorial aspects and possibly other aspects such as total or partial exemption from laws and decrees of the country concerned. . . . The zone has its own authority in which the central government functions are largely delegated.[34]

Physical access is restricted to those employed in these demarcated areas who are "often subject to special regulations (prohibition of labor disputes, for instance) [and] have to show special passes to enter it and often undergo a body check when they finish a day's toil."

Like the FTZs and EPZs, the areas of military prostitution around U.S. bases and sex tourism are spatially and socially separated from the rest of the country under designation as "camptowns" and "sex districts." To return to the specific case of Korea, a *zone* called America Town is even more extreme in its restricted accessibility and political-economic autonomy from the rest of the country: "What distinguishes America Town from the other camptowns is its physical isolation—it is completely walled off, with a guard posted at the gate—and its 'incorporated' status. America Town is not simply a place; it is a corporation, with a president and a board of directors who manages all the business and people living and working in it."[35] Similarly for sex tourism, as Truong points out, "in the peripheral tourist-receiving countries and particularly the low-income and small island countries, tourist resorts and hotels tend not to be well-integrated into the local economy."[36] Identifying India, Singapore, and Hong Kong as exceptions to the rule, Truong adds, "By and large, the tourist industry remains an enclave-like and footloose sector in less developed countries. Thus, on a local scale, enterprises engaged in the entertainment business, grand tours or other local services generally are not linked financially with other sub-branches of the service sector." As foreign ownership and/or control have been ingeniously disguised through various arrangements, it creates the appearance of local belonging and initiative.

Although this unmooring of work site from a particular nation-state as well as corporate headquarters could offer opportunities for greater international labor solidarity, it has often had the effect of producing a further estrangement. Unlike the recognizably geographical place names like Korea or Malaysia, these generic "zones" ring as somehow extraterrestrial. Indeed, some of these manufacturing zones have borne little correspondence to actual delineations of geographical contiguity or international borders. On the one hand, they are no longer restricted to certain outlying and coastal areas but are increasingly being carved into the interior expanses of certain countries as transnational firms, searching for even lower production costs, relocate certain production processes to more economically depressed rural areas.[37] Even *within* nation-state borders, some places are more or less amenable to the extraction of surplus value. On the other hand, there has been the formation of multinational "economic zones" such as the one reported amongst Malaysia, Thailand, and Indonesia.[38] Mitter's 1987 observation with regard to Mexican *maquiladoras* that the EPZ "has become an institutional concept rather than a territorial one" (41) could be applied to certain Asian contexts as well. As the social and geographical terrains of individual countries are increasingly fractured by the shifting presence of transnational capital, the official rationale that these "zones" benefit the interests of a cohesive and united nation and its worker-citizens is untenable.

The geographical distance of these workers and work sites is often buttressed by their temporal belatedness. Taking the capitalist industrialization and class formation of American and Western European economies in the nineteenth century as prototypical, low wages and sweatshop conditions in certain Asian locales are evaluated not in light of *contemporary* low wages and sweatshop conditions in the United States but compared to the conditions faced by American and European workers in earlier, darker times. One such unfortunate rhetorical move is to compare the labor exploitation of Asian women in the late-twentieth-century TNC factories to that of nineteenth-century "factory girls" in the United States or England. Reporting that the barracks housing workers in Taiwanese EPZs are "euphemistically called dormitories," Walden Bello and Stephanie Rosenfeld note that they "remind one of the living conditions in nineteenth-century Manchester."[39] In another instance noted in a 1983 essay by Cynthia Enloe, this asynchronous analogy appears motivated by a feminist linking of women's working conditions. While she initially describes the women textile workers in Southeast Asia as "experiencing the same hopes, frustrations and risks that their Western sisters did 150 years ago," Enloe proceeds in the next paragraph to emphasize their significantly different location within the nineteenth-century national and the twentieth-century transnational economies. The essay ends, however, by reanalogizing these Southeast Asian textile workers to "the 'Lowell girls' in 1830s Massachusetts, the needlewomen in nineteenth-century London, and the silk workers of Essex."[40] More recently, Miriam Ching Louie has noted, "For women, it's the Industrial Revolution repeated over and over again, relocated from the Triangle Factory fire that burned workers to death in 19th century America to South Korea's cramped chicken-coop sweatshops, Mexico's toxic maquiladoras, and China's Special Economic Zone workers' dormitories of today."[41] As much as this recursive characterization of labor conditions for female production workers may contest a linear teleology of capitalist development, it also insists on the same gender-class formation across time and space.[42] But, as Aihwa Ong notes about the Mexican maquiladoras and the Chinese SEZs, "Corporate reliance on mixed production systems in offshore sites has produced an increasingly heterogeneous workforce—including children, men, and imported labor."[43] Considered against the anachronistic figuration, the feminist rhetoric of international filiation—the women workers are sometimes called "our Asian sisters"—may not express a familial identification of shared circumstances as much as a hegemonic assertion of distinct, staggered maturities. One way to see these women and their work sites as contemporaneous is to keep in mind how "the very equipment produced in the [electronics] industry makes finely tuned long-distance coordination possible."[44] Another route would be to note how the establishment of sex tourism simultaneously or sometimes *before* the development of industrial manufacturing in certain countries—Thailand would be a good case in point—foregrounds different and even reversed trajectories of economic development: "While economists in industrialized societies presume that the 'service' economy, with its explosion of feminized job categories, follows a decline in manufacturing, policy-makers in many Third World countries have been encouraged by international advisers to develop service sectors before manufacturing industries mature."[45]

The simultaneous and interconnected deployments of Asian immigrant and Asian American women workers in both manufacturing assembly jobs and the sex services industry in the territorial United States also contests spatiotemporal distinctions. In contrast to a marked decline in manufacturing sectors in the past three decades, there has been an increase in the numbers of production jobs in a few industries and in certain metropolitan centers with significant immigrant populations from Asia and Latin America.[46] Writing in 1983 of how national statistics showing an absolute decline in the number of domestic manufacturing jobs from the mid-1960s through the 1970s belie "important shifts in the composition of the electronics workforce," Robert Snow adds, "In San Jose, the percentage of minority workers in the blue-collar workforce has doubled since 1966, and case studies indicate that immigrant workers make up a large portion of the electronics workforce in both San Jose and Boston."[47] Given that the wages in the electronics industry did not keep pace with the national increase in manufacturing wages, Snow further speculates, "Perhaps because of the low wages received by electronics production workers, the percentage of ethnic minorities in the blue-collar electronics workforce has increased considerably." In 1978 Rachel Grossman reported that 90 percent of the electronic assemblers in the Silicon Valley were women and "roughly half of them are of Asian and Latin origin, including Filipinas, Koreans, Vietnamese, Mexicans, Azoreans."[48] Chalsa Loo and Paul Ong have referred to the large numbers of Chinese immigrant women workers in Chinatown garment factories as constituting an "ethnic labor market."[49] In addition to lower wages, hard physical labor, long hours, and an unhealthful shop environment, there is widespread use of family-run subcontracting shops and homework.[50] Finally, in major U.S. cities and in outlying areas surrounding military bases in Hawaii, California, and throughout the South, Asian immigrant women are employed in similar kinds of entertainment and sex services in similarly dismal conditions. Their immigrant status, limited English skills, and lack of familiarity with local laws, social services, and transportation networks make these women further vulnerable to entrapment, extortion, and violence. In light of the similarities of their labor status and work conditions to women in Asia, it is difficult to argue that living and working in the late capitalist United States assures a better, more modern, and liberated existence for Asian/American women.

Here again, a tendency to mark them as spatially and temporally removed from an implicit center obscures the contemporaneity and continuity of these American sites of labor to the FTZs and EPZs in Asia. The dubbing of these American manufacturing sites as "underground economies" or "peripheral zones" charges them with an air of surreptitiousness and inconsequent marginality, and thereby marks them off from the rest of the domestic and transnational economy. However, the small factories owned and run by Asian immigrants in New York and Los Angeles serve as a crucial and well-integrated node in the multinational production process: "Even though New York companies ship piecework to factories in Taiwan, Singapore and Hong Kong, they still need factories that can quickly produce specialized or custom fashion lines in a matter of days. This so-called spot market business accounts for nearly all of the work performed in these [Chinatown] shops."[51] Referring to the growth in such jobs as a "resurgence" of outmoded practices, "the return of capital," or "the Third Worlding of the First World" reinforces the spatiotemporal relegation of labor exploitation to a less developed distant locale. For example, Mitter notes, "International capital is returning from Third World countries to the peripheral regions of the advanced West" (20–21). Richard Appelbaum describes this as "the reperipheralization of the core—the coming home of sweatshops to take advantage of the home market and cheap immigrant labor."[52] Coded in terms of a regression or a reversed colonization, these degraded work conditions have been justified as (however unfortunately) "necessary" to compete with lower-priced imports and to provide much desired jobs for "uneducated and unskilled" immigrants from Asia and Latin America who otherwise will swell the welfare rolls.[53] As racialized nonwhite and most likely "illegal" aliens, the argument goes, these work-ers are not entitled to the same employment conditions and benefits as are "real" Americans. As a persistent xenophobia, which is often speci-fied and shrouded as *only* against illegal immigration, trains its paranoid gaze on spectacularized bodies of Asian and Latina/o immigrant workers, the corporate firms and retail agents that plan and profit from their ex-ploited labor recede from critical view. Avtar Brah cogently reads this anti-immigrant fervor in the United States for how such "tropes of resent-ment construct the worker as an embodiment of capital rather than its contradiction."[54]

Although some post-1965 Asian immigrant women worked in similar jobs in their countries of origin, many others have entered the manufac-turing sector only after immigrating to the United States. Additionally considering that many of these women are college graduates, with some having worked as professionals before emigration, their entry into these low-paying, insecure job markets is thoroughly mediated by their immi-grant status, racist and sexist hiring practices, and institutional barriers to recertification by professional licensing boards in the United States. Contrary to the claims that this is a new development or a resurgence of "anachronistic" employment practices, the spatial segregation and inferior conditions that confront immigrant workers bear certain historical conti-nuities.[55] Low-paid and unhealthful physical labor has long been performed by immigrants whose socioeconomic mobility was constrained by their politically insecure "alien" status and limited English proficiency. Accord-ing to Morrison G. Wong, "the present-day garment shops in Chinatown are but lineal descendants of the Chinese guild that organized apparel fac-tories in California in the 1860s."[56] Arguing that the employment patterns of "Third World women" in the United States problematize the distinc-tion between *traditional* and *modern* forms of manufacturing, Saskia Sassen has proposed instead a distinction between *labor-intensive* and *capital-intensive* forms of production, which "overcomes the inadequacy of conceiving certain forms of organization of work, notably sweatshops and industrial homework, as pertaining to the traditional, non-modern sector, a notion that can easily be read to mean that these forms will become increasingly insignificant as modernization takes place." Rather than an anomalous exception, Sassen adds that the existence of sweatshops and homework "would seem to be integral to the functioning of advanced capitalism in the current historical phase."[57]

The deployment of Asian immigrant female workers in U.S. garment and electronics manufacturing suggests that the offshoring of production processes in Asian countries should be read in terms of increasing interpenetration across geopolitical boundaries. John Willoughby describes how "a series of monopoly capitalist enterprises [engage] in competition and cooperation over the whole vast territory of the Western world"[58] and, I would add, throughout Asia. Framing this dynamic largely as international competition ignores how class, gender, and racial inequalities are manipulated and exacerbated within individual nation-states. Here Willoughby alerts us to the "sharp distinction between those policies (both macroeconomic and institutional) that might make a region a more attractive field of accumulation and those policies that are designed to assist *a specific national fraction of capital*. These latter nationalistic state interventions are becoming less and less important, while the former policies retain their significance" (138, original italics). As early as 1983, June Nash argued that the dispersion of production be mapped in terms of corporate strategy and state planning rather than distinct spatial demarcations: "More than a uniformly defined or geographically delimited concept, the export-processing zone provides a series of incentives and loosened restrictions for multinational corporations by developing countries in their effort to attract foreign investment in export-manufacturing."[59] A more recent article on EPZs in Asia notes, "Another type of custom-free manufacturing that has been introduced is the Export Processing Factory (EPF) or Custom-Bonded Factory (CBF), which produces exports and receives preferential treatment irrespective of location."[60] It also points out that most investors in Asian EPZs have been "small firms from industrialized countries and increasingly from other developing countries such as the NICs." The authors add, "When an MNC does invest in a zone, it is more concerned with maintaining links with its own international production network than establishing links with the host economy to stimulate growth" (841). In addition to the "growth triangle" among Malaysia, Indonesia, and Thailand, other efforts have been made to establish economic zones across several national borders.[61] Finally, in the past decade, there has been a significant reduction of U.S.-based TNC investment and offshoring in certain Asian countries while some Asian TNCs are increasingly investing in the United States. For example, Korean semiconductor firms have established "outposts in the Silicon Valley of California."[62] Along with the massive transnational migrations of labor, this diversified and often volatile pattern of capital investment and accumulation renders the nation-state differently significant but not defining. As Saskia Sassen summarizes: "Economic globalization has reconfigured fundamental properties of the nation-state, notably territoriality and sovereignty. There is an incipient unbundling of the exclusive territoriality we have long associated with the nation-state. . . . the state is no longer the only site of sovereignty and the normativity that accompanies it."[63]

Such blurring and overlapping of national and regional boundaries calls for a critical deliberation about *how* distinctions amongst "Asian women," "American women," and "Asian American women" are and can be meaningful. On the first case in point, even as the transnational reconfigurations of capital and labor are contracting the physical distance between the United States and Asia, they have also provoked a reconsideration of the continental demarcation of "Asia." The singularly notable economic dominance of Japan has long troubled any such neat geographical distinctions. Aihwa Ong has argued, "the Japanese move into the Pacific Rim area recalls the prewar 'Great Co-Prosperity Sphere' strategy whereby Japan sought to make Asia the offshore base of Japanese capitalist expansion."[64] Japanese TNCs were often the first to move into the FTZs, before American and European firms; their investment presence was especially extensive in former colonies, Taiwan and South Korea.[65] More recently, Korean and Taiwanese-owned TNCs have been relocating production facilities to China, Vietnam, and Indonesia. To the homogenizing model of a New International Division of Labor (NIDL), Ngai Pun has proposed "an analytical framework of the New Regional Division of Labor in Asia, disclosing the specific movement of capital from industrialized sub-regions to developing sub-regions within Asia."[66] In this intracontinental "industrial restructuring" of the 1980s and 1990s, "newly industrialized countries provide the capital, control the technology and markets while the developing countries provide land and abundant workers. Southeast and South Asian countries thus become the destination for the relocation of factories by NICs from East Asia" (20). As clearly illustrated in this passage, the uneven development of transnational capitalism necessitates the breakdown and multiple specification of "Asia" into "South," "East," and "Southeast" *Asias*.

When "Asian" is deployed interchangeably with national designations, as often happens in the scholarship, it risks eliding such differences and inequalities. The murkiness with which continental and regional distinctions have been deployed is further exacerbated in the scholarship on sex tourism. One study clusters Korea, Thailand, and the Philippines together under the odd designation of "South-East Asia" as sites "where the most blatant and systematic organization of sex tourism can be found."[67] On the other hand, Japan is often categorized as part of the "West" or the "North" along with the United States, Canada, and Western European countries. Another scholar of sex tourism in "South-East Asia" notes this continentally anomalous position: "Although it is prevalent in Western capitalist nations, sex tourism has generally come to be associated with 'Western' (including Japanese), usually male visitors to the Third World."[68] Some have even argued that extensive participation of Japanese men as sex tourists has been fueled by a *racist* ethnocentrism. According to one Japanese critic of sex tourism, "It is partly 'the subconscious feelings of sexual and racial superiority of Japanese males,' former colonizers of South Korea, which account for Korea's popularity as a tourist destination."[69] Finally, the growing numbers of male tourists from South Korea, Taiwan, Singapore, and Hong Kong attest to how the contours of transnational sex tourism unsettle any sense of their shared "Asian" designation with the Thai and Filipina sex workers.

The shifting geographical terrain of transnational sex work in Asia also demands a critical reconsideration of the category of "Asian women." One result of the vociferous protests against sex tourism, which were waged by women's groups in Japan, Korea, and the Philippines in the 1970s and early 1980s has been a growth of sex services in tourist origin countries. Significant numbers of women from Korea, Taiwan, Thailand, and the

Philippines have been migrating to Japan to work in the domestic sex industry. In their study of this transnational labor migration, Hisae Muroi and Naoko Sasaki explore two axes of differentiation amongst women: (1) a "double standard" that divides Japanese wives from women who work as prostitutes, and (2) "important differences between the Asian women who work in prostitution-related activities in Japan."[70] Given the first strict demarcation of "good wives and other women," the authors argue that many Japanese women "find it easy to accept the norm that women who sell their bodies are a different type of woman, in a category of 'whores', racial difference marking this division with ease."[71] If other Asian women in Japan may be *racially* distinguished from Japanese women, Muroi and Sasaki also accent important national differences amongst the (im)migrant sex workers. Reporting that Korean and Taiwanese women enjoy "relatively secure working conditions," they explain:

> Japan has had a longer relationship with both Korea and Taiwan, especially through occupying these countries before World War II, and many Koreans and Taiwanese have already lived in Japan, so that women from these two countries have had easy access to Japan through their relatives or acquaintances. This entry time gap has allowed some Korean and Taiwanese women to establish some kind of status in Japanese society such as becoming a bar owner rather than a hostess or taking up permanent residence through marriage. (202)

In contrast, Thai women are subject to the worst working conditions, which they attribute largely to the fact that there are "many levels of brokers in the recruitment process."[72] Such complicated international disparities and shifting movements within *Asia* are elided through the materialization of a continental identity in the figure of "Asian women."

In light of how such shifts and movements of capital and laboring bodies within and across nations, regions, and continents trouble national, ethnic, and continental identifications, I propose to study how the assumption of "Asian women" as a coherent—and sometimes natural—category of working bodies has served two other discursive functions: (1) supporting the disembodied, rational logic of capital accumulation, and (2) managing the problem of knowing and representing these political economic phenomena and their working subjects. In several texts on the proliferation of offshore manufacturing in Asia, there is an implicit yet consistent privileging of a "logical" subjectivity attributed to transnational capital over and against the "natural" Asian female working bodies in the language of description, analysis, and even critique. Conjoining the two, Fuentes and Ehrenreich declare: "Women everywhere are paid lower wages than men. Since multinationals go overseas to reduce labor costs, women are the natural choice for assembly jobs" (12). Similarly, assuming that lower wages are a priori conditions of the Asian locales, Linda Y. C. Lim emphasizes the relocation of production as a "rational competitive response to changing international comparative cost advantages."[73] Describing employment practices in the U.S. and Britain, Swasti Mitter asserts: "The management strategy of global corporations . . . is to rely on a docile, non-unionized and casual workforce. If such labour is available near the market, it makes little sense to source production in offshore companies" (*Common Fate*, 21). Imbuing an aura of common sense obscures the dense transnational web of organizations and individual actors who compete and cooperate in shaping and maintaining these laboring sites and their wage levels. Such attribution of reason echoes and affirms the "laissez-faire policy" regarding personnel on the part of some TNC management who rationalize that "when confronted with inequalities in wages and conditions on a world-level, the firm must adapt to local conditions."[74] Rejecting this appeal to the "local" as "a kind of cultural relativism that accepts a given condition as inevitable and justifies conformity for retrogressive labor practices in functionalist terms," June Nash pointed out in 1983 how, despite the apparent spatial remoteness of these offshore plants, "the degree of centralized control is masked by 'harmonization' of operations between branches of the firm, such that what appears to be local decisions are the inevitable result of a series of conditioning factors initiated from the headquarters of the firm" (25). Further contesting the claims that preexisting local conditions dictate wage differentials, Nash clarified an important distinction: "Whereas wage *levels* are kept on line with local and national labor markets, new wage *systems* are often introduced. Job evaluations, merit systems, and detailed job descriptions are U.S. innovations that serve as mechanisms of control by the home office" (30, original italics). In making this distinction, Nash would contest how, according to the rationale of the TNC management, "acceptance of wage differentials . . . implies the need for labor exploitation to bring about the accumulation of capital" (26).

This privileging of the logic of capital accumulation also scores what

Julie Graham has identified as a "Marxist legacy of economic essentialism." She explains, "Though capital accumulation is ultimately an activity of individual firms (and policy-makers), it is more commonly construed as an inevitable concomitant of capitalist development, a 'tendential' law of capitalist development."[75] She locates this presumption of capital's "accumulation essence" as an analytical "problem of conferring ontological privilege upon a discursive point of entry" in the writings of the regulation school as well as those of what is labeled "flexible specialization" (50). I would add that this applies also to David Harvey's observation of a distinct mode of "flexible accumulation" in postmodernity. Dating its emergence to "the period from 1965 and 1973 [when] the inability of Fordism and Keynesianism to contain the inherent contradictions of capitalism became more and more apparent," Harvey emphasizes a move away from the mutual compromises of the capital-labor accord toward a greater "flexibility with respect to labour processes, labour markets, and patterns of consumption."[76] Focalizing these political-economic shifts largely through the increasingly flexible agency of capital, Harvey is bound to an implicit framework of spatiotemporal distancing of labor exploitation as a problem of underdevelopment elsewhere: "Organized labour was undercut by the reconstruction of foci of flexible accumulation in regions lacking previous industrial traditions, and by importation back into the older centres of the regressive norms and practices established in these new areas" (147). The very term "flexible accumulation" assumes the agile and versatile subject-position of capital and thereby renders as secondary those working bodies that are stifled and disciplined by this corporate and industrial reorganization. In another telling instance, Richard Applebaum differentiates a technological mode of capital flexibility in exploiting labor from an organizational mode as in subcontracting. Referring to the Marxist distinction amongst *constant capital* ("sunk investment in machinery and equipment"), *variable capital* ("the costs of living labor, as indicated by the wage bill"), and *surplus value* ("unpaid labor extracted by the capitalist"), Applebaum writes that "living labor can be broken down into nearly infinitesimal increments, enhancing the capitalist's flexibility in responding to changing market conditions."[77] From this more ambiguous construction of cause-and-effect, he continues with a more transitive locution: "*Labor, then, provides capitalists with infinite flexibility,* although of course labor's part in class struggle is to reduce that flexibility by speaking in one's voice, thereby taking on the 'lumpy' character of constant capital" (299, my italics).

Julie Graham remarks how certain epistemological priorities structure partial understandings and representations:

> The question of the entry point to social analysis is a question about the kinds of knowledge we wish to create. With capital accumulation as our entry point, we will produce knowledge of the causes and consequences of the growth of productive capital. This knowledge may be rich and fruitful, but it will also be specific. In its specificity, it may not be able to tell us much about the capitalist class process of exploitation or about the distribution of surplus labor in value form. (47)

Part of the challenge of trying to produce a knowledge of the capitalist class process of exploitation lies in how the very effort to describe, even if to condemn and critically analyze, these phenomena has been largely predetermined by the preferred terminology of the various corporate, military, and government interests. I think this could partially explain the paradoxical tendency to take a critical stance against labor exploitation and yet to affirm its inevitability. Swasti Mitter points to this discursive bias at two different points in her book. First, she notes the "semantically curious" naming of "free trade zones" because it "implies almost total freedom for the investing companies . . . and an almost complete lack of freedom for workers" (38), particularly on their right to unionize. On the category of "casual workers," she later remarks: "These predominantly female workers are called casual not because of a lack of commitment or experience on their part, but simply because their conditions of work have been deliberately casualized" (139). Although Mitter does not further analyze these semantic curiosities, I would extend her observations to note how even as the accumulating will of capitalism is credited with such positively valued human properties as freedom, reason, and good sense, the subject of corporate motivation and active implementation often drops out in the scenario of labor exploitation. The shifting of the modifier "casual" onto the workers, far from naming some ontological or occupational property, materializes even as it mystifies how *casualization* is a concerted management strategy of intermittent and uneven employment to fit fluctuating production needs.

Without invoking some omniscient planner, we might foreground the contours and mechanics of such *deliberateness* and attach that to a set of different subjects. Rachel Grossman offers an alternative deployment of "temporary" from modifying a kind of worker to "an expendable workforce": "The ability to lay their workers off at will is essential to the electronics firms, because the work is by definition temporary" (37). Lisa Lowe offers a very different locution of flexibility when she suggests that "contrary to the classical Marxist understanding that capital seeks 'abstract labor,' the use of Chinese immigrant labor demonstrates that even in the nineteenth-century, U.S. capital profited precisely from the 'flexible' racialization of Asian labor" (*Immigrant Acts,* 14). Writing about the more contemporary phenomenon of Filipina migrant labor, Grace Chang writes: "Migrant women workers from indebted nations are *kept pliable* not only by the dependence of their home countries and families on remittances, but also by stringent restrictions on immigrant access to almost all forms of assistance in the United States. Their vulnerability is further reinforced by U.S. immigration policies, designed to recruit migrant women as contract laborers or temporary workers who are ineligible for the protections and rights afforded to citizens."[78] Alongside racializing discourses and immigration restrictions, the prerogative to name hiring and firing practices has been crucial to an ongoing struggle to materialize the skewed terms and conditions of *flexible exploitation.*

The "accumulation essence" of capital has been materialized by a simultaneously presumed "exploitation essence" of these racialized and gendered working bodies. In contrast to such recurrent terms as "footloose industries" and "runaway shops," which oddly imbue the TNCs with an unencumbered and even fanciful subject-position, a nation's female labor force is often figured as one primordial fixture in a litany of other amenable features of the natural geography such as good shipping locations. The term "reservoir" is followed by various combinations of the following adjectives: abundant, cheap, young, female, unmarried, and unskilled.[79] Stating that "travel and trade are ancient endeavors in Southeast Asia—between specific kinds of people and regions engaged in exchanging resources," the editor of an area studies volume promises, " 'Resources,' and the social schemes surrounding them, will repeatedly surface . . . in amazingly diverse forms—from female bodies to primeval rain forests to cigarette lighters."[80] The workers are repeatedly referred to as "cheap, docile labor," as if depressed wages and workplace discipline were ontological properties unique to these women.[81] Here I would argue that the unexamined identification of "Asian women" with its assured aura of both racial commonality and continental distinction could work to reinforce such naturalizing figurations. When these laboring subjects are granted a degree of socioeconomic agency, they are figured as enabling corporate exploitation by "accepting" or being "willing" to work under such terms and conditions. The inferior conditions under which their bodies and labor power are mobilized are rendered as inevitable even for those who would vociferously decry their exploitation.

Despite this sense of a natural or beneficial fit, many development agendas initially envisioned a largely male workforce for export-oriented manufacturing. "Host governments," Aihwa Ong notes, "hoped that the large number of rural male migrants, the group thought to have the greatest potential for political unrest, would be absorbed by the new offshore industries."[82] Criticisms that women had been overlooked in this planning, in turn, led to the proliferation of studies and recommendations on "women in development" (WID). As Arturo Escobar argues:

> The fact that young women ended up being the optimal, and preferred, "docile, cheap labor force" was neither a coincidence nor the result of a sudden change of heart on the part of the male planners and Third World elites. The promotion of industrialization in the Third World through export platforms and free trade zones was happening at the same time that calls for "integrating women into development" were being hailed by international organizations. (175)

In addition to this historical convergence, the embodying of Asian women workers has been effected through specific disciplinary practices and discursive means. The newly postcolonial states in Hong Kong, South Korea, Taiwan, and Singapore actively and often violently suppressed labor organizing in order to prepare the grounds for and to maintain export-oriented industrialization.[83] In the case of Malaysia, Aihwa Ong describes how Taylorist scientific management technique, which "specifies exact bodily posture and requires tedious repetition of the same finger, eye, and limb movements, often for hours on end at the assembly line," was combined with "forms of spatial control [such as] the deployment of workers on the shop floor in relative isolation from each other but under the constant surveillance of foremen, an arrangement that induces self-monitoring."[84]

These strategically planned and coercively implemented measures of suppression and control are eclipsed by a persistent focus on certain "natural" characteristics of Asian women workers. One recurrent tendency has been the emphasis placed on their youth. While it is true that TNC factories employ female workers as young as fourteen—or in some cases even younger—many are adult women in their twenties, often married and/or with children. In her in-depth study of a "runaway shop" by an American TNC in Korea and the mostly middle-aged women workers who sustained a lengthy and innovative campaign for their unpaid wages and severance pay, Hyun Mee Kim points to how a 30 March 1989 article in the *Los Angeles Times* mistakenly described these workers as "young female assemblers."[85] Referring to them all as "factory girls," "bar girls" or "hospitality girls" charges them further with a premature docility. Implicit in this infantilization is the promise of achieving adult subjecthood in time. To the extent that this generic figuration of age and gender is accurate, the heavy concentration of young female workers is the effect of a consciously pursued recruitment, hiring, and promotion strategy on the part of the firms. As Aihwa Ong has noted, the TNC electronics assembly plants in Malaysia "attempted to limit the tenure of their female workers to the short span of their life cycle when they were most capable of intensive labor" (147). If younger women are thus recruited because TNC management sees potential for a longer period of exploitation, their youth, gender, and unmarried status are mobilized to justify lower wages and lack of job security. To minimize costs of hospital fees and maternity benefits—in addition to the loss of labor productivity—TNCs have deployed a range of tactics to control the sexual and reproductive lives of their workers. Fuentes and Ehrenreich cite this example: "In the Philippines' Bataan Export Processing Zone the Mattel toy company offers prizes to workers who undergo sterilization" (40). Here we can see how certain tactics of figuration and disciplinary employment practices reinforce one another.

Another related way of justifying the low wages paid to these workers is through the distinctions of "skilled" and "unskilled" labor. Arguing that "it is more accurate to speak of the jobs making a demand for easily trained labour, than for unskilled labour," Diane Elson and Ruth Pearson suggest that gendered encodings of labor skill precede and imprint the bodies of the women workers. They usefully argue, "To a large extent, women do not do 'unskilled' jobs because they are the bearers of inferior labour;

rather the jobs they do are 'unskilled' because women enter them already determined as inferior bearers of labour" (100). Gendered bodies are rendered as skilled or unskilled *before* their entry into the labor market, where they are matched to similarly categorized occupations and job tasks. However, technological innovations have radically reshaped the division of job tasks and consequently the definition of worker skills and qualifications. As Mitter reports, "The fragmentation of jobs has progressed, especially in manufacturing, to such an extent that the execution of the respective partial operations of even very sophisticated overall processes now often requires a training period of not more than a few weeks, even for a very young and inexperienced worker" (10). Note the complementary contrast here, in which sophistication modifies the manufacturing process while youth and inexperience characterize the worker. As much as it might relieve the human body from certain repetitive and monotonous tasks, mechanical and computerized automation has rendered the labor input of certain bodies as obsolete or, at best, supplementary to the work of the machinery. Aihwa Ong articulates this shift in terms of a mind/body division of labor: "The fragmentation of skills into simple procedures and the stripping away of individual judgment (separation of conception and execution) are intended by the system to treat workers as appendages of the machine" (71).

Here we would do well to keep in mind that the superfluity of worker skill, experience, or intelligence is a management strategy and motivated figuration, *not* an ontological fact or subjective experience. Concluding that "the impact of NT [new technology] has been more pronounced in the casualization of work than in bringing automation," Swasti Mitter adds, "The subdivision of the production process into simple elements offers capitalists an effective *means to cheapen* the manufacturing costs of commodities by maximum replacement of craft-skilled labour" (22). Granting that new technologies have certainly impelled a reassessment of job categories, I would argue furthermore that the very replacement and, indeed, displacement of "traditional" skills through technological innovation could render obsolete the categorical distinctions of skilled/unskilled and experienced/inexperienced insofar as these designations emerged from a historically and geographically specific mode of production. According to a suggestive locution by Rachel Grossman, "As highly compartmentalized segments of a multinational production process, the *jobs develop skills* with no application in other industries."[86] Even *within* the same industry in one national labor market, the particular skill of bonding, which is "the only part of the electronic process that comes to Southeast Asia," cannot be applied toward other jobs. In this structure, job skills inhere within the much more fleeting temporality of the production process rather than being taught, learned, and honed by and across specific working subjects over a longer period. However, as Grossman also points out, the use of certain tactics as "apprentice periods" during which the workers are paid less harks back to another, more enduring framework of craft and skills possession.

But if their youth imprints these working bodies with a lack of skill, it is seen to imbue them with two defining characteristics: "nimble fingers" and "docility." While such figuration might have been authored and disseminated by factory owners and government officials as a lure for TNC investment, I would argue that the compelling iconicity of the Asian female working body *as* "nimble fingers" has been partially effected through its repetition through the sympathetic transnational reporting and analysis of TNC assembly work. A 1981 article by Diane Elson and Ruth Pearson bore the title " 'Nimble Fingers Make Cheap Workers': An Analysis of Women's Employment in Third World Manufacturing."[87] Speaking more generically of women as a transnational category of working bodies, Elson and Pearson argue, "The famous 'nimble fingers' of young women are . . . the result of the training they have received from their mothers and other female kin since early infancy in the tasks socially appropriate to woman's role." As a more specific illustration, they explain that "since industrial sewing of clothing closely resembles sewing with a domestic sewing machine, girls who have learnt such sewing at home already have the manual dexterity and capacity for spatial assessment required." In their effort to put forth a strong social constructionist account of the "nimble fingers," Elson and Pearson end up homogenizing all Third World women: "It is in the context of the subordination of women as a gender that we must analyze the supposed docility, subservience and consequent suitability for tedious, monotonous work of young women in the Third World" (93). They push their argument so far as to contend that "self-repression is required for women to achieve an adequate level of docility and subservience." According to this formation, gender subordination universally precedes and prepares the ground for labor exploitation.

Even texts that criticize the stereotypes of Asian women as inherently nimble and docile are bound up in the discursive problematics. Several texts point out how this image emerged in the 1960s to justify and valorize EOI development. Indeed, the image of the "good worker" is of relatively recent manufacture, which contradicts the recurrent portrayal of the "natives" as lazy and unruly as a justification for territorial conquest and dispossession during the colonial era.[88] To demonstrate their point that the Asian governments actively produced and propagated a particular image of their female labor, Fuentes and Ehrenreich offer two compelling examples. A Malaysian brochure offers this alluring promise: "The manual dexterity of the Oriental female is famous the world over. Her hands are small, and she works fast with extreme care. . . . Who, therefore, could be better qualified by nature and inheritance, to contribute to the efficiency of a bench assembly production line than the Oriental girl?" (16).[89] A Royal Thai Embassy brochure suggests that "the relationship between the employer and the employees is like that of a guardian and a ward." Reading this Thai effort as "guarantee[ing] the submissive femininity of Eastern women in an attempt to attract American investment," Swasti Mitter describes it as "a highly selective photostudy of Thai womanhood: giggling shyly, bowing submissively, and working cheerfully on the assembly line" (45). The emphatic tone and decorous composition of these advertisements betray the calculated staging of these female bodies and beg the question of what other kinds of bodies are anticipated in this pitch. Rather than carefully examining the eroticized terms of such figurations, Fuentes and Ehrenreich—and Mitter after them—make recourse to a problematic analogy. Mitter offers no analysis in her description of the Thai brochure but rather quotes Fuentes and Ehrenreich: "Crudely put (and incidents like this do not inspire verbal delicacy), the relationship between many Third World governments and multinational corporations is not very different from the relationship between a pimp and his customers" (46). While this metaphor may render this transnational phenomenon legible within a certain Western, urban and implicitly racialized framework of pimp, prostitute, and customer, it also unduly confers a further sexual charge to the evidently eroticized pitch for TNC investment. Most unfortunately, it is the crude analogy that figures the Thai women workers *as* prostitutes, an identification that may be suggested but certainly not foreclosed by the textual details of the brochure. Indeed, the title, "Why We Woo Foreign Investments," positions the Malaysian government as the conventionally masculine suitor in contrast to the foreign investor, who is cast as the feminized object of this romantic pursuit. Finally, this generically sexualized triangulation of the Thai women workers, the Third World governments, and multinational corporations further mystifies the historical complexity and geopolitical density of transnational manufacturing that I outlined earlier.

In addition to assembly line production, there is also a common assumption of a natural or logical association between Asian female bodies and international sex work. Suggesting that "bases and prostitution have been assumed to 'go together'," Cynthia Enloe notes that while prostitution occurs near military bases all over the world, it has "attracted so much notoriety around bases in the poorer countries in the Third World" (*Bananas, Borders, Bases* 81). I would further argue that Asian female bodies have been the most visible icons of U.S. military–related prostitution. The plethora of Hollywood films and television shows on the Korean War and especially on the Vietnam War have portrayed Asian women primarily as prostitutes or bar girls. To recall from chapter 2, Suzie Wong was a prostitute and the primary set location for *The World of Suzie Wong* is a bar peopled by U.S. sailors and local Hong Kong women. Like the labels "casual labor" or "temporary worker," which transpose the terms and conditions of employment into features of an experiential or ontological identity, the parallel occupational category of "hospitality girls" is semantically curious. Placing the transnational labor of Asian women in export-oriented manufacturing alongside and against military prostitution and sex tourism allows for the interrogation of both the mechanized and eroticized enfigurations of these working bodies. How would military prostitution and sex tourism be recast and reconsidered if the women were described as performing *boring, repetitive, monotonous, low-paid, insecure, and unhealthful assembly work,* a task they are supposedly so suited for in the TNC factories? Even as their bodies are rendered as incidental and naturally woven fixtures of the mechanized assembly line, they also imbue these complex historical, economic, political, and cultural phenomena with a material and human grounding. In other words, Asian women workers come to *im-body* transnational capitalism, in the paradoxical sense of (mis)recognition *and* metaphorical closure intimated by the prefix.

To ask how and why these contradictory proprieties for factory discipline and erotic pleasure have become attached to Asian female working bodies, we might track how such figurations proceed by comparing and contrasting them to other racialized and gendered bodies. Explaining the corporate motivation for relocating production abroad, Mitter writes that "the promise of a docile young female workforce at the periphery stood in sharp contrast to the assertive and high-cost male workforce in the organized sectors of the 'First World'" (25). By fixing the two groups in terms of a binarily opposed but also complementary difference, this repeated juxtaposition also homogenizes the multiply different kinds of working bodies within the "periphery" and the "First World." In terms of transnational sex work, however, the women "over there" are more often set in contrast to women "back here." According to one repeatedly cited example, an advertisement in a Frankfurt paper promises, "Asian women are without desire for emancipation, but full of warm sensuality and the softness of velvet."[90] Here again, there needs to be a distinction made between how the promotional advertisements for sex tourism highlight the exotic and compliant sexuality of "Asian women" and how, in turn, their racial and sexual differentiation from women in the tourist-generating countries has been reasserted in the descriptive and analytical scholarship on sex tourism. Pointing to how "the tourist trade flourishes on the myth of docile black women," Mitter adds, "The differences between non-white females and their liberated white counterparts are continually emphasized in the enticements to sex tours" (67). Given the continuities and similarities of the kinds of work employing Asian women in Asia and "Asian American women" in the United States, what does it mean to identify and be identified as "Asian" *and* have access to the mantle of U.S. citizenship with its nationalized rewards variously posited of economic prosperity, social equality, and feminist liberation?

Such questions are foreclosed by an often unquestioned sense of urgency and solidarity behind the epistemological and representational endeavors about these sites and subjects of transnational labor. Beyond the developmental teleology of silence-to-voice or invisibility-to-visibility, I would accent the need to think through the very terms and conditions by which these working bodies are rendered into intelligible objects of knowledge and subjects of desire and social agency. In the previous three chapters, I situated a specific figuration of Asian/American women as writing subject, desiring body, or national citizen in a particular disciplinary location. However, their composition as transnational labor in the past three decades has taken place across a range of social science disciplines—including anthropology, sociology, economics, and political science—as well as in several interdisciplinary sites—most prominently in women's studies, Asian studies, development studies, and Asian American studies but also to a lesser extent in tourism studies and prostitution studies. In light of the proliferation of studies under such diverse disciplinary rubrics and fields of study, I would argue that a presumed coherence and ontological solidity of "Asian women" have been necessary to the variously situated knowledge claims about these subjects of transnational manufacturing, military prostitution, and sex tourism.

Taking the last as an example, I turn to one rather detailed explanation of how "the study of sex tourism is difficult because of several factors":

(i) the seeming blindness of many tourism researchers to actually acknowledge that a link exists between sex and the tourism industry, particularly in respect of sex as a motivating factor for travel and the sexual relationships between hosts and guests;

(ii) the extreme difficulties to be had in conducting research on tourism prostitution, which is typically an illegal informal activity, often with substantial crime connections, and which may place both researcher and subject at risk from brothel owners, criminal gangs and syndicates, and police and politicians who wish to keep the subject hidden and away from public examination;

(iii) the lack of common methodological and philosophical frameworks with which to explain the complex web of gender, productive, reproductive and social relations which surround sex tourism.[91]

Despite this very suggestive framing of the epistemological limits of existing modes of research and analysis as well as new challenges posed by this particular object of study, the author, C. Michael Hall, goes on to outline his own classification system of four different kinds of working subjects in tourism prostitution and asserts his own knowledge of "reality for many of the women involved in the sex tourism industry" that he "draws from empirical evidence" (148). Hall then interposes his own epistemological authority between "Western feminists" and "Asian women" as two geopolitically differentiated subjects and objects of knowledge: "The economic and social problems of Asian women tend to be viewed by Western feminists as stemming from the patriarchal nature of local cultures. Yet, there is not an undifferentiated Asian model of women and gender relations, although the state as a structure is dominated by patriarchal interests" (348). In emphasizing the determining significance of the *state* over the misguided and ethnocentric Western feminist emphasis on *culture,* Hall would differentiate "Asian women" by shifting from a continental to a smaller geographical unit: "Each region within South-east Asia needs to be examined in terms of its own particular set of gender, class, and social relations." This regionalization is supposed to strengthen his still generic knowledge-claims since "certain generalisations about the role and position of women within South-east Asia and development of sex tourism can be made" (149).

A growing number of representational endeavors that range from specifically disciplined studies to documentary videos have distinguished themselves as relaying the true *experiences, subjectivities,* and *voices* of the women workers. In *Patpong Sisters,* a rambling travelogue based on her Ph.D. fieldwork and subtitled *An American Woman's View of the Bangkok Sex World,* Cleo Odzer proclaims: "Charged with dedication . . . I decided to do something magnificent for the prostitutes of Patpong. My concern lay with the women of Patpong, whom I felt were unjustly condemned as abominations of society and disgraces to womanhood. . . . I wanted to spotlight what the Thai government wanted to hide."[92] She adds later, "Rather than viewing Patpong prostitutes as helpless victims of circumstance, I believed them to be clever women who saw opportunity and grasped it. I wanted to demonstrate how, as actors in their own ways, they chose logical courses for their lives" (22). The most extreme instance can be found in Marc Askew's essay "Strangers and Lovers: Thai Women Sex Workers and Western Men in the 'Pleasure Space' of Bangkok," which starts out by criticizing how preexisting representations that "center on Western male imaginings and encounters with the body of Thai women," tend to "downplay the role of women in these transactions."[93] While crediting previous researchers such as Truong who study sex tourism as a "political economy of underdevelopment" for having "done much to enlighten us about the structural basis and economic dynamics underpinning prostitution in the local and global context," Askew takes issue with how such accounts "reinforced assumptions of the victimhood of Southeast Asian women." Instead, he proposes to rescue the women from such figuration through his own studied account. The extended explication of his research methodology merits full citation:

The information used in this section is derived from the results of cumulative unstructured in situ interviews conducted with women in beer bars, go-go bars, and expatriate bars in Bangkok from 1993 to 1996. Information on over fifty women bar workers was gathered during this time. Of the range of methods employed in studies of prostitution, it was inappropriate to issue questionnaires or interview the women formally both because of the danger that this would pose to the quality of information and because it detracted from the importance of observing women at work, with friends, associates and customers. Like Odzer, I wanted a life-course perspective in addition to in situ observations; however, I did not reveal my objectives in asking the research questions. After the first interview which was conducted on formal lines outside a bar setting, I decided not to reveal any research was taking place in further meetings, disguising my identity (as per McKeganey and Barnard 1996: 11–16) as a researcher, but not as a drinker (which I am). "Interviews" thus comprised of conversations with women working at the venues, with the researcher playing the role of a regular drinker and then, as better and more continuous acquaintance was developed with particular women, "friend" and often "benefactor."[94]

This lengthy quotation underscores how the methodological terminology of the social sciences can be marshaled to rationalize one investigating subject's "necessary enmeshment" in the material conditions of his object of study. Askew's own knowledge-claims *about* Thai women sex workers are further fortified through his extended critique of the cinematic representation of Dennis O'Rourke's *The Good Woman of Bangkok*. Invoking his own "anthropological" expertise on Thai culture, Askew claims that the film's "dominant monologue form misrepresents Thai sociability and accepted ways of expressing emotion and problems" (114). From this more disciplined ground of authority, Askew is able to discern and to report "women's self-expressed understandings of their experiences and practices, as related to me in interviews and as expressed in women's language, in their self-conscious and reflexive expressions of being and acting and their daily activities with customers." One of Askew's key findings is to attribute "a conscious impulse toward 'experimentation'" as a key motivating force for his Thai female objects of study: "While clearly the motives for women's involvement in prostitution, of whatever type, are driven by economic necessity, there is a pattern of active rejection of aspects of Thai society and of a determination to transform their lifestyle, or at the very least to defy conventional social strictures on female behavior" (117).

Against such confident claims to espy, know, and then relay the interiority of these subjects, I will now consider two particular *modes* of composition—photography and ethnography—that have been deployed and how a third mode of inscription—variously called "life stories" or "autobiographical accounts"—works to elide the uneven play of representational power in the first two. In addition to the repeated circulation of the black-and-white photograph of the Filipina electronics assembler with which I began this chapter, images of Asian women at work are often included as visible illustrations alongside linguistic descriptions, most notably in the pamphlet "Women in the Global Factory" but also in the studies by Grossman, Elson and Pearson, Ong, and Eric Wolf. While Grossman's essay is illustrated with pages taken from TNC newsletters that feature black-and-white photographs of the workers in company-sponsored beauty pageants and fashion shows, she also points to the unreliability of photography in conveying the material conditions of these factories. "Although workplace conditions might look immaculate in photographs," she adds, "On an actual walk through a plant . . . the visitor often gags on the strong smell of chemicals, and a trial look through a microscope quickly produces dizziness or a headache."[95] Considering such representational limits of a photograph in testifying to the workers' experience of inhabiting such a workspace, what other discursive effects could such images produce? Referring to Charlie Chaplin's dramatic portrayal of a factory worker in the silent film *Modern Times,* Rey Chow explicates a second layer of automatization beyond the disciplining effects of mechanized labor: "Being 'automatized' means being subjected to social exploitation whose origins are beyond one's individual grasp, but it also means becoming a spectacle whose 'aesthetic' power increases with one's increasing awkwardness and helplessness. The production of the 'other' in this sense is both the production of class and aesthetic/cognitive difference."[96] She adds "the moment of visualization coincides, in effect, with an inevitable dehumanization in the form of a physically automatized object, which is produced as spectacular excess" (61).

The enforced visibility of women who work in military prostitution and sex tourism is even more persistently yet uncritically staged. That these frequently photographed bodies have become iconic of the large, complex transnational political economies of military prostitution and sex tourism is evident in the cover image of a 1993 *Time* magazine special issue on "world prostitution," which featured a Thai woman perched on the lap of a white male customer in a Bangkok bar.[97] Granted, the spatial structuring of sexual entertainment itself highlights the to-be-looked-at-ness of those particular workers who dance, strip, and perform live sex acts for the foreign male audience. The voyeuristic pleasure of the bars and clubs is taken to the by-now-infamous extreme of establishments that feature "one-way glass windows behind which are displayed dozens of women who can be selected by patrons according to the numbers pinned to their dresses."[98] However, I am interested in how these working bodies are "put on display" a second time through their photographic representation in various critical and analytical *studies* of these political-economic phenomena. In the past decade there have been a plethora of film and video documentaries on sex tourism and military prostitution, some of which have been produced by Asian American women. These include *The Good Woman of Bangkok* (dir. Dennis O'Rourke, 1991), *Sin City Diary* (dir. Rachel Rivera, 1993), *A Woman Being in Asia* (dir. Byun Young Joo, 1993), *The Women Outside* (dirs. Hye Jung Park and J. T. Takagi, 1995), and *Camp Arirang* (dirs. Diana Lee and Grace Lee, 1995). In addition to these moving images, many essays and books on the subject make some, if not extensive, use of photographs of the sex workers. More so than in film and video, these print textual representations beg the question of if and why the photographs of the denuded Asian women's bodies are necessary to their stated aims of exposing and critically analyzing the transnational phenomena. As a partial response, I will present a close reading of one particularly troubling text in this regard: *Let the Good Times Roll: Prostitution and the U.S. Military,* jointly authored by Saundra Pollock Sturdevant and Brenda Stoltzfus.

Let us begin by lingering on the material body of *Let the Good Times Roll* and keep in mind how a book like this is marketed as an appealing purchase to a prospective reader. The back cover announces:

> In *Let the Good Times Roll,* the women of the bar areas around U.S. bases in Okinawa, the Philippines, and the southern part of Korea speak about their lives with remarkable candor. In gripping and poignant narratives they describe their families and childhoods, the poor rural and urban areas they come from, life and work in the bar areas, and their attitudes

toward the bar owners, the American customers, and themselves. Two hundred powerful black-and-white photographs make vivid the lives, cultures, and economies that have been hidden from most Americans for so long.

Sturdevant is credited with having taken the photographs while Stoltzfus conducted the interviews on which the nine "oral herstories" are based: two Korean women and seven Filipinas, five who work in the Philippines and two who work in Okinawa. In addition to the photographs and life stories, the book includes short essays by feminist scholars and area specialists Aida F. Santos, Bruce Cumings, and Cynthia Enloe. This composite of three very different genres offers an interesting case study of *how* the titular subject of U.S. military prostitution in Asia can be apprehended and represented.

I will begin with the matter of whether and how the two hundred photographs are significant to this particular account. That these images have the power to "make vivid" the complex immensity of "lives, cultures, and economies" is confidently assumed, especially *against* their prior suppression and invisibility and specifically *for* the knowing-viewing agency identified as "most Americans." The illuminating value of these pictures is further buttressed in the preface as Sturdevant and Stoltzfus recount how it was "very difficult" and "almost impossible" to take them in often uncooperative circumstances, given that "a Euro-American woman photographing on the streets and in the bars with one or two cameras around her neck stood out."[99] The admittedly striking *difference* of the photographing subject here barely hints at the unequal political-economic terms of belonging and mobility, which enable and obstruct her representational endeavor. Her power to frame and shoot is immediately submerged in a celebratory milieu conducive to the willing cooperation of those being photographed: "However, the atmosphere on the streets and bars was one of partying, with a number of bar owners and managers giving permission to photograph." They add, "the few requests not to take pictures were immediately complied with." That the bar owners and managers allowed Sturdevant to photograph some scenes but not others, even if this was a rare case, qualifies the "authenticity" of these black-and-white images. The question of who decides to take a picture and of what becomes inverted as a question of who wanted a picture of what taken. Left out in this peculiar negotiation of permission and compliance between the "Euro-

American woman" and the "bar owners and managers" are the U.S. sol-
diers-customers and, more significantly, the Filipina and Korean women
whose variously denuded, numbered, contorted, and ogled working bodies are most prominently displayed in the book. Considering such representational force and unevenness, their "difficulty" is less a self-critical
acknowledgment of epistemological and methodological limitations in
composing the book than an additional promotion of these photographs as
ethically sound and, as such, more hard-earned and credible.

If they neglect to take up the thorny questions of their own representational motivation and practice, Sturdevant and Stoltzfus do articulate a
certain consciousness of a terrain of discursive struggle around the subject.
First, they describe an absence, or, more accurately, suppression of accounts
about the women who work in U.S. military prostitution: "It is almost as
if a shroud of silence has hovered over them in Vietnam, the Philippines,
Korea, Thailand, Okinawa, and Japan. The silence exists both because
prostituted women in the Third World are not considered important
enough to take note of and because the U.S. does not want publicity about
the GIs' off duty hours" (315). Second, they point out that "when the silence is broken and journalists, academics, and others write about this
topic, two dominant and seemingly disparate images come into play" (316).
Labeling these as "the happy hooker" and "the victim," they criticize these
"bad" images for "their simplistic and superficial treatment of prostituted
women . . . [which does] injustice to the variety and complexity of the
women's lives" (316). By obscuring their true depth and heterogeneity,
these flattened depictions prevent "most Americans" from identifying with
these Asian women:

> A primary function that such images as victim, ago-go dancer, and dis-
> eased—to add one more—serve is that of creating and maintaining dis-
> tance. Whether she is morally reprehensible, politically hopeless, a victim
> of poverty, or diseased, she is Other. She is in a different class, the class of
> women required by the U.S. military for the morale of its boys. Such dis-
> tance is important for the continuation of the bar areas and control over
> the women. (316)

Rather than extending their critique to consider how their own imaging
departs from or reproduces such representational tendencies, all their in-
dignant talk about the distancing effected through such stereotypes works

to distinguish their own well-meaning account from these misguided predecessors. If distance and depthlessness are the problems, Sturdevant and Stoltzfus pose intimacy and empathy with the women as methods of a better representation. In its assertion of "how different something appears when seen from the perspective of the women" (317), the following sentence slides seamlessly from the point of view of the women to the vision of Stoltzfus and Sturdevant: "Their lives, however, have rarely been photographed with much depth or complexity." Implicit in this critique is a promise that their visual rendering of the women will be deep and complex.

The question of *how* photography can mechanically reproduce the depth and complexity of human lives is displaced and enshrouded by a persistent recourse to the even greater truth of these women's "voices" as what *really matter.* Classifying the "women's life herstories" along with the photographs as the two "primary documents in this book," Sturdevant and Stoltzfus take some pains to explicate their methodological approach, first in the face-to-face interviews conducted with the women featured and later in their transcription and translation of those conversations. Fueled by the conviction that "in keeping with the goal of providing a venue for the women to speak about their lives, it was important to minimize the role of the interviewer," they relate their own very particular position as investigating subjects as follows:

> When dealing with matters of content, Brenda attempted to ask questions in as neutral a way as possible. However, complete neutrality and objectivity are not possible. In the Philippines the fact of the prior relationship between Brenda and the interviewees was a factor, whether large or small, in how the women told their stories. The authors' bias is that this relationship, where trust had been established, has resulted in the women speaking very freely about their lives. In Okinawa, however, the women also spoke with surprising openness. This could be attributed in part to the cathartic effect of telling one's story to someone who speaks your language and is sincerely interested in your life. (ix)

Rather than qualifying their visual and linguistic representation, this acknowledgment of possible "bias" claims a more intimate access to their interviewees, who might not have revealed so much to a less familiar and trustworthy interviewer. The authors' decision to identify seven of the nine women interviewed on a first-name basis only as Madelin, Lita, Manang, Glenda, Linda, Nan Hee, and Janet further reinforces this claim of intimacy.[100] These women are thus figured as almost unwitting speaking subjects whose life stories gush forth from their photographically documented bodies. Rather than insisting on another truth as hidden behind these tactics of creating a sense of immediacy and transparency, I would be interested in a further elaboration and explication of these dialogic terms and conditions: neutral interrogation, very free speech, anticipated degree of openness, and the relay of sincere interest.

Sturdevant and Stoltzfus also emphasize their avowed fidelity in the act of translation. Here, they admit that their "bias was toward keeping the original meaning even if the terminology was not necessarily what one would use in English, while also trying to allow the story to flow smoothly." Reminding their would-be readers that "these are oral herstories that have been transcribed, not written literature," they again stress, "Editing was done for reasons of length, the flow of the story, and redundancy. Words were not put in any woman's mouth" (ix–x). The conflicting protocols of translation between faithfulness to the original and regulating length and coherence in the second language are managed here through a faith in the process of transcription, *not* as the displacing transformation of spoken word to written text that it is, but as a correspondence of spoken word and its scriptive symbol. This is where the importance of the photographs comes into play in helping the multiply removed readers of this book to visualize a real body as the material origin and guarantor of these nine first-person life stories. Each story is told as uninterrupted first-person narration without any discernible breaks or traces of the interview questions that might have elicited the specific details. The interventions of the authors are visible only in the endnotes where they provide some supplementary data, relevant statistics, and English translations of the scattered Tagalog or Korean words and phrases.

If their methodological mediations are largely effaced in the composition of the individual life stories and their accompanying photographs, *Let the Good Times Roll* ends with a concluding essay by Sturdevant and Stoltzfus, which they describe in the preface as inaugurating "the process of pulling together threads from the other sources into an interpretive analysis" (x). Immediately qualifying that this task "is not a comprehensive academic analysis—deliberately not so," they explain: "To provide a comprehensive and structured analysis would be to take away from the voices of the women, and, in fact, to perpetuate the kind of domination already endured by them from various quarters. Such theorizing and analyzing would best be done by the women, themselves, who sell their sexual labor. We look forward to that day." By repudiating their necessary *work* of analysis and theorization as a gesture of epistemological domination of the women's *voices,* Sturdevant and Stoltzfus make it unthinkable that the subjects of these stories could possibly attempt such *thinking.* However, they also reserve for these women a special theoretical and analytical wisdom but relegate its potential articulation to an uncertain future, implying that "that day" has yet to arrive. In this separation and hierarchical valuation of the existing protocols of "academic and structured analysis" and the "women's voices," Sturdevant and Stoltzfus attempt to align and ally their own compositional construction with the latter, thereby eliding their own transnational agency in imposing coherence, and meaning onto the women's bodies and their lives. But this distinction disavows how *Let the Good Times Roll* is marked and marketed as a "Women's Studies/Asian Studies" book.

Against such elevation and relegation of the women's "voices" to a distant possibility, I would emphasize the awkward transnational work of rendering these subjects intelligible under specifically American regimes of representation and knowledge dissemination. If it may be easier to dismiss the constitutive superficiality of photographic reproduction, what about a graphic mode that promises a more probing and rigorous account of the distant "Asian women"—ethnography? Before considering this composition, I would recall the diacritically troubling and geopolitically unwieldly "Asian/American women" as a figure *for* epistemological critique of the prevailing division of knowledge and distribution of expertise. Which disciplines are charged with and most adequate for the study of the transnational laboring sites? Here a key challenge has been to account for the broader national and international dynamics that produce a certain racially and gender-specific class of laboring bodies linked by a common subordination to transnational capital *and* to attest to the individual and local experiences of these women as subjects and agents. The divisions of the social sciences into separate disciplines that study the political, economic, social, or cultural realms has exacerbated this dilemma.

A skewed tension between the "cultural" and the "economic" has marked the ascendance of development studies in the immediate postwar era as a significant intellectual and institutional site for the study of capitalist globalization and transnational labor. Arturo Escobar has discussed at length the "economic" bent of development studies. Noting the disciplinary training of the first WID advisor to the World Bank as a population economist, Escobar accents how the discursive proliferation around WID is an "institutionally constructed reality that is consonant with conceptualizations of development already put together in Washington, Ottawa, Rome, and Third World capitals" (179). The production and evaluation of certain standardized data such as annual per capita income also favored an economic conceptualization of problems and possible solutions. Against this disciplinary dominance, Escobar would argue that "culture" precedes and makes "economics." Here, he cites the work Charles Taylor on the "inscription of the economic onto the cultural":

> There are certain regularities which attend our economic behaviour, and which change only very slowly. . . . But it took a vast development of civilization before the culture developed in which people do so behave, in which it became a cultural possibility to act like this; and the discipline involved in so acting became widespread enough for this behavior to be generalized. . . . Economics can aspire to the status of science, and sometimes appear to approach it, because there has developed a culture in which a certain form of rationality is a (if not the) dominant value. (59)

When studied through the prism of what he calls "the anthropology of modernity," Escobar argues that the epistemological prioritization of the economic over the social and the cultural was reinforced by the functionalist demands of the postwar emergence of development agendas. He writes, "Development had to rely on the production of knowledge that could provide a scientific picture of a country's social and economic problems and resources. This entailed the establishment of institutions capable of generating such knowledge" (37). These sentences could be rewritten this way: "A scientific picture of a country's social and economic problems and resources was necessary to mandate the work of development." Given this mandate, Escobar suggests that economics was able to secure a more scientific grounding through development studies' emphasis on the total "area" or region to be studied rather than proceeding from the abstract and Eurocentric theories of the discipline as it had formed in relation to the "Western economy." If this accent on the "economic" was motivated by a belief that "the better and more widespread understanding of the workings of the economic system strengthened the hope of bringing material prosperity to the rest of the world," Escobar suggests that it also led to the slighting of the other dimensions. More than a benign neglect, the "organizing premise" of development economics was "the belief in the role of modernization as the only force capable of destroying archaic superstitions and relations at whatever social, cultural, and political cost" (39). Noting the exclusion of "people" from planning, Escobar later emphasizes that "culture was a residual variable, to disappear with the advance of modernization" (44).

Against the demotion of the cultural in development discourse, Escobar proposes "an approach to examining both the economy and its science as cultural constructions, a task for which few guideposts exist at this time" (58). He further casts what he labels "the Western economy" as not merely a "production system" but "an institution composed of systems of production, power, and signification" (59). All three systems, he adds, "should be seen as cultural forms through which human beings are made into producing subjects. The economy is not only, or even principally, a material entity. It is above all a cultural production, a way of producing human subjects and social orders of a certain kind." From this dematerialization of the economic as fundamentally and ultimately cultural, it follows that the transfiguration of "human beings" into "producing subjects" is also above all a cultural production. But what if these two generic categories were modified by gender, ethnicity, and nationality in the transfiguration of "Asian women" into "transnational labor"? The scare quotes around both subjects signal that *both* are discursive productions but also suggest that *each* works to materialize the other. It is a mistake to presuppose "Asian women" as analogous to "human beings" if what is meant by the latter is some primordial, generic ontology which precedes their degradation as "transnational labor" and to which they must be restored. Rather, their reciprocal consolidation works to elide how both are the products of certain regularities that attend our representational tactics in a culture in which it became a cultural possibility to act like this. This specification situates the previously surveyed si(gh)tings of Asian/American women *as* transnational labor in terms of what Escobar calls "cultural struggles" or "struggles not only for goods and services but also for the very definition of life, economy, nature, and society" (16).

I would extend this cultural framing to anthropological accounts of the subject. Reflecting on ethnography as the discipline's "distinctive mode of understanding reality," George E. Marcus credits its attentiveness to "the everyday life of those usually portrayed as victims" but also notes the slighting of "macrosociological questions" about "the constitution of major systems or processes." [101] Marcus contrasts the different underestandings of "culture" between the disciplinary assumptions of anthropology and the analytical framework of Marxism. While anthropologists are "accustomed to staging culture as a integral spatio-temporal isolate, not without its own internal contradictions, but at least with its own integrity against the world," Marcus argues, "This is much different from the Marxist emphasis, which views culture as a product of struggle; there is no self-contained integrity entailed in the concept." In a more extended elaboration that appears in the book *Anthropology and Cultural Critique,* coauthored with Michael M. J. Fischer, they credit June Nash along with Eric Wolf and Sidney Mintz for a "revitalization" of political-economy research in the discipline during the 1960s, but he also notes that "the status of culture and cultural analysis has been problematic in this most strongly developed strain of political-economy research within anthropology." [102]

The work of Aihwa Ong attempts what Marcus calls "an ethnography sensitive to its context of historical political economy." [103] Ong has published a monograph, *Spirits of Resistance and Capitalist Discipline: Factory Women in Malaysia* (1987), and several articles based on fieldwork "in and around free trade zones (FTZs) in Peninsular Malaysia from 1978 to 1980." [104] This work has sought to contest and to complicate a range of macrostructural frameworks and generic theoretical assumptions around industrialization, modernization, and class formation. In contrast to this critical stance, there is a repeated and confident invocation of disciplinary authority and specifically the method of fieldwork and ethnography. Ong's essay included in the 1983 collection *Women, Men, and the International Division of Labor* opens by rejecting "the labor aristocracy model" as "rather deterministic, obscuring social reality and the need for closer inspection of surface phenomena" (427). Instead, she goes on to assert that "anthropological research reveals that covert resistance and protests by local groups and isolated individuals are not absent below the surface political tranquility." Noting the "lack of a specific class consciousness" among "the semiskilled workers of the multinational corporations," Ong marshals both her own field observations and other anthropological studies to describe "Malay cultural prohibitions against expressions of anger and dissatisfaction," and adds, "Malay girls are socialized to be submissive and loyal in accordance with village notions of female modesty" (434).

In the preface to her expanded 1987 monograph, Ong states, "The voices of the neophyte factory women, in counterpoint to corporate images and in protest against public abuse, articulate an intersubjective mode of understanding the world." She then adds, "This study is thus a composition of many discordant voices, claiming no final authority. It is an unfolding story that remains to be told more fully by young women living in the shadowy recesses undisclosed by the electronic gaze of the twentieth century" (xv). Interwoven with these "voices" are maps, statistical tables, and black-and-white photographs of the field and its inhabitants. One photo shows "a factory woman doing the day's laundry before going to work" (98), while another shot of a factory interior with two women peering into microscopes is accompanied by the ironically quoted literary caption "'Through a glass darkly'" (176). As a common convention of "ethnographic realism," which proffers "some direct indication of fieldwork conditions and experiences," such visual documents as these photographs serve importantly as "symbolic markers of 'having really been there.'"[105] I wish to foreground the multiple temporalities enfolded in and by this weave of a present ethnographic inscription, an "unfolding story that remains to be told more fully" by the obscured voices of the "young women" and those female figures frozen photographically in the distant time-place of fieldwork. Studying this compositional flutter as a constitutive glitch of transnational knowledge production might suggest an intriguing alternative to the spatiotemporal fixing of Asian/American women as proper transnational labor.

In a 1990 essay that focuses on Malay women workers in Japanese TNC factories, Ong inscribes a more assured knowledge of her ethnographic subjects. While the fieldwork on which the article is based was undertaken in the years 1978–1980, Ong writes her account in the present tense, such as "Many women tell me they like to work in the factories mainly for the friends they make there" or "An operator reveals that 'I feel that if I work closely with men they will tell us whatever we ask'" ("Japanese Factories," 405–06). The Malay women workers that Ong interviewed are thus rendered in the text as synchronic figures of orality, sharing the time of the reader of this published account. While such ethnographic figurations may appear to surmount the problem of their spatiotemporal distancing,

I would cast them as implicating what Johannes Fabian has called the "aporetic composition" of anthropological findings. Marcus and Fischer explain:

> Ethnographies have in fact rarely reported what ethnographers actually see of the present in the field. There is a gap between the contemporaneity of fieldwork, during which the ethnographer and his subjects share the same immediate present, and the way these same subjects are temporally distanced from the back-home world of the ethnographer in his account derived from field research. (*Anthropology as Cultural Critique*, 96)

In composing a sense of intimacy and immediacy, the "ethnographic present" enables a smooth slide into penetrating and generic characterizations: "Kampung women who work in the nearby FTZ define their own self-images in opposition to the cultural alienation exhibited by urban-based workers" (415). Ong also claims that "the neophyte factory women identify with an intensified Islamic asceticism, which shapes a specific yet generic "gender consciousness of Malay factory women in rural Selangor" (422). Such knowing claims are set against the unwitting agency of the ethnographic subjects. Referring to the women's unarticulated "problems of felt oppression," Ong continues, "I wish here to discover, in the vocabulary and imagery of spirit possession, the unconscious beginnings of an idiom of protest against male control in the industrial situation" (417).

Recalling the "aporetic composition" of ethnography, I would underscore the disciplined transcription of these women workers into such legible subjectivities. James Clifford has argued that "so long as the guiding task of the work is to make the (often strange) behavior of a different way of life humanly comprehensible, ethnography's narrative of specific differences presupposes, and *always* refers to, an abstract plane of similarity." [106] In the review essay "The Gender and Labor Politics of Postmodernity," Ong moves from the focus on Malaysia and Malay factory women to a broader continental designation of "Asian women." It opens by asserting this temporal lag: "The literature on export-industrialization and the feminization of industrial work challenges theory to catch up with lived realities. Reports from the new frontiers of industrial labor reveal a widening gap between our analytical constructs and workers' actual experiences" (61). These "reports" are later characterized as "easily available studies, of uneven ethnographic and methodological quality, conducted between

1970 and 1990" (62), including her own 1987 monograph. In addition to the odd juxtaposition of a very broadly encompassing continent, Asia—which Ong sometimes interchanges with the more regionally specific designation of Southeast Asia—and a single, bounded nation-state, Mexico, Ong's discussion of "Asia" as a single unit has the effect of flattening out significant historical and geopolitical differences and discontinuities in the moments and sites of industrial labor as well as of ethnographic fieldwork. For instance, she marshals nationally and regionally specific studies published as early as 1981—which also means that the time of fieldwork was several years prior—to declare: "In Asia, the division of labor introduced by transnational firms separates managers and workers along lines of nationality, race, gender, and age. Central activities like research and finance are controlled by experts in the metropolitan headquarters, while the low-skilled and labor-intensive production processes employ young, poorly trained women in the offshore sites" (68). In thus referring to an ethnographic archive, Ong's overview discussion of workers and working conditions across Asia is split between a past tense inhabited by the ethnographic subjects and a present-tense accounting by those that Ong identifies as "ethnographers of Asian workers": "For instance, Salaff notes that in the Hong Kong working class, parents viewed daughters as 'poor long-term investments,' and working daughters saw themselves paying back their natal families. . . . In a Chinese Taiwan case, Kung observes that women working in FTZs fulfilled and expanded 'traditional roles/expectations of daughters.'" (69). The repeated invocation of the epistemological purchase of ethnographic research in these historically and geographically constrained studies enables certain synchronic, transnational generalizations about "Asian women" workers:

> Ethnographic findings reveal that disciplinary practices frequently define the industrial presentation and workings of the body. . . . electronics workers from Taiwan to Sri Lanka complain of the detail work that literally wears away at the "instruments of production"—for instance, eyes fitted to microscopes. Indeed, neophyte workers, whose sensibilities were shaped by peasant and/or preindustrial cultures, often challenge the work process for its dehumanizing effects and accompanying forms of social control. (73)

I would argue that rather than merely *found* over there and *reported* back here, such visceral yet generic attribution of laboring bodies and selves to "Asian women" works to materialize "ethnographic findings" but also to eclipse the particularly disciplined practices that produce and transmit such knowledges.[107]

In a more focused deliberation on the matter of ethnographic representation, Ong acknowledges how "a subfield of feminist discourse has expressed doubts as to the legitimacy and advisability of writing about other, less privileged women."[108] However, she argues, "ethnographic subjects can exercise power in the production of ethnographic knowledges," and explains: "How informants treat ethnographers, what they demand and withhold, is part of the process whereby they persuade us to provide 'a point of access' to cultural conversations in metropolitan centers. In recounting their stories of setbacks, courage, resourcefulness, and inventiveness, feminists help challenge and destabilize the truth-claims of Western cultural knowledges" ("Women Out of China," 353–54). It is important that the ethnographic subjects and the fieldwork location have shifted here from "Asian women" in Asia to informants that Ong identifies as "recent Asian female immigrants" in the United States, with whom she shares a "sense of shared marginalization in Chinese culture and history and in Western society that creates an ethnographic situation different from that of an ethnographer who descends into a village in some Third World country" (355). In expressing her "sympathy with their desire to change stereotypical Western perceptions of Chinese immigrant women," Ong accents the role of the ethnographer as a conduit *for* the informants' "life stories," which she upholds as "an especially powerful mechanism to convey authentic experiences and relationships between self and others." One more final detail to note is how Ong ends by framing this geographical location of ethnographic subjects and their ethnographers as demonstrating how "anthropology needs to reflect the postcolonial situations whereby we increasingly live inside, outside, and through East-West divisions."[109]

In this transnational, cross-generic, extradisciplinary reaching gesture, it appears that *Compositional Subjects* has come back to the messy matter of "life stories" *about* "Chinese immigrant women" *in* the United States. In the concluding chapter, I veer off yet again to track what I call "compositional struggles" in and through certain cultural productions by Korean/American women. I foreground specific works that grapple in compelling ways with the possibilities and limits of autobiographical, cinematic, historiographical, pictorial, photographic, and ethnographic representation that I have studied in the previous four chapters.

— historicize
— self reflexive
— med. of production ??
— disconnect temporal + spatial

Compositional Struggles

Re-membering Korean/American Women

The preceding four chapters have examined the agonistic interchanges amongst racial, national, ethnic, gender, and class designations that surface in varying accounts of Asian/American women across several compositional registers. The increasing legibility of Asian/American women through literary, cinematic, historiographic, photographic, and ethnographic inscriptions should not be reduced to a belated challenge of social particularity that can ultimately be incorporated into preexisting epistemological foundations. Instead, I have tried to show how the celebrated heralding of and the measured resistance to their relevance for "what really matters" can reveal much about the terms and conditions of emergence and belonging in a particular discipline. This final chapter turns to a select cluster of textual, pictorial, photographic, and cinematic compositions by Korean women, which critically and creatively *contend with*— rather than simply reproduce or repudiate—the fixations on and containments of Asian/American women that I have thus far analyzed. In thus narrowing my critical investigation to a more ethnonationally specific constituency, my aim is not to retreat into a more definite subpopulation that has been overlooked or marginalized within the larger grouping of Asian/American women. Instead, I continue to examine the categorical distinctions of "Asian," "Asian American," and "American" as they might bear on "women" in several directions. I have selected a cluster of works that interrogate the troubled interplay of ethnic, national, and racial identifications. All of the writers and artists whose work I discuss comprise that grouping of Koreans referred to as *il-chom o-se* or "1.5 generation," who were born in Korea but emigrated elsewhere as children. Their spatial-temporal liminality cannot be captured by the distinctions of native-born/foreign-born or Asian or American. While most of the works I will discuss are articulated from a U.S. location, I have chosen to include two very provocative pieces by Korean Canadian artist Jin-me Yoon in an effort to point to a multinational Korean diaspora that has been facilitated by an earlier history of U.S. military forays into the Korean peninsula. Although my inclusion of Yoon within the category of "Korean/American women" risks reasserting the hegemony of the United States in claiming the identification of "American" as a nationality, I again emphasize the intervening slash to mark the incomplete and precarious induction of Koreans as "Americans" in the United States. Furthermore, the comparative examination of Asian racialization and multiculturalism in the United States and Canada in these works may afford an opportunity to consider the different valences of a Korean identification beyond the binary axis of originary home and migratory destination.

The shifting and uncertain location of these works within and across the nation-state borders of Korea, the United States, and Canada complicates any fixed, homogeneous notion of both individual and collective identity as rooted in a single place, state, or culture. Instead, they interrogate the presuppositions of "rootedness" that work in various contexts to confine women "at home"—in the private sphere, in the patriarchal family with its matrix of compulsory heterosexuality, and in terms of a singular ethnonational loyalty—or to exclude them from claiming "home" in host countries in the context of immigration. In addition to contesting their categorization as *Asian Canadian* or *Asian American*, these Korean/American cultural productions demand consideration in relation to two other prevailing categories of identification. While their exploration of the historical imbrications of the United States in (South) Korea accent a Korean American *postcoloniality*, their sustained yet complicated *diasporic* orientations toward the Korean homeland unsettle any sense of the national boundaries of the United States—and Canada—as impermeable and autonomous.

These works also demand attention to their evidently awkward and often forced construction. They are critically engaged with the pitfalls of the desire for representation and the will to knowledge, some of which I have pointed to in the previous chapters: the transparency of language, the discreteness and telos of autobiography, the conciliatory resolution of narrative cinema, the selective production and maintenance of official archives, the elision of the constitutive force of dictation—the conversion of the spoken interview to the written text—and translation in ethnography, and the objectification of documentary photography. Their often fragmented, halting, and intertextual composition highlight the very doubts and dilemmas that confront cultural production against the disabling legacy of multiple colonizations, intranational divisions, diasporic scattering, racialization, and reculturation. In thus grappling with the very terms, conditions, and apparatus of legibility and visibility, these works are engaged in what I would call *compositional struggles* in two ways. First, all knowledge-claims and representational endeavors respond to, even if to contest, a range of prior claims and representations. Second, this always already embedded production necessitates attention not only to *what* is said but to questions of *why* and *how* this articulation differs from those previous claims. Put differently, such dialogical exigencies force attention to not only the content but the form, style, context, and material circuits of knowledge and representation. They are critical re-memberings of identity and its possible composition.

In placing these materially diverse cultural productions alongside and against each other, I seek to counter several persistent tendencies in their interpretation and reception. Despite their performative and deconstructive stagings, these works have not been immune to the kind of generic fixation that claims to see them as spoken by a singularly raced and gendered self, who is speaking for a larger ethnic or national constituency. On the other hand, if their attentiveness to the formal manipulations and material mediations of the apparatus of representation—writing, photography, and cinematography—resists such mimetic and metonymic closure, these works are alternately read only for their formal eccentricities and theoretical engagements, which often elide the significance of their critical investments in a very specific Korean/American history of colonization, immigration, racialization, and diasporic attachments.[1] The reading of an individual work as either ethnically generic or formally exceptional can be fortified when studied in isolation, especially under their respective disciplinary rubrics of literary studies, film studies, or art history. My focus on the resonant and particular ways in which each work is invested in and skeptical of both identification and representation seeks to resist such critical and disciplinary enclosures. We could then consider how they might challenge modes of representation and knowledge production in other disciplinary terrains such as history and anthropology.

While the works I survey attest to the political and epistemological possibilities opened up by the emergence of Korean/American women as investigating and representing subjects of scholarship, creative writings, and visual culture, I end by considering how they demand a critical reconsideration of how certain knowledge-claims and representational endeavors are authorized across different sites of interdisciplinary study. Put very schematically, Asian American studies and other ethnic studies—and, I would add, women's studies—often sanction an epistemological authority of "being," wherein the investigating or representing subject's shared racial-ethnic *identity* with her object(s) of study can imbue knowledge-claims with an especial legitimacy and experiential wisdom. In contradistinction, certain research and representational endeavors under the rubric of area studies often derive their epistemological authority from having "been-there,"[2] a more temporary relation of proximity through habitation of the place, region, nation, and/or area that one studies. In addition to language training, "fieldwork" experience in the place that one studies is a crucial requirement of area specialization.

Any easy distinction between or ranking of the epistemological assurances of "being" and "been-there"—between a more fixed and enduring ontology and an ascribed identity, on the one hand, and a more mobile and measured habitation and elective vocation, on the other—is interestingly troubled by the dynamic body of knowledge-claims by and about "women" in certain continental, national, and regional areas outside of the United States as well as those "women of color" in the United States, which could stake a claim to belong within two or all three rubrics. I end this chapter and this book on a more cautious note by considering how the epistemological and representational authority of "being" and "been-there" are marshaled by two film/video documentaries that have been produced by "Korean American" women on the subject of Korean women and U.S. military prostitution in Korea. While the subjects and locales depicted might place these documentaries under Asian studies or Korean studies, the identity of their producers and their exhibition and distribution in the United States situate them as part of the ongoing efforts by variously minoritized racial-ethnic groups to be active agents of the knowledge production about themselves. Then, too, the gendered and sexual dimensions of the topic, the Korean women pictured, and the gender identity of the documenting agents command their inclusion in women's studies. Such newly eccentric composites demand careful *and* critical interrogation.

I will begin with Theresa Hak Kyung Cha's *Dictée* because the book has been so important for not only myself but for several other emerging Korean/American writers and scholars.[3] *Dictée* is an internally diverse, fragmented, and contradictory text that precludes thematic encapsulation and generic fixation. Multilingually composed of parts in French, English, Greek, Chinese, and Korean, *Dictée* incorporates a range of compositions from translation exercises, Catholic religious texts, journalistic accounts, political petitions, and journal entries. In addition to these reprinted citations, there are several photographic reproductions of different found inscriptions: typed and handwritten letters, two full pages of what appears to be a scribbled draft by Cha in the process of writing the book, and a note etched into the walls of a Japanese mine by a Korean laborer. Many other visual images are also scattered throughout, ranging from several individual and group portraits of Korean women, historical photographs of Japanese colonial persecution of Koreans, including a mass anticolonial rally, a simple map of the divided Korean peninsula, anatomical diagrams in both English and Chinese, and still images from films such as Carl Dreyer's *Joan of Arc*.

The heterogeneous composition of the book could be read as accounting for the multicultural and multinational pressures that have wrought the peculiar and crisscrossed genealogy of a Korean/American female subject. While it includes significant details of the author's family history, the book rejects the singular narration and developmental trajectory of the autobiography, instead figuring identity as both internally fractured and embedded in other persons, discourses, and histories. Consequently, *Dictée* interrogates the broader historical and political grounds for delineating sameness and difference by presenting several instances of distinguished, unequal yet conjoined subject-positions: visitor-host, immigrant-native, mother-daughter, husband-wife, colonizer-colonized, student-teacher, performer-audience, addresser-addressee, protester-soldier, penitent-judge. The book points to the division of Korea into two adjoining yet hostile nation-states as a particularly striking illustration of the paradox of identity; the distinction of a "Korean" ethnonationality has been constituted by a long history of multiple foreign invasions, colonial recultrations, and transnational migrations. Such a manifold yet discontinuous genealogy propels a critical reworking of the fixed terms of both social identification and linguistic-visual representation, as demonstrated throughout the book.

Dictée illuminates how the authorized forms and methods of linguistic expression serve to legitimate certain social positions over others. The systematic suppression of the native language in favor of the colonizer's language, the patriarchal idealization of female silence, the racist devaluation of "pidgin" English, the religious obligation to make a true confession, and the classroom exercises for inducting students into normative grammar and spelling are all invoked as instances in which language is a formidable medium of social, political, and psychic subjection. Inasmuch as the postcolonial immigrant subject must bear the brunt of the differential authorization of identity via language, she also understands the capricious and forceful ways in which language is ordered and normalized to privilege certain speaking and writing bodies over others. The page numbered one in *Dictée* contains two paragraphs, the first written in French and the second in English. Describing a sparse verbal exchange between a traveling female subject and the "natives," the passages present the difficulty of expression and communication in a new environment as she cannot answer a seemingly innocuous query—"How was the first day?" The question seeks an account of the beginning of immigration and resettlement. As such, the very fact of its asking and any possible response can only reinforce the gulf between the recently transplanted female and the local "families." Both exchanges end not with a polite, coherent reply but an awkward assertion of her displaced status in both the French and English settings:

> . . . dire le moins possible virgule la résponse serait virgule ouvre les guillemets Il n'y a qu'une chose point ferme les guillemets Il y a quel qu'une point loin point ferme les guillemets

. . . at least to say the least of it possible comma the answer would be open quotation marks there is but one thing period There is someone period From a far period close quotation marks. (1)

The interrogators' expectations of a first-person telling are foiled by the striking absence of an "I" in the response. Instead, the response is cast as a generic third-person statement, as if referring to some other (ungendered) traveler.

Rather than some descriptive and anecdotal reportage, both paragraphs in French and in English are written out as detailed dictation, which shifts the context to the classroom and the unequal relationship of instructor and student. In a brilliant reading of what she calls the book's "aesthetics of infidelity," Lisa Lowe has pointed out that, in commanding the student to write out exactly what is spoken, "the founding premise of dictation recognizes an initial incommensurability between the oral and the written, revealing the purported aim of that identical reproduction to be internally contradictory."[4] By writing out each grammatical instruction, this perversely obedient writing subject also impedes the smooth, coherent flow of the narrative content of the passage, exposing a structural mismatch between language acquisition and authentic expression.

This impossibility of identical reproduction is further underscored as also a problem of translation. Pointing out significant differences between the French and English passages, Lowe reads this second staging of "non-equivalence" as a critique of the assumption of linguistic equivalence behind the ideal of faithful translation. She writes: "The ethos [of fidelity] not only levels and minimizes linguistic differences, but the presumption of equivalence masks the hierarchy of cultures operating in any differentiated linguistic relationship; the power of one nation state to determine not merely the language but the material conditions of another people is rendered largely invisible" (42). Rather than an experiential account of a female migrant, these passages of unruly dictation and "unfaithful" translation offer "a fictionalized amalgam that allegorizes the influences of both American imperialism and the earlier French missionary colonialism" (40). Thus, a third meaning of the first page emerges; from a telling story about the traveling woman to a transcribed exercise in dictation and translation, the page textually stages the competing linguistic force of two foreign incursions that preceded Korean immigration to the United States. Finally, this opening also foregrounds the ways in which different languages are hierarchically gendered. Pointing to how "the neutered translation of the female 'quequ'une' as 'someone' precisely underscores female gender as the particularity that proves untranslatable," Lowe adds, "In the dictation, femininity constitutes the deviant detail that makes visible the normalization of masculinity in the English language" (42).

Along with this rejection of assimilation, there is also an acknowledgment of the impossibility of an easy and immediate return to an untransformed Korean past with its mother tongue. After years of living abroad, the emigrant returns to Korea only to be met with suspicious queries and persistent reminders of her estrangement: "They ask you identity. They comment upon your ability and inability to speak. Whether you are telling the truth or not about your nationality. They say you look other than you say. As if you didn't know who you were" (57). There is yet another painful breach between this returning emigrant and the local natives. Later, when the narrator declares, "I speak in another tongue now, a second tongue, a foreign tongue" (80), she must transcribe this admission in the "foreign" English, which doubly inscribes the displacement of the "first" tongue. The coercive intimacies of language and identity are exacerbated by transnational migrations and resettlements, disrupting the fantasy of cultural identity as geographically circumscribable and inextricably affiliated with one corresponding language.

Given this multiple linguistic displacement, rather than presenting the struggle over language as the particular onus of the immigrant, *Dictée* continually points to the arbitrary and narrow rules of linguistic structures that mediate all enunciative efforts. The forceful and laborious aspects of language acquisition and of writing are thus highlighted in the book over and against any naturalized and often nativist terms of fluency. Such unnatural constructedness of language and literature is muted by the implicit and explicit hierarchies of differentially authorized speaking or writing positions, which often support differential social valuations along the axes of ethnicity, class, and gender. Instead of attempting to prove the (exceptional) linguistic command of one Korean immigrant subject, the book opens up a questioning of the racialized and gendered valuations of linguistic authority. For example, there are the strategic incorporations of "pidgin" or broken English, which is commonly associated with immigrants and specifically Asians in the United States and often invoked as a racist stereotype to degrade and dismiss its speakers. In a second set of translation exercises, there is a lengthy passage of such pidgin English:

> She call she believe she calling to she has calling
>
> because there no response she believe she calling . . .
> she hide all essential words link subject verb (15)

The incorporation of these words into the book without any readily identifiable ethnicized speaker or context contests the nativist and elitist requirements of correct speech and good literature. Directed to "translate" these words into French, the reader must grapple with them as comprehensible means of expression and in so doing question our own assumptions about linguistic normality and proficiency. Furthermore, given the book's pervasive focus on division and separation, brokenness here reflects the fundamental alienation of the speaking subject in language rather than signaling lack and otherness: "Cracked tongue. Broken tongue. Pidgeon. Semblance of speech" (75).

Even while the postcolonial immigrant is thus alienated and silenced along the many axes of language and social positioning, she is not completely innocent of their authorizing structures and effects. In a passage written as a religious confession, the penitent writes:

> *I am making up the sins. For the guarantee of ab-*
> *solution. In the beginning again, at zero. Before*
> *Heaven even. Before the Fall. All previous*
> *wrongs erased. Reduced to spotless. Pure . . .*
> *I am making the confession. To make words.*
> *To make a speech in such tongues. (16–17)*

The speaking subject of this Catholic contrition must submit to a ritualized form and more importantly to the requirement of truth, leaving little room for any act of personal imagination or invention in language. The religious overtones also point to the mythical sacrality of languages that further inhibits any deviation, even as it serves to buttress certain ethnic, gender, and class positions over others. "Making up" can mean atonement for some internalized wrongdoing or supplementing some accepted lack and deficiency.

"Making up" can also be taken as a conscious construction and even falsification. In thus authoring her own sins, she commits yet another transgression of the given commandments of enunciatory propriety, gesturing to her own powers of willful creation. Even more perversely, she deconstructs the hierarchical relationalities of disclosure and judgment that rely on and uphold absolutist truths. The confessional mode, which is closely associated with the genre of autobiography, is gradually transformed not as some unconscious emission of an individual truth but a calculated resolve "to make words" not under one linguistic system but in pluralized "tongues" and for various effects. If complicity and submission are built into language-use, literary production can also be a vehicle of linguistic recreations and ideological resistance: "She would take on their punctuation. She waits to service this. Theirs. Punctuation. . . . Seize upon the punctuation" (4). As in the ambivalent and split implications of her "making up" *her* sins, she will "take on" *their* language can mean not that she will assume the faithful execution of these rules of articulation, but that she will challenge their very definition and usage. This textual project is similarly transgressive both in content *and* in form. As such, it resists any autobiographical fixation that would reduce the text to some individual and sociological verity. *Dictée* continually frustrates the desire to locate a single person between its covers, redirecting attention to the illusory and capricious powers of language and to its own peculiar materiality as textual production.[5]

While the book so deftly problematizes language and literary production from several social and cultural locations, it is also a powerful exploration of the troubled contours of modern Korean history. The multiply layered foreign domination of Korea explodes any natural or commonsensical association between political autonomy, territorial integrity, and a continuous history. The long period of Japanese colonial rule, a devastating three-year "civil war," the division of the country, the postwar social unrest, the massive emigration of Koreans and the neocolonial domination of Korea by the United States are invoked throughout the book. This continuing history of intra-Korean conflict and splitting is significantly manifest in and through language. Noting "the different names for Korea claimed by North and South (*Chosen* and *Taehan Minkuk* respectively)," Elaine H. Kim writes:

The South Korean National Security Law long forbade citizens to speak about reunification or about North Korea except in negative terms. Under the provisions of that same law, making statements that might aid the "enemy"—North Korea—was punishable by imprisonment: for example, in the 1970s descriptions of the living conditions of Koreans around the U.S. military bases were considered taboo because they might "aid the enemy." The Korean language has been mutilated and manipulated in the interest of preserving the polarity between North and South Korea: certain words, such as *tong-mu* (friend, comrade), *uk-ap* (oppression) or *in-min* (the people, the masses) have not been used in South Korea because they connoted "Communism."[6]

The book intervenes into the distancing and marginalization of these historical episodes as having happened to other people at another time by pointing to their enduring significance, especially in the disruptions and separations that continue to this day. Just as it problematizes the generic parameters of autobiography, it draws critical attention to the writing of history as a discursive production that illuminates and occludes certain details. Rather than attempting a narrative recuperation of some smooth and discrete national history, *Dictée* foregrounds the historiographical dilemma of attempting to access the past by way of previously written accounts. For the task of redressing an episode, event, or person excluded from previous histories, the critical historiographer must "take on" those other accountings that have contributed to such erasure. There is no clean detour from this discursive web so that even as her own historiographical effort may have been impelled by the inadequacy or inaccuracy of these other accounts, she must recite them even as she attempts to contest those surviving documents. Furthermore, whatever information was gathered from records, monuments, archives, and primary and secondary texts is synthesized, ordered, and renarrated in the here and now. Every turn in this process calls attention to inaccessibility of the past as self-evident fact and forces a reckoning with the historiographical operation as a mediating and productive inscription.

The entire "Clio/History" section is a laying bare of precisely such detours, borrowings, and contortions in the writing of history. There are lengthy citations of three unidentified accounts, all ostensibly written by non-Koreans, describing the Japanese colonial domination of Korea. The

first is a clearly uninvested description of Japanese abuses, which nevertheless makes facile generalizations about both Japanese and Korean psy-
chologies. A few paragraphs later appears the second citation. These two
paragraphs are set off with two sets of quotation marks, signaling Cha's recitation as triply mediated. Once again written from the point of view of a
non-Korean, non-Japanese foreigner, this description of the violent clashes
between Japanese military forces and Korean insurgents is more critical of
Japanese actions and policies than the first foreign account. The following
citation appears under the title "SUPPRESSION OF FOREIGN CRITICISM" and
is dated 26 September 1907. Set off with a single set of quotation marks,
this reportage reads:

> We are informed that a bad fight took place about eight miles from Su-
> won on Sunday, September 12th. Thirty volunteers were surrounded by
> Japanese troops, and although no resistance was offered, they were shot
> down in the most cold-blooded fashion. This not being quite enough to
> satisfy the conquerors, two other volunteers who had been captured were
> brought out and were decapitated by one of the officers. We may men-
> tion that this news does not come from native sources; it comes from Eu-
> ropean. (31–32)

This most visceral critical documentation of Japanese atrocities against Koreans is most remarkable in its implicit distrust of "native sources." How is
the Korean diasporic subject to retrieve and reinvoke this "Korean" history
given this marked denial of Koreans as historical witnesses in the privileged
archives?

Right

If, as Elaine H. Kim points out, "Korean women's experiences of history have been buried under layers of male narratives, Korean, Chinese,
Japanese, and Western" (14), Cha does not simply turn to "native" sources
or official Korean archives to remember this history. In focusing attention
on two female subjects, the anti-colonial activist Yu Guan Soon and Cha's
mother Hyung Soon Huo, Cha resists the linear and authoritative narration of disciplined history. The three citations of foreign accounts in
the "Clio/History" section are interspersed with several paragraphs on the
young Korean woman patriot, Yu Guan Soon. Cha's biographical composition is striking in both its air of familiarity, referring to the subject by her
first name, and its present-tense narration:

Guan Soon is the only daughter born of four children to her patriot father and mother. From an early age her actions are marked exceptional. History records the biography of her short and intensely-lived existence. Actions prescribed separate her path from the others. The identity of such a path is exchangeable with any other heroine in history, their names, dates actions which require not definition in their devotion to generosity and self-sacrifice. (30)

As the passage proceeds beyond its initial provision of a few generic details about this figure, it becomes evident that this is not so much about this individual woman–patriot or the Japanese colonial abuses in Korea but the narrativizing apparatus of history, and specifically the generically restricted and contradictory positions it allocates for female subjects. Being "marked exceptional" for one's "self-sacrifice" points to the impossible generic fixation of women within many nationalist narratives. The passage notes the paradoxical historiographical operation that simultaneously privileges the individual as *unique* in her historical context and yet renders her a *generic* figure of self-denial in a broader discourse. Here, then, "the only daughter" who proves herself to be an "exceptional" actor in her historical milieu becomes transcribed as "any other heroine in history." The unidentified actor of the various transitive verbs "marked" and "prescribed" displaces the historical agency of the putative subject, which is presumably the reason for her especial memorialization in the first place.[7]

The book's reflections on twentieth-century Korean history are as much concerned with an effective mode of communicating across geographical distances as with memorializing the past. A crucial question here is the lack of foreign intervention into the colonial atrocities committed by Japan given the fact that such trustworthy, nonnative "eye-witness accounts" were available at the time. In so doing, Cha takes the concern about transnational communication and intervention beyond the narrow boundaries of a solely "Korean" problem:

To the other nations who are not witnesses, who are not subject to the same oppressions, they cannot know. Unfathomable the words, the terminology: enemy, atrocities, conquest, betrayal, invasion, destruction. They exist only in the larger perception of History's recording, that affirmed, admittedly and unmistakably, one enemy nation has disregarded the humanity of another. Not physical enough. Not to the very flesh and bone, to the core, to the mark, to the point where it is necessary to intervene, even if to invent anew, new expressions, for this experience, for this outcome, that does not cease to continue.

To the others, these accounts are about (one more) distant land, like (any other) distant land, without any discernible features in the narrative, (all the same) distant like any other. (33)

If such repetitive invocations of distance would try to rationalize and naturalize international detachment, Cha connects histories of Korea and the United States by full recitation of the "Petition from the Koreans of Hawaii to President Roosevelt." Written in Honolulu and dated 12 July, 1905, the letter presents a strenuously proper request by the Korean immigrant community for the United States to intervene on behalf of Korean independence from Japan. The Roosevelt administration did not respond positively to this request, indeed going on to sign the Taft-Katsura pact later that same year. As Elaine H. Kim points out, "This agreement allowed Japan free reign in Korea in return for her promise to allow the U.S. to dominate the Philippines, which had recently been acquired in the Spanish-American War" (10). Furthermore, until the formal end of Japanese colonial rule in 1945, the U.S. government continued to consider Koreans as "Japanese" nationals, subjecting them to the same restrictive immigration laws. Testifying to the early presence of Koreans in the United States, their abiding love for the Korean homeland in the face of both their geographical separation and its internal colonization, and the crucial role of the United States in the political fate of Korea in the twentieth century, the letter shrinks the transpacific expanse between the two lands and their histories to reveal a significant complicity and imbrication.

As it contracts geopolitical boundaries, *Dictée* also troubles temporal distinctions. Rather than accepting the relegation of Japanese colonization and the Korean War into the remote and finite past, these events are reinscribed in terms of their lingering significance in the present. The "Calliope/Epic Poetry" section reinscribes the mother's exile from the colonized Korean homeland as an important pre-text for the daughter's later emigration to the United States. Significantly, this narration begins at the moment of the mother's relocation away from her natal family to teach under the dictates of the Japanese imperial regime:

> Mother you are eighteen. It is 1940. You have just graduated from a teach-
> er's college. You are going to your first teaching post in a small village in
> the country. You are required by the government of Manchuria to teach
> for three years in an assigned post, to repay the loan they provided for you
> to attend the school. You are hardly an adult. You have never left your
> mother's, father's home. (48)

In lieu of the conventionally disinterested or laudatory third-person, past-
tense narration, the present tense, second-person address reads as alternately commanding and imaginary, in both cases significantly problema-
tizing it as a mimetic description of past events. This awkward locution also
testifies to the formative inflections and exclusions of gender in historical
accountings. Belying the heroic and masculinist self-importance of epic
poetry, this telling claims a multilocational genealogy of female resilience
and resistance.

The mother's exilic history and eventual return to the homeland are
again invoked in the "Melpomene/Tragedy" section. Written in the form
of a letter addressed to the mother on a return visit to Korea eighteen years
after emigrating, the immigrant daughter writes:

> Dear Mother,
>   4.19. Four Nineteen, April 19th, eighteen years later. Nothing has
> changed, we are at a standstill. I speak in another tongue now, a second
> tongue a foreign tongue. All this time we have been away. But nothing has
> changed. A stand still.
>   It is not 6.25. Six twenty five. June 25th 1950. Not today. Not this
> day. There are no bombs as you had described them. They do not fall,
> their shiny brown metallic backs like insects one by one after another. (80)

Recalling two prominently memorialized moments of modern history in
the Korean practice of numbering the month and day, these opening paragraphs alternately emphasize the present differences from *and* the continuities with these past events. This Korean daughter's sober and alienated
homecoming is set in stark contrast to the mother's hopeful and exuberant
return upon "liberation" from Japanese colonization:

> You knew it would not be in vain. The thirty six years of exile. Thirty six
> years multiplied by three hundred and sixty five days. That one day your
> country would be your own. This day did finally come. The Japanese were
> defeated in the world war and were making their descent back to their

country. As soon as you heard, you followed South. You carried not a single piece, not a photograph, nothing to evoke your memory, abandoned all to see your nation freed. (80–81)

Such expansive dreams of a free homeland would be soon undercut by national division and civil unrest, which imposed the nation's self-alienation all over again. Rather than a linear progression of exile and return, colonization and liberation, the letter goes on to declare a frustratingly recursive stasis: "Our destination is fixed on the perpetual motion of search. Fixed in its perpetual exile. Here at my return in eighteen years, the war is not ended. We fight the same war. We are inside the same struggle seeking the same destination" (81). Within such a collective legacy, the daughter of the exile is also frustrated in her desire for a definitive reconciliation with the homeland. Finding herself in the midst of a student protest for democratization that turns into a violent clash with the U.S.-backed Korean military, she recalls in her letter the mother's attempts to dissuade the brother from joining the student-led protests of 1960. It then goes on to focus on the tragic irony of Korean military men suppressing fellow Korean student demonstrators:

> The students. I saw them, older than us, men and women held to each other. They walk into the others who wait in their uniforms. Their shouts reach a crescendo as they approach nearer to the other side. Cries resisting cries to move forward. Orders, permission to use force against the students, have been dispatched. To be caught and beaten with sticks, and for others, shot, remassed, and carted off. They fall they bleed they die. They are thrown into gas into the crowd to be squelched. The police the soldiers anonymous they duplicate themselves, multiply in number invincible they execute their role. Further than their home further than their mother father their brother sister further than their children is the execution of their role their given identity further than their own line of blood. (83–84)

The unspecified deployment of "they" and "others" in this passage points to both the anonymity and the convergence of the supposedly oppositional groups engaged in this chaotic clash. The estrangement of the soldiers from their "own line of blood," echoing the displacement of the exile, demonstrates the vulnerability and fluidity of such fixed, biological ties. However, this alienation is not an unavoidable stage of individuation but is a "given identity"—the effect of consciously dispatched orders from above. While the section is critical towards the actions of the police and soldiers, a later passage describes them as acting out of certain patriotic concerns just as the students think of themselves as radical nationalists: "You are your post you are your vow in nomine patris you work your post you are your nation defending your country from your own countrymen" (86). This adversarial positioning of Korean against Korean, the division of the country in two, the continuing effects of colonization and the immigrant's sense of splitting in displacement are interconnected. It is precisely *within* such internal tensions and contestations that this Korean/American subject locates herself most assuredly. In contrast to the moments of the book detailing the linguistic barriers and bureaucratic mediations that mark her irrevocable estrangement from the Korean homeland, the most confident Korean identification is tendered at this moment: "I am in the same crowd, the same coup, the same revolt, nothing has changed. I am inside the demonstration I am locked inside the crowd and carried in its movement" (81). This first-person accounting with its double repetition of "in" and "inside" offers a stark contrast to the earlier repudiations of the returning emigrant. Through this writing of a self *inside* the reflection upon and the reinscription of a multiply fragmented Korean history and people, *Dictée* rejects the historicist and exclusive terms of national identification on both sides of the shifting U.S.-Korea border.

In addition to these linguistic recollections, the book also includes photographic traces of Korean history. There is the group portrait of Yu Guan Soon and her classmates on the back cover. Within the pages of the book, there are two interrelated sets of black-and-white photographs: three photographic reproductions that pertain to the Japanese colonial era and three photographic portraits of Korean women. In his essay "The Work of Art in the Age of Mechanical Reproduction," Walter Benjamin marks the paradoxical movement by which a work of art becomes liberated from its originary context and, by this process of displacement, is deprived of any claims to authenticity:

> . . . that which withers in the age of mechanical reproduction is the aura of the work of art . . . One might generalize by saying: the technique of reproduction detaches the reproduced object from the domain of tradition. . . . it substitutes the plurality of copies for a unique existence. And

in permitting the reproduction to meet the beholder or listener in his own particular situation, it reactivates the object reproduced. These two processes lead to a tremendous shattering of tradition which is the obverse of the contemporary crisis and renewal of mankind.[8]

This description of mobility in exile, of loss and shattering in the midst of reactivation and renewal strikingly resonates with the contours of immigrant experience. *Dictée* reactivates the photographic images of Korean history in an "American" context, while acknowledging their incommensurability with the moment and place of their original production as image. Their displacement is acutely illustrated by the complete absence of any descriptive captions that would identify their social and historical contents, the identity of the photographer, and the circumstances and motivations of their making.[9] Roland Barthes writes about two levels of codes in a photograph: the *denotative,* which refers to its mechanically produced analogy of the natural world, and the *connotative,* which is a specific cultural coding and interpretation of what is denoted:

> Thanks to its code of connotation, the reading of the photograph is thus always historical; it depends on the reader's "knowledge" just as though it were a matter of a real language [langue], intelligible only if one has learned the signs. . . . To find this code of connotation would thus be to isolate, inventoriate and structure all the "historical" elements of the photograph, all the parts of the photographic surface which derive their very discontinuity from a certain knowledge on the reader's part, or, if one prefers, from the reader's cultural situation. (28)

The historical significance and symbolic force of these three photographs are susceptible to dismissal and open to multiple reinterpretations as they appear in *Dictée* which is produced out of and circulates in a distant time and place.

Against the critical impulse to read these photographs as "dead" and "homeless" through such multiple reproductions and dispersals, I would argue that the book opens up the possibilities of their different legibility and significance within the history of Japanese colonization, American imperialism, and Korean/American immigration.[10] Put another way, these photographic details command differently situated viewers to grapple with their possible significance alongside and against the book's persistent interrogation of language, specifically in its autobiographical and historiograph-

ical manifestations. Only through some prior knowledge of Korean persecution under Japanese colonial rule and the 3.01 protest can the viewer recognize the long shot of a hillside crucifixion of three Korean males by uniformed Japanese soldiers on page 39 and a poor copy of the photograph of
a large yet indistinguishable crowd of Korean women, men, and children
gathered in Seoul to protest Japanese colonial rule. This shifting meaning
and meaninglessness of the photographic image is perhaps best illustrated
in the image on the frontispiece which is the most indecipherable of the
three and yet could also be viscerally evocative for a particularly knowing
viewer. It is such a poor reproduction that one can easily mistake it for an
etching instead of a photograph. The image shows the anonymous inscription in *Han-gul,* the Korean alphabet. Translating as "Mother, I want to see
you. I am hungry. I want to go to home," the message presages Cha's own
postcolonial separation from the Korean homeland and her writing up of
its hungers and yearnings in the rest of the book. However, its stark framing and odd placement in the text remind us that this is a printed reproduction of a photographic trace of the material inscription, which the
readers of *Dictée* must confront in such a multiply mediated form. In pointing to how the frontispiece poses a directional tension to the rest of the
book given that Korean reads top to bottom and right to left, Shelley Sunn
Wong underscores "the radical potential of Cha's formal strategies." She
explains, "By having the Korean sign virtually move off the page and out
of the textual composition, Cha signals the instability of that Korean sign
within the larger narrative framework of American life."[11] Stressing how
"Cha's Korean and Korean American references require that we step beyond the body of knowledge we in the West rely on and often hierarchize
as 'the best,'" Elaine H. Kim nicely frames *Dictée* as a "both/and text" that
"offers both an intensely emotional and personal exploration of individual
dreams and memory and a passionate polemic about history and politics"
("Poised on the In-Between," 22–23).

A similar exploration of Korean/American history and identity in and
through detailed manipulations of language can be discerned in the poetry
of Myung Mi Kim. Like *Dictée,* the language of Kim's 1991 collection, *Under Flag,* is dense, difficult, and often elusive. Any attempt to locate a singular poetic voice is punctuated by the inclusion of mechanical lists, transliterated yet untranslated passages of Korean, Latin words, excerpts from

naturalization examinations, and journalistic accounts of the Korean War.[12] It is further difficult to discern a coherent and knowing subject, for the poems are mostly descriptive or interrogative rather than declarative or purely self-reflexive. Denaturalizing language as expressive, communicative vehicle, the poems often highlight the very sounds of words, playing frequently with rhyme and alliteration such as "prattle done trattle gone just how far," "Callback fallback whip whippoorwill," "dead dead dead la la la/ trundle rondo." While there are more semantically clear moments in the volume, the unstable referentiality of much of this poetry is significantly bound up with a substantive interrogation of national and cultural identity in the context of foreign invasion, colonial domination, civil war, and the North/South division and the subsequent global scattering of the Korean people.

The title of the volume, "Under Flag," announces the text's prevailing concern with questions of national identification and citizenship. However, the force of political subjection in the pithy phrase is deflated by the unspecified nature of this national emblem—which flag?—which ultimately undermines instead of affirming its decidability. Historical and geographical signifiers slide from visceral specificity to bewildering generality. While the volume repeatedly deploys the vocabulary of geography— "the sea," "the fields," "gulch, mesa, peak," "The continent and the peninsula, the peninsula and the continent"—the proper names of specific locations are rarely and strategically invoked, emphasizing both the uprooted placelessness of the refugee and the selectively obsessive memory of the exile. Grammatical demarcations of time are also shifting and ambiguous with past, present and future temporalizations disrupting and then bleeding into each other. Marking its overwhelming prominence as defining historical moment, the 6.25 Korean War is inscribed not in the simple past but alternately in the present and in the conditional perfect tenses, admitting the lingering effects of what Walter Benjamin calls "a past charged by the time of the now . . . blasted out of the continuum of history" (261). Furthermore, the conditional perfect and the recurrence of "if" inscribe an imaginary negotiation of all that *could have been* under different historical trajectories. Many of the lines reverse the order of subject and verb, deflating any sense of human agency; yet they are without even the small sense of finality and clarity afforded by the question mark, further amplifying the mood of longing and curiosity wracked by doubts permeating the volume. All these details contribute to an abiding sense of estrangement from and mistrust of language as a medium for either personal expression or group identification. Pronouns and adverbial markers lack definite antecedents; the words "it," "them," "us," "then," and "there" literally hang at the end of each line. Such ambiguous syntactical positionings seem to express the uncertainties and sense of ruptured suspension of personal and communal displacements, and then, too, they appear to declare some taken-for-granted meaning within a particular collective consciousness.

The enterprise of speaking and writing as well as the ideological controls in and through language are unsettled from the first poem of the collection, "And Sing We." It begins with a compelling need for expression: "Must it ring so true / So we must sing it" (13). Given the title of the volume, the "it" here suggests a national anthem, an obvious site for the meeting of nationalism with language. The anthem is also an important pedagogical tool for the cultivation of patriotism in the young and impressionable. The reversal of the subject and verb in the title signifies collective identification as constituted in and through language. Furthermore, it emphasizes the vulnerability of the collective "we" against the ideological and sentimental weight of the anthem.

This surge of patriotic spirit, though expressed from within the nation-state borders of the United States, reaches for a place *elsewhere:* "To span even yawning distance / And we would be near then / What would the sea be, if we were near it" (13). The exiles' desire for the homeland would be so great as to minimize the expanse of ocean that separates them. Yet the uncertainty of this object of longing, indicated by a generic "it," underscores its remoteness; the singing—the remembering and imagined return through the vehicle of language—would have its limitations in fulfilling that hunger. Immediately following the lines I just quoted is a singular, lone word off to the right side of the poem, "Voice," and then: "It catches its underside and drags it back / What sounds do we make, 'n', 'h', 'g' / Speak and it is sound in time" (13). There is no innocent and permanent repatriation, only a repetition of fraught and yet temporary returns and expulsions that are mediated by language. But the special meanings of the words sung can be reduced to generic sounds that can be dissected into single letters in another language and thus alien(ated) from the singers. This opening poem thus posits language as a powerfully evocative and neutralizing force for maintaining a collective Korean identification amidst invasions, losses, and migrations. "Depletion replete with barraging / Slurred and taken over / Diaspora" (13). Any resettlement involves a transsubstantiation of both language and community.

In the face of such complications of identity and limitations of language, the response should not be a radical disassociation, a stubborn refusal to remember and represent. The first stanza on the next page posits:

> If we live against replication
> Our scripts stricken
> Black ants on tar: ponderous pending change
> Fable voices, fabled voices say to us (14)

We will always already be implicated in some (other's) context of representation. While it may enable "us" to guard its stories against the possible (mis)interpretations and judgments by others, the choice of silence will have the effect of erasing these specific narratives, and like "black ants on paper" the "we" will only be rendered inscrutable and incomprehensible as it waits passively for relief and cure. Meanwhile, others will continue to construct and circulate their embellished versions of us *to us*. Then, too, the "fable voices" become "fabled voices," undergoing necessary change into a mythologized pastness through time and across space.

In addition to these contending narratives, another imperative to speak is the force of one's own irrepressible memories of the homeland:

> And this breaks through unheralded—
>
> Sardines browned to a crisp over charcoal is memory smell
> elicited from nothing
>
> Falling in that way
>
> Um-pah, um-pah sensibility of the first grade teacher, feet firm
> on the pump organ's pedals, we flap our wings, butterfly wings,
> butterfly, butterfly fly over here (14)

Instead of a lateral movement backward in linear time, remembering is imaged as descent at several other points in the volume. Identity and subjectivity are not premised on a linear, individual development but involve a much more complicated and unpredictable process of doublings back, retrievals, and rememberings. The powerful pricks of memory smells and sounds are not always willfully invoked nor do they offer up a secure past. In addition to being uncalled for, "unheralded" suggests that such memories resist a discernible mark in their reappearance, signaling a certain untranslatability in this context. Rather, these reminders further exacerbate a sense of alienation and force the speaker to pose in turn, "Once we leave a place is it there" (14). This uncertain locution attests to memory as both an inescapable and unreliable mediator of place and identity.

The homeland left behind is not a site of certainty, purity, and wholeness. The title poem, "Under Flag," begins with one of the most declarative lines in the entire volume: "Is distance." The punctuation mark is significant for it rarely appears in the collection, its noticeable absence reinforcing the uncertainties and the often disarticulating effects of migration and resettlement. This unusual firm assertion, immediately following the national subjection signified by the title, marks the irretrievable nature of a coherent national identity not only through emigration but in the historical inheritance of imperial conquest and civil war that precedes emigration:

> Is distance. If she knows it
> Casting again and again into the pond to hook the same turtle
> Beset by borders conquered, disfigured (16)

The "Turtle Ship," which played a key role in the successful efforts to thwart foreign invasions, is a potent emblem of Korean national identity and sovereignty. Yet the repeated attempts to grasp and to recast that icon, and that too from a distance, are rendered futile by its already disfigured and therefore indiscernible contours.

Such elusiveness of ethnic identification is not internalized as an individual and group pathology; instead, the poem goes on to situate this difficulty within a multilayered critique of U.S. military intervention in Korea. The third stanza begins with a cryptic "Above: victims. / Below: Chonhui, a typical Korean town. In the distance, / a 155-mm shell has exploded" (16). The rationale of U.S. involvement relied crucially on the generic and dehumanizing construction of Koreans as "victims" of communism. Such superficial figuring of Koreans as objects of American pity and salvation covered over the fact that many were killed indiscriminately by U.S.-manufactured weapons of war. At the same time, the random violence perpetrated on the Korean people was justified by the inability of "American" troops and military leaders to distinguish the helpless "victims" from the willful "collaborators" of communism. Kim counters the ideological and discursive apparatus that forgoes local specificities—"a typical Korean town," as if they were all the same and interchangeable and ultimately disposable—by following up with these sensorial descriptions of both familial intimacy and individual bodies that were destroyed by the shell:

> Of elders who would have been sitting in the warmest part
> of the house with comforters draped around their shoulders
> peeling tangerines
> Of an uncle with shrapnel burrowing into shinbone
> for thirty years
>
> A wave of much white cloth (16–17)

The last line evokes an endless procession of mourners dressed in the traditional white clothes of funeral rites, indicating not just death but the lingering effects on the survivors. This cortege is set against another trail of havoc and destruction, the southbound evacuation of Koreans during the war:

> Handful of millet, a pair of never worn shoes, one chicken
> grabbed by the neck, ill-prepared for carrying,
> carrying through (17)

This trail is strewn with the physical evidence of lives disrupted and in the midst of hurried and harried displacement; but these harrowing reminders tell us nothing of where their owners were running from and of any definite destination as signaled in the too cryptic final line. Such losses and suffering experienced by Koreans are mitigated and ultimately displaced by figuring them as "typical victims."

Against these scenes of death and destruction, the poem challenges the naming of the war as a "civil war" between North and South by forcing the question of who were the key actors of this armed conflict. Kim interweaves journalistic accounts of the war that clearly highlight the ("heroic") deeds of the U.S.-Americans:

> At dawn the next morning, firing his machine gun, Corporal Leonard
>   H. was shot and
> instantly killed while stopping the Red's last attempts
> to overrun and take the hilltop
>
> The demoralized ROK troops disappeared but the handful of Americans,
> completely surrounded, held out for seven days against continuous
> attack, until all ammunition was exhausted
> General D.'s skillful direction of the flight was fully memorable
> as his heroic personal participation with pistol and bazooka (17)

These descriptions reveal the "Korean War" as a field for the exercise and display of American masculinity against the alien Red Koreans and the cowardly and less masculine Republican troops. Immediately after the above lines appears a litany of militaristic terms: "Grumman F9F / Bell H-130s / Shooting Stars / Flying Cheetahs" (17). These impersonally technical and cartoonish names belie their devastating capabilities, and they are followed by this ironic line: "They could handle them if they would only use the weapons we have / given them properly, said Colonel Wright." The inability of the ROK troops to utilize these American "tools" further cements their technological backwardness and inferior masculinity. Yet this condescending description reveals the estrangement of Korean soldiers from "their" own battles. It makes us ask, "What was Korean about the Korean War?" and in turn, "What was *not* Korean about the Korean War?" As Chungmoo Choi so cogently asks, who is the invisible subject of the intransitive verb "partition"?[13]

The above/below distinction also echoes the North/South division of Korea. Alluding to the postpartition practice of routine drills to prepare for the imminent bombing of South Korea by North Korea, the poem rejects this officially disseminated paranoia and asks: "And how long drill to subvert what borders are" (18). The following page describes the tragic estrangement of Koreans from Koreans as well as an imagined scenario of their possible reunion:

> What must we call each other if we meet there
> Brother sister neighbor lover   go unsaid what we are
> Tens of thousands of names
> Go unsaid the family name (19)

It is ambiguous as to where this "there" is. Refusing the arbitrary designation of the boundary between North and South, Kim reconstructs the thirty-eighth parallel not as a definitive barrier but as a midpoint, a negotiated place of reconciliation. It is perhaps in an uncertain Korean diasporic space—removed from both the comforting certainty of native birth but also the immediate paranoia of intranational division—that one can denaturalize the rigid bordering of North/South, and envision some moment of reunification, no matter how fleeting.

In the poem "Food, Shelter, Clothing" Kim focuses on the dynamics of migration and resettlement. After an opening of sensually descriptive images of rural domesticity in Korea, there is a startling break in tone with the lines "crossings and bearings / steadily pernicious" (21). Immediately following these lines appears this surreal figuration of linguistic adaptation: "She could not talk without first looking at others' mouths (which language?) / (pushed into) crevice a bluegill might lodge in" (21). The mouth, active organ of speech and communication, is here rendered as a passive receptacle housing some other presence and accommodating its needs. Then, too, the transoceanic voyage is figured as arduous, hard-earned, and yet unpredictable: "They had oared to cross the ocean / And where had they come to / These bearers of the homeland" (22). The uncertainty of destination betrays the considerable strains of emigration. Kim writes the following scene of arrival in decidedly militaristic and imperialistic terms, drawing an ironic comparison between their civilian immigration to the armed invasion of Korea by U.S. forces:

> Those landing amphibious (under cover of night)
> In a gangplank thud and amplification take
> Spot of ground. Fended it might remain
> Republic and anthem, spot and same spot
> How little space they take up given the land's reach
> All those whose feet had resounded
> Smear fear tyranny of attack
> Already the villages already the cities receding (23)

These lines are ambiguous as to whether they refer to a defense of the nation space against external attacks or to the attempts to retain a national identity amidst transnational migration. Their blurring points to the inextricable layering of Korean diasporic movements, especially to the United

States, within the history of Korea's colonizations. The "amplified" metaphors of their stealthy landing are ironically set against the subsequent descriptions that reveal that what they (can) lay claim to is a small space, merely a spot. As a reference to Korean immigration, these lines bring into relief the fears and insecurities of emigration against the suggestion of some strategic military aggression. This tension also interrogates the xenophobic figuration of Korean immigrants as part of a systematic invasion of the United States by "yellow hordes." The immigrants' attempts to hold onto some semblance of the country left behind—"Republic and anthem"—reflect a besieged sense of unwelcome residence and ultimately reveal the defensive futility of maintaining that "spot and same spot." Here, too, they must live in fear of violence and loss. Their geographical displacement and disenfranchised resettlement estrange them from both a past and a hopeful future, as both (home) village and (host) city slip beyond grasp.

The social marginalization and personal fragmentation of immigrant experience involve a substantial linguistic aspect. Along with the basic human requirements of food, shelter, and clothing—which are also the elementary desires of the besieged and transient evacuee—Kim posits language as crucial to sustenance. It is this hunger that is deprived for the newly arrived immigrant whose experience of linguistic and cultural dislocation is indicated by three widely dispersed words: "Descent   slur vowel." (26). In contrast to the American Dream's promise of acceptance and prosperity, immigration is figured as a degrading fall into the incoherence of a "slur" as well as the racist slurs that Koreans are often subject to; the slurred descent also signifies the deformation of familial genealogies through global scatterings, which further denature national identity. What is at the end of this trajectory may be (only) the meaningless isolation of a singular vowel—the individualist American "I."

One of the most provocative passages on the theme of language and identity appears at the end of "Food, Shelter, Clothing":

Geographical trodden shelter
Locate deciphering
        by force
As contour
Hurls
    ga ga ga ga (27)

The homes that one occupies are not as fixed and stable as one may (want to) think; neither are they unique and discrete but always already "trodden"—crossed over again and again by unknown others. The "shelter" is more than and less than a secure dwelling but an ever provisional positioning in relation to language. Comprehension and interpretation are the effects of specific positionalities and sociohistorical contexts. What comes forth shaped by the outlines of a mouth are not perfect expressions with inherent meanings but studied enunciations constructed under particular linguistic systems as strange as a bluegill fish.

Having to grapple with a multiplicity of languages can both deform and reform the diasporic's voice:

> No, "th", "th", put your tongue against the roof of your mouth,
> lean slightly against the back of your top teeth, then bring your bottom
> teeth up to
> barely touch your tongue and breathe out, and you should feel the
> tongue vibrating,
> "th", "th", look in the mirror, that's better (28)

These directives about how to make a sound that recent Korean immigrants have an especially difficult time with appears in the midst of "Into Such Assembly," a poem that powerfully reveals the interconnectedness of language proficiency with prevailing notions of social legitimacy and national identity. Recalling the mass naturalization ceremonies held in large assembly halls, the poem starts out with a simple U.S. citizenship examination question, "Do you read and write English?" From there, it goes on to pose more troubling questions about division and loss: "Who is mother tongue, who is father country?" and "What was given, given over?" "Ga, ga, ga, ga" is the accepted "American" sound of the incomprehensible prattle of an infant prior to her induction into coherent American/English. Yet, in another cultural-linguistic context, it is the careful repetition of the first letter of Han-gul. That a fluency in one language can get (mis)-taken as premature, inarticulate babble in another challenges the racism and cultural superiority that undergird the disdain of the recent immigrant by the native English speaker. Myung Mi Kim's poetry, more than inscribing one Korean/American woman's artistry, provocatively makes language a site of active political and ideological contestation.

I will now move to a discussion of some visual tactics of composing Korean/American women in the works of Yong Soon Min and Jin-me Yoon. The prominent presence of the United States, especially in the uniformed bodies of its military forces, in the social and political landscape of postwar South Korea is also the focus of two artworks by Los Angeles–based Yong Soon Min, which appear in the anthology *The Forbidden Stitch*. The title of a black-and-white drawing, "Back of the Bus, 1953," invokes the pre–Civil Rights racial segregation in the United States. However, in the back of this particular bus, three Korean women are seated next to each other. In addition to the directional cue given in the title, the viewer's attention is drawn to these female figures by three other conspicuous bodies of uniformed American GIs. Though they are seated in front of the women, all three men have their heads turned back toward these women. In contrast to their rearwards gaze, the other Korean passengers are oriented toward the front in various angles, and it is unclear whether they are averse or simply indifferent to the peculiar dynamics of looking between the two parties of Korean women and American soldiers occurring behind them. The spatial positioning of the Korean women in a socially disenfranchised location at the back of the bus and the clear interest that they appear to hold for the GIs, whose actively looking bodies separate the women from the other Korean passengers, combine for a striking pictorial allusion to the sexual objectification of Korean women's bodies by the imperialistic military gaze and the social ostracization of Korean women who are sexually associated with American soldiers by other Koreans. Even as a patriarchal, nationalist ideology of chaste and loyal femininity would castigate these women as sexually and ethnically "contaminated," thereby relegating them to the social margins, a broad segment of the South Korean population has directly or indirectly benefited from both the sexualized construction of Korean women and the specific political-economic phenomenon of military prostitution. While pointing to this legacy of stigmatizing certain Korean women's bodies, Min's graphic representation resituates them as sharing a common Korean socioeconomic space with the GIs and the other Koreans. The year 1953 marks the official end of the Korean War, but this periodization often hides the fact of the continued physical occupation by the United States. By linking that Korean historical moment to a phrase associated with domestic racial segregation, the piece makes important transnational linkages between U.S. military imperialism abroad and structural racism at home.

"American Friend" is a mixed-media piece that appears to be a sketched reproduction of a photograph. Two rows of Korean figures pose in this image, six men and three women. All of the men except for one are dressed in army fatigues. At the center of the group portrait is a bespectacled and uniformed white male body, evidently the "American Friend" of the title. The phrase is stenciled in large capitalized and emboldened letters at the bottom of the image, suggesting a generic reproducibility of this subject-position. These benevolent words are contrasted to the smaller, barely legible Han-gul that runs in the right upper corner of the image. What may appear to be a decorative or at best descriptive inscription reads very differently to a bilingual reader. Unlike English which reads from left to right, then top to bottom, the directionality of Han-gul is reversed, reading from top to bottom, right to left. The Han-gul text thus creates a kind of directional tension to the more prominent English words incorporated in this image. This writing on the wall also disrupts the semiotics of the image in its content which is translated as:

> Such a generous friend! You were our father's American friend who sponsored his immigration to the States after fighting together in the Korean War. Upon our father's request from America, you also got our mother a job on a U.S. army base in Seoul with which she supported her kids during the tough times just after the war.

This expression of gratitude turns to a sarcastic critique of U.S. military intervention in modern Korean history and politics in the second paragraph:

> Since our liberation from Japan, you influenced our political development by supporting the autocrat Syngman Rhee, and the military dictatorships of Park and Chun. You continue to share with us your economic and military might. You've even given us your valuable nuclear missiles!
> You've given us far more that we bargained for. How could we ever reciprocate?

While it is not indicated in the English translation, the phrase "Dear Friend" is persistently repeated in the Han-gul inscription. This has the effect of denaturalizing and demystifying the purported humanitarian aims, so that this affectionate appellative becomes increasingly accusatory of the hypocrisy of the United States government's concern for Korea's national security. The final question both condemns the lack of reciprocity in this neocolonial hegemony and suggests the determination to formulate some contentious rejoinder. Considering that "American Friend" looks very much like an official group portrait, Min's imposition of this critical caption renders this redrawing as resonantly "unfaithful to the original" but twice over by stressing the tactically composed and ideologically charged staging of the photographic archives of U.S. military occupation.

Jin-me Yoon, a multimedia artist based in Vancouver, British Columbia, has provocatively tackled similar questions around positioning and movement, identification and representation, specifically through photography and captioning. In *Souvenirs of the Self,* a metal rack displays numerous copies of a six-panel postcard series. Priced at a dollar, these cards are meant to be purchased and circulated, blurring the lines of artistic production and tourism-geared commodification, at once occupying a unique, localized installation and encouraging multiple, wide-ranging dispersals. In each of the six postcard images of *Souvenirs of the Self,* the same Asian female figure stands in various natural and constructed tourist sites in Banff, Canada, forcing the viewer to negotiate this raced and gendered body against some of the most sedimented signifiers of Canadian national identity. This project combines the conventional postcard photographs of widely recognized and picturesque locations and the conventional snapshots of individuals in these places. These are two distinct but related orders of the souvenir, which Susan Stewart separates out as "souvenirs of exterior sights, which most often are representations and are purchasable, and souvenirs of individual experience, which most often are samples and are not available as general consumer goods." [14] Indeed, the two specific examples of each that Stewart provides, the postcard and the photo album, are the forms of visual representation, memorialization, and circulation that Yoon works through in *Souvenirs of the Self.* What makes Yoon's compositions so effective is the blurring and mixing of their distinctions between public vs. private and multiple reproduction vs. authentic original.

Several reviewers and critics have pointed out the incongruity of the Canadian national landscape and the Asian female body in these scenes. [15] While both are the effects of selective *and* repetitive stagings, what is interesting about the perceived dissonance between the two is that the primordial naturalness of the first tends to be privileged over and against the alien and belated imposition of the second. The six photographs and their accompanying captions certainly challenge each viewer to make sense of or to imagine *how* this particular body has come to be in these particular spaces. The matter of her place of birth, nationality, current residence are not clarified but open to speculation. To apprehend this racialized and gendered body as inappropriate to the naturalized whiteness of the physical and social landscape of Canada bespeaks only one possible, albeit telling, apprehension. Here the public and monumental meanings of the souvenir are centered, while the simultaneous possibility of these images as the private record of a Canadian woman's travels is effectively elided.

When the female figure is highlighted, the monumental significance becomes elided. The neutral expression on the woman's face is apprehended as indicative of an amazing range of projected emotions and performative strategies from uneasiness to irony to humor to defiance depending on the (re)viewer.[16] The (auto)biographical collapsing of Jin-me Yoon, the artist, with the Asian female figure enables certain authoritative subjectivizations of this strangely doubled and split female subject. By underscoring the artist's biographical identity as a "Korean-born woman," some critics perceive both the photographed figure and the artwork itself as expressing the artist's pain of displacement and inappropriate otherness.[17] However, the specific suppositions and interpretive priorities of the (re)-viewer who cannot reconcile the body in the foreground with the background are eclipsed by the penetration of an authoritative gaze into her interiority. The physical stance or the facial expression of this figure may invite viewers to interpret and/or project certain emotional and psychic states beneath the surface of the body, but they cannot be reduced to an unmediated expression of the artist's own subjectivity and authorial intention. The inability or unwillingness to consider this visible woman as a staged figure bypasses the necessary tension in these images between "the self's" interior negotiations of physical occupation in shifting geopolitical sites and the staged public presentation of these sites and their native features. While some even acknowledge the photographed figure as a posed model, the possibility of "the scenery" as a constructed prop/studio for staging is not considered. Finally, presuming that "tourist" and "Canadian" are mutually exclusive identifications denies the full contestatory force of this piece, which operates more effectively only against the possibility that this female figure can be seen as coterminously Canadian and tourist.

Here, it may be useful to look at Yoon's strategy of captioning these postcard images. According to Susan Stewart:

> Temporally, the souvenir moves history into private time . . . [transforming] a generally purchasable, mass-produced object (the material souvenir) into private possession (the referent being "my trip to Philadelphia"). That remarkable souvenir, the postcard, is characterized by a complex process of captioning and display which repeats this transformation of public into private. First, as a mass-produced view of a culturally articulated site, the postcard is purchased. Yet this purchase, taking place within an "authentic" context of the site itself, appears as a kind of private experience as the self recovers the object, inscribing the handwriting of the personal beneath the more uniform caption of the social. (138)

Blurring the above distinction between personal signature and uniform caption, the six captions that appear on the back of each panel juxtapose a conventionally generic description of the place pictured with a more self-reflective sentence about a female subject identified only by the third-person pronoun "she."

Five of these captions begin by exhorting the reader to "Come and enjoy," "Feast," "Explore," "Indulge," and "Marvel over" the various sites. These commanding verbs highlight the pedagogical rather than merely descriptive nature of the accompanying text, whose intended readers are twofold in the postcard as it is purchased by a tourist-consumer and then mailed to a beloved addressee not to mention the countless others who may look but not buy these souvenirs. The accompanying captions that direct the visitor to "Feast your eyes on the picturesque beauty of this lake named to honour Princess Louise Caroline Alberta, daughter of Queen Victoria" or to "Indulge in the European elegance and grandeur of days gone by" celebrate a European pedigree for Canada. This romanticization of "European elegance and grandeur" can be effected only through a willful erasure of both the native populations displaced by the European settlers in the figuration of "the Canadian wilderness" as well as the non-European immigrants and their contributions to the establishment and growth of Canada. The unabashed nostalgia for the "days gone by" is riddled with a certain antipathy for the continued ethnic and cultural diversification of Canada through immigration.

The second sentences that complete the captions, which describe the thoughts and actions of an unspecified female subject, are more ambiguous and elliptical, and often they serve to mark a distance and alienation from both the speaking position and the intended audience of the first sentence. For example, against the directive to "Explore the riches to rags drama of this historic coal mining town," in the Bankhead panel, the second caption reads: "She discovers that Chinese workers lived on the other side of the slack heaps." While this caption points to the history of racial segregation and labor exploitation that is suppressed by the Eurocentric monumentalizations of Canadian history and geography, it is framed as a process of discovery and learning at the tourist site for this female subject. This discovery also suggests the erasure or marginalization of Asian Canadian histories from the dominant national historiographies of Canada that Asian Canadians are pedagogically subjected to.

Caught within such cultural and political dynamics, the process of identification is multiply split for this female subject. On the postcard of Banff Avenue, the caption reads, "She has trouble finding that perfect souvenir for herself." Often the Asian female body is both and neither the gazing tourist and the exotic object frozen under some gaze. For example, on the opening postcard image, the figure stands outside the Banff Park Museum. Behind to her right are glass cases lined with taxidermied animals. A sign hanging over her head reads "Cabinets of Curiosities, Objets bizarres." The accompanying text reads: "Marvel over the impressive collection of Western Canada's natural history museum. She looks with curiosity and imagines life beyond the rigid casings." The natural museum is one of the most powerful mechanisms by which arbitrary and historically shifting constructions of national identity are masked through artificially constructed tableaux of plant and animal life. Although this inscape is often signified in decidedly feminized terms, this Asian female body can only be partially caught in and by this naturalizing trope of Canadian national identity. Similarly, she can only be partially interpellated as the tourist who wields the power to look at the indigenous objects put on display. Liable to be identified equally with the often ethnicized "objets bizarres" *and* the more familiar feminized inscape of the nation, she occupies an impossible position inside/outside the "rigid casings" of ethnicity and gender as they intersect with geopolitical identifications. Therefore, she resists the exhortation to "marvel"—to become filled with surprise, astonishment, wonder, or amazed curiosity or perplexity—at these forcefully natural figures on display.

This resistance cannot be attributable merely to social alienation, because it is also a refusal to be interpellated into the naturalized and commodified mechanisms of national identification. On each postcard panel, three vertically arranged captions, written in Japanese, Chinese, and Korean proclaiming, "We too are the keepers of this land," attest to the differential processes of racialization and the incongruous connections of ethnic specificity and racial categorizations. While this trilingual declaration can serve as an empowering slogan that seeks to claim a space of entitlement for Asians in both the literal and figurative Canadian national landscape, it also simultaneously indicts an ongoing struggle for political and cultural recognition. In that vein, I read these vertical captions and their adjoining placement on "A 100% Canadian Product" as figuring the coalitional identity of "Asian Canadian," signaling not so much a shared origin in Asia but a product of Canada's own specific history of anti-Asian racism. The elision of ethnic distinctions in the face of racialized generalizations happens crucially on the visual level: "All Orientals Look Alike." That the specific ethnic identity of the Asian female figure is never elucidated on any of the six panels is an important detail that attests to the centrality of its critical engagement with the politics of Asian racialization. On this note, the trilingual caption challenges the bilingual debates, which proffer only two possible choices for the official language of a much-proclaimed "multicultural" Canada. The connections among geography, language, and community are never organic but forcefully dictated, and as such, they demand careful calibration.

The critics' collapsed identification of the female figure with the artist, especially as "Korean," undermines such strategic ambiguities of the work. Another strategic ambiguity is the legal, political status of the Asian female figure in terms of the country of birth, residence, and formal citizenship. The oft-asked question, "Where are you from?," is a declaration and reinforcement of the addressee's perceived alterity, her non-Canadianness, her nonnativeness in the eyes of the (native) interrogator. This query, rephrased slightly as "Where is she from?," is certainly provoked by but never resolved in *Souvenirs of the Self*. Tellingly, one critic phrases the interrogative thrust of the piece as, "Can this naturalized Canadian ever really fit comfortably and naturally into the Canadian landscape?" (Sheppard, "Jin-me Yoon," 35). But how is any body's legal nationality thus visible?

Souvenirs of the Self works most effectively not as an expression of the artist's personal cultural schizophrenia or uncertainty about Canadian naturalization but as a critical staging of the vapid slogans and commodified circuits of multiculturalism. Here "otherness" is domesticated, translated, neatly packaged, bought and sold. The work resists the comforting illusions of both completeness and individual possession in its built-in command to fragment each perforated panel from the other five and to dispense them from origin to multiple destinations. In this light, the awkward title, "Souvenirs of the Self," needs further critical unpacking beyond simply an autobiographical gesture. There is a crucial distinction between *myself* and "the self," which raises questions about the assumptions of authenticity and transparency that come to bear on minoritized cultural productions. The reproducibility and the transferability of this self problematize a core essence that could be distilled and memorialized into a souvenir. The construction of a narrowly delimited minoritized subject also serves to affirm the selfsame subject, and the piece resists both these moves of marginalization and consolidation.

Here it is important to consider the implications of the doubled and split medium of *Souvenirs of the Self.* Both the postcard and the tourist's photographs are geographically displaced representations, meaning they only achieve their full significance elsewhere from their point of originary production. Postcards are purchased at the tourist spot—before that they are most likely manufactured/printed elsewhere as well—and mailed to people in far-off locations, as a sign or proof of the traveler's physical presence at the tourist site. The photo of the self against the tourist attraction functions more in terms of memory, but it will not materialize until the traveler has returned "home" to develop the negatives. Both the postcard and the photograph must then achieve their full realization elsewhere from the place that is pictured.

Yoon further tests the limits of the mythical lure of origins in her 1993 installation piece *Screens,* as well as in the photo essay derived from the installation that was published in *Ms.* magazine. Elements of Yoon's life are much more evident, but the piece is less an individual autobiographical statement than it is a fragmented and internally conflictual collage about the complications of the mother–daughter relationship within a history of colonialism, war, and transnational migration. The piece incorporates black-and-white photographs in varying sizes and states of replication, which are interspersed amongst three inscriptions written by the same hand in Han-gul and dated to 1968, 1952, and 1992. In its very composition, *Screens* provokes the question of origin and authenticity. For example, despite the remote dating of the first two inscriptions, the same writing style of all three signals a contemporaneous composition. Also, the most clearly identifiable photographs, the immigrant family portrait and the war-time school picture, are framed as over-the-shoulder shots of a disembodied hand holding a passport and a scrapbook, suggesting a mediating subject between the viewer of the photo-essay and these documentary photographs.

Screens opens with the skewed photograph of the hand holding open a Korean passport that bears the regulation black-and-white photograph of the artist, her mother, and two younger sisters. The first full page contains Han-gul text that surrounds three centered images of the top half of an A-frame house, the top of a woman's head with her hair parted in the middle and pulled back in the traditional Korean style, and the lower part of a house at street level. The text is a reinscription of a letter dated 4 January 1968, written by a Korean immigrant woman from her new home in Vancouver to her parents in Korea. It is evident in this first correspondence back home to Korea following immigration to Vancouver that the mother and three daughters in the preceding passport photograph have been separated from and then recently reunited with the father, who had immigrated at an unspecified earlier moment. Although she writes that "it is nice that the family is living together," this note of pleasure is immediately undercut by a parenthetical qualification that reads, "In reality, the work is difficult and we are living in the basement." The photograph of the house is severed into two halves, noting the family's subterranean living quarters but also suggestive of the racial stratification and economic downgrading that confronts many Asian middle-class immigrants to Canada as well as the United States.

The letter also renders the artist as a figure of the mother's own compositional efforts. The oldest daughter Jin-me's quick and eager acculturation to her new environment, and the two younger sisters' differently expressed desires to emulate the older sister's blithe use of the English language, are traced back to the mother's own youthful fascination with the United States and her romanticized reaction to the presence of a U.S. naval ship in Kun-san, South Korea, in the midst of the Korean War. A later page offers another inscription in Han-gul by the mother, again fragmented and arranged around three other photographs, melding text and image. Dated "Summer, 1952," the passage translates into:

> An American naval ship came into the Kun-san Harbor, and so the whole school took a group field trip to look at the ship. For me, used to seeing only motorboats and seeing such a large American ship for the first time made it seem like a palace. I ate the American candy ("Do-ro-pus" ["Drops"]) that the big-nosed American man gave us for visiting the ship, and it was truly delicious. Usually before then the American soldiers were mostly frightening. If a ship is this big and nice, how much nicer can America be! Perhaps I may go there if only in my dreams? [my translation]

Considered against the first page, the above passage demonstrates how immigration to Canada and the attendant expectations were in a large sense shaped by this indelible history of U.S. military occupation and what Chungmoo Choi calls the "material fetishism" for made-in-the-U.S.A. commodities by Koreans and the "colonization of consciousness," which revolved heavily around a longing to enter the colonial metropole that was held out as an elusive, distant promise.

As much as *Screens* incorporates elements of the artist's life history, both the installation and the photo-essay are consciously staged presentations, which raise questions about various forms of identification and memorialization. The recourse to the proper name of Jin-me Yoon casts the piece as an autobiographical statement about her relationship to her mother. However, if we set this interpretive lure aside, it becomes evident that several female figures are presented in the work, and the central subject is the Korean immigrant mother, who is the author of all three inscriptions. These textual signs as well as her appearance in the various photographs highlight this woman as a historical subject of colonization, civil war, migration, and acculturation. The passport photo of the immigrant Korean woman and the three daughters is not an innocent family portrait but a proof of identity that assures international passage. In the specific context of Korean emigration to Canada and the United States, this family photo is a strange product of two intersecting forms of patriarchal political systems. In Korea, married women do not take the husband's last name and children are registered through their patrilineage. It is only on immigration that married Korean women take the last names of their husband and children. As such, this passport photograph is a historically specific and politically mediated form of family record. The uncanny details in the late restaging of the initial photograph, such as the expression of their faces, the mother's black glasses and white pearls, the rounded collars on the zippered sweater worn by the eldest daughter, come off as perverse, bespeaking a futile and disturbing desire for recuperation. The most troubling detail is the inappropriate pigtails on the now-adult eldest daughter. Even as this staging signals the impossibility of return, it also casts doubt on the "original" passport portrait as authenticating tool of identification for the state, which must rely on the fiction of photographic mimesis. The black-and-white photographs of the wartime encounter with the American naval ship are presented in three clearly mediated framings. Resembling the opening photo, the image on the top-left is a photograph of a page from a scrapbook, taken from an over-the-shoulder subjective point of a view of a female subject. Although the image is mediated through this viewer, the identity of this female subject is not given. The two other images are enlarged fragments of the large group photo, focusing on the young Korean schoolchildren in one and on the American naval officers in the other. This recomposition interposes another viewing subject that mediates our own views of the photograph. The handwritten Korean text is also a reproduction and a careful staging. This is all the more evident in the photo-essay incarnation where they alternately wend themselves around or cut across the center of the geometrically positioned images. Both the immigrant Canada-to-Korea letter and the wartime journal entry also pose problems of authenticity and translation, containing in themselves already transliterated traces and clear inscriptions of English.

Souvenirs of the Self and *Screens* attest to Jin-me Yoon's critical interrogation of the visual and linguistic forms by which personal identity is measured, circulated, and assured in the late-twentieth-century geopolitics of transnational travels and migrations: the postcard, the souvenir, the passport, the family photo album are image-texts that move and are moved by bodies. Yoon's works are a challenge to the power of naming and identification within that convoluted spatiotemporal terrain, which ranges from the most hegemonic designations of otherness to the resistant potentials for their deconstruction and rearticulation. What to call these female figure(s)? What possibilities for naming can be transmitted through the visual? Put differently, which social identifications can be visually encoded and interpreted? They invite their viewers to imagine possible responses as well as to pose more questions from our specific locations, the temporary but also enabling addresses at which we receive and apprehend these images and words. That both pieces centrally incorporate forms of correspondence in the postcard and the letter back home suggests that they must reach their fullest complexity at these multiple elsewheres, displacing any singular origination.

From the groundbreaking work of Theresa Hak Kyung Cha in pieces such as *Passages/Paysages* and *EXILEE,* there has been a strong strain of innovative films and videos produced by Korean/American women, which bring together both a passionate and critical exploration of identity *and* a rigorous "laying bare" of the apparatus of cinematic representation. Kim Su Theiler's stunning 1993 16mm short film, *Great Girl,* attempts to pin down an elusive Korean female subject-position in its search for a Korean maternal body in the strange and incomprehensible terrain of the Korean homeland. The experimental techniques laid bare in the film are linked to the subject matter of a Korean American adoptee attempting to piece together a tenuous connection to Korea from the fragments of memory, crude anecdotes, hearsay, chance encounters, bureaucratic documents, and American popular culture. The elusiveness of a Korean identity in such a context of near-total severance of cultural and familial connections is formally expressed in the film's heterogeneous and often disorienting form, which combines jarring cuts, colored tints, dramatic stagings of select movements against stark backdrops, obviously artificial model landscapes, and disjunction between the audio and the images. An actress, Anita Chao, credited as "K. aka Cho Suk Hi," performs the roles of two central female figures in the piece. K. is a young adult with long hair, made-up face, and brash speech and mannerisms, the initial a reference to the filmmaker's name. Cho Suk Hi is portrayed with a shoulder-length bob much like the photo in an adoption document and dressed in clothing reminiscent of young Korean girls. The adoption document of a young Korean girl identifies her as, among other physical characteristics, "Yellow" in complexion and also notes her "Discovery Place and Date." The title of the film is then flashed in three languages; besides the English "Great Girl," there are the Korean characters Sok Hee and the commensurate Chinese characters.

The Korean adoptee's separation from the homeland is a peculiarly fraught one, in which the possibility of "return" is laden with an even greater degree of uncertainty and struggle. The audience learns of her return and attempts to retrace her past first through confusing voice-over conversations between a young, English-speaking woman, her Korean translator, and a group of Korean residents about her possible identity and their confused and contending memories of who and where she could have been. In the earlier inquisition with a Korean man, possibly about the orphanage she stayed in before emigrating, the translator tells the adoptee in halting English, "There's not exist, so not important," to which she responds, "But it exists in my mind . . . you know . . . it's the only documentation." In a later exchange, two Korean women attempt to recall whether she is the girl that they knew as a child. The girl expresses her frustration and difficulty in comprehending. The translator relates to her only this puzzling but suggestive phrase: "You were very white and white." The women also say that she was called by different names, Suk Hi and Soon Mi, further exacerbating the linguistic gulf that separates her.

Accompanying these unseen conversations are shots of K. performing two activities differently associated with Korean womanhood. In the first scene following the opening titles, K. is sitting on the floor peeling apples on a low Korean table covered with pages of a Korean newspaper. She proceeds to cut the apples into bite-sized pieces and place them on a serving plate. This activity commonly associated with a refined Korean femininity is performed with an awkwardness—the peelings are thick and the pieces are misshapen—that suggests both her desire and inability to "be a Korean woman." The lone, stark setting of this performance denaturalizes these actions, and not just for the culturally estranged Korean female adoptee. The second sequence of actions begins with an overhead shot of K. cutting off her hair, eventually showing the entire floor space around her to be covered by the shorn locks. It then proceeds to a low-angle close-up of K. sweeping up the hair. These images could be taken to signify various things, including the practice of poor Korean women who cut and sold their hair in the postwar era of poverty as well as a later reference to the mother's job as a *yi-bahl-sa*. They can also suggest the fragmentation, loss, and recuperation of a Korean female identity for the adoptee.

The following sequence is an interview setting with Cho Suk Hi, here dressed in what looks like a schoolgirl uniform of a white blouse and black blazer, which offers a clear contrast to the stark white backdrop. While the framing is a conventional medium close-up of the interviewee's head and shoulders, the decontextualized setting and the slightly asynchronous audio track recall the experimental techniques of Trihn Minh-ha's *Surname Viet, Given Name Nam*. The distant and echolike voice-over begins: "My name was Cho Suk Hi. I went to Tongduchon to see if I can find out information about my orphanage and my mother." She addresses the camera directly, with a hesitant tone of voice and nervous mannerisms. The voice-over goes on to describe a series of new clues from various people as well as new frustrations in the attempt to gather information. A city reporter leads her to the gardener of her orphanage who leads her indirectly to the vice president of a hotel who "thinks he knows a woman who could be my mother." But this too proves to be more confusing that enlightening: "When this woman and I meet, we don't recognize the other. Just to make sure, she circles around to see the other side of my face. Her daughter had gotten a scar from a bicycle accident." In the accompanying close-up shot of Cho Suk Hi, she does not mouth the words but begins to brush her hair to one side as the camera begins to circle around to the viewer's left. While this camera movement mimics the motion of the woman-mother, rather than intensifying identification and emotional investment, this moment of (possible) rediscovery and reunion is revealed as a cinematic construction with the slow revelation of the film's camera crew now brought into our field of vision.

In shadowy, side profile, K. recites various occupations in Korean and in English as she looks forlornly off into space. When she says "doctor," she looks down to check a cheat sheet in her hands, betraying a lack of fluency in Korean as well as a particularly doubtful attitude about this respected profession in particular. The dark lighting and half-turned face reinforce the mood of uncertainty here. This shot is intercut with a frontal head shot of K. under harsh white lighting and background, with a lone bulb hanging to the right. Speaking with more confidence and attitude, she begins, "Well, when I would tell people, friends, where my mother and I lived, what she did . . . ," thus giving a context for the strained litany of the preceding scene. The film abruptly cuts back to the previous recitation scene as she states, "doctor. *ui-sa.* businessperson. *sil-up-ga.* scholar.

hak-ja." Then, after a moment of slight hesitation when she silently plays with her hair, she utters the word *yi-bahl-sa.* K. does not translate this last into English, revealing a slippage along both class and gender lines that could not be discerned without some knowledge of Korean language and society. Meaning barber or haircutter, *yi-bahl-sa* is also a euphemism for women who work in barbershops where sexual favors can be purchased. The suggestion of shame in this refusal/inability to make this particular translation is immediately displaced by cutting back to the more confident K. as she describes people's uncomfortable and insensitive reactions to the disclosure of her personal history:

> . . . they would pause. Then they would tell stories like the one about the cab driver who bombed the beauty shop. The girls hadn't treated him properly. Or the one about the Korean American boy who had heard that he can get a hand job with a shave. He had to check it out, so he went and when he opened his eyes in mid-shave, he found out that the barber was giving him his erotic massage and not—what?—the delicate young maiden he expected. I don't know what people are thinking. What is on their minds?

Rather than simply internalizing the sexist and elitist terms of degradation of those women who must work as yi-bahl-sa, Theiler shapes the sequence in such a way as to effect a frank critique and interrogation of the misogynist exploitation of and violence toward Korean women's bodies. The grainy night footage of the streets of Korea that fills the middle of this soliloquy also gestures to a broader social context, but the frontal face shot of K. returns at the end to punctuate the mocking and critical tone of the words.

K.'s relating of the barbershop anecdote significantly marks the differential experiences of return for Korean Americans to the "homeland." This anecdote is a humorously circulated one amongst Korean Americans, especially males, who return to Korea and exploit the experience as a chance to purchase sexual labor from local women, aided significantly by unequal dollar-won exchange rates and shielded by distance from their "homes" in the United States. But the film recites it here to mark the differential desires and stakes invested in the return to the homeland, which are centrally organized around class, gender, sexuality, and, for the adoptee, ethnicity as well.

Even though K. retains only scattered images and incidents from her childhood in Korea, there are several allusions to the low socioeconomic status of her biological mother. In addition to the hair-cutting sequence discussed above, the connection between domestic poverty and an international political economy, built on poor women's bodies, is perhaps most strikingly depicted in a scene in which the female figure tapes two American dollar bills to her naked belly, beneath her shirt. This image can be taken to mean both the adoptee's status as a commodity and also an image of paranoid hoarding, alluding to an economic impoverishment that caused her transnational adoption. Other flashes suggest more clearly that K.'s mother was a sex worker for the American military clientele. The orphanage where she was supposed have been is located in Tong-du-chon, which is one of the most infamous sites of U.S. military-related prostitution in South Korea. In the sequence immediately following the scene of taping the dollar bills, the young Cho Suk Hi, is slowly awakened by a flirtatious bilingual conversation wafting in from the next room. An American male voice says, "I've never played this. I play poker all the time with the guys on the base, but I've never seen these." A Korean woman's voice speaks to him teasingly, and it becomes evident that she is teaching him to play *hwa-toh,* a Korean card game associated with the lower classes and which has special gender inflections associating it with "fallen" women. The girl's eyes are wide open by the end of the scene in which the woman's playful giggles dissolve into the sounds of a jet plane taking off—a premonition of her later transcontinental flight to the United States. In the following scene the young girl is shown sitting on the floor and shuffling the hwa-toh cards when the older woman, noticing her actions from off camera, asks in Korean, "Oh, Sook Hee, you too want to play hwa-toh?" This third, slightly different name should be noted. When the mother concedes that she will teach her "just this once," the young girl responds in Korean, "Mom, teach me like you did for your friend." This sequence impresses on the audience how the lingering memories of such motherly affection are qualified by the prominent and indelible marks of the U.S. presence in South Korea.

Making reference to her bureaucratically processed and reconstituted subject position as a transnational adoptee, a shot of a meat-processing plant with audio of an annoying buzzing and eerie music is intercut with an extreme close up of Cho Suk Hi's head, as the audio of heavy, plodding footsteps and barely discernible shadows show a male figure methodically encircling her as if performing some kind of careful examination. Abruptly, she is knocked backward and out of the frame. The following moving shot of a blue-tinted terrain with a shadowy presence hovering above further extends a sense of vulnerability and dread. In the next scene, the young girl in a colorful dress sits in front of some stage steps, once more against a white backdrop. She is innocuously blowing bubbles with her own saliva when an unidentified male approaches and stands before her on the right edge of the screen, the low-angle of the frame showing only his legs next to the crouched figure of the girl, who must look up at him. The unequal position of these two figures represents the power differentials between girl-child and male adult. He hands this female figure a piece of paper, which she proceeds to rip into pieces and then eats. This ingestion viscerally enfigures the transnational adoptee as an indelible product of various channels of institutionalized paperwork.

Great Girl ends with an old, faded color photograph of the narrator-filmmaker as a young girl, what she refers to as "a photo taken of me to give to my parents," which besides her adoption documents and passport is one of few clues to this irretrievable identity: "My American mom gave it to me some years later. It wasn't enough, so I went back to Korea in a way to create my own documents and memories that exist now only in my mind." The identification of "American mom" imbues a distinct nationality to motherhood, denaturalizing the homologies of mother and motherland, family and nation. The piece ends with the image of yet another Korean female sweeping and mopping a small room in an obviously working-class home. A map of Korea hangs on the wall, with only the southern half visible to the camera, which is positioned outside this room. Acting not as leading frontispiece but as a closing reminder or echo, this truncated image of the "homeland" connects the history of national partition, the subsequent military buildup of the South with the aid of the United States to this diasporic female subject's irretrievable Korean identity, an effect of international economic disparities and foreign military occupation. This, then, is the "home" that she has provisionally constructed.

While I have thus far emphasized the innovative and resistant force of these heterogeneous yet resonant compositional gestures, I want to now turn to a more worrisome discussion about the ways in which various aspects of Korean history and current socioeconomic and cultural conditions have been the site of intense political investment as well as the object of aesthetic representation and knowledge production by Korean American women. The expository documentary in film and video, with its seemingly unmediated presentation of "real" persons and phenomena, is an especially fraught site for these tangled dynamics of Korean Americans' representing Korea and Korean women. Two documentaries by Korean American women filmmakers seek to address the historical and political-economic phenomenon of U.S. military–related prostitution in South Korea: Hye Jung Park and J. T. Takagi's *The Women Outside* and *Camp Arirang*, directed and produced by Diana Lee and Grace Lee. I should clarify that Takagi is Japanese American, so I will be referring mainly to the other three through the identification "Korean American." First, I want to underscore the act of documentation not as a transparent presentation *of* the real but as a transitive production or construction *with*, suggestive of both translation and displacement of an object of documentation by a differently located documenting subject. Second, the specifically cinematic example of documentation often positions the producer as a subject looking at a socioeconomically depressed, geographically delineated population, marking the separation and inequality that always already distinguish the two parties—the one documenting and the other documented.

In her book titled *They Must Be Represented: The Politics of Documentary*, thus foregrounding the operation of power/knowledge in the presumed urgency to represent those who, in the other half of Marx's pronouncement, "cannot represent themselves," Paula Rabinowitz writes, "One goes somewhere as a documentarian—Polynesia, Alabama, Poland, downtown; the documentarian is drawn elsewhere by an other. Documentary is based on exchange."[18] Citing what Brian Winston names as "the tradition of the victim in documentary production," Jay Ruby has described the process by which certain persons and social groups have been "tranformed into aesthetic creations, news items and objects of our pity and concern."[19] He adds further that "society condones this action because it is assumed that the act of filming will do some good—cause something to be done." This promise of documentary film production to provoke sympathy for the oppressed and exploited and to enable social change takes on added dimensions when members of groups that have been historically denied the rights and the resources of public cultural representation take on the act of documentation, of themselves and other others. In this instance, Ruby writes, "the documentary is not only an art form, it is a social service and a political act."

With these mutually troubling descriptions of documentary filmmaking in mind, I would situate *The Women Outside* and *Camp Arirang* at an awkward intersection of two kinds of visual production with different trajectories of development as well as often antagonistic aims: (1) ethnographic documentaries about a specific group of people living at a geographical distance and under different circumstances than those of both the filmmaker(s) and the primary audience located in the United States, and (2) efforts by variously minoritized groups in the United States such as Asian Americans to produce a self-generated visual public culture that more accurately and humanely represents their specific experiences and circumstances against the distorted and narrow figurations manufactured by the dominant culture. On this point, it is important to note that both pieces have been funded by the National Asian American Telecommunications Association, which is itself funded largely through the "minority" funding initiative of the Corporation for Public Broadcasting, and *The Women Outside* was partly funded by and also aired on PBS as part of its "Minority POV" series. Furthermore, they have been screened at several regional Asian American Film Festivals. "Autoethnographies" and "subject-generated documentaries" are two terms that have been proposed for this odd intersection.

Questions of representational power and its uneven, forceful practice become especially knotted in these two instances of Korean/American women traveling to their distant "homeland"—whether by birth or by an imaginarily sustained ethnonational affiliation—to document "native" Korean women, whose images and voices will be edited and projected back in the United States. In one important sense, these efforts to *publicize*—to bring to American public attention—the exploitative deployment of Korean women's sexual labor in service of U.S. military occupation of South Korea can be seen as expressing an anti–imperialist diasporic attachment by Korean Americans, born and/or residing in the United States. They also articulate an international feminist solidarity by "American women" concerned about the plight of Asian women caught in the oppressive webs of globalized, militarized, and sexualized capitalism.

Without denying the need for and the resistant possibilities of such transnational and feminist affiliations, I would underscore the important differences between the image-makers and the subjects that they have put on display. While a shared ethnic and gender identification as "Korean women" might suggest a greater intimacy-via-sameness between the documentary makers and the sex workers, resulting in a more complex and sympathetic portrayal, these pieces are not unmediated "self-representations," either of the Korean American women documentarians or the Korean women sex workers. Here it becomes crucial to bear in mind the spatiotemporal fissures between the audiovisual recording of the Korean women in Korea and the belated and geographically removed contexts of their editing, projection, reception, and circulation in the United States. More significantly, there are differential and unequal dynamics of power, control, and exposure in operation that demand critical vigilance: Who controls the gaze of the camera? Whose bodies are put on display, and how so? Who is the intended audience for these visualizations? Who directs the flow of questions and who must provide testimony? Who provides illustrative experiential data and who articulates historical and political analysis? Who is credited as author? These and other questions, which have been insistently posed in the ongoing critique of journalistic and ethnographic documentaries, are never seriously taken up in either *The Women Outside* or *Camp Arirang*. Rather than merely condemning the documentarians for (re)deploying certain problematic representational techniques, I want to suggest that these pieces are instructive precisely in demonstrating the untenability of any innocent and self-effacing gesture of transnational diasporic or feminist affiliation, in this case, between Korean American women and Korean women. Both pieces presume a certain urgency to "expose" or "uncover" this history and contemporary reality, especially against their prior suppression and distortion in public discourse. At the end of *Camp Arirang,* the narrator asserts, "In the shadow of every military excursion are countless untold tales of women recruited to comfort soldiers." In the opening of *The Women Outside,* after mentioning that in forty years, over one million Korean women worked in the camptowns, the narrator adds, "Their lives, however, are not part of the official U.S. or Korean history."

Since the arrival of the first contingent of U.S. GIs to the Korean peninsula with the outbreak of the Korean War in 1950, there has been a complex and bidirectional flow of bodies, cultural practices, and socioeconomic arrangements between the United States and Korea. The transnational production and circulation of these documentaries, then, interestingly parallels this thoroughly transnational character of U.S. military–related prostitution, and both pieces offer up some significant data and insightful analysis on this point. For example, one sequence in *Camp Arirang* describes how shifting racial formations in the United States have been literally implemented on the bodies of Korean women sex workers. In the initial post–Korean War years of U.S. military occupation, there was a strict racial segregation of bars, clubs, and the women who worked in them between those catering to white vs. black soldiers. The racist segregation and hierarchy of the United States were transplanted to the camptowns so that white soldiers would not dance with or patronize those Korean women known to associate with black soldiers. In the post–Civil Rights era, the U.S. Army commanders threatened bar owners to order the women to treat all GIs equally, regardless of race or color. All the while, the black/white racial segregation of both the clubs and the women who work in them has remained pretty much intact until today, now attributed to the self-selecting social "preferences" of the American soldiers. In an interview in *The Women Outside,* Elaine H. Kim emphasizes the important connections between camptown prostitution in Korea and Korean/American presence in the United States: "Many Koreans in the United States today can trace their immigration to a woman who married an American serviceman, black or white, and sponsored another relative, who then sponsored in piggyback fashion the rest of the Korean immigrant community." *The Women Outside* also illustrates significant continuities between the sex industries in the United States and the U.S. military–occupied parts of Asia, when it "returns" to the United States in the latter half to point out how Korean immigrant women engage in similar types of labor in massage parlors and clubs in major metropolitan regions as well as the camptowns surrounding military bases in Hawaii and in the "heartlands" of the continental United States.

Critique

The productive force of such important insights into this "American" history of imperialism, immigration, racialized and sexualized labor across the U.S.-Korea divide are undercut by the filmmakers' often problematic representation of Korean women sex workers, both as the most visible bodies on display and as the object of commentary and analysis by various "expert" witnesses. Both films rely heavily on montage sequences of location footage of the camptowns that show the English neon signage of the clubs and bars, the American soldiers out on the streets, and most prominently the Korean women who work there, as a kind of local visual detail. While this is a stock device of documentaries, the thorny question of "informed consent" on the part of the subject being filmed becomes especially significant when we see footage of denuded Korean women pole-dancing in bars or propositioning GIs, which appears to be filmed with hidden cameras. As *Camp Arirang* briefly acknowledges but does not adequately take up, many of these Korean women are resistant to publicity precisely because they are socially ostracized for the kinds of work they do. Therefore, both documentaries are undergirded by an unexplicated tension between the filmmakers' goals to make the phenomenon of military prostitution and the Korean women involved *visible* and to accommodate the women's own desires for privacy and anonymity.

The prominent and naturalistic presentation of the bodies and voices of real Korean women sex workers appears especially stark against the disembodied female narrators of the two films and the various "talking heads" of a few GIs, U.S. Army commanders, politicians, and Korean, Korean/ American, and American feminist scholars, who provide historical background and social analysis throughout. The controlling power and presence of the Korean American women filmmakers is most detectable in a few interview sequences with Korean women sex workers in *The Women Outside*, where we can hear a female interviewer—presumably one of the filmmakers, but never visible in the frame or otherwise identified—asking questions. Even the feminist, anti-imperialist scholars who speak authoritatively about and sometimes on behalf of the Korean women sex workers throughout the piece are significant as voices, and not so much as bodies-to-be-looked at. Indeed, the "objective" location footage of Korean women at work in the camptowns often accompanies these expert voice-overs as visible illustration of the point being made. I want to turn to a few specific details from the two films that illustrate this tension between the objectification and subjectivization of the Korean women sex workers.

In addition to the location shots, *Camp Arirang* switches back and forth amongst four interviewees: an African American GI and a white American retired Army officer, who had both been stationed in South Korea, and a Korean American woman professor, Katharine Moon, who provides the historical background and sociopolitical analysis. The fourth and the most prominently featured interviewee is Youn Ja Kim, a former sex worker and madam, now turned missionary working with biracial children of Korean mothers and American GI fathers who have abandoned them. In introducing Kim to the audience at the beginning of the film, the narrator explains that "unlike others who prefer anonymity, Kim was willing to discuss life as a camptown prostitute." Except for this brief statement, the reluctance of the Korean women sex workers to be documented is never directly addressed by the narrator/documentarians even though the tension between anonymity and visibility is apparent in several other details.

In the most telling sequence, *Camp Arirang* records Youn Ja Kim as she returns to the room she used to rent when she was working as a camptown prostititute. Kim and the camera crew come to the home of one of Kim's former neighbors, who ask repeatedly not to be filmed, one of the women going so far as to retreat from the camera with her face shielded. As the situation becomes more tense when a male authority arrives on the scene to tell Kim and the crew to leave the area, the bodies of some of the crew come into view. However, there is no clarification of these women's identities and the documentary never addresses the troubling implications of this particular exchange.

Besides the interviews with Youn Ja Kim, the induction of Korean women mainly to provide first-person experiential testimony to support the broad observations and analyses articulated by the GIs and the Korean/ American woman scholar is done through four or five brief segments scattered throughout the film, in which a female voice-over tells a personal anecdote. These women are identified only by first name, which appears on screen inside quotation marks, suggesting a pseudonym, at the beginning of each narration. For example, in the first such instance introduced by the intertitle of "Su Jin" and followed by nighttime footage of the camptown area, a voice-over performance recalls:

> I was fourteen when I first visited an American camptown. My friend was working at the "Top Gun" club. I was curious, so I followed her there. She wanted to live with her American GI, but she had a debt to the club. So she took me to her room and left me there to work in her place.

This is immediately followed by Professor Katharine Moon explaining the debt-bondage system. The documentary does not provide any other information on "Su Jin" and it does not explain whether this is a pseudonym or why it is being presented in this obviously disguised yet also mediated manner. Other disembodied voices under the names of "Jin Su," "Sora," and "Hae Ran" speak fleetingly about physical violence, the threat of AIDS, racial politics between black and white GIs, and the abuse and abandonment that many Korean women who marry GIs face when they do manage to immigrate to the United States. Although these snippets may attest to the multiple hazards that Korean women sex workers must negotiate, the circumspect but unexplained manner of presentation reduces the Korean women in these edited, translated, and performed verbal anecdotes to generic, experiential voices of an endangered population, who lack specifically complicated histories and who cannot articulate the kind of broader analysis that the other "talking-head" interviewees and the narrator are shown to possess.

In addition to a willful disregard of certain women's desires *not* to be documented, *Camp Arirang* effects a further displacement of their agency through an oblique effort at subjectivization, by having the various other bodies from the former American GI to the Korean/American feminist scholar speak authoritatively on the thoughts and desires of the Korean women sex workers. In one striking instance of a Korean/American woman speaking for and on behalf of Korean women, Katharine Moon declares:

> I have never met a prostitute or read about a prostitute or heard about a prostitute who wanted to stay a prostitute forever. These women have goals. Their basic goal is to marry a U.S. serviceman so that they can leave the country, Korea, that has basically thrown them away. They want to go to America and start a new life where the prostitution will not follow them.

Very briefly, I want to note how the subjectivization of these "other" women happens here on two levels: the claim to know what all of "these women" want, and the assertion that, not unlike us, they want what we want and have—a life in America.

The Women Outside begins with a dramatic shot of a Korean woman dancing in a white *hanbok,* the traditional dress for women. A female narrator begins the audio voice-over:

> In Korea, all girls are taught that a good woman obeys her father first, then her husband and finally her son. She must be chaste and obedient and

willing to sacrifice all for the family. That's what a good woman is; that's what *we're* taught. (my emphasis)

First of all, any sentence that begins, "In Korea, all girls . . . ," should be immediately suspect. The "three obediences" of Confucian patriarchy have been tiresomely invoked in a wide range of discussions of "Asian women" or "Korean women." I find this a problematic move along the lines of what I explored in the previous chapter as the spatiotemporal distancing of other women, not only to a distant place, but to an earlier moment in a single teleolology of human, and also feminist, development. However, the collective plural pronoun "we" configures the women sex workers and the female narrator, speaking here apparently *for* the disembodied filmmakers, as one homogeneous group, collapsing important differences that preclude any such totalizing claims.

At fifty-two minutes, which is standard for television broadcast, *The Women Outside* is twice as long as *Camp Arirang,* incorporating more interviewees with expertise, including Cynthia Enloe, Elaine Kim, and even a uniformed Army commander, speaking officially for the U.S. military. As such, it is more polished, complex, and layered than *Camp Arirang.* The biggest difference between the two films is that *The Women Outside* contains direct interviews with three present and former Korean women sex workers. Through the ways in which they were framed, filmed, and also later edited, two of these women, Yang Hyang Kim and Jun Mi Han, emerge prominently as two starkly contrasting figures. In their speaking sequences, Kim is framed in straight-on close-ups and faces the camera directly, much like the "expert" commentators. Although the filmmakers decided to caption what she says in English in transcribed subtitles, Kim's English is more than proficient, albeit accented and sometimes grammatically awkward. Han, for her part, speaks only in Korean, and, more significantly, she is framed in such a way that she never addresses the camera directly. In the sequences that are meant to show them in their "real" and "everyday" environments, Kim is shown walking to a women's center, getting tutored in English, and cooking an American dinner for her white GI boyfriend. Later in the film, after her marriage and immigration to the United States, Kim is filmed enacting a stereotypical portrait of American middle-class domesticity—seeing her husband off to work, playing the piano, and grocery shopping. Meanwhile, Han is shown putting makeup on

— cht gove people who also believe
they are doing progressive

in preparation for the night's work and walking around the camptown, flirting with and propositioning soldiers. Clearly, Kim emerges as the comprehensible and redeemable subject, while Han, both in her heavily made-up appearance and pessimistic outlook and by the filmmakers' framing and editing, emerges as the subject that is doomed to misery and, therefore, not a productive site for the investment of the viewer's sympathetic identification. Here I want to emphasize that I'm not speaking about them as real people but as contrasting character-positions in the narrative and moral arc that is woven by the documentary. Indeed, Kim literally gets the last word, now as an expectant mother, living in Hawaii and tearfully declaring her dream of taking her child to Burger King. For me, it is this clear juxtaposition of the two women and the directing of narrative investment toward the rehabilitated Korean woman sex worker that exposes this documentary effort as a partial construction, revealing much more about the documentarians as well as the American audience they are appealing to than the Korean women sex workers.

I want to emphasize that my contention with the two documentaries is not meant as a wholesale rejection of publicizing and even visualizing the conditions that these Korean women workers negotiate. Although it is evident for the most part that the filmmakers' sympathies lie with the Korean women sex workers and against the American GIs, especially those who have exploited, abused, mistreated the women featured, such decent intentions when realized through an uncritical logic and practice of documentation are ultimately insufficient. One can cast this act as the question "Korean American Women Saving Korean Women from American Men?" Some readers will recognize it as a messy reformulation of Gayatri Spivak's phrase "White men saving brown women from brown men," with an important detour through Rey Chow's rephrasing, "Brown man saving brown women from white men" in her critique of Malek Alloula's book *The Colonial Harem,* specifically what Chow describes as his "self-appointed gesture of witnessing"(39) on behalf of the variously denuded women in the postcards.[20] Chow continues: "Even though the male critic sympathizes with the natives, his status as invisible writing subject is essentially different from, not identical with, the status of the pictures in front of us" (39). With that in mind, I read these documentaries not as failures in the accurate representation of real, suffering Korean women but as illustrative demonstrations of how even such well-meaning anti-imperialist and feminist endeavors must work through the radically unequal relations between the two different subjects of these visual productions: the Korean women sex workers and the Korean/American women documentarians. Instead of a refusal to represent, the challenge is to bring these issues to a transnational public discourse, without forgetting and, more pointedly, without effacing our own specific positionalities as "American" investigating subjects. The difference is most pointed in this case because as citizens of the (neo)colonial metropole, Korean/American women traveling to Korea, with either notebook or camera in hand (and ideally a grant or two), are entitled to certain rights and privileges, most significantly and paradoxically the right to (re)enter the United States, which the documentaries themselves present as a kind of ultimate wish fulfillment for these Korean women sex workers in military camptowns. In any case, we are not doing anything *for* them. One approach would be to foreground the material specificities, in all their unavoidable inequalities and contingencies, of our particular historical moment that would enable one set of Asian/American feminist investigating subjects to travel elsewhere to locate, encounter, negotiate, and finally to visually stage the bodies and subjectivities of other Asian women. This would temper the impulse toward any grandiose, homogenizing, and disembodied claims about and on behalf of those Korean women sex workers. A sustained critical interrogation of the methods by which certain subjects must be made into bodies on display, as a kind of visible evidence of our narrativizing and even critical analysis, can serve as the point of departure for imagining and more importantly practicing alternate methods of documentation, representation, and composition.

The interrogations of social identity and geographical location in these works also provoke the question of their proper belonging in terms of women's studies, Asian American studies, American studies, and Asian studies. Insofar as they could be taken to enlarge the racial, national, and gender scope of each of these "studies," especially as a means to fill a prior lack or to correct an earlier misrepresentation, they are apt to be apprehended and celebrated for their greater truth and authenticity. There needs to be a critical vigilance about how such ready inclusions—and, I might add, some lingering refusals—of "Asian women" or "Asian American women" as noteworthy subjects can be premised on a resistance to considering their theoretical, methodological, and epistemological interventions *and* limitations within these interdisciplinary fields. To take women's stud-

Need to reconsider these 2 categories

ies as an example, they force a critical reconsideration of the relation between two categories: women of color and Third World women. Two differently problematic tendencies have characterized the delineation and circulation of these two categories in women's studies. At times they have
been seen to constitute two distinct social and geopolitical constituencies;
one popular taxonomy of different feminist frameworks identifies them as
"multicultural feminism" and "global feminism."[21] More often, they have
become collapsed into a big murky category of other women who are
distinguished in relation to white women or Western women. Here I
would venture that this blurring can also be attributed to the variously self-
identified "women of color" and "Third World women" who have argued
for the similarity and continuity of racial-ethnic women in the United
States, the United Kingdom, and other "Western" locations *and* women in
a range of formerly colonized and Third World nations on the basis of both
a shared experience and common political goals across national borders.
Often, such transnational identifications have achieved their coherence
largely if not mainly through a problematic differentiation from undifferentiated "white women," "Western women," and/or "First World feminism."[22] Within the terms of such blurring and bifurcation, cultural representations and knowledge-claims such as *The Women Outside* and *Camp
Arirang* hold out the promise of multiple redemptions through their inclusion and approbation in women's studies as part of a mandate of racial diversification and international expansion. Against such lures, I would insist
on taking them on as an opportunity for self-critical reflection on the two
grounds of epistemological authority outlined earlier by considering how
such texts might circulate as objects of study in other interdisciplinary terrains. To that end, one would need to be somewhat informed about the
historical formation of these studies and their ongoing intellectual and institutional contours as interdisciplinary fields, specifically in relation to the
established or traditional disciplines. A careful *and* critical examination of
how "Asian women" and "Asian American women" might be positioned
within and across American studies, Asian studies, and Asian American
studies could productively extend the study of the tensions and collisions
of identity, disciplinarity, and interdisciplinarity that *Compositional Subjects*
has attempted to incite.

notes

Introduction

1 Judy Yung, "Appendix: A Chronology of Asian American History," in *Making Waves: An Anthology of Writings By and About Asian American Women,* ed. Asian Women United of California (Boston: Beacon Press, 1989), 423–31. See also James Moy, *Marginal Sights: Staging the Chinese in America* (Iowa City: University of Iowa Press, 1993), 11.

2 Noting important spatiotemporal differences, there are suggestive resonances here to Michel Foucault's analysis of the shift in disciplinary economies and their tactics of subjection, from a concern with the criminal *body* as tortured spectacle to the criminal *soul* as object of investigation and rehabilitation, especially what he terms the "body politic": "a set of material elements and techniques that serve as weapons, relays, communication routes and supports for the power and knowledge relations that invest human bodies and subjugate them by turning them into objects of knowledge." *Discipline and Punish: The Birth of the Prison,* trans. Alan Sheridan (New York: Vintage, 1979), 28.

3 For a detailed discussion of this act and other legislative and public policy efforts to delimit the presence of Asian female bodies in the United States, see Sucheng Chan's essay, "The Exclusion of Chinese Women, 1870–1943," in *Entry Denied: Exclusion and the Chinese Community in America, 1882–1943,* ed. Sucheng Chan (Philadelphia: Temple University Press, 1991). Chan points out a significant monetary factor that would deter the immigration official from being fully convinced: "Any ship captain who violated this statute would be charged with a misdemeanor and fined between $1,000 and $5,000 or be imprisoned from two to twelve months. The state commissioner of immigration, headquartered in San Francisco, was given considerable incentive to enforce the law: He could retain 20 percent of all fees and commissions he collected as he carried out his duties" (98).

4 Julie Thompson Klein, *Interdisciplinarity: History, Theory, and Practice* (Detroit: Wayne State University Press, 1990), 21–22.

5 Taking off from René Girard's critical exploration of the dynamics of "discipleship" in an eighteenth-century monastery, John Mowitt points out that

even as their shared interest in a particular object may bring different agents together in the first place, their relation to the object is mediated by inter-subjective dynamics of competition and judgment. While those perceived as closer to the sacred object (of study) are exemplified, admired, and envied, certain others are designated for ostracization and ultimately expulsion. The purported object of their shared study then is ultimately displaced in and by this fundamentally "rivalrous structure" of disciplinarity. *Text: The Genealogy and an Anti-Disciplinary Object* (Durham: Duke University Press, 1993).

6 Invoking the critical studies of disciplinarity that have been put forth by Bourdieu and Foucault as supporting "the picture of disunified science where local patches of coherence must be laboriously produced" (75), Lenoir sug-gests rather that we approach disciplines as "heterogeneous families of social, organizational, and scientific-technical practices packaged as disciplinary programs in order to take advantage of the allocation of resources within a specifically configured political economy of institutions and neighboring dis-ciplinary fields." (Timothy Lenoir, "The Discipline of Nature and the Na-ture of Disciplines," in *Knowledges: Historical and Critical Studies in Discipli-narity,* ed. Ellen Messer-Davidow et al. [Charlottesville: University Press of Virginia, 1993]). Stephen Turner offers a starker formulation of disciplines as "cartels that organize markets for the production and employment of stu-dents by excluding those job-seekers who are not products of the cartel." ("What Are Disciplines? And How Is Interdisciplinarity Different?," in *Prac-tising Interdisciplinarity,* ed. Peter Weingart and Nico Stehr [Toronto: Univer-sity of Toronto Press, 2000]).

7 Arjun Appadurai, "Diversity and Disciplinarity as Cultural Artifacts," in *Dis-ciplinarity and Dissent in Cultural Studies,* ed. Cary Nelson et al. (New York: Routledge, 1996), 34.

8 Accenting what she calls "the political history of words," Donna Haraway opens her agile tracking of the diverse travels of "gender" with this helpful prompt: "The value of an analytical category is not necessarily annulled by critical consciousness of its historical specificity and cultural limits." "Gen-der for a Marxist Dictionary," in *Simians, Cyborgs, and Women* (New York, Routledge, 1991), 130.

9 Yen Le Espiritu, *Asian American Panethnicity: Bridging Institutions and Identities* (Philadelphia: Temple University Press, 1992), 32. Michael Omi and Howard Winant characterize "Asian American" as an example of a "racial move-ment" that sought to name a "common identity," which "reflected the sim-ilarity of treatment that various groups . . . received at the hands of state institutions." *Racial Formations in the United States: From the 1960s to 1990s* (New York: Routledge, 1994), 89. Susie Hsiuhan Ling attributes the origin to "young women activists, already involved in the progressive Asian Amer-ican Movement." "The Mountain Movers: Asian American Women's Move-

ment, 1968–1976" (master's thesis, University of California at Los Angeles, 1984), 5.

10   The numerous and various feminist critiques of the racial, sexual, and class-based exclusions and marginalization of "feminism" are often figured as a belated response to some preceding, coherent, and stable articulation by straight, white, and middle-class women. However, I would argue that dissentions and contestations over "women" as a unified identity have been there *all along* even if they may not be recorded in official historiographies. Against the appeal to retain some universal concept of "women," Denise Riley is correct to stress that the "instabilities of the category ['women'] are the *sine qua non* of feminism" and that "feminism is the site for the systematic fighting out of stability—which need not worry us." *"Am I That Name?": Feminism and the Category of 'Women' in History* (Minneapolis: University of Minnesota Press, 1988), 4, original italics. See also Angela Davis, *Women, Race, and Class* (New York: Vintage, 1981), and Katie King, *Theory in its Feminist Travels: Conversations in U.S. Women's Movements* (Bloomington: Indiana University Press, 1994).

11   *Asian Women* (Berkeley: Asian Women's Journal Workshop, 1971), 4.

12   *Asian American Women* (Palo Alto: Stanford University, 1976), 2.

13   Three collections published in the early 1970s bear the hyphenated "Asian-American" in their titles. See *Asian-American Authors,* ed. Kai-Yu Hsu and Helen Palunbinskas (Boston: Houghton Mifflin, 1976); *Asian-American Heritage: An Anthology of Prose and Poetry,* ed. David Hsin-Fu Wand (New York: Washington Square Press, 1974); and *Aiiieeeee!: An Anthology of Asian-American Writers,* ed. Frank Chin et al. (Washington, D.C.: Howard University Press, 1974).

14   The categorical distinction between "Asian" and "Asian American" has been inconsistently blurred by the ambivalent impulses of claiming an unqualified "American" identity and maintaining cultural and political affiliations to various "Asian" countries. The inclusion of Pacific Islanders within or alongside "Asian" has also been contested, especially after the U.S. Bureau of the Census introduced "Asian or Pacific Islander" in the 1990 census, which encompasses nineteen Asian nations and nineteen Pacific islands.

15   Katheryn M. Fong, "Feminism Is Fine, But What's It Done for Asian America?" *Bridge: An Asian American Perspective* 6:4 (winter 1978): 21.

16   William Wei, *The Asian American Movement* (Philadelphia: Temple University Press, 1993), 92.

17   See Rita Fujiki Elway, "Strategies for Political Participation of Asian-Pacific Women," in *Civil Rights Issues of Asian and Pacific Americans: Myths and Realities* (Washington, D.C.: U.S. Commission on Civil Rights, 1979); Esther Ngan-ling Chow, *Acculturation of Asian American Professional Women* (Wash-

ington, D.C.: Department of Health and Human Services, National Institutes of Mental Health, 1982).

18 In the San Francisco Bay Area, Asian Immigrant Women Advocates (AIWA), founded in 1983, continues to serve low-income women workers. Established in 1984, the New York Asian Women's Center directed itself to the problem of domestic violence. See William Wei, *The Asian American Movement,* 79–86.

19 In addition, in 1980, Dexter Fisher edited and published *The Third Woman: Minority Women Writers of the United States* (Boston: Houghton Miffllin, 1980), which contained a section titled "Asian American Women."

20 Genny Lim and Judy Yung, "Introduction," *Bridge: An Asian American Perspective* (1978): 5.

21 Barbara Noda, Kitty Tsui, and Z. Wong, "Coming Out: We Are Here in the Asian Community," *Bridge: An Asian American Perspective* 7:1 (spring 1979): 22. Also featured in the issue was Kitty Tsui's poem "A Chinese Banquet," which would be published again in 1983 as part of a poetry volume titled *The Words of a Woman Who Breathes Fire.*

22 Barbara Noda, "Asian American Women: Two Special Issues of *Bridge: An Asian American Perspective,*" *Conditions* 6 (1980): 203–211.

23 Nellie Wong, "Asian American Women, Feminism and Creativity," *Conditions* 7 (1981): 177–184.

24 Throughout the 1980s and into 1990s, there would be a number of single-authored texts as well as edited collections written by Asian American women under shifting composite formations announcing a lesbian, bisexual, and/or queer identification. For anthologies, see *Between the Lines: An Anthology of Pacific/Asian Lesbians,* ed. Connie Chung, Alison Kim, and A. K. Lemeshewsky (Santa Cruz: Dancing Bird Press, 1987), and *The Very Inside: An Anthology of Writing by Asian and Pacific Islander Lesbian and Bisexual Women,* ed. Sharon Lim-Hing (Toronto: Sister Vision Press, 1994). For single-author texts, see Willyce Kim, *Dancer Dawkins and the California Kid* (Boston: Alyson, 1985), and *Dead Heat* (Boston: Alyson, 1988). Previously, Kim published *Eating Artichokes* (Oakland: Women's Press Collective, 1972), and *Under the Rolling Sky* (Oakland: Maud Gonne, 1976). See also Merle Woo, *Yellow Woman Speaks* (Seattle: Radical Women, 1986), and Kitty Tsui, *The Words of a Woman Who Breathes Fire* (San Francisco: Aunt Lute, 1983). In her review essay "Landmarks in Literature by Asian American Lesbians" (*Signs: Journal of Women in Culture and Society* 18:4 [1993]: 936–43, 936), Karin Aguilar-San Juan notes the historical and political significance of Tsui's poetry volume to the articulation of "Asian American lesbian" identification. Aguilar-San Juan also includes Asian Canadian women in the category of "Asian American lesbian," citing the *Fireweed Anthology* as well as Sky Lee's *Disappearing Moon Café.* In citing the publication of these Asian American lesbian writers in the 1970s and 1980s as one of two historical cir-

cumstances that made "queer Asian American studies" possible, Alice Hom and David Eng write that "Their work helped to give shape to a public and recognizable Asian American lesbian subject within larger feminist circles." ("Introduction," in *Q & A: Queer in Asian America,* ed. David Eng and Alice Y. Hom [Philadelphia: Temple University Press, 1998], 3.)

25 Mitsuye Yamada, "Invisibility Is an Unnatural Disaster: Reflections of an Asian American Woman," in *This Bridge Called My Back: Writings by Radical Women of Color,* ed. Gloria Anzaldúa and Cherríe Moraga (Latham, N.Y.: Kitchen Table/Women of Color Press, 1982), 11.

26 In contradictory tension to its rhetoric of organic and coherent emergence, other passages of Yamada's essay work to fissure the category of "Asian American women" along class lines: "For the past eleven years I have busied myself with the usual chores of an English teacher, a wife of a research chemist, and a mother of four rapidly growing children. I hadn't even done much to shatter this particular stereotype: the middle class woman happy to be bringing home the extra income and quietly fitting into the man's world of work. When the Asian American woman is lulled into believing that people perceive her as being different from other Asian women (the submissive, subservient, ready-to-please, easy-to-get-along-with Asian woman), she is kept comfortably content with the state of things. She becomes ineffectual in the milieu in which she moves. The seemingly apolitical middle class woman and the apolitical Asian woman constituted a double invisibility, so to speak" (12).

27 Some other related subheadings and their dates of approval are "Asian American women artists" (1 November 1995), "Asian American lesbians" (12 December 1996), and "Asian American women employees" (23 June 1997). I would like to acknowledge Joan Ariel, the Women's Studies librarian at U.C. Irvine, and Lydia Shahid for this information.

28 Asian Women United of California, eds., *Making Waves: An Anthology of Writings By and About Asian American Women* (Boston: Beacon Press, 1989). The editorial preface to the 1997 follow-up, titled *Making More Waves: New Writing by Asian American Women,* ed. Elaine H. Kim, Lilia V. Villanueva, and Asian Women United of California, and also published by Beacon Press, identifies Asian Women United of California as "a nonprofit organization founded in 1976 to promote the socioeconomic and general welfare of Asian American women" (xi). Asian Women United has produced other books, including Diane Yen-Mei Wong and Elaine H. Kim, *Dear Diane: Questions and Answers for Asian American Women* (Oakland: Asian Women United of California, 1983), and Elaine H. Kim with Janice Otani, *With Silk Wings: Asian Women at Work* (San Francisco: Asian Women United of California, 1983). This collective has also produced several video documentaries, including *With Silk Wings: Asian American Women At Work,* a four-part series produced during 1983–85; *Slaying the Dragon* (1987); and *Art to*

Art: Expressions by Asian American Women (1993). In 1988 a separate group called Asian Women United of New York collected writings and art works by Asian/American women into a special issue of the journal *IKON*, specially titled *Without Ceremony (IKON* 9).

29 Asian Women United, "Preface," in *Making More Waves: New Writings by Asian American Women,* ed. Asian Women United (Boston: Beacon Press, 1997), xi.

30 Omi and Winant define "racial formation" as "the sociohistorical process by which racial categories are created, inhabited, transformed, and destroyed." They further clarify that this is "a process of historically situated *projects* in which human bodies and social structures are represented and organized." *Racial Formations in the United States,* 55–56, original italics.

31 Sucheta Mazumdar, "General Introduction: A Woman-Centered Perspective," in *Making Waves,* 16.

32 Esther Ngan-ling Chow, "The Development of Feminist Consciousness Among Asian American Women," *Gender and Society* 1:3 (1987): 285.

33 In addition to their narrower grouping, these volumes express a growing contention around a proper group categorization. For instance, Kehaulani Kauanui and Ju Hui "Judy" Han contest the ways in which "Asian Pacific Islander" is used interchangeably with "Asian American." Pointing to the social phenomenon of interracial sexual relations, they write: "A unique set of implications for Pacific Islanders, which are closer in nature to Native American/indigenous people's concerns than to Asian Americans' anxieties of 'outdating'." "'Asian Pacific Islander': Issues of Representation and Responsibility," in *The Very Inside: An Anthology of Writing by Asian and Pacific Islander Lesbian and Bisexual Women,* ed. Sharon Lim-Hing (Toronto: Sister Vision Press, 1994), 378.

34 The popular reader of women's history, *Unequal Sisters: A Multicultural Reader in U.S. Women's History,* ed. Ellen Carol DuBois and Vicki L. Ruiz (New York: Routledge, 1990) includes essays on Chinese American women and Japanese American women by Judy Yung and Valerie Matsumoto. See also the heavily sociological collection *Race, Class, and Gender: Common Bonds: Different Voices,* ed. Esther Ngan-ling Chow et al. (Thousand Oaks, Calif.: Sage, 1996), and Teresa L. Amott and J. A. Matthaei, *Race, Gender, and Work: A Multicultural Economic History of Women in the United States* (Boston: South End Press, 1991).

35 See *Home to Stay: Asian American Women's Fiction,* ed. Sylvia Watanabe and Carol Bruchac (Greenfield Center, N.Y.: Greenfield Review Press, 1990); *The Politics of Life: Four Plays by Asian American Women,* ed. Velina Hasu Houston (Philadelphia: Temple University Press, 1993); and *Unbroken Threads: An Anthology of Plays by Asian American Women,* ed. Roberta Uno (Amherst: University of Massachusetts Press, 1993). This genre specification

parallels similar trends in the publishing of Asian American writings in general. For ethnic-specific collections, see *Writing Away Here: A Korean/American Anthology*, ed. Hyun Yi Kang (Oakland: Korean American Arts Festival Committee, 1994); *Contours of the Heart: South Asians Map North America*, ed. Sunaina Maira and Rajini Srikanth (New York: Asian American Writers' Workshop, 1996); *Watermark: Vietnamese American Poetry and Prose*, ed. Barbara Tran, Monique T. D. Truong, and Luu Truong Khoi (New York: Asian American Writers' Workshop, 1998). For genre-specific collections, see *The Open Boat: Poems from Asian America*, ed. Garrett Hongo (New York: Doubleday, 1993); *Premonitions: The Kaya Anthology of New Asian North American Poetry*, ed. Walter K. Lew (New York: Kaya Productions, 1995); *Charlie Chan Is Dead: An Anthology of Contemporary Asian American Fiction*, ed. Jessica Hagedorn (New York: Penguin Books, 1993); *Between Worlds: Contemporary Asian-American Plays*, ed. Misha Berson (New York: Theater Communications Group, 1990); and *On a Bed of Rice: An Asian-American Erotic Feast*, ed. Geraldine Kudaka (New York: Anchor Books/Doubleday, 1995).

36 Bradford M Smith, "The Measurement of Narcissism in Asian, Caucasian, and Hispanic American Women," *Psychological Reports* 67:3 (December 1990): 779–85; Regina G. Ziegler, Robert N. Hoover, et al., "Migration Patterns and Breast Cancer Risk in Asian-American Women," *Journal of the National Cancer Institute,* 85:22 (17 November 1993): 1819–27; Kristy Lucero, Roberta A. Hicks, et al., "Frequency of Eating Problems Among Asian and Caucasian College Women," *Psychological Reports* 71 (1991): 255–58; Lawrence D. Hammer, Darrel M. Wilson, et al., "Impact of Pubertal Development Among White, Hispanic, and Asian Female Adolescents," *Journal of Pediatrics* 118: 6 (June 1991): 975–80; Diane C. Fujino, Sumie Okazaki, and Kathleen Young, "Asian-American Women in the Mental Health System: An Examination of Ethnic and Gender Match Between Therapist and Client," *Journal of Community Psychology* 22:2:164–76; Connie S. Chan, "Asian-American Women: Psychological Responses to Sexual Exploitation and Cultural Stereotypes," *Women and Therapy* (1987): 33–38.

37 *Discipline and Punish:* Note the rousing self-help title of Phoebe Eng's *Warrior Lessons: An Asian American Woman's Journey into Power* (New York: Pocket Books, 1987), which suggests one possible sedimentation and commodification of the earlier efforts at individual and group naming.

38 Some of the more interesting distinctions that Julie Thompson Klein outlines are (1) bridge building between two disciplines vs. restructuring one or both disciplines; (2) reformist vs. traditionalist; and (3) synoptic/conceptual vs. pragmatic/instrumental. In attempting to avoid "the continuing opposition of disciplinarity and interdisciplinarity," Klein calls for a composite mix of both in a "disciplined interdisciplinarity," which has "a

grounding in the cognate disciplines" but also "moves outward from mastery of disciplinary tools." *Interdisciplinarity,* 106.

39 Klein attributes the term "critical interdisciplinarity" to two different sources in her two books. In *Crossing Boundaries* (1996), she credits David Marcell, who contrasted it to "mere disciplinarity" in discussing American Studies. In her 1990 study, Klein cites Arthur Kroker, who distinguished it from "vacant interdisciplinarity" in his call for a Canadian Studies that is based on "a new relation of intellectuality, a vigorous pluralism that requires 'an active migration beyond the disciplines to a critical encounter with different perspectives on the Canadian situation'." *Interdisciplinarity,* 96.

40 Lisa Lowe, *Immigrant Acts: On Asian American Cultural Politics* (Durham: Duke University Press, 1996), 40.

41 Lisa Lowe, 'The International Within the National: American Studies and Asian American Critique," *Cultural Critique* 40 (1998): 29–47.

42 Wahneema Lubiano, "Like Being Mugged by a Metaphor: Multiculturalism and State Narratives," in *Mapping Multiculturalism,* ed. Avery F. Gordon et al. (Minneapolis: University of Minnesota Press, 1996), 70.

43 See "Towards a Contending Pedagogy: Asian American Studies as Extracurricular Praxis," in *Teaching Asian America: Diversity and the Problem of Community,* ed. Lane Ryo Hirabayashi (New York: Rowman and Littlefield, 1997).

44 Klein, *Interdisciplinarity,* 77.

45 Michael Omi and Dana Y. Takagi have very usefully historicized this process of disciplining of Asian American studies in the context of the "waning of radical political movements in the 1980s." They write: "We feel that the absence of a sustained and coherent radical theory of social transformation led to a retreat to more mainstream, discipline-based paradigmatic orientations. Contributing to this trend was the increasing 'professionalization' of the field in academic settings, the demands of tenure and promotion for faculty members, and the entrance of newcomers to the field trained in specific disciplines who had not participated in the new social movements of the previous decades. The result of this has been the contraction of space for dialogue across the disciplines—one which could have critically interrogated disciplinary boundaries and fostered cross-disciplinary perspectives." "Thinking Theory in Asian American Studies," *Amerasia Journal,* 21, nos. 1–2 (1995): viii.

46 Michael Omi and Howard Winant's identification of the state's two responses to contestatory "racial projects" offers some suggestive parallels with the institutional fate of these "identity-based knowledge formations." They distinguish "absorption" to refer to the state's adoption of certain challenges through moderate reforms while "insulation" describes the further marginalization of other demands that cannot be readily absorbed. *Racial Formation in the United States,* 85.

1 Generic Fixations: Reading the Writing Self

1 Harold Bloom, ed., *Asian-American Women Writers* (Philadelphia: Chelsea House Publishers, 1997), xi. As evident in this epigraph, the hyphen is affixed to the adjectival deployment but not to the plural noun "Asian Americans."

2 Bloom, "The Analysis of Women Writers," in *Asian-American Woman Writers,* xii.

3 On this matter, the Library of Congress classification for *Asian-American Women Writers* is worth noting: "1. American literature—Asian American authors—History and criticism. 2. American literature—Asian American authors—Bio-bibliography. 3. American literature—Women authors—History and criticism. 4. American literature—Women authors—Bio-bibliography. 5. Asian Americans in literature. 6. Women and literature—United States."

4 Sarah Blackburn, "Notes of a Chinese Daughter," *Ms.* 5:7 (January 1977): 39.

5 King-kok Cheung, "Re-viewing Asian American Literary Studies," in *An Interethnic Companion to Asian American Literature,* ed. King-kok Cheung (New York: Cambridge University Press, 1998), 10. The prominence of the text in defining but also thereby confining the field is well noted by Leslie Bow's acknowledgement of "the positive effect of having Amy Tan's voice out in a mainstream literary market, which is only just beginning to see Asian American literature as more than *The Woman Warrior.*" "Cultural Conflict/Feminist Resolution in Amy Tan's The Joy Luck Club," in *New Visions in Asian American Studies,* ed. Franklin Ng et al. (Pullman: Washington State University Press, 1994), 92.

6 Edward Iwata, "Word Warriors," *Los Angeles Times* (24 June 1990).

7 Elaine H. Kim, "'Such Opposite Creatures': Men and Women in Asian American Literature," *Michigan Quarterly Review* (1990): 79.

8 Diana Ketchum, "Maxine Hong Kingston: Oakland's 'Woman Warrior' Talks about Life as a Literary Star," *Oakland Tribune* (24 June 1990). The article quotes Kingston as saying, "The *Woman Warrior* came from deep within myself, from the place where I am still a child. *China Men,* on the other hand, is the work of a mature woman who is strong enough to look outward and describe others. In *Tripmaster Monkey,* I leave the egocentric narrator behind altogether." The admitted personal intimacy of *The Woman Warrior* is attenuated here by the developmental trajectory away from that text as well as by the emphasis on the labor of textual production as well as the mediation of a narrator that is distinguished from a writing self.

9 For the most extensive study of the published reviews of Kingston's three books, see Curtiss J. Rooks Jr. and Jon Panish, "The Dilemma of the Ethnic Writer: A Case Study of Maxine Hong Kingston," in *Bearing Dreams, Shaping Visions: Asian Pacific American Perspectives,* ed. Linda A. Revilla et al. (Pul-

man: Washington State University Press, 1993). The authors set out by asserting, "Reviews themselves often declare the 'spokespersonship' of an ethnic author and thereby set the context in which the work is read and understood by the public at large. Such we believe has been the case of Maxine Hong Kingston" (129). Of the twenty-seven reviews they examined, they observe that "Overwhelmingly . . . they discuss her book as a chronicle either of Hong Kingston's developing self or of the people and events that have been important in her life, or as both" (130). While they resist and discount those published efforts to read *The Woman Warrior* as accurately documenting Chinese village life or as universally representing the oppression of women, Rooks and Panish would generically figure Kingston the author as "instead depicting a way of knowing and learning for the Chinese American women of her generation" (131) and of speaking to "a particular sensibility of the Chinese American" (133).

10 This blurb, attributed to John Leonard of the *New York Times*, appears on the back cover of the book.

11 Paul Craig, "An Outsider's Understanding: Maxine Hong Kingston's Chronicles of Chinese-Americans Earn a TV Tribute," *Sacramento Bee* (25 November 1990). In a 1981 interview Kingston expresses dismay at the tendency to reduce these textual productions as transparent documentation of her self, life, and ethnic community: "I've met people who read my books and think they've got it. It's awful—some people read it and say to their Chinese-American friends, 'I understand you now—I've read this book about you." Arturo Islas, "Interview with Maxine Hong Kingston," in *Women Writers of the West Coast Speaking of Their Lives and Careers,* ed. Marilyn Yalom (Santa Barbara: Capra, 1983), 11–19.

12 After the 1990 publication of *The Tripmaster Monkey,* categorized as "Fiction," Kingston claims to have alienated much of her female readership, who found this third book with its brash, fast-talking, and sometimes misogynist male protagonist a radical departure from her earlier books: "I have lost *Ms.* Magazine and others in my audience who wanted to hear the same voice forever. The compensation is that I have a new audience of people who never heard of me before." (Ketchum, "Maxine Hong Kingston.")

13 G. Thomas Couser, *Altered Egos: Authority in American Autobiography* (New York: Oxford University Press, 1989), 230.

14 Cited in Shari Benstock, "Authorizing the Autobiographical," in *The Private Self: Theory and Practice of Women's Autobiographical Writings,* ed. Shari Benstock (Chapel Hill: University of North Carolina Press, 1988), 11.

15 Kim, "'Such Opposite Creatures,'" 71.

16 Philippe Lejeune, *On Autobiography,* ed. Paul John Eakin, trans. Katherine Leary (Minneapolis: University of Minnesota Press, 1989), 12, original italics. In the foreword, Eakin notes how, by drawing attention to the defining significance of a singular proper name inscribed on the title page *and* in

the narrated story, Lejeune "shifted the fulcrum of the genre from the extratextual state of authorial intention to the sign of intention present in the text" (ix).

17 Maxine Hong Kingston, *The Woman Warrior: Memoirs of Girlhood Among Ghosts* (New York: Vintage, 1977). "Brave Orchid" emerges in the middle of the section titled "Shaman," in which a daughter-narrator tells the story of "my mother." Later, the narrator affirms the authenticity of this name, unchanged through the pressures of marriage and immigration to the United States: "Nor did she change her name: Brave Orchid. Professional women have the right to use their maiden names if they like. Even when she emigrated, my mother kept Brave Orchid, adding no American name nor holding one in reserve for American emergencies" (77). In the next section, titled "At the Western Palace," an omniscient third-person narrator displays no familial relation to the two female protagonists, Brave Orchid and Moon Orchid. The opening of the final section that immediately follows further complicates this shifting narrator-protagonist relationship. "The Song for a Barbarian Reed Pipe" opens, "What my brother actually said was, 'I drove Mom and Second Aunt to Los Angeles to see Aunt's husband who's got the other wife'" (163). This is followed by a dialogue with another sibling who presses the brother for more details of the trip, to which he replies that he was not present for some of the scenes described in the preceding section and that he does not remember. The ellipses and mediations are further amplified by the narrator's subsequent disclosure, "In fact, it wasn't me my brother told about going to Los Angeles; one of my sisters told me what he'd told her. His version of the story may be better than mine because of its bareness, not twisted into designs" (163).

18 See Sidonie Smith, *A Poetics of Women's Autobiography: Marginality and the Fictions of Self-Representation* (Bloomington: Indiana University Press, 1987). Smith characterizes the first chapter as "the biographical story of a no-name aunt" (52). Malini Johar Schueller turns the purposely generic anonymity into a proper name in referring to "the No Name aunt." *The Politics of Voice: Liberalism and Social Criticism from Franklin to Kingston* (Albany: SUNY Press, 1992), 152. See also Susan Stanford Friedman, "Women's Autobiographical Selves," in *The Private Self,* ed. Shari Benstock; and Stephanie A. Demetrakopolous, "The Metaphysics of Matrilinealism in Women's Autobiography," in *Women's Autobiography: Essays in Criticism,* ed. Estelle C. Jelinek (Bloomington: Indiana University Press, 1980).

19 Sau-ling Cynthia Wong, "Necessity and Extravagance in Maxine Hong Kingston's *The Woman Warrior*: Art and the Ethnic Experience," *MELUS* 15:1 (spring 1988): 5. Consequently, Brave Orchid is referred to as "Maxine's mother." In a 1991 essay, Wong again notes, "As a child though, Maxine is capable only of posing a Chinese system against an American system: when aunt Moon Orchid goes mad, drawing curtains and locking doors

against invisible enemies, Maxine and her siblings erroneously conclude, 'Chinese people are very weird'" (Sau-ling Wong, "Immigrant Autobiography: Some Questions of Definition and Approach," in *American Autobiography: Retrospect and Prospect,* ed. Paul John Eakin [Madison: University of Wisconsin Press, 1991], 183). As I have pointed out above, this reading oddly transposes a subjective struggle of the young female character onto the episode featuring Moon Orchid, which is written in a distanced yet omniscient third-person and offering glimpses only into the interiority of Brave Orchid and Moon Orchid. Moreover, the narration foregrounds Moon Orchid's bewildered perceptions of her sister's children, whose own point of view is expressed in a startling shift in the cryptic final sentence of this section, "All her children made up their minds to major in science or mathematics" (Maxine Hong Kingston, *The Woman Warrior,* 160). Another critic, King-kok Cheung, notes, "As the lyrical ending intimates, Maxine has worked the discords of her life into a song" ("'Don't Tell': Imposed Silences in *The Woman Warrior* and *The Color Purple,*" *PMLA* [1987]: 170). Making some attempt at a distinction, Paul John Eakin refers to the protagonist-narrator as "Kingston's 'Maxine'" (*Touching the World: Reference in Autobiography* [Princeton: Princeton University Press, 1992], 200). Both Rachel Lee and Leslie W. Rabine refer to a narrator as "Maxine" (Lee, "Claiming Land, Claiming Voice, Claiming Canon: Institutionalized Challenges in Kingston's *China Men* and *The Woman Warrior,*" in *Reviewing Asian America: Locating Diversity,* ed. Wendy L. Ng et al. [Pullman: Washington State University Press, 1995]; and Rabine, "No Lost Paradise: Social Gender and Symbolic Gender in the Writings of Maxine Hong Kingston," in *Revising the Word and the World: Essays in Feminist Literary Criticism,* ed. Veve Clark et al. [Chicago: University of Chicago Press, 1993]). A most interesting clarification of names is offered by Paul Outka: "To avoid confusion and to respect an important difference, in the essay I will refer to Maxine Hong Kingston the protagonist of *The Woman Warrior* as 'Maxine,' and to Maxine Hong Kingston the author of *The Woman Warrior* as 'Kingston'" ("Publish or Perish: Food, Hunger, and Self-Constructions in Maxine Hong Kingston's *The Woman Warrior,*" *Contemporary Literature* 38, no. 3 [1997]: 482, footnote 3).

20 G. Thomas Couser, *Altered Egos,* 230. Contrasting *The Woman Warrior* with Jade Snow Wong's *Fifth Chinese Daughter,* Shirley Geok-lin Lim sees that "the ideological choice of speaking as a Chinese or an American is reflected in the author's choice of pen names" so that "Maxine Hong Kingston, married to an Anglo-American, adopted her Anglo husband's name" ("The Tradition of Chinese American Women's Life Stories," 256). The odd triangulation of ethnic and gendered markers of naming produces awkwardness, given that referring to her as "Kingston" in accordance with other protocols of authorial invocation erases her Chinese/Asian identity. This is

especially so when a reading is centered on ethnicity, as in "The Dilemma of the Ethnic Writer," where Curtiss J. Rooks Jr. and Jon Panish elect to refer to a more awkwardly named "Hong Kingston" throughout, as if in strategic defiance of this erasure. There are also two cases of opting to refer to a "Hong Kingston," which might be explained in terms of the feminist contexts of publication. See E. M. Broner, "Stunning Sequel to *Woman Warrior*," *Ms.* 9, no. 2 (August 1980): 28, 30. In the index to the critical collection *De/Colonizing the Subject*, edited by Sidonie Smith and Julia Watson, the author is listed under "H" as "Hong Kingston, Maxine."

21 Biddy Martin, "Lesbian Identity and Autobiographical Difference(s)," in *Life/Lines: Theorizing Women's Autobiography*, ed. Bella Brudzki and Celeste Schenck (Ithaca: Cornell University Press, 1988): 116.

22 Michel Foucault, *Language, Counter-Memory, Practice: Selected Essays and Interviews*, ed. and trans. Donald F. Bouchard (Ithaca: Cornell University Press, 1977), 116.

23 On the other hand, the critical shorthand that privileges a single authorial last name leads Harold Bloom to mistakenly re-deploy "Kingston" as a natal surname. In noting that "the text is in fact populated by numerous characters drawn from the Chinese-American community of Kingston's youth," Bloom reports, "The Kingstons' tradition of passing down myths and family history profoundly influenced the future author, who would incorporate much of these memories into her novels" (*Asian-American Women Writers*, 37). In crediting the formative influence of the Kingstons, this improper naming, taken as such, could actually work to undermine the autobiographical and sociological transparency of the text.

24 Trinh T. Minh-ha, *Woman, Native, Other: Writing Postcoloniality and Feminism* (Bloomington: Indiana University Press, 1989), 6.

25 I take this locution from Katie King, "Bibliography and a Feminist Apparatus of Literary Production," *TEXT* 5 (1999): 91–103.

26 Elaine H. Kim, "'Such Opposite Creatures,'" 79.

27 For edited collections, see Estelle C. Jelinek, ed., *Women's Autobiography: Essays in Criticism* (Bloomington: Indiana University Press, 1980); Shari Benstock, ed., *The Private Self: Theory and Practice of Women's Autobiographical Writings* (1988); Margaret Culley, ed., *American Women's Autobiography: Fea(s)ts of Memory* (Madison: University of Wisconsin Press, 1992); and Julia Watson and Sidonie Smith, eds., *De/Colonizing the Subject: The Politics of Women's Autobiography* (Minneapolis: University of Minnesota Press, 1992). A notable exception to this ubiquity of *The Woman Warrior* in women's autobiographical criticism is *Life/Lines: Theorizing Women's Autobiography* (Ithaca: Cornell University Press, 1988), edited by Bella Brodzki and Celeste Schenck. While not naming *The Woman Warrior*, Brodzki and Schenck do apologize for a specific absence: "Asian women's autobiographies, despite our strenuous efforts to include them, remain underrepre-

sented in our collection" ("Introduction," 13). For monographs, see Sidonie Smith, *A Poetics of Women's Autobiography: Marginality and the Fictions of Self-Representation* (Bloomington: Indiana University Press, 1987); and Liz Stanley, *The Auto/biographical I: The Theory and Practice of Feminist Auto/biography* (Manchester: Manchester University Press, 1992). See also Faith Pullin, "Enclosure/Disclosure: A Tradition of American Autobiography by Women" in *First Person Singular: Studies in American Autobiography* (New York: St. Martin's Press, 1988).

28 See Stephanie A. Demetrakopolous, "The Metaphysics of Matrilinealism in Women's Autobiography: Studies of Mead's *Blackberry Winter,* Hellman's *Pentimento,* Angelou's *I Know Why the Caged Bird Sings,* and Kingston's *The Woman Warrior,*" in *Women's Autobiography,* ed. Estelle Jelinek; and Suzanne Juhasz, "Toward a Theory of Form in Feminist Autobiography: Kate Millet's *Flying* and *Sita;* Maxine Hong Kingston's *The Woman Warrior,*" in *Contemporary American Writers,* ed. Catherine Rainwater et al.

29 Roberta Rubenstein, *Boundaries of the Self: Gender, Culture, Fiction* (Chicago: University of Chicago Press, 1987), 165.

30 Bella Brodzki and Celeste Schenck, "Introduction," in *Life/Lines: Theorizing Women's Autobiography,* 1, original italics.

31 Shari Benstock, "Introduction," in *The Private Self,* 20.

32 In her review essay, Jeanne Costello also notes the awkwardness of the "sudden introduction, in the last chapter, of a Chinese-American woman's autobiography . . . into a discussion that has been solely limited to English texts." "Taking the 'Women' out of Women's Autobiography: The Perils and Potentials of Theorizing Female Subjectivities," *Diacritics* (summer/fall 1991): 126.

33 Sidonie Smith, *A Poetics of Women's Autobiography,* 150.

34 Sidonie Smith and Julia Watson, "Introduction," in *De/Colonizing the Subject,* ed. Julia Watson and Sidonie Smith, xvii.

35 In her essay in the volume, Caren Kaplan offers a different mapping of a greater continuity and complicity in outlining the "essential categories of autobiography, especially as adopted by Western feminism in the last twenty years—the revelation of individuality, the chronological unfolding of a life, reflections and confessions, the recovery of a suppressed identity." "Resisting Autobiography: Out-law Genres and Transnational Feminist Subjects," in *De/Colonizing the Subject,* ed. Julia Watson and Sidonie Smith, 81.

36 Julia Watson, "Unspeakable Differences: The Politics of Gender in Lesbian and Heterosexual Women's Autobiographies," in *De/Colonizing the Subject,* ed. Julia Watson and Sidonie Smith, 139.

37 Michael M. J. Fischer, "Ethnicity and the Post-Modern Arts of Memory," in *Writing Culture: The Poetics and Politics of Ethnography,* ed. James Clifford and George E. Marcus (Berkeley: University of California Press, 1986), 195.

38 Michel de Certeau, *The Writing of History,* trans. Tom Conley (New York: Columbia University Press, 1988).

39 Liz Stanley, *The Auto/biographical I: The Theory and Practice of Feminist Auto/biography* (Manchester: Manchester University Press, 1992), 70.

40 Leigh Gilmore, *Autobiographics: A Feminist Theory of Women's Self-representation* (Ithaca: Cornell University Press, 1994), 2.

41 Schueller, *The Politics of Voice,* 143.

42 Lee Quinby, "The Subject of Memoirs: *The Woman Warrior's* Technology of Ideographic Selfhood," in *De/Colonizing the Subject,* ed. Julia Watson and Sidonie Smith.

43 Kathryn Van Spanckeren reads the generic titling of book as expressing the writer's ethnocultural identity: "Kingston's presentation of her work as nonfictional 'memoirs' situates it within the classical Chinese canon." "The Asian Literary Background of *The Woman Warrior,*" in *Approaches to Teaching Kingston's "The Woman Warrior,"* ed. Shirley Geok-lin Lim (New York: Modern Language Association, 1991), 44. For an interesting counterperspective to this impulse to trace the text back to Asia or specifically to China and Chinese culture, see Zhang Ya-jie, "A Chinese Woman's Response to Maxine Hong Kingston's *The Woman Warrior,*" MELUS 13, nos. 1–2 (1986): 103–7. Zhang begins, "*The Woman Warrior,* a favorite book of many of my American friends, should have been a very interesting book for me, as I was a visiting professor from the People's Republic of China." In the next paragraph she expresses her initially lackluster impression because "the stories in it seemed somewhat twisted, full of American imagination." The emphatically *American* creative source and reader appreciation of the book is clearly distinguished from Zhang's own reaction: "Furthermore, some of Kingston's remarks offended my sense of national pride." Zhang does agree with the autobiographical fixation, disclosing how she "felt that Kingston held too much bitterness against her mother and her Chinese origin" (103).

44 Ed Iwata, "Word Warriors," *Los Angeles Times* (11 September 1989). The patriarchal cast of Chin's polemical alignment of autobiography and interracial heterosexuality as expressions of racialized submission, which are inimical to "yellow art" and "yellow artists," takes on a blatantly martial and homophobic masculinism in his essay, "This Is Not an Autobiography," where he argues that "the fighter writer uses literary forms as weapons of war, not an expression of ego alone, and does not [waste] time with dandyish expressions of feeling and psychological attitudinizing." Quoted in King-kok Cheung, "The Woman Warrior versus The Chinaman Pacific: Must a Chinese American Critic Choose Between Feminism and Heroism?" in *Conflicts in Feminism,* ed. Marianne Hirsch et al. (New York: Routledge, 1990), 238–39.

45 King-kok Cheung, "Reviewing Asian American Literary Studies," 10. As summarized by Robert G. Lee, Chin and his fellow male writers, most no-

tably Jeffrey Paul Chan and Benjamin Tong, object to the book "on the grounds that it is insufficiently rooted in the historical experience of the Chinese in America; that it distorts the traditional myths and legends on which it relies; and that, as a result, it exoticizes the Chinese aspect of the Chinese American experience, thereby catering to the Orientalist prejudices of its white audience." See "*The Woman Warrior* as an Intervention in Asian American Historiography," in *Approaches to Teaching Kingston's "The Woman Warrior,"* 52.

46 Elaine H. Kim, "'Such Opposite Creatures,'" 75.

47 Shirley Geok-lin Lim, "Feminist and Ethnic Literary Theories in Asian American Literature," *Feminist Studies* 19, no. 3 (fall 1993): 573.

48 Lisa Lowe, *Immigrant Acts,* 74.

49 King-kok Cheung, "The Woman Warrior Versus The Chinaman Pacific," 238.

50 Leslie Bow, "For Every Gesture of Loyalty, There Doesn't Have To Be a Betrayal: Feminism and Cultural Nationalism in Asian American Literature," in *Who Can Speak?: Authority and Critical Identity,* ed. Judith Roof et al. (Urbana: University of Illinois Press, 1995), 37.

51 Jinqui Ling, *Narrating Nationalisms: Ideology and Form in Asian American Literature* (New York: Oxford University Press, 1998), 115. King-kok Cheung, in "The Woman Warrior Versus The Chinaman Pacific," similarly maps a staggered trajectory from ethnonationalist foundation to feminist intervention and attributes the "beginning" of Asian American literature to *Aiiieeeee!:* "This androcentric solution to racist representation was bound to be challenged sooner or later. The catalyst came in the form of Maxine Hong Kingston's *The Woman Warrior* (1976)" (348).

52 While he imbues the *Aiiieeeee!* editors with such historical and political importance, Ling also acknowledges that their efforts to construct a "provisional unity" was "structurally deficient because it prioritized a (straight) male gender as a sufficient ground for ethnic solidarity." *Narrating Nationalisms,* 27.

53 To buttress this point, Ling cites Sara Evans's very broad observation about how some Southern women made this argument in the nineteenth century and during the civil rights movement. *Personal Politics: The Roots of Women's Liberation in the Civil Rights Movement and the New Left* (New York: Knopf, 1979).

54 Leslie Bow attributes the "source" of the debates to "the power that the white media wields in seeming to valorize one Asian American voice at a time." "For Every Gesture of Loyalty," 36.

55 Rooks and Panish observe that "for the non-Asian American, there seems to be a need to read this book as a melting pot story." Indeed, they end their essay by questioning the "lack of Asian American representation among reviewers": "Do the publishers and editors feel that an Asian American

reviewer will be accorded less credibility by the white audience?" "The Dilemma of the Ethnic Writer," 133, 138.

56 Elaine H. Kim, "'Such Opposite Creatures,'" 79.

57 Robert G. Lee, "The Woman Warrior as an Intervention in Asian American Historiography," 52.

58 Sau-ling Cynthia Wong, "Autobiography as Guided Chinatown Tour? Maxine Hong Kingston's *The Woman Warrior* and the Chinese-American Autobiographical Controversy," in *Multicultural Autobiography: American Lives,* ed. James Robert Payne (Knoxville: The University of Tennessee Press, 1992), 248–49.

59 Elaine H. Kim, *Asian American Literature: An Introduction to the Writings and Their Social Context* (Philadelphia: Temple University Press, 1982), 59.

60 It is worth pondering why this impasse has not had the same kind of "defining" force for interdisciplinary women's studies. I would hazard a guess that this may have much to do with the decreased probability that *The Woman Warrior* could be misread as about *all women* as there have been significantly more other books by women authors to discourage a purely metonymic reading of this one text. Rachel Lee has offered a more confident explanation of what she sees as the "qualitatively different institutional incorporation" of *The Woman Warrior* and *China Men:* "I wish to suggest that *The Woman Warrior* has been validated through its successful incorporation into Women's Studies programs, while China Men sits uncomfortably between English literature and Ethnic Studies programs. Portraying a female subject shaping an identity, *The Woman Warrior* appears non-threatening to Women's Studies departments, which can easily embrace it as a young progeny, and luckily, one which might deflect accusations of white feminist dominance." "Claiming Land, Claiming Voice, Claiming Canon" (157).

61 Sau-Ling Cynthia Wong, "Necessity and Extravagance in Maxine Hong Kingston's *The Woman Warrior,*" 4.

62 Shirley Lim, "Twelve Asian-American Writers," 57.

63 Robert G. Lee reads Chin's charge against *The Woman Warrior* as a "fake" book as bound up in his desire to locate an "authentic" Chinese American formal aesthetics in a "heroic" Chinese literary and cultural tradition. In insisting upon the possibility of a pure, authentic cultural identity, such a binary construction of Western "fakeness" and Chinese "realness" echoes the Orientalist discourse of absolute cultural alterity. Furthermore, Lee argues that "[t]he reconstruction of Chinese American history premised on an 'authenticity' in the form of an idealized heroic past simply recapitulates the male domination at the center of Orientalism." "*The Woman Warrior* as an Intervention in Asian American Historiography," 62.

64 Yen Le Espiritu, *Asian American Women and Men: Labor, Laws and Love* (Thousand Oaks, Calif.: Sage Publications, 1997), 136, 137.

65 Stephen Sumida, "Afterword," in *Growing up Asian American: An Anthology,* ed. Maria Hong (New York: Morrow, 1993), 402.

66 Lisa Lowe, "Canon, Institutionalization, Identity: Contradictions for Asian American Studies," in *The Ethnic Canon: Histories, Institutions, Interventions,* ed. David Palumbo-Liu (Minneapolis: University of Minnesota Press, 1994), 53, 54.

67 David R. Shumway, *Creating American Civilization: A Genealogy of American Literature as an Academic Discipline* (Minneapolis: University of Minnesota Press, 1994), 12.

68 Maxine Hong Kingston, "Personal Statement," in *Approaches to Teaching Kingston's "The Woman Warrior,"* 23.

2 Cinematic Projections: Marking the Desirous Body

1 Marina Heung, "Representing Ourselves: Films and Videos by Asian American/Canadian Women," in *Feminism, Multiculturalism, and the Media: Global Diversities,* ed. Angharad N. Valdiva (Thousand Oaks, Calif.: Sage Publications, 1995), 84.

2 Renee E. Tajima, "Lotus Blossoms Don't Bleed: Images of Asian Women," in *Making Waves: An Anthology of Writings By and About Asian American Women,* ed. Asian Women United (Boston: Beacon Press, 1989), 309.

3 Eugene Franklin Wong, *On Visual Media Racism* (New York: Arno Press, 1978), 27.

4 Elaine H. Kim, "Asian Americans and American Popular Culture," in *Dictionary of Asian American History,* ed. Hyung-chan Kim (Westport, Conn.: Greenwood Press, 1989), 108, my italics.

5 Renee Tajima, "Cinemaya," in *Making More Waves: New Writing by Asian American Women,* ed. Elaine H. Kim et al. (Boston: Beacon Press, 1997), 317.

6 Marina Heung is quite correct in her description of *Slaying the Dragon* as delineating "the injuries inflicted on the professional and personal lives of Asian women" ("Representing Ourselves," 86). She then adds, "Although it regrettably uses a male voice-over in its narrative and features a predominantly male roster of 'experts,' it nevertheless surveys a panoply of Asian women—actresses, producers, journalists, students—whose images and voices counteract the one-dimensional celluloid stereotypes with which they are juxtaposed" (86). I am more skeptical about the oppositional force of these first-person testimonies.

7 Hagedorn immediately tempers this plurally professed fatalism with a more knowing, cultivated skepticism: "When there are characters who look like us represented in a movie, we have also learned to view between the lines, or add what is missing." "Asian Women in Film, No Joy, No Luck," *Ms.* (January/February 1994): 74–79. The title is an obvious negation of Wayne

Wang's cinematic adaptation of Amy Tan's novel *The Joy Luck Club,* which Hagedorn criticizes as *perpetuating* stereotypical images, especially of the Chinese immigrant mothers as victims.

8   Connie S. Chan, "Asian-American Women: Psychological Responses to Sexual Exploitation and Cultural Stereotypes," *Women and Therapy* (1987): 34–35. Cited in JeeYeun Lee, "Why Suzie Wong Is Not a Lesbian: Asian and Asian American Lesbian and Bisexual Women and Femme/Butch Gender Identities," in *Queer Studies: A Lesbian, Gay, Bisexual, and Transgender Anthology,* ed. Brett Beemyn et al. (New York: New York University Press, 1996), 130.

9   Sumi K. Cho, "Asian Pacific American Women and Racialized Sexual Harassment," in *Making More Waves,* 165.

10 Helen Zia, "Violence in Our Communities: Where Are the Asian Women?," in *Making More Waves,* 212.

11 JeeYeun Lee, "Why Suzie Wong Is Not a Lesbian," 130. Pushing this point even further toward a still more specific constituency, Lee argues, "Asian women who are both bisexual and feminine or femme occupy an even more overdetermined position that renders them extremely invisible as queers." In an essay included in the same volume, Patricia L. Duncan admits to an intensely felt incongruity between her "s/m identity and an Asian-American identity," as partially borne by the prevailing stereotypes of Asian female sexual submissiveness. "Identity, Power, and Difference: Negotiating Conflict in an S/M Dyke Community," in *Making More Waves,* 88.

12 Yen Le Espiritu, "Race, Class, and Gender in Asian America," in *Making More Waves,* 137.

13 Gina Marchetti, *Romance and the "Yellow Peril": Race, Sex, and Discursive Strategies in Hollywood Fiction* (Berkeley: University of California Press, 1993), 5. An earlier version of my own narrative analysis was published as "The Desiring of Asian Female Bodies: Interracial Romance and Cinematic Subjection," *Visual Anthropology Review* 9:1 (spring 1993): 5–21.

14 Gina Marchetti, *Romance and the "Yellow Peril,"* 1.

15 Marchetti's classification results in a greater concentration of Asian male–white female relationships in the rape, captivity, and seduction scenarios while Asian female–white male couplings dominate the scenarios of salvation, sacrifice, tragedy, and assimilation.

16 While I cannot discuss them in detail here, I would add two other films to this cluster of cinematic representations of "Asian American women" and interracial romance. *Golden Gate* (dir. John Madden, 1993) tackles the anticommunist persecution of Chinese immigrants in the 1950s and links it to the emergence of Asian American politics in opposition to the war in Vietnam and racism in the United States. *Heaven and Earth* (dir. Oliver Stone, 1993) traces the life story of one woman from her childhood in Vietnam to her later immigration to the suburbs as the wife of an American GI. Both

films bear the imprint of Asian American authorship. Tony-winning Chinese American playwright David Henry Hwang wrote the screenplay for *Golden Gate* while *Heaven and Earth* is adapted from the two autobiographies by Le Ly Hayslip, who also served as an on-location advisor during the production of the film.

17 While this is certainly attributable to a difference between linguistic and visual media, it could easily be argued that there are alternate routes of cinematic representation *not* taken by Kelly and Yamamoto.

18 The only interaction that is not sexually charged is the scene in which an African American man informs her that slavery is no longer legal and that she should be free.

19 While Alan Parker is credited for both directing and writing the film, details of plot, setting, and character resonate with accounts of the Internment written by Japanese Americans, especially Jeanne Wakatsuki's memoir, *Farewell to Manzanar.* There are many coincidences in the two stories, such as the emasculation of a tyrannical Japanese father, a strong older brother, and the repeated use of the phrase "shigata ga nai." One scene in which the Kawamura siblings destroy their old Japanese phonograph records as a way of venting their confusion and suppressed rage about the evacuation orders is reminiscent of Mrs. Wakatsuki smashing all of her nice dishware rather than sell to a scavenger. Such similarities further point to another possible (mis)appropriation of Asian American "autobiographical" narratives.

20 Sara Frankel, "American Lesson, British Eyes: 'Paradise' Director Alan Parker Attacks U.S. Social Problem Through Love Story," *The San Francisco Examiner* (23 December 1990). Parker's superficial appropriation of this deplorable historical event is evident in the ironic but potentially misleading title, *Come See the Paradise.*

21 Joe Baltake, "Love Story Weakens Heartfelt Pulse of Pain in 'Paradise'," *Sacramento Bee* (1 February 1991).

22 This disclaimer was begrudgingly added following protests from the Asian American community, and a $100 million suit was filed for defamation against the studio, which was later dropped.

23 Teresa de Lauretis, *Alice Doesn't: Feminism, Semiotics, Cinema* (Bloomington: Indiana University Press, 1984), 113.

24 See my "The Desiring of Asian Female Bodies: Interracial Romance and Cinematic Subjection." In contrast to Marchetti's observation of a mythical emplotment of conflict and resolution for the white American male subject, the interracial narrative of both *Golden Gate* (1993) and *Heaven and Earth* (1993) ends not with the lovers' happy (re)union but with the tormented psyche and suicidal death of the white male protagonist. Indeed, each film continues on to show the female protagonist creating a happy, productive life.

25 See Eugene Wong, *On Visual Media Racism.*

26 Sollors, *Beyond Ethnicity: Consent and Descent in American Culture* (New York: Oxford University Press, 1986). See especially chapter 4, "Romantic Love, Arranged Marriage, and Indian Melancholy." See also Mary V. Dearborn, *Pocahontas's Daughters: Gender and Ethnicity in American Culture* (New York: Oxford University Press, 1986), where Dearborn notes more specifically that "interracial and interethnic unions between Caucasian men and non-white women form an important theme in American fiction written by women of color." Cited by Marchetti, *Romance and the "Yellow Peril,"* 117.

27 Richard Dyer, "Introduction to Film Studies," in *The Oxford Guide to Film Studies,* ed. John Hill and Pamela Church Gibson (Oxford: Oxford University Press, 1998), 3. I have chosen this text to focus on extensively since the writing and publication of such comprehensively organized and pedagogically oriented "guides" attest to one possible composition of a field-formation.

28 Patricia White, "Feminism and Film," in *The Oxford Guide to Film Studies,* 118.

29 If feminist film studies was thus founded on such "structuring omissions," White also counterposes its relative marginality in relation to the cinematic avant-garde: "Economically accessible and institutionally alternative, avant-garde film has given a significant place to American women since at least the 1950s; yet the movement has been pervaded by a male heroic modernism. . . . While feminist film theory has consistently championed formal experimentation, the avant-garde's ethos of personal experience can be seen to foreclose consistent socio-political critique, and frequently, significant engagement with audiences" ("Feminism and Film," 177).

30 Lester D. Friedman, ed. *Unspeakable Images: Ethnicity and the American Cinema* (Urbana: University of Illinois Press, 1991), 5.

31 Ella Shohat, "Ethnicities-in-Relation: Toward a Multicultural Reading of American Cinema," in *Unspeakable Images,* 215.

32 Ella Shohat and Robert Stam, *Unthinking Eurocentrism: Multiculturalism and the Media* (New York: Routledge, 1994), 178.

33 The three strengths of "the analysis of repeated, ultimately pernicious constellations of character traits" that Shohat and Stam outline are: (1) "revealing the oppressive patterns of prejudice in what might at first glance have seemed random and inchoate phenomena"; (2) "highlighting the psychic devastation inflicted by systematically negative portrayals on those groups assaulted by them, whether through internalization of the stereotypes themselves or through the negative effects of their dissemination"; and (3) "signaling the social functionality of stereotypes, demonstrating that they are not an error or perception but a form of social control" (198). And, for "theoretical pitfalls," see pp. 198–200. Characterizing the analytical move on the part of "less subtle critics" of stereotypes who "reduce a complex variety of portrayals to a limited set of reified formulae" as liable to "repro-

ducing the very racial essentialism they were designed to combat" (198), Shohat and Stam add that such criticism often "ignores the historical instability of the stereotype." On the charge of "moralism," Shohat and Stam explicate that insofar as stereotype analysis seeks to adjudge "the relative virtues of fictive characters (seen not as constructs but as if they were real flesh-and-blood people) and the correctness of their actions," it remains wedded to a moral framework of negative and positive, which is the "favored ground" of racist discourse. Following from this privileging of character as unit of analysis, Shohat and Stam finally argue that the focus on "the individual character, rather than larger social categories (race, class, gender, nation, and sexual-orientation) . . . misses the ways in which social institutions and cultural practices, as opposed to individuals, can be misrepresented."

34 Robyn Wiegman, "Race, Ethnicity, and Film," in *The Oxford Guide to Film Studies,* 158.

35 Rey Chow, "Film and Cultural Identity," in *The Oxford Guide to Film Studies,* 169.

36 Robyn Wiegman, *American Anatomies: Theorizing Race and Gender* (Durham: Duke University Press, 1995), 8–9.

37 Hubert Howe Bancroft, "Mongolians in America," in *Essays in Miscellany* (San Francisco: The History Company Publishers, 1890), 309–10 and 315–20. Cited in Wong, *On Visual Media Racism,* vi, note 12.

38 Cited in Elaine H. Kim, "Asian Americans and American Popular Culture," 101. Here we should keep in mind that these textual figures are specified as Chinese.

39 In the rare instance of a chromatic difference, a darker-hued Chinese male body is pictured in contrast to the lighter-hued and rosier white female face and body. See "The Pigtail Has Got to Go" in *Puck* (October 1898); this image is featured in *The Coming Man: Nineteenth-Century American Perceptions of the Chinese,* ed. Philip Choy et al. (Seattle: University of Washington Press, 1994), 103.

40 Cited in Sharon Willis, *High Contrast: Race and Gender in Contemporary Hollywood Films* (Durham: Duke University Press, 1997), 4.

41 The noncorrespondence of yellow as a hue to the heterogeneity of skin colors among Asians did not discourage the Asian American student activists of the 1960s and 1970s from attempting to reappropriate "Yellow" as a politically defiant and indeed radical identification. In the summer of 1968, students at the University of California, Los Angeles, organized a conference titled "Are You Yellow?" (Susie Hsihuan Ling, "The Mountain Movers: Asian American Women's Movement in Los Angeles," *Amerasia Journal* 15:1 [1989]: 65). William Wei describes a conference on "Asian American Experience in America—Yellow Identity," which was held at the University of California, Berkeley, on 11 January 1969, as a significant early site of

"Asian American" political articulation (*The Asian American Movement,* 12). Given that this "Yellow Power" sought to emulate the symbolic and political force of "Black Power," it offers another way of considering the analogic possibilities and limits between Asian American and African American racial formations.

42 James Snead, *White Screen, Black Images* (New York: Routledge, 1994), 5. Cited in Willis, *High Contrast,* 217–18, note 5.

43 Sharon Willis, *High Contrast,* 4.

44 Richard Dyer, *White* (New York: Routledge, 1997), 42.

45 "For much of history," Dyer points out, "white people have sought to make themselves look white of hue" (48). As an example, he cites Michel Chevreul's 1839 book, which enumerated "a huge range of 'white skins' that had to be taken into account, including 'more than rosy,' 'a tint of orange mixed with brown,' 'more yellow than orange,' 'a little blue' and so on."

46 Carl Louis Gregory, *Condensed Course in Motion Picture Photography,* 317, original capitalization. Cited in Dyer, *White,* 91. Dyer notes the "remarkable racial resonance" of this passage, but does not explore it beyond the citation. According to William K. Everson, "the black-and-white silent film was a rarity" through the 1920s: "A rich amber was the standard color, and to this were added different color stocks for appropriate moods or effects; green for scenes of terror, blue for night scenes, red for fire scenes, and often subtle combinations of stock." *American Silent Film* (London: Oxford University Press, 1978), 10.

47 Despite all of these surface modifications and gestural affectations, there was an almost naive commitment to a faithful mimicry of a distinctively authentic original "body": "One of the most sophisticated techniques developed by the industry is a product of the famed Westmore family of cosmetologists. Philip Ahn, the well-known Korean American actor, sat as a model for Wally Westmore who poured a jelly substance into Ahn's eyes. The resultant jelly mold was then transferred to clay, and finally to rubber, after which the pieces were used to Orientalize Akim Tamiroff for *The General at Dawn*" (Wong, *On Visual Media Racism,* 42–43).

48 Wong notes that while white actors and sometimes even black actors were cast to play Asian characters, there was not one instance he could trace in which an Asian actor was cast to play a white character or a black character. He notes the same protocol of substitutions for Native American characters, which were sometimes played by white and black actors, even as no Native American actors could play white or black roles.

49 This quote evinces how specific casting practices configured the legibility of both "oriental" and "occidental" embodiments while being quite indifferent to persons. As long as the argument against "yellowfacing" white actors for Asian roles is premised on a criterion of racial authenticity and cinematic mimesis, it misses the point that white actors have *not* displaced "real

Asians" insofar as it is the fact of the individual actor's dramatic range and flexibility, and the performative and corporeal malleability of the white body in general, which are put on cinematic display. Indeed, Wong concludes from his interviews with various Asian American actors that their professionally ideal scenario is one in which any actor can play any role, meaning that Asian actors should be considered for non-Asian roles. Only in the face of the realization that this is not pragmatic do some Asian actors arrive at the compromised demand that, if they must be shut out of the massive number of white film roles, the relatively miniscule number of Asian roles should be performed by Asian actors.

50 Thomas W. Bohn and Richard Stromgren, *Light and Shadows* (Port Washington, N.Y.: Alfred Publishing Company, 1975), 192–93. Cited in Wong, *On Visual Media Racism,* 56, note 146.

51. Raymond Durgnat, "The 'Yellow Peril' Rides Again," *Film Society Review* 5 : 2 (October 1969): 36. Cited in Wong, *On Visual Media Racism,* 57, note 148.

52 Dorothy B. Jones, *The Portrayal of China and India on the American Screen, 1896–1955: The Evolution of Chinese and Indian Themes, Locales, and Characters as Portrayed on the American Screen* (Cambridge, Mass.: Center for International Studies, MIT, 1955), 12.

53 Timothy J. Lyons, "Hollywood and World War I, 1914–1918," *Journal of Popular Film* 1 : 1 (winter 1972): 20. Cited in Wong, *On Visual Media Racism,* 75, note 182.

54 Jones, *Portrayal:* Prince of Wales, 2; Lord Newton, 2–3.

55 Charles Merz, "When the Movies Go Abroad." *Harper's Monthly Magazine* (January 1926). Cited in Jones, *Portrayal,* 3.

56 Through the establishment of a national film commission, the French government took perhaps the most extensive measures to protect its national image from negative representation not only in the eyes of the domestic French audiences but also those of viewers worldwide. To thwart the attempts by American film producers to cut out those scenes that might possibly be deemed offensive to the French for release in France, the commission decreed that any imported "motion picture must be presented in the exact integral form in which it was shown in the country of origin [U.S.], with dialogue unaltered in the original language" (Jones, *Portrayal,* 3). To further discourage the production of anti-French depictions, the commission held the power "to ban the entire output of any company from France should that company show anywhere in the world a picture which the commission adjudged as detrimental to French prestige" (3).

57 Will Hays, quoted in Edward G. Lowry, "Trade Follows Film," *Saturday Evening Post* (7 November 1925). Cited in Jones, *Portrayal,* 4–5.

58 Jones points out in footnotes that this phrase was slightly amended after World War II when "the United States was included as one of the nations

to be represented fairly, and the words, 'other nations' was changed to read 'all nations'" (5, note 7). Although this could be read as a modest recognition of the national particularity of the United States and of American cinema, I would argue that, on the contrary, it reconfigures the Association of Motion Picture Producers as a supranational agency, above and beyond any ethnocentric and nationalistic prejudices.

59 Cited in Wong, *On Visual Media Racism,* 92.

60 Paul K. Whang, "Boycotting American Movies," *The World Tomorrow* (August 1930). Cited in Wong, *On Visual Media Racism,* 114.

61 Ruth Vasey, "Foreign Parts: Hollywood's Global Distribution and the Representation of Ethnicity," *American Quarterly* 44:4 (December 1992): 630.

3 Historical Reconfigurations:
Delineating Asian Women as/not American Citizens

1 Reverend J. C. Holbrook, "Chinadom in California," *Hutching's California Magazine* (September 1859).

2 Lisa Lowe, *Immigrant Acts: On Asian American Cultural Politics* (Durham: Duke University Press, 1996), 4, original italics.

3 James Moy, *Marginal Sights: Staging the Chinese in America* (Iowa City: University of Iowa Press, 1993), 9. He also adds that while non-Chinese actors almost always performed Chinese characters, there was a production at Rickett's Circus in New York on 13 July 1796 advertising a "young Chinese."

4 Quoted in Judy Yung, *Chinese Women of America: A Pictorial History* (Seattle: University of Washington Press, 1987), 15.

5 Instead, Liang claims that the first Chinese female immigrant came to New York in 1879. "Fighting for a New Life: Social and Patriotic Activism of Chinese American Women in New York City, 1900–1945," *Journal of American Ethnic History* 17:2 (winter 1998): 36, footnote 1.

6 Cited in Yung, *Chinese Women of America,* 15.

7 Cited in Yung, *Chinese Women of America,* 17.

8 Quoted in Dan Caldwell, "The Negroization of the Chinese Stereotype in California," *Southern California Quarterly* 53 (June 1971): 128.

9 Caldwell, "Negroization," 128.

10 Several scholars have recently challenged the overemphasis on prostitution in earlier historiography, pointing to the sizable presence of wives of laborers. Sucheng Chan includes prostitutes as one of six different categories of Chinese women in the United States during the period of exclusionary immigration laws. *Entry Denied: Exclusion and the Chinese Community in America, 1882–1943,* ed. Sucheng Chan (Philadelphia: Temple University Press, 1991). See also George Anthony Peffer, "From Under the Sojourner's Sha-

dow: A Historiographical Study of Chinese Female Immigration to America, 1852–1882," *Journal of American Ethnic History* (spring 1992).

11 Lucie Cheng Hirata, "Chinese Immigrant Women in Nineteenth-Century California," in *Asian and Pacific American Experiences: Women's Perspectives,* ed. Nobuya Tsuchida (Minneapolis: University of Minnesota Press, 1982), 40–41.

12 Neil Larry Shumsky, "Tacit Acceptance: Respectable Americans and Segregated Prostitution, 1870–1910," *Journal of Social History* 19 (summer 1986). Although the clientele for Chinese prostitution comprised Chinese immigrant males and non-Chinese men, it was further sanctioned under the racist and sexist logic that providing Chinese men with necessary sexual release would keep these lascivious men away from (white) American women. Others have proposed that Chinese prostitution in the United States was also useful for certain capitalists who sought to maintain the split family structure in which the family stayed back in China, in that it helped justify lower wages and harsher conditions for their Chinese male workforce.

13 Lucie Cheng Hirata, "Free, Indentured, Enslaved," *Signs: A Journal of Women in Culture and Society* 5:1 (autumn 1979): 5.

14 Reverend A. W. Loomis, "Chinese Women in California," *Overland Monthly* (April 1869): 345–46.

15 Ibid., 349. While decrying prostitution, Loomis argues that these Chinese females "deserve our pity" since they were forced into "their course of prostitution." Additionally, the author recommends that a special home be established as a place of refuge and reform for these Chinese women: "Here is a field for the exercise of benevolence; and this community, young as is this country, is not behind any Eastern city in its proportion of noble women, who only need to be told where there is want to be relieved, sorrow to be assuaged, or wrong to be redressed, and they are there with all a woman's sympathy and quick perception, contriving and executing means to meet the exigencies of the occasion" (348).

16 Chan, "The Exclusion of Chinese Women," in *Entry Denied: Exclusion and the Chinese Community in America, 1870–1943* (Philadelphia: Temple University Press, 1991), 97.

17 *Alta California* (22 June 1866). Cited in Chan, "The Exclusion of Chinese Women," 98.

18 Ivan Light, "From Vice District to Tourist Attraction: The Moral Career of American Chinatowns, 1880–1940," *Pacific Historical Review* 43 (August 1974). Light makes note of how "some white visitors apparently felt free to engage 'sing-song' girls in aberrant sexual practices which they would have blushed even to mention to the most jaded of white harlots." He then asserts that to exploit "persistent rumors about the alleged difference in the 'slant' of the vagina of white and Chinese women . . . Chinese prostitutes developed the ten-cent 'lookee' for the curious" (371). Here then is another

troubling display of Chinese female bodies premised on their alleged physiological peculiarities.

19 Yuji Ichioka, "Ameyuki-San: Japanese Prostitutes in Nineteenth-Century America," *Amerasia Journal* 4, no. 1 (1977).

20 Noting the anomalous presence of Japanese prostitutes in Butte, Montana, in 1884, which was recorded in Japanese consular reports, Ichioka infers that they probably came via Hong Kong where they were taken initially to work for the large number of Chinese male laborers and then "rerouted to America as prostitutes in Chinese labor camps" ("Ameyuki-San," 4). This transnational traffic of women within Asia and its linkages to the United States merits further study.

21 Cited in Stuart Creighton Miller, *The Unwelcome Immigrant: The American Image of the Chinese, 1785–1882* (Berkeley: University of California Press, 1974), 154.

22 Chan, "The Exclusion of Chinese Women," 100. In the case of *Ex parte Ah Fook,* Chan cites one California Supreme Court associate who affirmed the credibility of the commissioner's judgment comparing "the authority given the state commissioner of immigration to exclude the Chinese women to the power given a health officer, who could isolate those ill of contagious diseases, or those who have been in contact with such, or the powers to prohibit the introduction of criminals or paupers. These powers are employed, not to punish offenses committed without our borders, but to prevent the entrance of elements dangerous to the health and moral well-being of the community" (101).

23 Charles J. McClain, *In Search of Equality: The Chinese Struggle Against Discrimination in Nineteenth-Century America* (Berkeley: University of California Press, 1994), 57.

24 McClain, *In Search of Equality,* 58.

25 See the entry on "Page Law of 1875" in *The Asian American Encyclopedia,* ed. Franklin Ng (New York: Marshall Cavendish, 1995); 1192–93. It continues, "While the law also established much less severe penalties for individuals engaged in the coolie trade, the numbers of male immigrants rendered individual interrogation a logistical impossibility."

26 "Page Law of 1875," 1193.

27 Yung, *Unbound Feet: A Social History of Chinese Women in San Francisco* (Berkeley: University of California Press, 1955), 24.

28 While historians have given differing assessments of the effectiveness of the Page Law in restricting Chinese prostitution, Sucheng Chan and Judy Yung both conclude that it "succeeded in reducing not only the number of Chinese prostitutes but also the overall number of Chinese immigrant women." Yung, *Unbound Feet,* 32.

29 This is Chan's primary argument in "The Exclusion of Chinese Women": "Contrary to the common belief that laborers were the target of the first

exclusion act, the effort to bar another group of Chinese—prostitutes—preceded the prohibition against laborers. Given the widely held view that all Chinese women were prostitutes, laws against the latter affected other groups of Chinese women who sought admission into the country as well" (95).

30 Yen Le Espiritu, *Asian American Women and Men: Labor, Laws, and Love* (Thousand Oaks, Calif.: Sage Publications, 1997), 18.

31 Joan B. Trauner, "The Chinese as Medical Scapegoats in San Francisco, 1870–1905," *California History* 57 (spring 1978): 75.

32 Cited in Joyce M. Wong, "Prostitution: San Francisco Chinatown, Mid- and Late-Nineteenth Century," *Bridge: An Asian American Perspective* 6 (winter 1978): 25.

33 Cited in Trauner, "The Chinese as Medical Scapegoats," 75.

34 Cited in "Chinatown: Declared a Nuisance!" (report, San Francisco, California, 10 March 1880). In advocating the exclusion of Chinese immigration, Toland also invoked a more practical reason on behalf of the medical profession; he testified that if Chinese were allowed to continue living in such moral and physical squalor, "It will fill our hospitals with invalids, and I think it would be a great relief to the younger portion of our committee to *get rid of them*" (5, original italics).

35 "Chinatown: Declared a Nuisance!" In the attached "Memorial on Chinatown," submitted to the mayor and the board of health by the Investigating Committee of the Anti-Chinese Council, Workingmen's Party, there is this panic about contamination and degeneration, focused on drug use and prostitution in Chinatowns: "There it is from whence leprosy, this inherent factor, this inbred disease of Chinese, is infused into our healthy race by the using, the sucking of opium-pipes, which have been handled by the already afflicted. From thence, from houses of prostitution, grows and steadily infuses itself slowly but surely an incurable and hereditary curse, ultimately destroying whole nations through the instrumentality of Chinese prostitutes, who, in destroying our young men, implant into them the germs of leprosy and other loathsome, constitutional and hereditary disorders, which will be handed down, through our present and past laxity concerning the enforcement of hygienic laws, to our children and children's children" (12). Citing the "germ theory" of disease as "now an acknowledged fact in the science of medicine," the report goes on to warn against the consumption of any and all products, including clothing, fabrics, and cigars, manufactured by the Chinese and points to the contagious force of Chinese servants. The report displaces the labor of Chinese immigrants, in sex work, manufacturing, and domestic work by figuring this triangulation as "a perfect network of contagion and infection" (13). See also Yung, *Unbound Feet*, 32.

36 Despite the emphasis on the Chinese women, prostitution in Chinatown was sustained by a complex and stratified network of brothel owners, po-

licemen, and non-Chinese prostitutes as well as Chinese and non-Chinese male customers: "In 1885, there were approximately seventy brothels in SF's Chinatown. White prostitutes in Chinatown bordellos 'obtained their patronage almost exclusively from the Chinese themselves.' According to San Francisco police, the 'better class' of Chinese prostitutes catered exclusively to a Chinese trade and would 'not allow white men at all.' Only the seedier Chinese prostitutes took white clients. However, such women were numerous enough that, according to a San Francisco policeman, 'great numbers of young [white] men visit Chinawomen.'" Light, "From Vice District to Tourist Attraction," 310–11.

37 "Chinatown: Declared a Nuisance!" 5.

38 Cited in Light, "From Vice District to Tourist Attraction," 311.

39 Benjamin S. Brooks, *The Chinese in California,* (1876), 3, original italics. Given the fluid and heterogeneous racial and ethnic composition of both native and newly arriving bodies in California at this time, it is impossible to determine the specific referent for "white" here.

40 Yung, *Unbound Feet,* 23. Yung cites *In re Ah Quan* and *The Case of the Chinese Wife (Ah Moy)* as key cases that barred the entry of wives of laborers.

41 Quoted in Adam McKeown, "Transnational Chinese Families and Chinese Exclusion, 1875–1943," *Journal of American Ethnic History* 18:2 (winter 1999): 73–110.

42 Chan, "The Exclusion of Chinese Women," 132.

43 M. G. C. Edholm, "A Stain on the Flag," *The Californian* (February 1892), 159.

44 "Chinese Slavery," *San Francisco Chronicle* (17 April 1892).

45 Charles Frederick Holder, "Chinese Slavery in America," *North American Review* (September 1897): 288–94.

46 Ichioka, "Ameyuki-san," 2. Noting that Japanese prostitutes were brought to the United States by Japanese men as early as the late 1880s, Ichioka claims that they were divided into three categories delineated by the racial and ethnic identity of their male clientele: "The Hakujin-tori catered exclusively to white men, the Shinajin-tori had Chinese customers, and the Nihonjin-tori dealt with Japanese. This division of prostitutes no doubt mirrored not only white American prejudices but Japanese ones as well" (10).

47 Ichioka also distinguishes this case for Japanese American history as "the first Japanese-related litigation to reach the U.S. Supreme Court." "Ameyuki-san," 19, footnote 24.

48 Hyung-chan Kim, ed., *A Legal History of Asian Americans, 1790–1990* (Westport, Conn.: Greenwood Press, 1994), 77.

49 Ichioka, "Ameyuki-san," 17.

50 William S. Bernard, "A History of U.S. Immigration Policy," in *Immigration* (Cambridge: Belknap Press of Harvard University Press, 1982), 93.

51 Despite protests on the part of Koreans to be recognized as Koreans, their

categorization as Japanese by the U.S. government, demonstrating an implicit acceptance of the legitimacy of Japan's hostile colonization of Korea, continued until the end of the Second World War in 1945.

52 Bernard, "A History of U.S. Immigration Policy," 94.

53 Sucheng Chan writes: "Anthropologists classified some of the inhabitants of the Indian subcontinent as 'Aryans,' but no one was sure whether Aryans were Caucasians and whether the latter referred only to whites. Between 1910 and 1917, immigration officials tried to minimize the number of Asian Indians coming in by using administrative regulations, but a clause in the 1917 Immigration Act finally enabled them to stop the influx." *Asian Americans: An Interpretive History* (Boston: Twayne Publishers, 1991), 55.

54 Ronald Takaki, *Strangers from a Different Shore* (New York: Little, Brown, 1989), 14. Takaki notes, "The 1924 law was amended in 1930 to allow the entry of Asian wives of American citizens married after June 1930" (497, footnote 20).

55 "Facing a three to one male-female ratio in the Chinese community, thousands of Chinese-American soldiers married women in China and brought them to the United States. Between 1946 and 1953, over seven thousand Chinese entered as war brides. . . . Filipinos, too, were bringing wives here. After becoming citizens through service in the U.S. Armed Forces, Filipino men sent for their families. Meanwhile the Korean War began a new Korean immigration: between 1950 and 1965, some 17,000 Koreans entered, most of them as nonquota spouses of American citizens." Takaki, *Strangers from a Different Shore,* 417.

56 This racial bar was doubly compounded for those Asian Americans, but especially for Japanese Americans, who fought in the war. As many scholars have pointed out, even though the wartime internment of Japanese Americans was a flagrant denial of their citizen status, many Japanese American soldiers sought to prove their loyalty to the nation-state by way of military service. As Teresa K. Williams describes, "With the rigorous support of the Japanese American Citizens League that assisted Nisei (second-generation) Japanese Americans to marry and bring home native Japanese women, the GI Fiancées Act was enacted in 1946. This permitted the Japanese fiancées of US servicemen to enter the U.S. without an immigrant status." "Marriage Between Japanese Women and U.S. Servicemen Since World War II," *Amerasia Journal* 17:1 (1991): 143. This convergence of the military's needs for male bodies with a broader Japanese American political project of reasserting their citizen status resulted in a gender-skewed postwar immigration. Williams estimates that 55,000 to 100,000 Japanese women have subsequently come to the United States as "international brides."

57 Bill Ong Hing, *Making and Remaking Asian America Through Immigration Policy, 1850–1990* (Palo Alto: Stanford University Press, 1993), 68.

58　Jeff H. Lesser, "Always 'Outsiders': Asians, Naturalization, and the Supreme Court," *Amerasia Journal* 12:1 (1985–86): 84.

59　Eileen Boris, "The Racialized Gendered State: Constructions of Citizenship in the United States," *Social Politics* (summer 1995): 167.

60　Citing as evidence Harold Hyman's *A More Perfect Union: The Impact of the Civil War and the Reconstruction of the Constitution* (New York: Knopf, 1973), which describes how Senator Charles Sumner "won the inclusion of African descendents, skirting Orientals about whom western Republicans were sensitive," Lesser adds, "Thus, in effect, the act was a Republican compromise which explicitly excluded Chinese, so that persons of African descent might become citizens." "Always 'Outsiders,'" 84–85.

61　Charles J. McClain, "Tortuous Path, Elusive Goal: The Asian Quest for American Citizenship," *Asian Law Journal* 2, no. 3 (1995): 36.

62　Cited in Lesser, "Always 'Outsiders,'" 86.

63　Cited in Kim, *A Legal History of Asian Americans,* 120–21.

64　Cited in Lesser, "Always 'Outsiders,'" 87.

65　Paraphrased by McClain, "Tortuous Path, Elusive Goal," 49.

66　See Benedict Anderson, *Imagined Communities* (London: Verso, 1991).

67　Quoted in Lesser, "Always 'Outsiders,'" 88, original italics.

68　Gary R. Hess points out, "Between 1923 and 1926, the naturalization certificates of nearly sixty Indians were cancelled. Authorities did not act against Indians who had served in the American army during the war. The loss of citizenship made these Indians 'stateless persons' and also meant the loss of citizenship for the many American women who had married Indians." "The 'Hindu' in America: Immigration and Naturalization Policies and India, 1917–1946," *Pacific Historical Review* 38 (1991): 69.

69　Kim, *A Legal History of Asian Americans,* 121. In his book *White By Law: The Legal Construction of Race* (New York: New York University Press, 1996), Ian F. Haney López surveys a greater range of court cases on racial categorization and asks: "Why is it that all but one of the fifty-two prerequisite cases turned on whether the applicant was White, when every case was litigated after 1870, the year naturalization became equally available to Blacks?" (50–51). He adds, "Indeed, some immigrants, for example the Chinese, were initially categorized as Black, suggesting that for some, attempting to naturalize as a 'white person' was the more difficult route" (51). While López offers the possibility that the geographically specific nature of "persons of African nativity or descent" may also have discouraged taking this path toward naturalization, he attributes greater force to how "immigrants to this country quickly learn the value of being White rather than Black, and thereby learn to cast themselves as Whites"(52).

70　McClain, "Tortuous Path," 46.

71　Lowe, *Immigrant Acts,* 20.

72 Virginia Sapiro, "Women, Citizenship, Nationality," *Politics and Society* 13 (1984): 5.

73 Boris, "The Racialized Gendered State," 167.

74 Ian F. Haney López, *White By Law: The Legal Construction of Race,* 46.

75 Lauren Berlant, *The Anatomy of National Fantasy: Hawthorne, Utopia, and Everyday Life* (Chicago: University of Chicago Press, 1991), 11–12.

76 Sapiro, "Women, Citizenship, Nationality," 2. She also adds: "This change was one of the first items on the agenda of feminists at the time women obtained the right to vote; to the National Women's party it ranked along with an equal rights amendment to the Constitution as a necessary step in the completion of the task of full citizenship for women" (2–3).

77 Reed Ueda, "Naturalization and Citizenship," in *Immigration,* 135.

78 Quoted in Kathryn Fong, "Asian Women Lose Citizenship," *The San Francisco Journal* (29 December 1976), 12.

79 Cited in Berlant, *The Anatomy of National Fantasy,* 13.

80 Fong notes: " The complexity of individual cases arising out of the citizenship and marriage laws made it necessary for Congress to amend these laws to cover all the exceptions. The Act of June 25, 1936, the Act of July 2, 1940, the Act of October 14, 1940 (also known as the Nationality Act of 1940), the 1953 and 1971 editions of the Department of Justice's Laws Applicable to Immigration and Nationality all have provisions dealing with the naturalization rights of American-born women who were affected by the 1922 Cable Act" ("Asian Women Lose Citizenship," 12).

81 Lowe, *Immigrant Acts,* 10.

82 Katie King, *Theory in its Feminist Travels: Conversations in U.S. Women's Movements* (Bloomington: Indiana University Press, 1994), 112.

83 Anne McClintock, "Family Feuds: Gender, Nationalism, and the Family," *Feminist Review* 44 (summer 1993).

84 Homi K. Bhabha, ed., *Nation and Narration* (New York: Routledge, 1990), 300.

85 Quoted in Appleby, Hunt, and Jacob, *Telling the Truth About History* (New York: Norton, 1994), 154.

86 Takaki, *Strangers from a Different Shore,* 11.

87 Chan, *Asian Americans,* xiv.

88 Gary Okihiro, *Margins and Mainstreams: Asians in American History and Culture* (Seattle: University of Washington Press, 1993), 156.

89 Takaki, *Strangers from a Different Shore,* 7. All quotations in this paragraph are taken from p. 7.

90 Appleby, Hunt, and Jacob, *Telling the Truth About History,* 200.

91 L. Ling-chi Wang attributes the authorship of this term to Yuji Ichioka. "A Critique of *Strangers From a Different Shore,*" *Amerasia Journal* 16:2 (1990): 76.

92 In "Chinese Immigrant Women in the Nineteenth-Century," Lucie Cheng

Hirata notes how "white observers tended to emphasize the exotic or the evil, and Chinese writers tried to counter with exaltations of a few upper-class or highly educated women." Although this suggests a terrain of situated knowledge production and discursive struggle, she adds, "Hidden from history are the experiences of the majority of early Chinese immigrant women, who tried to survive within a complex structure." Hirata then characterizes her essay as "only the beginning in uncovering the history" (51).

93 Pointing out "lapses in the syntax constructed by the law of a place," Michel de Certeau writes, "Therein they symbolize a return of the repressed, that is, a return of what, at any given moment, has become unthinkable in order for a new identity to become thinkable." *The Writing of History* (New York: Columbia University Press, 1988), 4.

94 Okihiro, *Margins and Mainstreams,* 67–68.

95 Sucheta Mazumdar makes a similar point to "relocate" Asian American women in Asia during the male-dominated immigration of Chinese, Punjabi, and Filipinos to the United States, arguing that "when these migrant husbands returned they took back a bit of America with them and transformed their own cultural and social worlds." "Beyond Bound Feet: Relocating Asian American Women," *Magazine of History* (summer 1996): 25.

96 Okihiro, *Margins and Mainstreams,* 92.

97 This can be seen in the very titles of classic texts such as Sheila Rowbotham, *Hidden from History: Rediscovering Women in History from the Seventeenth Century to the Present* (New York: Pantheon Books, 1974); Gerda Lerner, *The Majority Finds its Past: Placing Women in History* (Oxford: Oxford University Press, 1979); and Anne Firor Scott, *Making the Invisible Woman Visible* (Urbana: University of Illinois Press, 1984).

98 Ellen Carol DuBois and Vicki L. Ruiz, eds., *Unequal Sisters: A Multicultural Reader in U.S. Women's History* (New York: Routledge, 1990), xv, xii.

99 Recall that George A. Peffer's historiographical critique of the dominance of the "sojourner" theory is titled "From Under the Sojourner's Shadow."

100 Donna Gabaccia, *From the Other Side: Women, Gender, and Immigrant Life in the U.S., 1820–1990* (Bloomington: Indiana University Press, 1994), 139.

101 Michel Foucault, "The Historical *a priori* and the Archive," in *The Archaeology of Knowledge and the Discourse of Language,* trans. A. M. Sheridan Smith (New York: Pantheon, 1972), 128.

102 Lucie Cheng Hirata, "Free, Indentured, Enslaved," 6.

103 George Anthony Peffer contends that the historiographical dominance of the "sojourner" and "restrictive (patriarchal) culture" theories of gender imbalance has discouraged scholarly attention to the Chinese immigrant women who *were* here in significant numbers in the nineteenth century. Instead, he calls for a more qualified approach: "The sojourner mentality

may explain why the majority of Chinese wives failed to join their husbands in the United States, but relying upon this theory alone to account for their enduring scarcity in America's Chinatowns demands a universal fidelity to inflexible cultural mores which was, in fact, neither exhibited nor demanded in Chinese village life." "From Under the Sojourner's Shadow," 58.

104 Chan, "The Exclusion of Chinese Women," 95.

105 Espiritu, *Asian American Women and Men,* 17.

106 Gloria L. Kumagai, "The Asian Women in America," *Bridge: An Asian American Perspective* (winter 1978): 17. Claiming that "the lives of Chinese immigrant women have been patterned on the Confucian ethic," Kumagai further concludes, "The cultural values of passivity and submission are passed on to Chinese American females who are born in this country." This increasingly Americanized graphing of descent and influence from Confucian culture to Chinese immigrant women to Chinese American females is posited as a model for the other ethnic women who come *after,* both in terms of the years of immigration and in the narrative order in this historical account. The Chinese origin sets the "pattern" that the case of Japanese women partially resembles but also differs from; the two ethnonational groups then set the template for the other ethnonational groups to come: "Besides Asian women of Chinese and Japanese ancestry, there are other women of Asian ancestry in this country, i.e. Korean, Filipino, Vietnamese, South Sea Islands, and Hawaiian. Early immigration patterns of these groups are similar to those of Chinese and Japanese: men came first and in greater numbers than women."

107 The nineteenth-century Chinese prostitute appears in the earliest discursive productions of and by Asian/American women. The 1971 student publication *Asian Women* included an article titled "Forgotten Women" by Gayle Louie. In addition to the works cited already, see Joan Hori, "Japanese Prostitution in Hawaii During the Immigration Period," in *Asian and Pacific American Experiences: Women's Perspectives,* ed. Nobuya Tsuchida. (Minneapolis: University of Minnesota Press, 1982), 56–65.

108 Hirata, "Free, Indentured, Enslaved," 8. In her brief account of Ah Toy, who arrived in 1849 from Hong Kong and "soon became infamous as the earliest and most famous Chinese courtesan in San Francisco," Judy Yung asserts, "Ah Toy's fame as a prostitute and the sensational newspaper coverage of Chinese prostitution led to the rise of another early stereotype of Chinese women—that of the prostitute." *Chinese Women of America,* 15.

109 Ichioka, "Ameyuki-San," 1.

110 Espiritu, *Asian American Women and Men,* 31.

111 Indeed, Joyce M. Wong draws an uninterrupted heritage that links Chinese women's involvement in prostitution in the nineteenth century to "Asian American women" in the 1980s: "The blatant degradation of Chi-

nese womanhood in the mid- and late-nineteenth century seems endless as Asian American women today are confronted with racist-sexist remarks and leering looks equating them with wartime prostitutes or present-day prom queens." "Prostitution," 28.

112 "Page Law of 1875," 1193.

113 Ichioka, "Ameyuki-san," 2.

114 For an interesting visual representation, see the reproduction of the "Official Map of Chinatown in San Francisco," identified in the caption as "Prepared under the supervision of the Special Committee of the Board of Supervisors, July 1885" and notating the location of "white prostitution houses" along with "Chinese gambling houses, prostitution houses, opium places, joss house." Wong, "Prostitution," 26.

115 Peffer, "From Under the Sojourner's Shadow," 42–43. Robert McClellan notes how "statistics were developed which were designed to prove that the Chinese population contributed a disproportionate share of the criminal population in the United States. One table based on the 1890 census showed that although the Chinese and Japanese made up less than a quarter of one percent of the foreign population, they were responsible for more than one and one quarter percent of homicides in the United States" (37). This table is attributed to an article on "Immigration and Crime" by Sydney G. Fischer, published in the September 1896 issue of *Popular Science Monthly*. McClellan also cites an article bearing the same title by a W. M. F. Rand in *The Journal of Social Science* (February 1890). This suggests an early instance of entangled webs of knowledge and identity formations, which produce the "Chinese" or "Asian immigrant" as a social problem. See *The Heathen Chinee: A Study of American Attitudes Toward China, 1890–1905* (Columbus: Ohio State University Press, 1971).

116 Loomis, "Chinese Women in California," 345.

117 A significant instance of such self-narration includes a brief unit titled "Story of Wong Ah So," which was collected, translated into English, edited, and published in 1946 as part of the "Social Science Source Documents" produced by the Social Science Institute at Fisk University. Attached to a very brief first-person narration is a copy of a primary document titled "Letter from Wong Ah So to her Mother Found in Suitcase After Arrest in Fresno, February 7, 1924." The archives of the mission homes also contain letters and journals written by the Chinese female residents.

118 Sucheng Chan notes: "The new element that has crept into historical studies of Asian Americans done in the last decade and a half is the concept of agency—a central idea in the new social history. Although most of the current generation of Asian American historians seldom make such a claim themselves, they are very much a part of the movement to write 'history from below. .' . . [Asian Americans] are depicted as people fully

capable of weighing alternatives, making choices, asserting control over the circumstances they face, and helping to change the world in which they live." "The Writing of Asian American History," *Magazine of History* 10:4 (summer 1996): 14.

119 Sidney Stahl Weinberg makes a similar observation in her critical assessment of the subdiscipline of "Immigration History" when she writes, "In most social history, women usually have been subsumed under 'family' with little consideration of their distinctive roles within or outside the home." "The Treatment of Women in Immigration History: A Call for Change," *Journal of American Ethnic History* 11 (summer 1992): 31.

120 Hirata, "Free, Indentured, Enslaved," 23.

121 Tong, *Unsubmissive Women: Chinese Prostitutes in Nineteenth-Century San Francisco* (Norman, Okla.: University of Oklahoma Press, 1994), xi.

122 Tong does incorporate other texts, especially those that have been produced since the publication of Hirata's essay, such as Anne M. Butler's *Daughters of Joy, Sisters of Misery,* Julia Kristeva's *About Chinese Women,* and Ruthanne Lum McCunn's *Thousand Pieces of Gold,* which he generically categorizes as a "biographical novel." This book serves an especially useful purpose in the subjectivization process because the projected interiority of Lalu Nathoy in McCunn's narration is read not only as a transparent window onto Nathoy's own subjectivity and personal history but also as a representative example for other Chinese immigrant women of the nineteenth century. For instance, Tong states on p. 42: "Few women sold into prostitution expressed resentment against their parents. When Lalu Nathoy first learned that her parents were planning to sell her, she rationalized that she had been sold so that the 'family could live.'" Tong also cites *Thousand Pieces of Gold* in his bibliography. Donna Gabaccia similarly incorporates this book in her comparative historical study of immigrant women, *From the Other Side.*

123 An illustrative passage reads: "This book explores the lives of Chinese prostitutes in San Francisco as a case study of women who not only survived subjugation but also, in many cases, summoned the strength to change their fate. In many ways, this is a portrayal of the 'powers of the weak'— the interaction of women's oppression and women's power. The Chinese women pressed into commercialized sex in this cosmopolitan city of the American West were hardly passive victims of their fate. Rather, under circumscribed conditions, they opposed their oppression and, if the opportunity arose, left the sexual commerce for better fortunes" (*Unsubmissive Women,* xix). Sucheng Chan also notes this in her historiographical overview: "However, Tong, in his eagerness to demonstrate that even the most oppressed individuals possess agency, overstates the extent to which prostitutes were able to overcome the restrictive conditions under which they lived" ("The Writing of Asian American History," 17).

124 Joyce M. Wong claims, "Of the small number of Chinese women who came to America in these early days, a good many of them unwillingly became prostitutes" ("Prostitution," 23.) As illustrative evidence, Wong quotes (on p. 17) the testimony given by an unnamed "slave girl" that appears in G. B. Densmore's *The Chinese in California: Description of Chinese Life in San Francisco, Their Habits, Morals and Manners* (San Francisco: Pettit and Russ, 1888).

125 Appleby, Hunt, and Jacob write, "Historians' questions turn the material from the past into evidence, for evidence is only evidence in relation to a particular account. . . . the objects that compose the supporting evidence come under scrutiny. Evidence adduced to an explanation can never be kept secret in a society that prizes historical knowledge, and it is the accessibility of evidence in publicly supported archives, libraries, and museums that sustains the historical consciousness of this culture. An audience of peers derives its power from equal access to the evidence and to publication, a reminder that democratic practices have an impact far beyond the strictly political. They permit replicability and testing, honest and often stormy controversy." *Telling the Truth About History,* 261. But this does not consider how the very production and preservation of what would and could later count as such public, accessible evidence are scored by unequal power and resources.

126 Hori, "Japanese Prostitution in Hawaii During the Immigration Period," 63.

127 Hirata, "Free, Indentured, Enslaved," 27.

128 Appleby, Hunt, and Jacob, *Telling the Truth About History,* 11.

129 Lowe, *Immigrant Acts,* 104, 110.

130 MaryKim DeMonaco, "Disorderly Departure: An Analysis of the United States Policy Toward Amerasian Immigration," *Brooklyn Journal of International Law* 15, no. 3 (1989): 661, 662.

131 DeMonaco, "Disorderly Departure," 668, 680.

132 In an excellent critical reframing of the 1965 act, Eithne Luibheid points out that the privileging of "family reunification" was predicated on a very particular vision of the family to be reunited. Citing David Reimer's book *Still the Golden Door: The Third World Comes to America* (New York: Columbia University Press, 1992) on how "the attorney general predicted that only about five thousand Asians would come as a result of the new law," Luibheid argues that the larger numbers of Asian immigrants after 1965 was "clearly an unintended consequence," which also accompanied an actual decrease in immigration from Mexico and Latin America. "The 1965 Immigration and Nationality Act: An 'End' to Exclusion?" *Positions* 5:2 (1997): 506–07.

133 Joan Scott, *Gender and the Politics of History* (New York: Columbia University Press, 1988), 30.

4 Disciplined Embodiments:
Si(gh)ting Asian/American Women as Transnational Labor

1   I am referring to Lynn Duggan's black and white photo of the "Ricoh watch factory, The Philippines" that appears on p. 14 of Annette Fuentes and Barbara Ehrenreich, *Women in the Global Factory* (Boston: South End Press, 1983). It is again reproduced in a very different context as one of the decorative visuals in the "Feminism and the Critique of Colonial Discourse" issue of *Inscriptions* nos. 3/4 (1988): 78.

2   Judith Butler, *Bodies That Matter: On the Discursive Limits of "Sex"* (New York: Routledge, 1994), 9, original italics.

3   Some would argue that migrant labor is an even more compelling type of transnational labor, but I have chosen to emphasize manufacturing and sex work in certain Asian and American locales in an effort to trouble the fixed distinction of these two sites. The case of migrant Filipinas is especially notable as evident in the following demographics: "In 1991, women constituted a larger portion of the country's overseas workforce (41 percent) than its domestic workforce (36 percent). Of those overseas, approximately 70 percent are women working as domestic servants in middle- and upper-middle class homes in the U.S., Britain, Europe, Japan, and the Middle East." Grace Chang, "The Global Trade in Filipina Workers," in *Dragon Ladies: Asian American Feminists Breathe Fire,* ed. Sonia Shah (Boston: South End Press, 1997), 134.

4   This is noted for Taiwan in Hu Tai-Li, "The Emergence of Small-Scale Industry in a Taiwanese Rural Community," in *Women, Men, and the International Division of Labor,* ed. June Nash et al. (Albany: The State University of New York Press, 1983).

5   Dennis Shoesmith, ed., *Export Processing Zones in Five Countries: The Economic and Human Consequences* (Hong Kong: Asia Partnership for Human Development, 1986), 23.

6   Ibid.

7   Diane Elson and Ruth Pearson, "'Nimble Fingers Make Cheap Workers': An Analysis of Women's Employment in Third World Manufacturing," *Feminist Review* 7 (1981): 90.

8   Fuentes and Ehrenreich, *Women in the Global Factory,* 37–38.

9   Aihwa Ong, *Spirits of Resistance and Capitalist Discipline: Factory Women in Malaysia* (Albany: The State University of New York Press, 1987): 146.

10 Elson and Pearson, "'Nimble Fingers Make Cheap Workers'," 89.

11 Arturo Escobar, *Encountering Development: The Making and Unmaking of the Third World* (Princeton: Princeton University Press, 1995), 178. Following Nüket Kardam, Escobar attributes authorship of the phrase "women in development" to "the women's committee of the Washington D.C. chapter of

the largest nongovernmental organization (NGO), the Society for International Development."

12 Rachel Grossman, "Women's Place in the Integrated Circuit," *Southeast Asia Chronicle* 66 (January-February 1979): 3.

13 Fuentes and Ehrenreich, *Women in the Global Factory,* 37.

14 A 1993 article on Sri Lanka reported, "Manufacturing grew by 9% and is expected to leap further this year with the recent commission of about 130 new garment factories, a Premasda [the late authoritarian president who was assassinated on 1 May 1993] pet scheme to take industrial employment to the villages." An accompanying photo of Sri Lankan women working at textile machines bears the caption "Manufacturing has grown by leaps and bounds." Hamish McDonald, "Ahead of the Neighbours: New Sri Lankan Government Says Reforms Will Continue," *Far Eastern Economic Review* (20 May 1993): 67–68.

15 Cynthia Enloe, "Women Textile Workers in the Militarization of Southeast Asia," in *Women, Men, and the International Division of Labor,* ed. June Nash and Maria Patricia Fernandez-Kelley (Albany: State University of New York Press, 1983), 407–08.

16 Saundra Sturdevant and Brenda Stoltzfus, "Disparate Threads of the Whole: An Interpretive Essay," in *Let the Good Times Roll: Prostitution and the U.S. Military in Asia* (New York: The New Press, 1992), 306.

17 Katharine H. S. Moon, "Prostitute Bodies and Gendered States in U.S.-Korea Relations," in *Dangerous Women: Gender and Korean Nationalism,* ed. Elaine H. Kim and Chungmoo Choi (New York: Routledge, 1998), 148.

18 Moon, "Prostitute Bodies and Gendered States in U.S.-Korea Relations," 147.

19 Aida F. Santos, "Gathering the Dust: The Bases Issue in the Philippines," in *Let the Good Times Roll,* ed. Sturdevant and Stoltzfus, 33, 37.

20 Thanh-Dam Truong, *Sex, Money, and Morality: Prostitution and Tourism in Southeast Asia* (London: Zed Books, 1990), 162.

21 Elaine H. Kim, "Sex Tourism in Asia: A Reflection of Political and Economic Inequality," *Critical Perspectives of Third World America* 2 : 1 (fall 1984): 216.

22 According to C. Michael Hall, "Australian criminal elements made substantial investments in the sex industry in Angeles City near Clark Air Force Base in the Philippines, prior to its being closed, in order to offer sexual services to Australian tourists as well as American servicemen." ("Gender and Economic Interests in Tourism Prostitution: The Nature, Development, and Implications of Sex Tourism in South-east Asia," in *Tourism: A Gender Analysis,* ed. Vivian Kinnaird et al. [Chichester: John Wiley and Sons, 1994], 151.) In support, Hall cites an article by a W. Bacon in the 19 April 1987 issue of the *Times,* which reported that "Australians now have

a financial interest in more than 60 percent of 500 bars and 7,000 prostitutes around the [Clark Air Force] base."

23 Truong, *Sex, Money, and Morality*, 162–63.

24 Kim, "Sex Tourism in Asia," 216.

25 Wendy Lee, "Prostitution and Tourism in South-east Asia," in *Working Women: International Perspectives in Labour and Gender Ideology*, ed. Nanneke Redclift et al. (London: Routledge, 1991), 91.

26 Kim, "Sex Tourism in Asia," 216.

27 Johannes Fabian, *Time and the Other: How Anthropology Makes Its Objects* (New York: Columbia University Press, 1983). Fabian examines how the differential and staggered temporalizations of *contemporary* societies and cultures are mapped spatially in terms of a singular evolutionary slope, in which other cultures occupy a lower, earlier point in contradistinction to the higher, more advanced point occupied by the anthropologist and the audience of her/his ethnographic account. Fabian notes a related tendency that he calls "visualism"—"a cultural, ideological bias toward vision as the 'noblest sense' and toward geometry qua graphic-spatial conceptualization as the most 'exact' way of communicating knowledge" (106).

28 Johannes Fabian, *Time and the Other*, 87.

29 Arturo Escobar, *Encountering Development*, 23. He adds, "Thus, statistics such as per capita gross national product, life expectancy at birth, and infant mortality rate [emphasize] what people are deprived of (as is implied by poverty)."

30 Wolfgang Sachs, cited in Escobar, *Encountering Development*, 23.

31 Arturo Escobar, *Encountering Development*, 24.

32 Morag Bell, "Images, Myths, and Alternative Geographies of the Third World," in *Human Geography: Society, Space, and Social Science*, ed. Derek Gregory et al. (Minneapolis: University of Minnesota Press, 1994), 184.

33 Arturo Escobar, *Encountering Development*, 3, 123.

34 Tsuchaya Takeo, *Free Trade Zones and the Industrialization of Asia*, quoted in Swasti Mitter, *Common Fate, Common Bond: Women in the Global Economy* (London: Pluto Press Limited, 1986), 40.

35 Katharine Moon, *Sex Among Allies: Military Prostitution in U.S.-Korea Relations* (New York: Columbia University Press, 1997), 18.

36 Truong, *Sex, Money, and Morality*, 126.

37 In the case of Thailand, this movement from the cities to the countryside reflects a convergence of both TNC profit seeking and national economic plans. The shortage of workers in Bangkok "has firms striking out for the provinces, where the minimum wage is some 23% lower" with the added incentive of tax breaks offered by the Thai government in its attempts to equalize urban and rural wage disparities. See Gordon Fairclough, "Slaves to Fashion," *Far Eastern Economic Review* (28 July 1994).

38 See Michael Vatikiotis, "Three's Company: Malaysia, Thailand, Indonesia Forge Development Zone," *Far Eastern Economic Review* (5 August 1993).

39 Walden Bello and Stephanie Rosenfeld, *Dragons in Distress: Asia's Miracle Economies in Crisis* (San Francisco: Institute for Food and Development Policy, 1990), 218.

40 Cynthia Enloe, "Women Textile Workers in the Militarization of Southeast Asia," 409, 422.

41 Miriam Ching Louie, "Breaking the Cycle: Women Workers Confront Corporate Greed Globally," in *Dragon Ladies: Asian American Feminists Breathe Fire*, ed. Sonia Shah (Boston: South End Press, 1997), 122.

42 This tendency to analogize these centuries-apart labor formations has a parallel in the assumptions that Third World industrialization would follow the particular industrialization trajectory of the nineteenth century. Citing Cheryl Payer's work on the Third World debt crisis as produced partially by a development blueprint, which was based on certain assumptions of how these borrowing countries would proceed to pay back the loans, Escobar explicates: "The main fact these models overlooked, however, was that the historical context of the Third World after World War II and that of the U.S. and England a century earlier were completely different. Although countries of the center became industrialized at a time when they could dictate the rules of the game and extract surpluses from their colonies (albeit not always and not in every colonial possession), Third World countries in the postwar period had to borrow under the opposite conditions . . . [including] a position of subordination in terms of policy formation" (*Encountering Development*, 83).

43 Aihwa Ong, "The Gender and Labor Politics of Postmodernity," in *The Politics of Culture in the Shadow of Capital*, ed. Lisa Lowe et al. (Durham: Duke University Press, 1997), 65.

44 Rachel Grossman, "Women's Place in the Integrated Circuit," 4.

45 Cynthia Enloe, *Bananas, Beaches, Bases: Making Feminist Sense of International Politics* (Berkeley: University of California Press, 1990), 36.

46 From the mid-1940s to the mid-1980s, factory employment declined from one-third to one-fifth of the U.S. work force. See Richard J. Barnet and John Cavanagh, *Global Dreams: Imperial Corporations and the New World Order* (New York: Touchstone, 1995).

47 Robert Snow, "The New International Division of Labor and the U.S. Workforce: The Case of the Electronics Industry," in *Men, Women, and the International Division of Labor*, ed. June Nash and Maria Patricia Fernandez-Kelley, 41, 43, 45. As a sociologist Snow expresses frustration with the disciplinary prejudice of the existing archive since "most of the available social science literature dealing with the relationship between overseas investment and domestic employment has been written by economists." He continues:

"Their findings are commonly based upon econometric models that, in turn, rest upon a variety of assumptions about the workings of the economy. They tend to discuss future trends, not those that have actually transpired" (44). This future orientation poses a different kind of disciplined impossibility of coeval representation to the problem of anthropological representation analyzed by Johannes Fabian. In addition to this "hypothetical" aspect, Snow also expresses dissatisfaction at how the literature deals with questions at "a very high level of statistical aggregation," which "tends to conceal the different dynamics at work in various industries" (45). Instead, he suggests that "it is useful to examine national, state, and county or metropolitan statistics *over time* . . . to examine the *historical record* of electronics" (48, my italics).

48 Rachel Grossman, "Women in the Integrated Circuit," 15.

49 Chalsa Loo and Paul Ong, "Slaying Demons with a Sewing Needle: Feminist Issues for Chinatown's Women," *Berkeley Journal of Sociology* 27 (1982): 77–87. See also Miriam Ching Louie, "Immigrant Asian Women in Bay Area Garment Sweatshops: 'After Sewing, Laundry, Cleaning, and Cooking, I Have No Breath Left to Sing,'" *Amerasia Journal* 18: 1 (1992): 1–26, and *Global Production: The Apparel Industry in the Pacific Rim,* ed. Edna Bonacich et al. (Philadelphia: Temple University Press, 1994), especially the introduction and Lucie Cheng and Gary Gereffi, "U.S. Retailers and Asian Garment Production."

50 The conditions in the Los Angeles garment industry, as described by a workers' rights group, are reminiscent of published accounts of working conditions in Asia: "Ta Bounyong and Jit Lao, natives of Thailand, work at a sewing factory in the heart of Koreatown. They make about $30 a day, hunched over a sewing machine for close to 15 hours, six days a week." The report continues: "Ta and Jit both complain of breathing difficulties. Nongyao Varanond of the Asian Health Project in the L.A.'s Crenshaw district says that garment workers often suffer from headaches, sleeplessness, shortness of breath, and severe chest pains—symptoms she attributes to dust and chemicals left on the fabrics from dyeing and finishing. Many Asian garment workers have no health care, often pass up meals because of the pressure of piecework, and suffer from ulcers and hypertension. When they go home, their work-induced medical problems are compounded by the air pollution in their neighborhoods." Eric Mann, *L.A.'s Lethal Air* (Los Angeles: WATCHDOG Organizing Committee of the Labor/Community Strategy Center, 1991): 25.

51 Alexander Reid, "New Asian Immigrants, New Garment Center," *New York Times* (5 October 1986).

52 Richard Applebaum, "Multiculturalism and Flexibility: Some New Directions in Global Capitalism," in *Mapping Multiculturalism,* ed. Avery F. Gordon et al. (Minneapolis: University of Minnesota Press, 1996), 298.

53 As early as 1983, an article on the sweatshop conditions in New York's garment industry gave these two racially loaded justifications while also blaming the 1965 liberalization of immigration laws for this labor exploitation. See William Serrin, "Combating Sweatshops Is an Almost Futile Task," *New York Times* (13 October 1983).

54 Avtar Brah, *Cartographies of Diaspora: Contesting Identities* (London: Routledge, 1996), 201.

55 In tracing the relegation of "racial-ethnic women" to a "colonial economy" within the United States, Evelyn Nakano Glenn underscores "institutional barriers that undercut their ability to compete in the labor market." "Racial Ethnic Women's Labor: The Intersection of Race, Gender, and Class Oppression," *Review of Radical Political Economics* 17:3 (1985): 4, 5.

56 Morrison G. Wong, "Chinese Sweatshops in the United States: A Look at the Garment Industry," in *Research in the Sociology of Work: A Research Annual,* ed. Ida H. Simpson et al. (New York: JAI Press, Inc., 1983), 358. This predominantly male composition of Chinatown garment workers only shifted to a mostly female labor force after World War I.

57 Saskia Sassen, "Notes on the Incorporation of Third World Women into Wage-Labor through Immigration and Off-Shore Production," *International Migration Review* 18 (winter 1984): 148.

58 John Willoughby, "Nationalism and Globalism: Beyond the Neo-Leninist Tradition," *Rethinking Marxism* 4. 1 (spring 1991): 138.

59 June Nash, "Introduction," in *Women, Men, and the International Division of Labor,* viii.

60 Hoosang Amirahmadi and Weiping Wu, "Export Processing Zones in Asia," *Asian Survey* 35:9 (September 1995): 833.

61 These include the Indonesia-Malaysia-Singapore (IMS) Growth Triangle, the East ASEAN Growth Area (EAGA), which incorporates parts of Brunei, Indonesia, Malaysia, and the Philippines, and the Tumen River Economic Development Area (TREDA), which includes areas of North Korea, Russia, and China with important cooperation with Japan and South Korea. See Kevin G. Cai, "Is a Free Trade Zone Emerging in Northeast Asia in the Wake of the Asian Financial Crisis?" *Pacific Affairs* 7:1 (Spring 2001).

62 Byung Moon Byun, "Recent Developments of the Korean Semi-Conductor Industry," *Asia Review* 34. 8 (August 1994): 710.

63 Saskia Sassen, *Globalization and its Discontents* (New York: The New Press, 1998), 81.

64 Aihwa Ong, "The Gender and Labor Politics of Postmodernity," 64. I would qualify this parallel by heeding important historical and geopolitical differences between the prewar and contemporary contexts of Japan's economic dominance.

65 Japanese capital accounted for almost 88 percent ($77.7 million) of the total foreign investment in the Masan Free Export Zone (FEZ) in its first four

years of operation (1971–1975). In Taiwan, where there was significant investment by overseas Chinese, Japanese capital investment still managed to comprise 41.8 percent of total investment in 1980. Dennis Shoesmith, *Export Processing Zones in Five Countries*, 25, 38.

66 Ngai Pun, "Theoretical Discussions on the Impact of Industrial Restructuring in Asia," *Silk and Steel: Asian Women Workers Confront Challenges of Industrial Restructuring* (Hong Kong: Committee for Asian Women, 1995), 18. Werner Sengenberger notes, "The bulk of exchange occurs within the Northern Triad (the United States, the European Union and Japan)." Relating how "the share of inward investment in the developing countries has fallen to 24 percent in the early 1990s from 27 percent in the mid-1980s, he concludes, "From this angle, it is doubtful whether we can truly speak of 'globalization'." Instead, he observes an economic "regionalism": "Rather than an increasingly borderless world-economy, we see freer circulation of capital, goods, and labor within regional groupings of countries" ("International Labour Standards in a Global Economy: The Issues," in *International Labor Standards and Economic Interdependence,* ed. Werner Sengenberger and Duncan Campbell [Geneva: International Institute for Labor Studies, 1994], 6). Providing the examples of such conglomerations as the EU, NAFTA, MERCOSUR, and APEC, Sengenberger proposes that "the economy has grown increasingly international and partly global." This subdivided yet uneven political economic topography poses challenges for conceptualizing let alone enforcing a common and consistent set of labor standards. As Sengenberger points out, there have been efforts to include "a clause in GATT that would restrict or halt the trade in goods whose production was not in conformity with basic labor standards, and ensure that the liberalization of markets is accompanied by improved rather than deteriorating conditions of work" (8). These so-called social clauses have been opposed by "developing countries" who suspect that such measures "would diminish their comparative advantage vis-à-vis the developed countries, and amount to disguised protectionism on the part of high-cost countries" (8).

67 Wendy Lee, "Prostitution and Tourism in South-East Asia," 79.

68 C. Michael Hall, "Gender and Economic Interests in Tourism Prostitution," 142.

69 "Kisaeng Tourism," *ISIS International Bulletin* 13 (1979): 23–25, cited in Wendy Lee, "Prostitution and Tourism in South-East Asia," 91.

70 Hisae Muroi and Naoko Sasaki, "Tourism and Prostitution in Japan," in *Gender, Work, and Tourism,* ed. M. Thea Sinclair (London: Routledge, 1997), 180.

71 Muroi and Sasaki, "Tourism and Prostitution in Japan," 201. Wendy Lee also cites a 1980 article by S. Takazato, which "claims that [Japanese women] prefer their husbands to use prostitutes overseas and that they find it easier to accept *an Asian rather than a Japanese* prostitute because 'Third

World' women are looked down on, thereby confirming them in their racist feeling of superiority" ("Prostitution and Tourism in South-East Asia," 91, my italics).

72 Hisae Muroi and Naoko Sasaki, "Tourism and Prostitution in Japan," 204. Satoko Watenabe attributes to these migrant Thai sex workers in Japan a far greater agency in effecting structural and conceptual transformations: "They may be creating a new wage division within Japan's sex industry as well as in the sector of women in general, but they can also be understood as multinational workers who, by moving across the artificial barriers of nation-state borders, are, at least to some extent, breaking down the international wage hierarchy and recomposing the structure and distribution of power within the working class against capital's control." See "From Thailand to Japan: Migrant Sex Workers as Autonomous Subjects," in *Global Sex Workers: Rights, Resistance, and Redefinition,* ed. Kamala Kempadoo et al. (New York: Routledge, 1998), 122.

73 Linda Y. C. Lim, "Capitalism, Imperialism, and Patriarchy: The Dilemma of Third World Women Workers in Multinational Factories," in *Women, Men and the International Division of Labor,* ed. June Nash and Maria Patricia Fernandez-Kelley, 72.

74 June Nash, "The Impact of the Changing International Division of Labor on Different Sectors of the Labor Force," in *Women, Men, and the International Division of Labor,* ed. June Nash and Maria Patricia Fernandez-Kelley, 24.

75 Julie Graham, "Fordism/Post-Fordism, Marxism/Post-Marxism: The Second Cultural Divide?" *Rethinking MARXISM* 4:1 (spring 1991): 50.

76 David Harvey, *The Condition of Postmodernity* (London: Basil Blackwell, 1990), 147.

77 Richard Applebaum, "Multiculturalism and Flexibility," 299.

78 Grace Chang, "The Global Trade in Filipina Workers," 133, my italics.

79 In a more ominous vein, Katharine Moon describes how in the early 1970s "the USFK authorities also targeted Korean prostitutes as the main source of 'the reservoir' of venereal disease transmission among U.S. servicemen." *Sex Among Allies,* 146.

80 Jill Forshee, "Introduction," in *Converging Interests: Traders, Travelers, and Tourists in Southeast Asia,* ed. Jill Forshee et al. (Berkeley: International and Area Studies, University of California, 1999), 3.

81 Cynthia Enloe has noted along more generically gendered lines: "It has become commonplace to speak of 'cheap, women's labor.' The phrase is used in public policy discussions as if cheapness were somehow inherent in women's work." *Bananas, Beaches, Bases,* 160.

82 Aihwa Ong, "The Gender and Labor Politics of Postmodernity," 63.

83 Citing the work of "Asianists [who] stress the role of the state in securing conditions for profitable export-oriented industrialization," Aihwa Ong

writes, "State suppression of workers in traditional industries greatly weakened labor movements [in Hong Kong, South Korea, Taiwan, and Singapore] *before* large-scale industrialization was undertaken." "The Gender and Labor Politics of Postmodernity," 67, my italics.

84 Perhaps in an attempt to counter the prevalent figuration of these women workers as inherently docile, Ong is a bit too emphatic in positing that this is "a form of body discipline especially intolerable to neophyte factory women." "The Gender and Labor Politics of Postmodernity," 72.

85 Hyun Mee Kim, "Labor Politics and the Women Subject in Contemporary Korea." (Ph.D. diss., University of Washington, 1995), 297. I would like to thank the author for sharing her dissertation with me.

86 Rachel Grossman, "Women's Place in the Integrated Circuit," 8, my italics.

87 Published in *Feminist Review* 7 (1981). Delia Aguilar recalls how in a course on feminism that she taught in Manila, "we discussed . . . how women's 'nimble fingers' and 'docility' ('genetic' credentials authenticated by a garment factory president we interviewed, who also cites women's ability to sit patiently) qualify them for low-paid employment on the assemblyline." "Lost in Translation: Western Feminism and Asian Women," in *Dragon Ladies: Asian American Feminists Breathe Fire,* ed. Sonia Shah (Boston: South End Press, 1997), 162.

88 Aihwa Ong points out how in the nineteenth century, "British perceptions of Malay peasants evolved into an image of the 'indolent native.'" *Spirits of Resistance and Capitalist Discipline,* 15.

89 This passage has been widely cited in other accounts and analyses of Asian women and the global assembly line, but its original source is unclear. In crediting Fuentes and Ehrenreich for her citation of this passage, Mitter refers to its title as "Why We Woo Foreign Investment" (*Common Fate, Common Bond,* 45). However, in her 1979 article, Rachel Grossman attributes it to a brochure titled "Malaysia: The Solid State for Electronics" previously quoted in an essay by Linda Lim. Also, according to Grossman, "Why We Woo Foreign Investment" was the title of an article in the 27 November 1978 edition of the *New Straits Times* ("Women in the Integrated Circuit," 35.) Finally, Aihwa Ong identifies the brochure as authored by the Federal Industrial Development Authority in 1975 ("Japanese Factories, Malay Workers: Class and Sexual Metaphors in West Malaysia," in *Power and Difference: Gender in Island Southeast Asia,* ed. Jane Monnig Atkinson et al. [Stanford: Stanford University Press, 1990], 405.)

90 Cited in C. Michael Hall, "Sex Tourism in South-east Asia," in *Tourism and the Less Developed Countries,* ed. David Harrison (London: Belhaven, 1991), 67.

91 C. Michael Hall, "Gender and Economic Interests in Tourism Prostitution," 143–44.

92 Cleo Odzer, *Patpong Sisters* (New York: Arcade Publishing, 1994).

93 Marc Askew, "Strangers and Lovers: Thai Women Sex Workers and Western Men in the 'Pleasure Space' of Bangkok," in *Converging Interests: Traders, Travelers, and Tourists in Southeast Asia,* ed. Jill Forshee et al., 109–10.

94 Ibid., footnote 15.

95 Rachel Grossman, "Women in the Integrated Circuit," 13.

96 Rey Chow, *Writing Diaspora: Tactics of Intervention in Contemporary Cultural Studies* (Bloomington: Indiana University Press, 1993), 60–61.

97 Mark Askew cites this cover photograph as an example of the "global marketing of city-images" of Bangkok as "a city of prostitutes."

98 Elaine H. Kim, "Sex Tourism in Asia," 218. A black-and-white photograph of just such a display decorates the book cover of *Night Market: Sexual Cultures and the Thai Economic Miracle,* by Ryan Bishop and Lillian S. Robinson (New York: Routledge, 1998).

99 Saundra Pollock Sturdevant and Brenda Stoltzfus, *Let the Good Times Roll,* ix. In Okinawa, especially, "photography was very difficult due to the involvement of the Yakuza (the Japanese mafia) in the sale of sexual labor." They further explain: "In every club, there was a large sign saying 'Photography is prohibited.' . . . In short, it was almost impossible to take photographs inside the clubs, and using a camera on the streets had to be done with some care as well. By speaking in Chinese, Saundra was able to take photographs inside one club owned by an Okinawan woman who had lived in Taiwan" (viii).

100 Although they do admit that "a few [women] chose to hide their identities by changing their names and not being photographed" (ix), they do not explicitly identify which of the nine women featured wanted this anonymity and invisibility. However, it can be discerned that the five women in the Philippines are identified by name in the photographs accompanying their stories, while the photos that illustrate the stories of the other four women in Korea and Okinawa are generic "location shots."

101 George E. Marcus, "Contemporary Problems of Ethnography in the Modern World System," in *Writing Culture: The Poetics and Politics of Ethnography,* ed. James Clifford (Berkeley: University of California Press, 1986), 171, note 4, and 168.

102 George E. Marcus and Michael M. J. Fischer, *Anthropology as Cultural Critique: An Experimental Moment in the Human Sciences* (Chicago: University of Chicago Press, 1986), 34, 36.

103 George E. Marcus, "Contemporary Problems of Ethnography," 167.

104 Aihwa Ong, "Global Industries and Malay Peasants in Peninsular Malaysia," in *Women, Men, and the International Division of Labor,* ed. June Nash and Maria Patricia Fernandez-Kelley, 426.

105 George E. Marcus and Dick Cushman, "Ethnographies as Texts," *Annual Review of Anthropology* (1982): 33. Maps and photographs are also included in Diane L. Wolf, *Factory Daughters: Gender, Household Dynamics, and Rural Industrialization in Java* (Berkeley: University of California Press, 1992).

106 James Clifford, "On Ethnographic Allegory," in *Writing Culture: The Poetics and Politics of Ethnography,* ed. James Clifford (Berkeley: University of California Press, 1986), 101.

107 Interestingly, Ong contests what she sees as Gayatri Spivak's generic Marxist figuration of the "subproletariat" woman as "the paradigmatic subject" of the international division of labor and argues instead that "there is no such overwhelmingly class-determined, cross-cultural female figure, but rather a multiplicity of historically situated subjects at the intersections of particular local-global power structures who by engaging in local struggles define who they are in *cultural* terms" ("Gender and Labor Politics," 91–92, note 63, my italics).

108 Aihwa Ong, "Women Out of China: Traveling Tales and Traveling Theories in Postcolonial Feminism," in *Women Writing Culture,* ed. Ruth Behar and Deborah A. Gordon (Berkeley: University of California Press, 1995), 353.

109 However, Ong would dissociate these "recent Asian female immigrants" from the purview of ethnic studies, wherein "the tendency is to make pedagogical claims of a Chinese American identity and to ignore other ways of being Chinese in America that go beyond claiming a rightful citizenship in the United States" (ibid., 368, note 10). Oddly, rather than reference any work produced in Asian American studies, she cites Fischer's 1986 essay, "Ethnicity and the Post-Modern Arts of Memory" and its discussion of "being a Chinese-American."

5 Compositional Struggles: Re-membering Korean/American Women

1 An illustrative instance of this interpretive impulse can be seen in Anne Cheng, "Memory and Anti-Documentary Desire in Theresa Hak Kyung Cha's *Dictée," MELUS* 23, no. 4 (winter 1998): 119–33.

2 As Julian Steward describes in tracing the rapid growth of area studies programs during World War II, in the federal government's rush to gather information about various regions and cultures, "They enlisted the assistance of everyone who had been to foreign areas—scholars, explorers, business men, travelers" (*Area Research: Theory and Practice* [New York: Social Science Research Council, 1950], xii). The hyphenated locution I use comes from Richard Lambert's 1973 review of area studies as he is discussing his own methodological difficulty in identifying who counts as an area spe-

cialist: "Among American-based academics, we faced the problem of defining which ones have an 'area competence.' Members of the potential universe vary tremendously from one-shot, short-term 'been-theres' to senior specialists with many areas of experience and full command of one or more languages in the area" (*Language and Area Studies Review* [Philadelphia: The American Academy of Political and Social Science, 1973], 8). I would venture that the ready distinction of area studies from both women's studies and ethnic studies stems from the very promise and premise of a separation of the investigating subject and those s/he studies that is struc-tured by the geographical separation of U.S. scholars and their foreign areas.

3 Theresa Hak Kyung Cha, *Dictée* (New York: Tanam Press, 1982). Portions of the following discussion of *Dictée* are taken from my longer essay, "The 'Liberatory Voice' of Theresa Hak Kyung Cha's *Dictée*," in *Writing Self, Writing Nation: Essays on "Dictée,"* ed. Elaine H. Kim and Norma Alarcón. (Berkeley, Calif.: Third Woman Press, 1993). Sections of the discussion of Myung Mi Kim and Kim Su Theiler have also appeared in my essay "Remembering Home," in *Dangerous Women: Korean Women and Nationalism,* ed. Elaine H. Kim and Chungmoo Choi (New York: Routledge, 1998), 249–90.

4 Lisa Lowe, "Unfaithful to the Original," 39. Noting how "dictation is at once the sign for the authority of language in the formation of the student, a model for the conversion of the individual into a subject of discourse, through the repetition of form, genre, and example, and a metaphor for the many regulating reproductions to which the narrator is subject in spheres other than the educational," Lowe argues that "in the very literal inclusion of the punctuation instructions themselves, it 'seizes upon the punctuation' to render explicit the disciplinary artifice of dictation, exploiting the contingent spaces in the dictation in order to voice a 'failed' subjection, affirming departures for the pedagogical model of formation" (40–41).

5 A significant part of this peculiar textual materiality is the large number of visual images, which alternately disrupt and illuminate the arrangement of words. The time-worn ruins on the front cover and the two birdlike figures on p. 167 are unidentified and reinforce the placelessness of the diasporic, articulated at several moments. Anatomical diagrams in English of the human throat and mouth are inserted in the midst of a poetic reflection on the physicality of speaking and the visceral struggles around articulation: "Cracked tongue. Broken tongue" (75). A simple map of the Korean peninsula cleaved by a thick black line labeled "DMZ" prefaces a powerful critique of the unnatural manipulations behind a nation and a people monstrously severed from itself: "Labyrinth of deceptions. No enduring time. Self devouring. Devouring itself. Perishing all the while. Insect that eats itself" (88).

6 Elaine H. Kim, "Poised on the In-between: A Korean American's Reflections on Theresa Hak Kyung Cha's *Dictée*," in *Writing Self, Writing Nation,* ed. Elaine H. Kim and Norma Alarcón.

7 Kim writes, "Not only does Cha choose Yu Guan Soon as a central figure for *Dictée;* she also reclaims Yu's story from official Korean History, which emphasizes the details of her torture and death, probably to underscore the virtue of individual female self-sacrifice for the benefit of the group while encouraging Korean nationalism. Cha recasts the story by emphasizing instead Yu's agency—her leadership of the "resistant group" she formed, her refusal to be pushed aside by movement activists because she was young and female, and her courageous 'backtalk' to the Japanese captors who eventually murdered her. Thus Cha's story has an ambivalent relationship to the Korean nationalist narrative" ("Poised on the In-Between," 16).

8 Walter Benjamin, *Illuminations* (New York: Schocken, 1969), 221.

9 Roland Barthes writes in an essay titled "The Photographic Message": "Naturally, even from the perspective of a purely immanent analysis, the structure of the photograph is not an isolated structure; it is in communication with at least one other structure, namely the text—title, caption or article—accompanying every press photograph. The totality of the information is thus carried out by two different structures (one of which is linguistic)." *Image, Music, Text,* trans. Stephen Heath (New York: Hill and Wang, 1977), 16.

10 Choosing to view these photographs as expressing Cha's own "antidocumentary desire," Anne Anlin Cheng argues: "*Dictée* suggests that modern Korea exists only as a history of found images—even, of dead images. The black-and-white photo of that student demonstration and subsequent massacre is homeless because *that* 'original' event was homelessness itself, a story lost." "Memory and Anti-Documentary Desire in Theresa Hak Kyung Cha's *Dictée,*" 120.

11 For a nicely suggestive reading of the significance of the frontispiece, see Shelley Sunn Wong's essay, "Unnaming the Same: Theresa Hak Kyung Cha's *Dictée,*" in *Writing Self, Writing Nation,* ed. Kim and Alarcón, 107.

12 Myung Mi Kim, *Under Flag* (Berkeley: Kelsey Street Press, 1991).

13 Chungmoo Choi writes in her essay "The Discourse of Decolonization and Popular Memory: South Korea," "the dominant narrative of South Korean history long acknowledged liberation as a gift of the allied forces, especially of the U.S.A., since Koreans were excluded from the liberation process itself. . . . Such a narrative has delegitimated the Koreans as valid agents of both nation-building and the subsequent military and economic dependence on the Cold War superpowers, although to a differing degree in the North than in the South. The transitive verbs "to liberate" and "to partition" presuppose a subject (or subjects), who is external to the action and yet administers it, and a passive receiver (the object) upon which such actions are performed." *Positions* 1:1 (spring 1993): 80.

14 Susan Stewart, *On Longing: Narratives of the Miniature, the Gigantic, the Souvenir, the Collection* (Durham: Duke University Press, 1993), 138.

15 In many critical discussions of Jin-me Yoon's works, there is an assiduous specification of the artist as "Asian," "Asian-Canadian," "Korean," "Korean Canadian," or even "South Korean." Christine Boyanoski refers to "the artist herself (a young woman of Asian descent)" in "Similar Differences: Canada and Australia Compared," *Art Monthly* (March 1992): 7–10. Characterizing Yoon's work as "propos[ing] matrilineal linkages that defy patriarchal Confucian tradition in Korean culture," Robin Laurence writes that Yoon "invents her own form of ancestor worship . . . locating herself, finding a 'story' through recovering the stories of her forebears in Korea" ("Fresh, Forceful Works Explore Creation of Identity," *Vancouver Sun* [6 March 1994]). Brenda Lefleur notes how the "Scandinavian sweater" is "worn by a woman of South Korean heritage" ("Review of *Between Views and Points of View*," *Versus*, no. 4 [1995]: 28). Writing about the critical reception of black art, Charles Gaines points out that the relationship of art criticism to the art work is mutually productive and constraining in a broader discursive struggle: "Works of art are complex events; their true complexity is revealed in criticism and its attempt to circumscribe the boundaries of art. Criticism idealizes representation and consequently distances the viewer from actuality. This is evident in the way marginalized discourse has been used to reduce complex experiences to overarching themes that relieve us of the responsibility of having to deal with the works themselves" (*The Theater of Refusal: Black Art and Mainstream Criticism,* ed. Catherine Lord [Irvine: Fine Arts Gallery, University of California, Irvine, 1993], 20). Note the resonance with the generic fixations of difference in literary criticism that I discussed at length in chapter 1. An earlier version of my discussion of Yoon's two works appears as "The Autobiographical Stagings of Jin-me Yoon," in *Jin-me Yoon: Between Departure and Arrival* (Vancouver, B.C.: Western Front Gallery, 1998): 23–42.

16 One reviewer apprehends a progression of emotional states in the six panels: "At the end, photographed with a party of people on a bus tour with their oriental driver/guide, she looks a little less uncomfortable, a little less out of place (is there a suggestion of a smile on her face?)." Allan Sheppard, "Jin-Me Yoon: Souvenirs of the Self—(Re)inventing (One)self in (Alien)-nation," *Canadian Link* (September 1991): 35.

17 Sarah McFadden writes: "Photographs of the Korean-born artist posing deadpan before the tourist sites of western Canada look like episodes from an identity crisis brought on by cultural dislocation." "Report from Istanbul: Bosporus Dialogues," *Art in America* 81:6 (June 1993): 55.

18 Paula Rabinowitz, *They Must Be Represented: The Politics of Documentary* (London: Verso, 1994): 6.

19 Jay Ruby, "Speaking For, Speaking About, Speaking With, or Speaking Alongside: An Anthropological and Documentary Dilemma," *Visual Anthropology Review* 7:2 (fall 1991): 52.

20 Gayatri Spivak, "Can the Subaltern Speak?" in *Marxism and the Interpretation of Culture,* ed. Cary Nelson et al. (Urbana: University of Illinois Press, 1988), 297; Rey Chow, "Where Have All the Natives Gone?" in *Writing Diaspora: Tactics of Intervention in Contemporary Cultural Studies* (Bloomington: Indiana University Press, 1993), 39.

21 In *Feminist Frameworks,* the editors identify two different forces: multicultural feminism and global feminism. In the editorial introduction, Jaggar and Rothenberg describe a new section on "Multiculturalism" in the third edition as replacing an earlier section on "Feminism and Women of Color" in the second edition, a change that reflects how "issues raised by women of color have moved from the margins to the center of feminist concerns" (123). If "multicultural feminism" is attentive to "sex/gender, sexuality, class, *and* race," "global feminism" adds a critical lens on imperialism and postcoloniality. Charlotte Bunch is credited with inventing the term, which carries "the difficult question of how to value cultural diversity and at the same time oppose domination rationalized by appeals to either tradition or modernization" (124). The editors' logic of inclusion is motivated by the belief that "such abuses [as in Latin America] should receive the widest possible publicity" but also because it raises a theoretical issue, namely, that apparently nongendered issues like national liberation, military dictatorship, and democracy are "women's issues." Alison M. Jaggar and Paula S. Rothenberg, eds. *Feminist Frameworks: Alternative Theoretical Accounts of the Relations Between Men and Women* (New York: McGraw-Hill, 1993), 124. For a persuasive critique of "global feminism," see Inderpal Grewal and Caren Kaplan, "Introduction: Transnational Feminist Practices and Questions of Postmodernity," in *Scattered Hegemonies: Postmodernity and Transnational Feminist Practices,* ed. Inderpal Grewal and Caren Kaplan (Minneapolis: University of Minnesota Press, 1994). See also their essay, "Transnational Feminist Cultural Studies: Beyond the Marxist/Post-Structuralism/Feminism Divides," *Positions* 2:2 (fall 1994): 430–45.

22 Another alternately named constituency, "racial ethnic women," proposed in 1985 by sociologist Evelyn Nakano Glenn, derive their socioeconomic commonality through their similarities with each other as much as by their difference from "white women." "Racial Ethnic Women's Labor: The Intersection of Race, Gender, and Class Oppression," *Review of Radical Political Economics* 17:3 (1985).

bibliography

Adler, Judith. "Origins of Sightseeing." *Annals of Tourism Research* 16 (1989): 7–29.

Aguilar, Delia. "Lost in Translation: Western Feminism and Asian Women." In *Dragon Ladies: Asian American Feminists Breathe Fire,* ed. Sonia Shah. Boston: South End Press, 1997.

Aguilar-San Juan, Karin. "Landmarks in Literature by Asian American Lesbians." *Signs: A Journal of Women in Culture and Society* 18, no. 4 (1993): 936–43.

Amirahmadi, Hoosang, and Weiping Wu. "Export Processing Zones in Asia." *Asian Survey* 35:9 (September 1995): 828–49.

Anderson, Benedict. *Imagined Communities: Reflections on the Origin and Spread of Nationalism.* London: Verso, 1991.

Anzaldúa, Gloria, and Cherríe Moraga, eds. *This Bridge Called My Back: Writings by Radical Women of Color.* Latham, N.Y.: Kitchen Table/Women of Color Press, 1982.

Appadurai, Arjun. "Diversity and Disciplinarity as Cultural Artifacts." In *Disciplinarity and Dissent in Cultural Studies,* ed. Cary Nelson et al. New York: Routledge, 1996.

Applebaum, Richard. "Multiculturalism and Flexibility: Some New Directions in Global Capitalism." In *Mapping Multiculturalism,* ed. Avery F. Gordon et al. Minneapolis: University of Minnesota Press, 1996.

Appleby, Joyce, Lynn Hunt, and Margaret C. Jacob, *Telling the Truth About History.* New York: Norton, 1994.

Aquino, Belinda A. "The History of Philipino Women in Hawaii." *Bridge: Asian American Perspective* 7 (1977): 17–21.

Asian American Women. Palo Alto: Stanford University Asian American Student Alliance, 1976.

Asian Women. Berkeley: University of California, 1971.

Asian Women United of California, ed. *Making Waves: An Anthology of Writings By and About Asian American Women.* Boston: Beacon Press, 1989.

———. *Making More Waves: New Writings by Asian American Women.* Boston: Beacon Press, 1997.

Askew, Marc. "Strangers and Lovers: Thai Women Sex Workers and Western Men in the 'Pleasure Space' of Bangkok." In *Converging Interests: Traders, Travelers, and Tourists in Southeast Asia,* ed. Jill Forshee et al. Berkeley: International and Area Studies, University of California at Berkeley, 1999.

Barnet, Richard J., and John Cavanagh. *Global Dreams: Imperial Corporations and the New World Order.* New York: Touchstone, 1995.

Barthes, Roland. *Image, Music, Text.* Trans. Stephen Heath. New York: Hill and Wang, 1977.

Bell, Morag. "Images, Myths, and Alternative Geographies of the Third World." In *Human Geography: Society, Space, and Social Science,* ed. Derek Gregory et al. Minneapolis: University of Minnesota Press, 1994.

Bello, Walden, and Stephanie Rosenfeld. *Dragons in Distress: Asia's Miracle Economies in Crisis.* San Francisco: Institute for Food and Development Policy, 1990.

Benjamin, Walter. *Illuminations.* New York: Schocken Books, 1968.

Benstock, Shari. "Authorizing the Autobiographical." In *The Private Self: Theory and Practice of Women's Autobiographical Writings,* ed. Shari Benstock. Chapel Hill: University of North Carolina Press, 1988.

Berlant, Lauren. *The Anatomy of National Fantasy: Hawthorne, Utopia, and Everyday Life.* Chicago: University of Chicago Press, 1991.

Bernard, William S. "A History of U.S. Immigration Policy." In Richard A. Easterlin et al., *Immigration.* Cambridge: The Belknap Press of the Harvard University Press, 1982.

Berson, Misha. *Between Worlds: Contemporary Asian-American Plays.* New York: Theater Communications Group, 1990.

Bhabha, Homi K., ed. *Nation and Narration.* New York: Routledge, 1990.

Bishop, Ryan, and Lillian S. Robinson. *Night Market: Sexual Cultures and the Thai Economic Miracle.* New York: Routledge, 1998.

Blackburn, Sarah. "Notes of a Chinese Daughter." *Ms.* (January 1977): 39–40.

Bloom, Harold, ed. *Asian-American Women Writers.* Philadelphia: Chelsea House Publishers, 1997.

Boris, Eileen. "The Racialized Gendered State: Constructions of Citizenship in the United States." *Social Politics* (summer 1995): 160–80.

Bow, Leslie. "Cultural Conflict/Feminist Resolution in Amy Tan's *The Joy Luck Club.*" In *New Visions in Asian American Studies,* ed. Franklin Ng et al. Pullman: Washington State University Press, 1994.

———. "For Every Gesture of Loyalty, There Doesn't Have To Be a Betrayal: Feminism and Cultural Nationalism in Asian American Literature." In *Who Can Speak?: Authority and Critical Identity,* ed. Judith Roof et al. Urbana: University of Illinois Press, 1995.

Bowles, Gloria. "Is Women's Studies an Academic Discipline?" In *Theories of*

Women's Studies, ed. Gloria Bowles and Renate Duelli Klein. Boston: Routledge and Kegan Paul, 1983.

Boxer, Marilyn. "For and About Women: The Theory and Practice of Women's Studies in the United States." In *Reconstructing the Academy,* ed. Elizabeth Minnich et al. Chicago: University of Chicago Press, 1988.

Brah, Avtar. *Cartographies of Diaspora: Contesting Identities.* London: Routledge, 1996.

Brodzki, Bella, and Celeste Schenck, eds. *Life/Lines: Theorizing Women's Autobiography.* Ithaca: Cornell University Press, 1988.

Broner, E. M. "Stunning Sequel to *Woman Warrior.*" *Ms.* (August 1980): 28, 30.

Brooks, Benjamin S. *The Chinese in California. To the Committee on Foreign Relations of the United States Senate.* N.p., 1876.

Brown, Wendy. "Injury, Identity, Politics." In *Mapping Multiculturalism,* ed. Avery F. Gordon et al. Minneapolis: University of Minnesota Press, 1996.

Bunch, Charlotte. "Prospects for Global Feminism." In *Feminist Frameworks: Alternative Theoretical Accounts of the Relations Between Men and Women,* ed. Alison M. Jaggar and Paula S. Rothenberg. New York: McGraw-Hill, 1993.

Butler, Judith. *Bodies That Matter: On the Discursive Limits of "Sex."* New York: Routledge, 1994.

Butler, Judith, and Joan W. Scott, eds. *Feminists Theorize the Political.* New York and London: Routledge, 1991.

Byun, Byung Moon. "Recent Developments of the Korean Semi-Conductor Industry." *Asia Review* 34, no. 8 (August 1994): 710.

Caldwell, Dan. "The Negroization of the Chinese Stereotype in California." *Southern California Quarterly* 53 (June 1971): 123–33.

Castagnozzi, Mary. "Maxine Hong Kingston Discusses Her Writing." *East/West* (13 May 1981).

Cha, Theresa Hak Kyung. *Dictée.* New York: Tanam Press, 1982.

Chai, Alice Yun. "An Asian American Woman's View of the CR Sessions." *Women's Studies Quarterly* 9, no. 3 (fall 1981): 16.

———. "Towards a Holistic Paradigm of Asian American Women's Studies: A Synthesis of Feminist Scholarship and Women of Color's Feminist Politics." *Women's Studies International Forum* 8, no. 1 (1985): 59–66.

Chakrabarty, Dipesh. "Postcoloniality and the Artifice of History: Who Speaks for 'Indian' Pasts?" *Representations* 37 (1992): 1–26.

Chan, Connie S. "Asian-American Women: Psychological Responses to Sexual Exploitation and Cultural Stereotypes." *Women and Therapy* (1987): 33–38.

———. "Issues of Identity Development Among Asian-American Lesbians and Gay Men." *Journal of Counseling and Development* 68, no. 1 (September/October 1989): 16–20.

Chan, Sucheng. "The Exclusion of Chinese Women, 1870–1943." In *Entry*

Denied: Exclusion and the Chinese Community in America, 1882–1943, ed. Sucheng Chan. Philadelphia: Temple University Press, 1991.

———. *Asian Americans: An Interpretative History.* Boston: Twayne Publishers, 1991.

———. "The Writing of Asian American History." *Magazine of History* 10, no. 4 (summer 1996): 8–17.

Chang, Grace. "The Global Trade in Filipina Workers." In *Dragon Ladies: Asian American Feminists Breathe Fire,* ed. Sonia Shah. Boston: South End Press, 1997.

Chen, May Ying. "Teaching a Course on Asian American Women." In *Counterpoint: Perspectives on Asian America,* ed. Emma Gee. Los Angeles: Asian American Studies Center, University of California, Los Angeles, 1976.

Cheng, Anne. "Memory and Anti-Documentary Desire in Theresa Hak Kyung Cha's *Dictée.*" *MELUS* 23, no. 4 (winter 1998): 119–33.

Cheng, Lucie, and Edna Bonacich, eds. *Labor Immigration Under Capitalism: Asian Workers in the United States Before World War II.* Berkeley: University of California Press, 1984.

Cheng, Lucie, and Gary Gereffi. "U.S. Retailers and Asian Garment Production." In *Global Production: The Apparel Industry in the Pacific Rim,* ed. Edna Bonacich et al. Philadelphia: Temple University Press, 1994.

Cheung, King-kok. "'Don't Tell': Imposed Silences in *The Woman Warrior* and *The Color Purple.*" *PMLA* (1988): 162–74.

———. "The Woman Warrior Versus The Chinaman Pacific: Must a Chinese American Critic Choose Between Feminism and Heroism?" In *Conflicts in Feminism,* ed. Marianne Hirsch et al. New York: Routledge, 1990.

———. "Re-viewing Asian American Literary Studies." In *An Interethnic Companion to Asian American Literature,* ed. King-kok Cheung. New York: Cambridge University Press, 1998.

Chicago Cultural Studies Group. "Critical Multiculturalism." *Critical Inquiry* 18 (1992): 530–55.

Chin, Frank, Jefferey Paul Chan, Lawson Fusao Inada, and Shawn Wong, eds. *Aiiieeeee!: An Anthology of Asian-American Writers.* Washington D.C.: Howard University Press, 1974.

———. *The Big Aiiieeeee!: An Anthology of Chinese American and Japanese American Literature.* New York: Meridian, 1991.

"Chinatown Declared a Nuisance!" Report, San Francisco, California (10 March 1880).

"Chinese Slavery." *San Francisco Chronicle* (17 April 1892).

Ching Louie, Miriam. "Immigrant Asian Women in Bay Area Garment Sweatshops: 'After Sewing, Laundry, Cleaning, and Cooking, I Have No Breath Left to Sing.'" *Amerasia Journal* 18, no. 1 (1992): 1–26.

———. "Breaking the Cycle: Women Workers Confront Corporate Greed

Globally." In *Dragon Ladies: Asian American Feminists Breathe Fire,* ed. Sonia Shah. Boston: South End Press, 1997.

Cho, Sumi K. "Asian Pacific American Women and Racialized Sexual Harassment." In *Making More Waves: New Writing by Asian American Women,* ed. Elaine H. Kim et al. Boston: Beacon Press, 1997.

Choi, Chungmoo. "The Discourse of Decolonization and Popular Memory: South Korea." *Positions: East Asia Cultures Critique* 1, no. 1 (spring 1993): 77–102.

———. "Transnational Capitalism, National Imaginary, and the Protest Theater in South Korea." *boundary 2* 22, no. 1 (spring 1995): 235–61.

Chow, Esther Ngan-ling. "The Development of Feminist Consciousness Among Asian American Women." *Gender and Society* 1, no. 3 (1987): 284–99. Reprinted in *Race, Class, and Gender: Common Bonds, Different Voices,* ed. Esther Ngan-ling Chow et al. Thousand Oaks, Calif.: Sage, 1996.

Chow, Rey. *Writing Diaspora: Tactics of Intervention in Contemporary Cultural Studies.* Bloomington: Indiana University Press, 1993.

———. "Film and Cultural Identity." In *The Oxford Guide to Film Studies,* ed. John Hill et al. Oxford: Oxford University Press, 1998.

Choy, Philip B., Lorraine Dong, and Marlon K. Hom. *The Coming Man: Nineteenth-Century American Perceptions of the Chinese.* Seattle: University of Washington Press, 1994.

Chu, Judy. "Asian American Women's Studies Courses: A Look Back at Our Beginnings." *Frontiers* 3, no. 3 (1986): 96–101.

Chung, Connie, Alison Kim, and A. K. Lemeshewsky, eds. *Between the Lines: An Anthology of Pacific/Asian Lesbians.* Santa Cruz: Dancing Bird Press, 1987.

Clifford, James. *The Predicament of Culture: Twentieth-Century Ethnography, Literature, and Art.* Cambridge: Harvard University Press, 1988.

———. "Diasporas." *Cultural Anthropology* 9, no. 3 (1994): 302–38.

Clifford, James, and George E. Marcus, eds. *Writing Culture: The Poetics and Politics of Ethnography.* Berkeley: University of California Press, 1986.

Costello, Jeanne. "Taking the 'Woman' out of Women's Autobiography: The Perils and Potentials of Theorizing Female Subjectivities." *Diacritics* (summer/fall 1991): 123–34.

Couser, G. Thomas. *Altered Egos: Authority in American Autobiography.* New York: Oxford University Press, 1989.

Coyner, Sandra. "Women's Studies as an Academic Discipline: Why and How to Do It." *Theories of Women's Studies,* ed. Gloria Bowles and Renate Duelli Klein. Boston: Routledge and Kegan Paul, 1983.

Craig, Paul. "An Outsider's Understanding: Maxine Hong Kingston's Chronicles of Chinese-Americans Earns a TV Tribute." *Sacramento Bee* (25 November 1990).

Culley, Margaret, ed. *American Women's Autobiography: Fea(s)ts of Memory.* Madison: University of Wisconsin Press, 1992.

Davis, Angela Y. *Women, Race, and Class.* New York: Vintage, 1981.

———. "Gender, Class, and Multiculturalism: Rethinking 'Race' Politics." In *Mapping Multiculturalism,* ed. Avery F. Gordon et al. Minneapolis: University of Minnesota Press, 1996.

de Certeau, Michel. *The Writing of History.* New York: Columbia University Press, 1988.

de Lauretis, Teresa. *Alice Doesn't: Feminism, Semiotics, Cinema.* Bloomington: Indiana University Press, 1984.

———. *Technologies of Gender: Essays on Theory, Film, and Fiction.* Bloomington: University of Indiana Press, 1987.

DeMonaco, MaryKim. "Disorderly Departure: An Analysis of the United States Policy Toward Amerasian Immigration." *Brooklyn Journal of International Law* 15, no. 3 (1989): 641–709.

Demetrakopolous, Stephanie A. "The Metaphysics of Matrilinealism in Women's Autobiography: Studies of Mead's *Blackberry Winter,* Hellman's *Pentimento,* Angelou's *I Know Why the Caged Bird Sings,* and Kingston's *The Woman Warrior.*" In *Women's Autobiography: Essays in Criticism,* ed. Estelle C. Jelinek. Bloomington: Indiana University Press, 1980.

Denison, D. C. "The Interview." *Boston Sunday Globe* (28 July 1991).

Densmore, G. B. *The Chinese in California: Description of Chinese Life in San Francisco.* San Francisco: Pettit and Russ, 1880.

Derrida, Jacques. *The Ear of the Other: Otobiography, Transference, Translation.* Edited by Christie V. McDonald. Translated by Peggy Kamuf. New York: Schocken Books, 1985.

Doezema, Jo. "Forced to Choose: Beyond the Voluntary vs. Forced Prostitution Dichotomy." In *Global Sex Workers: Rights, Resistance, and Redefinition,* ed. Kamala Kempadoo et al. New York: Routledge, 1998.

DuBois, Ellen Carol, and Vicki L. Ruiz, eds. *Unequal Sisters: A Multicultural Reader in U.S. Women's History.* New York: Routledge, 1990.

Duncan, Patricia L. "Identity, Power, and Difference: Negotiating Conflict in an S/M Dyke Community." In *Queer Studies: A Lesbian, Gay, Bisexual and Transgender Anthology,* ed. Brett Beemyn and Mickey Eliason. New York: New York University Press, 1996.

Dyer, Richard. *White.* London: Routledge, 1997.

———. "Introduction to Film Studies." In *The Oxford Guide to Film Studies,* ed. John Hill and Pamela Church Gibson. Oxford: Oxford University Press, 1998.

Eakin, Paul John. *Touching the World: Reference in Autobiography.* Princeton: Princeton University Press, 1992.

Easterlin, Richard A., et al. *Immigration.* Cambridge: Belknap Press of Harvard University Press, 1982.

Edholm, M. G. C. "A Stain on the Flag." *The Californian* (February 1892): 159–70.

Elson, Diane and Ruth Pearson. "'Nimble Fingers Make Cheap Workers': An Analysis of Women's Employment in Third World Manufacturing." *Feminist Review* 7 (1981): 87–107.

Eng, David, and Alice Y. Hom, eds. *Q & A: Queer in Asian America.* Philadelphia: Temple University Press, 1998.

Eng, Phoebe. *Warrior Lessons: An Asian American Woman's Journey into Power.* New York: Pocket Books, 1999.

Enloe, Cynthia H. "Women Textile Workers in the Militarization of Southeast Asia." In *Men, Women, and the International Division of Labor,* ed. June Nash and Mary Patricia Fernandez-Kelley. Albany: The State University of New York Press, 1983.

———. *Bananas, Beaches, Bases: Making Feminist Sense of International Politics.* Berkeley: University of California Press, 1990.

Escobar, Arturo. *Encountering Development: The Making and Unmaking of the Third World.* Princeton: Princeton University Press, 1995.

Espiritu, Yen Le. *Asian American Panethnicity: Bridging Institutions and Identities.* Philadelphia: Temple University Press, 1992.

———. "Race, Class, and Gender in Asian America." In *Making More Waves: New Writing by Asian American Women,* ed. Elaine H. Kim et al. Boston: Beacon Press, 1997.

———. *Asian American Women and Men: Labor, Laws, and Love.* Thousand Oaks, Calif.: Sage Publications, 1997.

Fabian, Johannes. *Time and the Other: How Anthropology Makes Its Object.* New York: Columbia University Press, 1983.

Fairclough, Gordon. "Slaves to Fashion." *Far Eastern Economic Review* (28 July 1994): 64–65.

Fischer, Michael M. J. "Ethnicity and the Post-Modern Arts of Memory." In *Writing Culture: The Poetics and Politics of Ethnography,* ed. James Clifford and George E. Marcus. Berkeley: University of California Press, 1986.

Fisher, Dexter, ed. *The Third Woman: Minority Women Writers of the United States.* Boston: Houghton Mifflin, 1980.

Fong, Katheryn M. "Asian Women Lose Citizenship." *San Francisco Journal* (29 December 1976): 12.

———. "Feminism Is Fine, But What's It Done for Asian America?" *Bridge: Asian American Perspective* 6, no. 4 (winter 1978): 21–22.

Forshee, Jill. "Introduction." In *Converging Interests: Traders, Travelers, and Tourists in Southeast Asia,* ed. Jill Forshee et al. Berkeley: International and Area Studies, University of California, 1999.

Foucault, Michel. *The Archaeology of Knowledge and the Discourse of Language.* Translated by A. M. Sheridan Smith. New York: Pantheon Books, 1972.

———. *Language, Counter-Memory, Practice: Selected Essays and Interviews.* Edited and translated by Donald F. Bouchard. Ithaca: Cornell University Press, 1977.

———. *Discipline and Punish: The Birth of the Prison.* Translated by Alan Sheridan. New York: Vintage, 1979.

———. *Power/Knowledge: Selected Interviews and Other Writings 1972–1977.* Edited by Colin Gordon. New York: Pantheon, 1980.

Friedman, Lester, ed. *Unspeakable Images: Ethnicity and the American Cinema.* Urbana: University of Illinois Press, 1991.

Friedman, Susan Stanford. "Women's Autobiographical Selves: Theory and Practice." In *The Private Self: Theory and Practice of Women's Autobiographical Writings,* ed. Shari Benstock. Chapel Hill: University of North Carolina Press, 1988.

Fuentes, Annette, and Barbara Ehrenreich. *Women in the Global Factory.* INC Pamphlet #2. Boston: South End Press, 1983.

Fujitomi, Irene, and Diane Wong. "The New Asian-American Women." In *Asian-Americans: Psychological Perspectives,* ed. Stanley Sue and Nathaniel N. Wagner. Palo Alto: Science and Behavior Books, Inc, 1973.

Gabaccia, Donna. *From the Other Side: Women, Gender, and Immigrant Life in the U.S., 1820–1990.* Bloomington: Indiana University Press, 1994.

Gaines, Charles. *The Theater of Refusal: Black Art and Mainstream Criticism,* ed. Catherine Lord. Irvine: Fine Arts Gallery, University of California, Irvine, 1993.

Gilmore, Leigh. *Autobiographics: A Feminist Theory of Women's Self-Representation.* Ithaca: Cornell University Press, 1994.

Glenn, Evelyn Nakano. "Racial Ethnic Women's Labor: The Intersection of Race, Gender, and Class Oppression." *Review of Radical Political Economics* 17, no. 3 (1985): 86–108.

Gordon, Ann D., Mari Jo Buhle, and Nancy Schrom Dye. "The Problem of Women's History." In *Liberating Women's History: Theoretical and Critical Essays,* ed. Berenice A. Carroll. Urbana: University of Illinois Press, 1976.

Gordon, Linda. "U.S. Women's History." In *The New American History,* ed. Eric Foner. Philadelphia: Temple University Press, 1990.

Graham, Julie. "Fordism/Post-Fordism, Marxism/Post-Marxism: The Second Cultural Divide?" *Rethinking MARXISM* 4, no. 1 (spring 1991): 39–58.

Gramsci, Antonio. *Selections from the Prison Notebooks.* New York: International Publishers, 1971.

Grewal, Inderpal, and Caren Kaplan. "Introduction: Transnational Feminist Practices and Questions of Postmodernity." In *Scattered Hegemonies: Postmodernity and Transnational Feminist Practices,* ed. Inderpal Grewal and Caren Kaplan. Minneapolis: University of Minnesota Press, 1994.

———. "Transnational Feminist Cultural Studies: Beyond the Marxism/Post-structuralism/Feminism Divides." *Positions: East Asia Cultures Critique* 2:2 (fall 1994): 430–45.

Grossman, Rachel. "Women's Place in the Integrated Circuit." *Southeast Asia Chronicle*. Special Issue: "Changing Role of Southeast Asian Women" 66 (January-February 1979): 2–17.

Gunn, Giles. *Thinking Across the American Grain: Ideology, Intellect, and the New Pragmatism*. Chicago: University of Chicago Press, 1992.

Hagedorn, Jessica. "Asian Women in Film: No Joy, No Luck." *Ms.* (January/February 1994): 74–79.

Hall, C. Michael. "Sex Tourism in South-east Asia." In *Tourism and the Less Developed Countries*, ed. David Harrison. London: Belhaven, 1991.

———. "Gender and Economic Interests in Tourism Prostitution: The Nature, Development, and Implications of Sex Tourism in South-east Asia." In *Tourism: A Gender Analysis*, ed. Vivian Kinnaird et al. Chichester: John Wiley and Sons, 1994.

Hall, Stuart. "The Meaning of New Times." In *New Times: The Changing Face of Politics in the 1990's*, ed. Stuart Hall et al. London: Verso, 1990.

———. "The Local and the Global: Globalization and Ethnicity." In *Culture, Globalization, and the World System*, ed. Anthony D. King. Binghamton: State University of New York at Binghamton, Department of Art History, 1991.

———. "Old and New Identities, Old and New Ethnicities." In *Culture, Globalization, and the World System*, ed. Anthony D. King. 1991.

———. "Culture, Community, Nation." *Cultural Studies* 7, no. 3 (October 1991): 349–63.

———. "When Was 'the Post-Colonial'? Thinking at the Limit." In *The Post-Colonial Question: Common Skies, Divided Horizons*, ed. Iain Chambers at al. London: Routledge, 1996.

Haraway, Donna. "A Manifesto for Cyborgs: Science, Technology, and Socialist Feminism in the 1980's." *Socialist Review* 80, 15:2 (March/April 1985): 65–107.

———. "Ecce Homo, Ain't (Ar'n't) I a Woman, and Inappropriated Others: The Human in a Post-Human Landscape." In *Feminists Theorize the Political*, ed. Judith Butler et al. New York and London: Routledge, 1991.

———. *Simians, Cyborgs, and Women: The Reinvention of Nature*. New York, Routledge, 1991.

Harvey, David. *The Condition of Postmodernity*. London: Basil Blackwell, 1990.

Hatta, Julie, and Claire Koga. "An Interview with Connie Young Yu." *Asian American Women* (May 1976): 45.

Hayakawa, Lee S. "Coroners' Reports as a Historical Source for Asian American History." In *Asian Americans: Comparative and Global Perspectives*, ed. Shirley Hune et al. Pullman: Washington State University Press, 1991.

Heath, Stephen. *Questions of Cinema*. Bloomington: Indiana University Press, 1981.

Hess, Gary. "The 'Hindu' in America: Immigration and Naturalization Policies and India, 1917–1946." *Pacific Historical Review* 38 (1991): 59–79.

Heung, Marina. "Representing Ourselves: Films and Videos by Asian American/Canadian Women." In *Feminism, Multiculturalism, and the Media: Global Diversities*, ed. Angharad N. Valdivia. Thousand Oaks, Calif.: Sage Publications, 1995.

Heyzer, Noeleen, ed. *Daughters of Industry: Work Skills and Consciousness of Women Workers in Asia*. Kuala Lumpur: Asian Pacific Development Center, 1988.

Hill, John, and Pamela Church Gibson, eds. *The Oxford Guide to Film Studies*. Oxford: Oxford University Press, 1998.

Hing, Bill Ong. *Making and Remaking Asian America Through Immigration Policy, 1850–1990*. Palo Alto: Stanford University Press, 1993.

Hirata, Lucie Cheng. "Free, Indentured, Enslaved: Chinese Prostitutes in Nineteenth-Century California." *Signs: A Journal of Women in Culture and Society* 5:1 (autumn 1979): 3–29.

———. "Chinese Immigrant Women in Nineteenth-Century America." In *Asian and Pacific American Experiences: Women's Perspectives*, ed. Nobuya Tsuchida. Minneapolis: University of Minnesota Press, 1982.

Holbrook, Rev. J. C. "Chinadom in California." *Hutching's California Magazine* (September 1859).

Holder, Charles Frederick. "Chinese Slavery in America." *North American Review* 165:3 (1897): 288–94.

Hori, Joan. "Japanese Prostitution in Hawaii During the Immigration Period." In *Asian and Pacific American Experiences: Women's Perspectives*, ed. Nobuya Tsuchida. Minneapolis: University of Minnesota Press, 1982.

Hsu, Kai-Yu, and Helen Palunbinskas, eds. *Asian-American Authors*. Boston: Houghton Mifflin, 1976.

Hune, Shirley. *Teaching Asian American Women's History*. Washington, D.C.: American Historical Association, 1997.

———. *Asian Pacific American Women in Higher Education: Claiming Visibility and Voice*. Washington, D. C.: Association of American Colleges and Universities, 1998.

Ichioka, Yuji. "Ameyuki-san: Japanese Prostitutes in Nineteenth-Century America." *Amerasia Journal* 4, no. 1 (1977): 1–21.

———. "The Early Japanese Immigrant Quest for Citizenship: The Background of the 1922 Ozawa Case." *Amerasia Journal* 4, no. 2 (1977): 1–22.

Islas, Arturo. "Interview with Maxine Hong Kingston." In *Women Writers of the West Coast Speaking of Their Lives and Careers*, ed. Marilyn Yalom. Santa Barbara, Calif.: Capra, 1983.

Iwata, Edward. "Hot Properties: More Asian Americans Suddenly Are Winning Mainstream Literary Acclaim." *Los Angeles Times* (11 September 1989).

———. "Word Warriors." *Los Angeles Times* (24 June 1990).

Iwataki, Miya. "The Asian Women's Movement: A Retrospective." *East Wind* (spring/summer 1983): 35–37.

Jameson, Fredric. *Postmodernism, or the Cultural Logic of Late Capitalism.* Durham: Duke University Press, 1990.

Jelinek, Estelle C., ed. *Women's Autobiography: Essays in Criticism.* Bloomington: Indiana University Press, 1980.

Jones, Dorothy B. *The Portrayal of China and India on the American Screen, 1896–1955: The Evolution of Chinese and Indian Themes, Locales, and Characters as Portrayed on the American Screen.* Cambridge: Center for International Studies, MIT, 1955.

Juhasz, Suzanne. "Maxine Hong Kingston: Narrative Technique and Female Identity." In *Contemporary American Women Writers,* ed. Catherine Rainwater et al. Lexington: University of Kentucky Press, 1983.

Jun, Helen Heran. "Contingent Nationalisms: Renegotiating Borders in Korean and Korean American Women's Oppositional Struggles." *Positions: East Asia Cultures Critique* 5, no. 2 (fall 1997): 325–55.

Kabanni, Rana. "The Salon's Seraglio." *Europe's Myths of Orient.* London: Macmillan, 1986.

Kafka, Phillipa. *(Un)doing the Missionary Position: Gender Asymmetry in Contemporary Asian American Women's Writing.* Westport, Conn.: Greenwood Press, 1997.

Kang, Laura Hyun Yi. "The Desiring of Asian Female Bodies: Interracial Romance and Cinematic Subjection." *Visual Anthropology Review* 9, no. 1 (spring 1993): 5–21.

———. "The Liberatory Voice of Theresa Hak Kyung Cha's *Dictée*." In *Writing Self, Writing Nation: Essays on* Dictée, ed. Elaine H. Kim and Norma Alarcón. Berkeley: Third Woman Press, 1994.

———. "Si(gh)ting Asian/American Women as Transnational Labor." *Positions: East Asia Cultures Critique* 5, no. 2 (fall 1997): 403–37.

———. "Towards a Contending Pedagogy: Asian American Studies as Extracurricular Praxis." In *Teaching Asian America: Diversity and the Problem of Community,* ed. Lane Ryo Hirabayashi. New York: Rowman and Littlefield, 1997.

Kaplan, Amy. "Romancing the Empire: The Embodiment of American Masculinity in the Popular Historical Novel of the 1890s." *American Literary History* 2, no. 4 (winter 1990): 659–90.

Kaplan, Caren. "Resisting Autobiography: Out-Law Genres and Transnational Feminist Subjects." In *De/Colonizing the Subject: The Politics of Women's Autobiography,* ed. Sidonie Smith and Julia Watson. Minneapolis: University of Minnesota Press, 1992.

———. *Questions of Travel: Postmodern Discourses of Displacement.* Durham: Duke University Press, 1996.

Ketchum, Diana. "Maxine Hong Kingston: Oakland's 'Woman Warrior' Talks About Life as a Literary Star." *Oakland Tribune* (24 June 1990).

Kim, Elaine H. *Asian American Literature: An Introduction to the Writings and their Social Context.* Philadelphia: Temple University Press, 1982.

———. "Sex Tourism in Asia: A Reflection of Political and Economic Inequality." *Critical Perspectives of Third World America* 2, no. 1 (fall 1984): 214–32.

———. "Asian American Literature and the Importance of Social Context." *ADE Bulletin* 80 (1985): 34–41.

———. "Defining Asian American Realities Through Literature." *Cultural Critique* 6 (spring 1987): 87–111.

———. "Asian Americans and American Popular Culture." In *Dictionary of Asian American History,* ed. Hyung-chan Kim. Westport, Conn.: Greenwood Press, 1989.

———. "'Such Opposite Creatures': Men and Women in Asian American Literature." *Michigan Quarterly Review* (1990): 68–93.

———. "Poised on the In-Between: A Korean American's Reflections on Theresa Hak Kyung Cha's *Dictée.*" In *Writing Self, Writing Nation: Essays on Theresa Hak Kyung Cha's "Dictée,"* ed. Elaine H. Kim and Norma Alarcón. Berkeley: Third Woman Press, 1994.

———. "'Bad Women': Asian American Visual Artists Hanh Thi Pham, Hung Liu, and Yong Soon Min." In *Making More Waves: New Writing by Asian American Women,* ed. Elaine H. Kim et al. Boston: Beacon Press, 1997.

Kim, Hyung-chan, ed. *Dictionary of Asian American History.* Westport, Conn.: Greenwood Press, 1989.

———. *A Legal History of Asian Americans, 1790–1990.* Westport, Conn.: Greenwood Press, 1994.

———. ed. *Asian Americans and Congress: A Documentary History.* Westport, Conn.: Greenwood Press, 1996.

Kim, Hyun Mee. "Labor Politics and the Women Subject in Contemporary Korea." Ph.D. dissertation. University of Washington, 1995.

Kim, Min-Jung. "Moments of Danger in the (Dis)continuous Relations of Korean Nationalism and Korean American Nationalism." *Positions: East Asia Cultures Critique* 5, no. 2 (fall 1997): 357–89.

Kim, Myung Mi. *Under Flag.* Berkeley: Kelsey Street Press, 1991.

King, Katie. "Bibliography and a Feminist Apparatus of Literary Production." *Text* 5 (1990): 91–103.

———. *Theory in Its Feminist Travels: Conversations in U.S. Women's Movements.* Bloomington: Indiana University Press, 1994.

Kingston, Maxine Hong. *The Woman Warrior: Memoirs of a Girlhood Among Ghosts.* New York: Vintage, 1977.

Klein, Julie Thompson. *Interdisciplinarity: History, Theory, and Practice.* Detroit: Wayne State University Press, 1990.

———. *Crossing Boundaries: Knowledge, Disciplinarities, and Interdisciplinarities.* Charlottesville: University Press of Virginia, 1996.

Kumagai, Gloria L. "The Asian Women in America." *Bridge: An Asian American Perspective* (winter 1978): 17–20.

Lambert, Richard D. *Language and Area Studies Review.* Philadelphia: The American Academy of Political and Social Science, 1973.

Laurence, Robin. "Fresh, Forceful Works Explore Creation of Identity." *Vancouver Sun* (6 March 1994).

Lee, A. Robert, ed. *First Person Singular: Studies in American Autobiography.* New York: St. Martin's Press, 1988.

Lee, JeeYeun. "Why Suzie Wong Is Not a Lesbian: Asian and Asian American Lesbian and Bisexual Women and Femme/Butch/Gender Identities." In *Queer Studies: A Lesbian, Gay, Bisexual, and Transgender Anthology,* ed. Brett Beemyn et al. New York: New York University Press, 1996.

———. "Toward a Queer Korean American Diasporic History." In *Q & A: Queer in Asian America,* ed. David Eng et al. Philadelphia: Temple University Press, 1996.

Lee, Rachel. "Claiming Land, Claiming Voice, Claiming Canon: Institutionalized Challenges in Kingston's *China Men* and *The Woman Warrior.*" In *Reviewing Asian America: Locating Diversity,* ed. Wendy L. Ng et al. Pullman: Washington State University Press, 1995.

Lee, Robert G. "*The Woman Warrior* as an Intervention in Asian American Historiography." In *Approaches to Teaching Kingston's* The Woman Warrior, ed. Shirley Geok-Lin Lim. New York: Modern Language Association, 1991.

Lee, Wendy. "Prostitution and Tourism in South-east Asia." In *Working Women: International Perspectives in Labour and Gender Ideology,* ed. Nanneke Redclift et al. London: Routledge, 1991.

Lefleur, Brenda. "Review of *Between Views* and *Points of View.*" *Versus,* no. 4 (1995): 27–30.

Lejeune, Philippe. *On Autobiography.* Ed. Paul John Eakin. Trans. Katherine Leary. Minneapolis: University of Minnesota Press, 1989.

Lenoir, Timothy. "The Discipline of Nature and the Nature of Disciplines." In *Knowledges: Historical and Critical Studies in Disciplinarity,* ed. Ellen Messer-Davidow et al. Charlottesville: University Press of Virginia, 1993.

Lesser, Jeff H. "Always 'Outsiders': Asians, Naturalization, and the Supreme Court." *Amerasia Journal* 12, no. 1 (1985–86): 83–100.

Liang, Hua. "Fighting for a New Life: Social and Patriotic Activism of Chinese American Women in New York City, 1900–1945." *Journal of American Ethnic History* 17, no. 2 (winter 1998): 22–39.

Light, Ivan. "From Vice District to Tourist Attraction: The Moral Career of American Chinatowns, 1880–1940." *Pacific Historical Review* 43 (August 1974): 367–94.

Lim, Linda Y. C. "Capitalism, Imperialism, and Patriarchy: The Dilemma of Third World Women Workers in Multinational Factories." In *Women, Men, and the International Division of Labor,* ed. June Nash and Maria Patricia Fernández-Kelly. Albany: The State University of New York Press, 1983.

Lim, Shirley Geok-Lin, ed. *Approaches to Teaching Kingston's* The Woman Warrior. New York: Modern Language Association, 1991.

———. "The Tradition of Chinese American Women's Life Stories: Thematics of Race and Gender in Jade Snow Wong's *Fifth Chinese Daughter* and Maxine Hong Kingston's *The Woman Warrior.*" In *American Women's Autobiography: Fea(s)ts of Memory,* ed. Margaret Culley. Madison: University of Wisconsin Press, 1992.

———. "Feminist and Ethnic Literary Theories in Asian American Literature." *Feminist Studies* 19, no. 3 (fall 1993): 571–95.

———. "Twelve Asian-American Writers: In Search of Self-Definition." *MELUS* 13, no. 2 (1986): 57–78.

Lim-Hing, Sharon. *The Very Inside: An Anthology of Writing by Asian and Pacific Islander Lesbian and Bisexual Women.* Toronto: Sister Vision Press, 1994.

Ling, Amy. "Chinese American Women Writers: The Tradition Behind Maxine Hong Kingston." In *Redefining American Literary History,* ed. A. LaVonne Brown Ruoff et al. New York: Modern Languages Association, 1990.

Ling, Jinqui. *Narrating Nationalisms: Ideology and Form in Asian American Literature.* New York: Oxford University Press, 1998.

Ling, Susie Hsihuan. "The Mountain Movers: Asian American Women's Movement, Los Angeles, 1968–1976." Master's Thesis. University of California at Los Angeles, 1984.

Liu, Sandra. "Passion and Commitment: Asian American Women in Hollywood." In *Making More Waves: New Writings by Asian American Women,* ed. Elaine H. Kim et al. Boston: Beacon Press, 1997.

Loo, Chalsa, and Paul Ong. "Slaying Demons with a Sewing Needle: Feminist Issues for Chinatown's Women." *Berkeley Journal of Sociology* 27 (1982): 77–87.

Loomis, Reverend A. W. "Chinese Women in California." *Overland Monthly* (April 1869): 344–51.

López, Ian F. Haney. *White By Law: The Legal Construction of Race.* New York: New York University Press, 1996.

Lott, Juanita Tamayo, and Canta Pian. *Beyond Stereotypes and Statistics: Emer-*

gence of Asian and Pacific American Women. Washington, D.C.: Organization of Pan Asian American Women, 1977.

Louie, Miriam Ching. "Immigrant Asian Women in Bay Area Garment Sweatshops: 'After Sewing, Laundry, Cleaning and Cooking, I Have No Breath Left to Sing.'" *Amerasia Journal* 18, no. 1 (1992): 1–26.

———. "Breaking the Cycle: Women Workers Confront Corporate Greed Globally," in *Dragon Ladies: Asian American Feminists Breathe Fire,* ed. Sonia Shah. Boston: South End Press, 1997.

Lowe, Lisa. "Heterogeneity, Hybridity, Multiplicity: Marking Asian American Differences." *Diaspora* 1, no. 1 (spring 1991): 24–44.

———. *Critical Terrains: French and British Orientalisms.* Ithaca: Cornell University Press, 1992.

———. "Unfaithful to the Original: The Subject of *Dictée.*" In *Writing Self, Writing Nation: Essays on Theresa Hak Kyung Cha's "Dictée,"* ed. Elaine H. Kim and Norma Alarcón. Berkeley: Third Woman Press, 1994.

———. "Canon, Institutionalization, Identity: Contradictions for Asian American Studies." In *The Ethnic Canon: Histories, Institutions, Interventions,* ed. David Palumbo-Liu. Minneapolis: University of Minnesota Press, 1994.

———. *Immigrant Acts: On Asian American Cultural Politics.* Durham: Duke University Press, 1996.

———. "Work, Immigration, Gender: Asian 'American' Women." In *Making More Waves: New Writings by Asian American Women,* ed. Elaine H. Kim et al. Boston: Beacon Press, 1997.

———. 'The International Within the National: American Studies and Asian American Critique." *Cultural Critique* 40 (1998): 29–47.

Lu, Lynn. "Critical Visions: The Representation and Resistance of Asian Women." In *Dragon Ladies: Asian American Feminists Breathe Fire,* ed. Sonia Shah. Boston: South End Press, 1997.

Lubiano, Wahneema. "Like Being Mugged by a Metaphor: Multiculturalism and State Narratives." In *Mapping Multiculturalism,* ed. Avery F. Gordon et al. Minneapolis: University of Minnesota Press, 1996.

Luibheid, Eithne. "The 1965 Immigration and Nationality Act: An 'End' to Exclusion." *Positions: East Asia Cultures Critique* 5, no. 2 (fall 1997): 501–22.

Luluquisen, Esmina M. *The Health and Well-being of Asian and Pacific Islander American Women.* Oakland: Asians and Pacific Islanders for Reproductive Health, 1995.

McCaughey, Robert A. *International Studies and Academic Enterprise: A Chapter in the Enclosure of American Learning.* New York: Columbia University Press, 1984.

McClain, Charles J. *In Search of Equality: The Chinese Struggle Against Discrimination in Nineteenth-Century America.* Berkeley: University of California Press, 1994.

————. "Tortuous Path, Elusive Goal: The Asian Quest for American Citizenship." *Asian Law Journal* 2 (1995): 33–60.

McClellan, Robert. *The Heathen Chinee: A Study of American Attitudes Toward China, 1890–1905.* Columbus: Ohio State University Press, 1971.

McClintock, Anne. "'No Longer a Future in Heaven': Women and Nationalism in South Africa." *Transition* 51 (1991): 104–23.

————. "The Angel of Progress: Pitfalls of the Term 'Post-colonialism'." *Social Text* 31–32 (1992): 1–15.

————. "Family Feuds: Gender, Nationalism, and the Family." *Feminist Review* 44 (summer 1993): 61–80.

McCunn, Ruthanne Lum. *Thousand Pieces of Gold.* Boston: Beacon Press, 1981.

McDonald, Hamish. "Ahead of the Neighbours: New Sri Lankan Government Says Reforms Will Continue." *Far Eastern Economic Review* (20 May 1993): 67–68.

McDonald, Paul. "Film Acting." In *The Oxford Guide to Film Studies,* ed. John Hill and Pamela Church Gibson. Oxford: Oxford University Press, 1998.

McFadden, Sarah. "Report from Istanbul: Bosporus Dialogues." *Art in America* 81:6 (June 1993)" 55–57.

McKeown, Adam. "Transnational Chinese Families and Chinese Exclusion, 1875–1943." *Journal of American Ethnic History* 18, no. 2 (winter 1999): 73–110.

Marchetti, Gina. *Romance and the "Yellow Peril": Race, Sex, and Discursive Strategies in Hollywood Fiction.* Berkeley: University of California Press, 1993.

Marcus, George E., and Michael M. J. Fischer. *Anthropology as Cultural Critique: An Experimental Moment in the Human Sciences.* Chicago: University of Chicago Press, 1986.

————. "Contemporary Problems of Ethnography in the Modern World System." In *Writing Culture: The Poetics and Politics of Ethnography,* ed. James Clifford et al. Berkeley: University of California Press, 1986.

Marcus, George E., and Dick Cushman, "Ethnographies as Texts." *Annual Review of Anthropology* (1982): 25–69.

Martin, Biddy. "Lesbian Identity and Autobiographical Difference(s)." In *Life/Lines: Theorizing Women's Autobiography,* ed. Bella Brodzki and Celeste Schenck. Ithaca: Cornell University Press, 77–103.

Matsui, Yayori. *Women's Asia.* London: Zed Books, 1989.

Mazumdar, Sucheta. "General Introduction: A Woman-Centered Perspective of Asian American History." In *Making Waves: An Anthology of Writings By and About Asian American Women,* ed. Asian Women United. Boston: Beacon Press, 1989.

Mies, Maria. *Patriarchy and the Accumulation of Capital.* London: Zed Press, 1984.

Miller, Stuart Creighton. *The Unwelcome Immigrant: The American Image of the Chinese, 1785–1882.* Berkeley: University of California Press, 1974.

Mitter, Swasti. *Common Fate, Common Bond: Women in the Global Economy.* London: Pluto Press, 1986.

Mohanty, Chandra, "Under Western Eyes . . ." In *Third World Women and the Politics of Feminism,* ed. Chandra Mohanty et al. Bloomington: Indiana University Press, 1991.

———. "Defining Genealogies: Feminist Reflections on Being South Asian in North America." In *Our Feet Walk the Sky,* ed. Women of the South Asian Diaspora. San Francisco: Aunt Lute Books, 1993.

Moon, Katharine. *Sex Among Allies: Military Prostitution in U.S.-Korea Relations.* New York: Columbia University Press, 1997.

———. "Prostitute Bodies and Gendered States in US-Korea Relations." In *Dangerous Women: Gender and Korean Nationalism,* ed. Elaine H. Kim and Chungmoo Choi. New York: Routledge, 1998.

Morgen, Sandra, ed. *Gender and Anthropology: Critical Reviews for Research and Teaching.* Washington, D.C.: American Anthropological Association, 1989.

Mowitt, John. *Text: The Genealogy and an Anti-Disciplinary Object.* Durham: Duke University Press, 1993.

Moy, James. *Marginal Sights: Staging the Chinese in America.* Iowa City: University of Iowa Press, 1993.

Mulvey, Laura. "Visual Pleasure and Narrative Cinema." *Screen* 16, no. 3 (autumn 1975): 6–18.

Muroi, Hisae, and Naoko Sasaki. "Tourism and Prostitution in Japan." In *Gender, Work, and Tourism,* ed. M. Thea Sinclair. London: Routledge, 1997.

Nash, June "The Impact of the Changing International Division of Labor on Different Sectors of the Labor Force." In *Women, Men, and the International Division of Labor,* ed. June Nash and Mary Patricia Fernández-Kelly. Albany: The State University of New York Press, 1983.

Neale, Steve. "The Same Old Story: Stereotypes and Difference." In *The Screen Education Reader: Cinema, Television, Culture,* ed. Manuel Alvarado et al. New York: Columbia University Press, 1993.

Ng, Franklin, ed. *The Asian American Encyclopedia.* New York: Marshall Cavendish, 1995.

———. *Asian American Women and Gender.* New York: Garland Publishing, 1998.

Niranjana, Tejaswini. *Siting Translation: History, Post-Structuralism, and the Colonial Context.* Berkeley: University of California Press, 1993.

Noda, Barbara. "Asian American Women: Two Special Issues of *Bridge: An Asian American Perspective,*" *Conditions: a Magazine of Writings by Women with an Emphasis on Writings by Lesbians* 6 (1980): 203–11.

Noda, Barbara, Kitty Tsui, and Z. Wong. "Coming Out: We Are Here in the Asian Community." *Bridge: An Asian American Perspective* 7, no. 1 (spring 1979): 22–24.

Noh, Eliza. "'Amazing Grace, Come Sit on My Face,' or Christian Ecumenical Representations of the Asian Sex Tour Industry." *Positions: East Asia Cultures Critique* 5, no. 2 (fall 1997): 439–65.

Nomura, Gail M. "Interpreting the Historical Experience." In *Frontiers of Asian American Studies: Writing, Research, and Commentary,* ed. Gail M. Nomura at al. Pullman: Washington State University Press, 1989.

———. "Revisioning Asian/Pacific American History." In *Bearing Dreams, Shaping Visions: Asian Pacific American Perspectives,* ed. Linda A. Revilla et al. Pullman: Washington State University Press, 1993.

Nowrojee, Sia, and Jael Silliman. "Asian Women's Health: Organizing a Movement." In *Dragon Ladies: Asian American Feminists Breathe Fire,* ed. Sonia Shah. Boston: South End Press, 1997.

Odzer, Cleo. *Patpong Sisters: An American Woman's View of the Bangkok Sex World.* New York: Arcade Publishing, 1994.

Okihiro, Gary Y. "The Idea of Community and a 'Particular Type of History'." In *Reflections on Shattered Windows,* ed. Gary Y. Okihiro. Pullman: Washington State University Press, 1988.

———. *Margins and Mainstreams: Asians in American History and Culture.* Seattle: University of Washington Press, 1993.

O'Merry, Rorry. *My Wife in Bangkok.* Berkeley: Asia Press, 1990.

Omi, Michael, and Howard Winant. *Racial Formation in the United States: From the 1960s to 1990s.* New York: Routledge, 1994.

Omi, Michael, and Dana Y. Takagi. "Thinking Theory in Asian American Studies." *Amerasia Journal,* 21, nos. 1–2 (1995).

Ong, Aihwa. "Global Industries and Malay Peasants in Peninsular Malaysia." In *Women, Men, and the International Division of Labor,* ed. June Nash and Maria Patricia Fernandez-Kelley. Albany: The State University of New York Press, 1983.

———. *Spirits of Resistance and Capitalist Discipline: Factory Women in Malaysia.* Albany: The State University of New York Press, 1987.

———. "Japanese Factories, Malay Workers: Class and Sexual Metaphors in West Malaysia." In *Power and Difference: Gender in Island Southeast Asia,* ed. Jane Monnig Atkinson et al. Stanford: Stanford University Press, 1990.

———. "The Gender and Labor Politics of Postmodernity." In *The Politics of Culture in the Shadow of Capital,* ed. Lisa Lowe et al. Durham: Duke University Press, 1997.

———. "Woman Out of China: Traveling Tales and Traveling Theories in Postcolonial Feminism." In *Women Writing Culture,* ed. Ruth Behar and Deborah A. Gordon. Berkeley: University of California Press, 1995.

Osumi, Megumi Dick. "Asians and California's Anti-Miscegenation Laws." In *Asian and Pacific American Experiences: Women's Perspectives,* ed. Nobuya Tsuchida. Minnneapolis: University of Minnesota Press, 1982.

Outka, Paul. "Publish or Perish: Food, Hunger, and Self-Constructions in Maxine Hong Kingston's *The Woman Warrior." Contemporary Literature* 38, no. 3 (1997): 447–83.

Peffer, George Anthony. "From Under the Sojourner's Shadow: A Historiographical Study of Chinese Female Immigration to America, 1852–1882." *Journal of American Ethnic History* (spring 1992): 41–67.

Pullin, Faith. "Enclosure/Disclosure: A Tradition of American Autobiography by Women." In *First Person Singular: Studies in American Autobiography.* New York: St. Martin's Press, 1988.

Pun, Ngai. "Theoretical Discussions on the Impact of Industrial Restructuring in Asia." In *Silk and Steel: Asian Women Workers Confront Challenges of Industrial Restructuring.* Hong Kong: Committee for Asian Women, 1995.

Quinby, Lee. "The Subject of Memoirs: *The Woman Warrior*'s Technology of Ideographic Selfhood." In *De/Colonizing the Subject: The Politics of Women's Autobiography,* ed. Sidonie Smith and Julia Watson. Minneapolis: University of Minnesota Press, 1992.

Riley, Denise. *"Am I That Name?": Feminism and the Category of "Women" in History.* Minneapolis: University of Minnesota Press, 1988.

Rooks Jr., Curtiss J., and Jon Panish. "The Dilemma of the Ethnic Writer: A Case Study of Maxine Hong Kingston." In *Bearing Dreams, Shaping Visions: Asian Pacific American Perspectives,* ed. Linda A. Revilla et al. Pullman: Washington State University Press, 1993.

Rosenbrock, H. H. "Can Human Skill Survive Microelectronics?" In *Implementing New Technologies: Choice, Decision, and Change in Manufacturing,* ed. Ed Rhodes et al. Oxford: Basil Blackwell, 1985.

Rothschild, Matthew. "Babies for Sale: South Koreans Make Them, Americans Buy Them." *Progressive* (January 1988): 18–23.

Rubenstein, Roberta. *Boundaries of the Self: Gender, Culture, Fiction.* Chicago: University of Chicago Press, 1987.

Rubin, Gayle. "The Traffic in Women: Notes on the Political Economy of Sex." In *Toward an Anthropology of Women,* ed. Rayna Reiter. New York: Monthly Review Press, 1975.

Safran, William. "Diasporas in Modern Societies: Myths of Homeland and Return." *Diaspora.* 1, no. 1 (spring 1991): 83–99.

Said, Edward. *Orientalism.* New York: Random House, 1979.

———. *The World, the Text, the Critic.* Cambridge: Harvard University Press, 1983.

———. *Culture and Imperialism.* New York: Vintage, 1993.

Sapiro, Virginia. "Women, Citizenship, Nationality." *Politics and Society* 13 (1984): 1–26.

Sassen, Saskia. *Globalization and Its Discontents*. New York: New Press, 1998.

———. "Notes on the Incorporation of Third World Women into Wage-Labor Through Immigration and Off-Shore Production." *International Migration Review* 18 (winter 1984): 1144–67.

Schramm, Sarah Slavin. "Women's Studies: Its Focus, Idea Power, and Promise." In *Women's Studies: An Interdisciplinary Collection,* ed. Kathleen O'Connor Blumhagen et al. Westport, Conn.: Greenwood Press, 1977.

Schueller, Malini Johar. *The Politics of Voice: Liberalism and Social Criticism from Franklin to Kingston*. Albany: The State University of New York Press, 1992.

Schwartz, Benjamin I. "Presidential Address: Area Studies as a Critical Discipline." *Journal of Asian Studies* 40, no. 1 (November 1980): 15–25.

Scott, Joan W. *Gender and the Politics of History*. New York: Columbia University Press, 1988.

———. "The Problem of Invisibility." In *Retrieving Women's History: Changing Perceptions of the Role of Women in Politics and Society,* ed. S. Jay Kleinberg. Oxford: Berg/Unesco, 1988.

———. "Women's History." In *New Perspectives on Historical Writing,* ed. Peter Burke. University Park, Pa.: Pennsylvania State University Press, 1992.

———. "Experience." In *Feminists Theorize the Political,* ed. Joan W. Scott et al. New York: Routledge, 1993.

Sengenberger, Werner, and Duncan Campbell, eds. *International Labor Standards and Economic Interdependence*. Geneva: International Institute for Labor Studies, 1994.

Serrin, William. "After Years of Decline, Sweatshops Are Back." *New York Times* (12 October 1983).

———. "Combating Garment Sweatshops Is an Almost Futile Task." *New York Times* (13 October 1983).

Shank, Barry. "Conjuring Evidence for Experience: Imagining a Post-Structuralist History." *American Quarterly* 36, no. 1 (spring 1995): 81–92.

Sharpe, Jim. "History from Below." In *New Perspectives on Historical Writing,* ed. Peter Burke. University Park, Pa.: The Pennsylvania State University Press, 1992.

Sheppard, Allan. "Jin-Me Yoon: *Souvenirs of the Self*—(Re)inventing (One)self in (Alien)nation." *Canadian Link* (September 1991): 35.

Shohat, Ella. "Ethnicities-in-Relation: Toward a Multicultural Reading of American Cinema." In *Unspeakable Images: Ethnicity and the American Cinema,* ed. Lester D. Friedman. Urbana: University of Illinois Press, 1991.

———. "Notes on the 'Post-Colonial'." *Social Text* 31–32 (1992): 99–113.

Shumsky, Neil Larry. "Tacit Acceptance: Respectable Americans and Segregated Prostitution, 1870–1910." *Journal of Social History* 19 (summer 1986): 665–79.

Shumway, David. *Creating American Civilization: A Genealogy of American Literature as an Academic Discipline.* Minneapolis: University of Minnesota Press, 1994.

Smith, Sidonie. *A Poetics of Women's Autobiography: Marginality and the Fictions of Self-Representation.* Bloomington: Indiana University Press, 1987.

Smith, Sidonie, and Julia Watson, eds. *Women, Autobiography, Theory: A Reader.* Madison, Wis.: University of Wisconsin Press, 1998.

Snow, Robert. "The New International Division of Labor and the U.S. Workforce: The Case of the Electronics Industry." In *Men, Women, and the International Division of Labor,* ed. June Nash and Mary Patricia Fernandez-Kelley. Albany: The State University of New York Press, 1983.

Spillers, Hortense J. "Mama's Baby, Papa's Maybe: An American Grammar Book." *Diacritics* 17, no. 2 (1987): 65–81.

Spivak, Gayatri Chakravorty. "Displacement and the Discourse of Woman." In *Displacement: Derrida and After,* ed. Mark Krupnick. Bloomington: Indiana University Press, 1983.

———. "Can the Subaltern Speak?" In *Marxism and the Interpretation of Culture,* ed. Cary Nelson et al. Urbana: University of Illinois Press, 1988.

———. "The Political Economy of Women as Seen by a Literary Critic." In *Coming to Terms: Feminism, Theory, Practice,* ed. Elizabeth Weed. New York: Routledge, 1989.

———. "In a Word. Interview." *Differences* 1 (summer 1989): 124–56.

———. *The Post-Colonial Critic: Interviews, Strategies, Dialogues.* Edited by Sarah Harasym. New York: Routledge, 1990.

———. "Diasporas Old and New: Women in the Transnational World." *Textual Practice* 10, no. 2 (1996): 245–269.

Stacey, Judith. "Can There Be a Feminist Ethnography?" In *Women's Words: The Feminist Practice of Oral History,* ed. Sherna Gluck et al. New York: Routledge, 1991.

Stanley, Liz. *The Auto/biographical I: The Theory and Practice of Feminist Auto/biography.* Manchester: Manchester University Press, 1992.

———. "On Auto/biography in Sociology." *Sociology* 27, no. 1 (February 1993): 41–53.

Steward, Julian H. *Area Research: Theory and Practice.* New York: Social Science Research Council, 1950.

Stewart, Susan. *On Longing: Narratives of the Miniature, the Gigantic, the Souvenir, the Collection.* Durham: Duke University Prtess, 1993.

Stock-Morton, Phyllis. "Finding Our Own Ways: Different Paths to Women's History in the United States." In *Writing Women's History: International Perspectives,* ed. Karen Offen et al. Bloomington: Indiana University Press, 1991.

Sturdevant, Saundra Pollock, and Brenda Stoltzfus. *Let the Good Times Roll: Prostitution and the U.S. Military in Asia.* New York: The New Press, 1992.

Sumida, Stephen. "Afterword." In *Growing Up Asian American: An Anthology,* ed. Maria Hong. New York: William Morrow, 1993.

Tajima, Renee E. "Lotus Blossoms Don't Bleed: Images of Asian Women." In *Making Waves: An Anthology of Writings By and About Asian American Women,* ed. Asian Women United. Boston: Beacon Press, 1989.

Takagi, Dana. "Maiden Voyage: Excursion into Sexuality and Identity Politics in Asian America." In *Making More Waves: New Writings by Asian American Women,* ed. Elaine H. Kim et al. Boston: Beacon Press, 1997.

Takaki, Ronald. *Strangers from a Different Shore.* New York: Little, Brown, 1989.

———. ed. *From Different Shores: Perspectives on "Race" and Ethnicity in America.* London: Oxford University Press, 1987.

Tang, Vincent. "Chinese Women Immigrants and the Two-Edged Sword of Habeas Corpus." In *The Chinese American Experience: Papers from the Second Annual Conference on Chinese American Studies,* ed. Genny Lim. San Francisco: The Chinese Historical Society of America and The Chinese Culture Foundation of San Francisco, 1980.

Tong, Benjamin R. "'Ornamental Orientals' and Others: Ethnic Labels in Review." *Focus: Notes from the Society for The Psychological Study of Ethnic Minority Issues* 1, no. 2 (June 1990): 8–9.

Tong, Benson. *Unsubmissive Women: Chinese Prostitutes in Nineteenth-Century San Francisco.* Norman, Okla.: University of Oklahoma Press, 1994.

Trauner, Joan B. "The Chinese as Medical Scapegoats in San Francisco, 1870–1905." *California History* 57 (spring 1978): 70–87.

Trinh, T. Minh-ha. "Not You/Like You: Post-Colonial Women and the Interlocking Questions of Identity and Difference." *Inscriptions* 3/4 (1988): 71–77.

———. *Woman, Native, Other: Writing Postcoloniality and Feminism.* Bloomington: Indiana University Press, 1989.

Truong, Thanh-Dam. *Sex, Money, and Morality: Prostitution and Tourism in Southeast Asia.* London: Zed Books, 1998.

Tsui, Kitty. *The Words of a Woman Who Breathes Fire.* San Francisco: Aunt Lute, 1983.

Turner, Stephen. "What Are Disciplines? And How Is Interdisciplinarity Different?" In *Practising Interdisciplinarity,* ed. Peter Weingart and Nico Stehr. Toronto: University of Toronto Press, 2000.

Ueda, Reed. "Naturalization and Citizenship." In Richard A. Easterlin et al., *Immigration.* Cambridge: The Belknap Press of the Harvard University Press, 1982.

Vasey, Ruth. "Foreign Parts: Hollywood's Global Distribution and the Representation of Ethnicity." *American Quarterly* 44, no. 4 (December 1992): 617–42.

Vatikiotis, Michael. "Three's Company: Malaysia, Thailand, Indonesia

Forge Development Zone." *Far Eastern Economic Review* (5 August 1993): 58–59.

Wand, David Hsin-Fu, ed. *Asian-American Heritage: An Anthology of Prose and Poetry*. New York: Washington Square Press, 1974.

Wang, L. Ling-chi. "A Critique of Strangers From a Different Shore." *Amerasia Journal* 16, no. 2 (1990): 71–80.

Watenabe, Satoko. "From Thailand to Japan: Migrant Sex Workers as Autonomous Subjects." In *Global Sex Workers: Rights, Resistance, and Redefinition*, ed. Kamala Kempadoo et al. New York: Routledge, 1998.

Watson, Julia. "Unspeakable Differences: The Politics of Gender in Lesbian and Heterosexual Women's Autobiographies." In *De/Colonizing the Subject: The Politics of Gender in Women's Autobiography*, ed. Sidonie Smith and Julia Watson. Minneapolis: University of Minnesota Press, 1992.

Watson, Julia, and Sidonie Smith, "De/Colonization and the Politics of Discourse in Women's Autobiographical Practices." In *De/Colonizing the Subject: The Politics of Women's Autobiography*, ed. Sidonie Smith and Julia Watson. Minneapolis: University of Minnesota Press, 1992.

Wei, William. *The Asian American Movement*. Philadelphia: Temple University Press, 1993.

Weinberg, Sidney Stahl. "The Treatment of Women in Immigration History: A Call for Change." *Journal of American Ethnic History* 11 (summer 1992): 25–31.

White, Hayden. *The Content of the Form: Narrative Discourse and Historical Representation*. Baltimore: The Johns Hopkins University Press, 1987.

White, Patricia. "Feminism and Film." In *The Oxford Guide to Film Studies*, ed. John Hill and Pamela Church Gibson. Oxford: Oxford University Press, 1998.

Wiegman, Robyn. *American Anatomies: Theorizing Race and Gender*. Durham: Duke University Press, 1995.

———. "Queering the Academy." *Genders* 26 (1997): 3–22.

———. "Race, Ethnicity, and Film." In *The Oxford Guide to Film Studies*, ed. John Hill and Pamela Church Gibson. Oxford: Oxford University Press, 1998.

Williams, Teresa K. "Marriage Between Japanese Women and U.S. Servicemen Since World War II." *Amerasia Journal* 17, no. 1 (1991): 135–54.

Willis, Sharon. *High Contrast: Race and Gender in Contemporary Hollywood Film*. Durham: Duke University Press, 1997.

Willoughby, J. 1991. "Nationalism and Globalism: Beyond the Neo-Leninist Tradition." *Rethinking Marxism* 4, no. 1 (spring 1992): 134–42.

Women of South Asian Descent Collective, ed. *Our Feet Walk the Sky: Women of the South Asian Diaspora*. San Francisco: Aunt Lute Books, 1994.

Wong, Ah So. "Story of Wong Ah So—Experiences as a Prostitute." Nashville: Social Science Institute, Fisk University, 1946.

Wong, Eugene Franklin. *On Visual Media Racism.* New York: Arno Press, 1978.

Wong, Joyce Mende. "Prostitution: San Francisco Chinatown, Mid- and Late-Nineteenth Century." *Bridge: An Asian American Perspective* 6 (winter 1978): 23–28.

Wong, Morrison G. "Chinese Sweatshops in the United States: A Look at the Garment Industry." In *Research in the Sociology of Work: A Research Annual,* ed. Ida H. Simpson et al. New York: JAI Press, Inc., 1983.

Wong, Nellie. "Asian American Women, Feminism and Creativity." *Conditions* 7 (1981): 177–84.

Wong, Sau-Ling Cynthia. "Necessity and Extravagance in Maxine Hong Kingston's *The Woman Warrior:* Art and the Ethnic Experience." *MELUS* 15, no. 1 (spring 1988): 3–26.

———. "Immigrant Autobiography: Some Questions of Definition and Approach." In *American Autobiography: Retrospect and Prospect,* ed. Paul John Eakin. Madison: University of Wisconsin Press, 1991.

———. "Autobiography as Guided Chinatown Tour? Maxine Hong Kingston's *The Woman Warrior* and the Chinese-American Autobiographical Controversy." In *Multicultural Autobiography: American Lives,* ed. James Robert Payne. Knoxville: University of Tennessee Press, 1992.

———. "Denationalization Reconsidered: Asian American Cultural Criticism at a Theoretical Crossroads." *Amerasia Journal* 21, nos. 1–2 (winter–spring 1995): 1–27.

Wong, Shelley Sunn. "Unnaming the Same: Theresa Hak Kyung Cha's *Dictée.*" In *Writing Self, Writing Nation: Essays on Theresa Hak Kyung Cha's "Dictée,"* ed. Elaine H. Kim and Norma Alarcón. Berkeley: Third Woman Press, 1994.

Yamada, Mitsuye. "Invisibility Is an Unnatural Disaster: Reflections of an Asian American Woman." *Bridge: An Asian American Perspective* (winter 1978): 12.

———. "Asian American Women and Feminism." In *This Bridge Called My Back: Writings by Radical Women of Color,* ed. Gloria Anzaldúa and Cherríe Moraga. Latham, N.Y.: Kitchen Table/Women of Color Press, 1982.

———. "Invisibility Is an Unnatural Disaster: Reflections of an Asian American Woman." In *This Bridge Called My Back: Writings by Radical Women of Color,* ed. Gloria Anzaldúa and Cherríe Moraga. Latham, N.Y.: Kitchen Table/Women of Color Press, 1982.

Yoshimoto, Mitsuhiro. "The Difficulty of Being Radical: The Discipline of Film Studies and the Postcolonial World Order." *Boundary 2* 18, no. 3 (fall 1991): 242–57.

Yung, Judy. *Chinese Women of America: A Pictorial History.* Seattle: University of Washington Press, 1987.

————. "Appendix: A Chronology of Asian American History." In *Making Waves: An Anthology of Writings By and About Asian American Women,* ed. Asian Women United of California. Boston: Beacon Press, 1989.

————. "The Social Awakening of Chinese American Women as Reported in Chung Sai Yat Po, 1900–1911." In *Unequal Sisters: A Multicultural Reader in U.S. Women's History,* ed. Ellen Carol DuBois and Vicki L. Ruiz. New York: Routledge, 1990.

————. "Unbinding the Feet, Unbinding Their Lives: Chinese Immigrant Women in San Francisco, 1902–1931." In *Asian Americans: Comparative and Global Perspectives,* ed. Shirley Hune et al. Pullman: Washington State University Press, 1991.

————. *Unbound Feet: A Social History of Chinese Women in San Francisco.* Berkeley: University of California Press, 1995.

Zhang Ya-jie. "A Chinese Woman's Response to Maxine Hong Kingston's *The Woman Warrior.*" *MELUS* 13, nos. 1–2 (1986): 103–7.

Zia, Helen. "Violence in Our Communities: 'Where Are the Asian Women?'" In *Making More Waves: New Writing by Asian American Women,* ed. Elaine H. Kim et al. Boston: Beacon Press, 1997.

Zinsser, Judith P. *History and Feminism: A Glass Half Full.* New York: Twayne, 1993.

Index

Espiritu, Yen Le, 65, 75, 151–52
Ethnography, 199–201, 210–14; and
ethnic autobiography, 46–48
Everson, William K., 293 n.46

Fabian, Johannes, 176, 212, 310 nn.27
and 28
Far Eastern Economic Review, 301 n.14,
310 n.37, 311 n.38
Feminism, 5, 7–11, 59–60, 272 n.10;
and film, 96–98, 269–70, 291 n.29
Filipinas/os: bars to immigration,
131; racial categorization of, 131
Film studies, 76, 96–98; ethnicity
and race in, 97–99; feminist,
96–98, 291 n.29; stereotype
criticism in, 76, 98–99, 291–92
n.33. *See also* Cinema
Fischer, Michael, 46–48, 210, 212
Fong, Katheryn M., 302 n.80
Foucault, Michel: *Discipline and Pun-
ish,* 17–18, 272 n.2; "The Histori-
cal *a priori* and the Archives," 149–
50; *Language, Counter-Memory,
Practice,* 35–36
Free Trade Zones (FTZ), 168, 177–78
Friedman, Lester D., 97–98
Friedman, Susan Stanford, 40–41
Fuentes, Annette, and Barbara
Ehrenreich, 187, 195

Gabaccia, Donna, 149
Gilmore, Leigh, 49–50
Glenn, Evelyn Nakano, 149
Good Woman of Bangkok, The (Dennis
O'Rourke), 200
Graham, Julie, 188–89
Grossman, Rachel, 181, 190, 193–94,
201

Hagedorn, Jessica, 73, 288 n.7
Hall, C. Michael, 198–99, 309 n.22

Haney López, Ian F., 138–39,
301 n.69
Haraway, Donna, 272 n.8
Harvey, David, 188
Hess, Gary R., 301 n.68
Heung, Marina, 71, 73, 288 n.6
Hing, Bill Ong, 132
Hirata, Lucie Cheng, 118, 151–52,
159, 302–3 n.92, 304 n.108
History: historiography, 150–60,
225–27; U.S. archives, problem of,
149–50, 154, 155–57; women's,
148–49
Holbrook, Reverend J. C., 114
Hom, Alice, and David Eng, 275
n.24
Hori, Joan, 159
Hutching's California Magazine, 114,
118

Ichioka, Yuji, 129, 152–53, 297 n.19,
299 nn.46 and 47
Immigration, U.S.: policies, 1–2,
126–32
India: and Hollywood films, 112–13
Indian Americans, 137
Interdisciplinarity, 18; "trenchant
interdisciplinarity," 20–21

Japanese, 129–30; Gentlemen's
Agreement, 130; restriction on
immigration, 129–30
Jones, Dorothy B., 109–13, 294 n.56
Juhasz, Suzanne, 41

Kaplan, Caren, 284 n.35
Kauanui, Kehaulani, and Ju Hui
"Judy" Han, 276 n.33
Kim, Elaine H., 38; *Asian American
Literature: An Introduction to the
Writings and Their Social Context*
(1982), 61–62; "Poised on the

Laura Hyun Yi Kang is Associate Professor of Women's Studies and Comparative Literature at the University of California, Irvine.

Library of Congress Cataloging-in-Publication Data

Kang, Laura Hyun Yi
Compositional subjects : enfiguring Asian/American women / Laura Hyun Yi Kang.
p. cm.
Includes bibliographical references and index.
ISBN 0-8223-2883-6 (cloth : acid free paper)—
ISBN 0-8223-2898-4 (pbk.: acid free paper)
1. Asian American women—Social conditions. 2. Asian American women—Study and teaching. 3. Asian Americans—Ethnic identity. 4. Asian Americans—Study and teaching. 5. Asian Americans—Cultural assimilation. 6. Asian American women in literature. 7. Categorization (Psychology) 8. United States—Ethnic relations. 9. United States—Intellectual life. 10. Universities and colleges—United States—Curricula—Social aspects.
I. Title.
E184.06 K36 2002
305.895073—dc21   2001007612

217 NW 3rd Apt. A
32601 gulb